Peter Smith
Lecturer in Economics
University of Southampton

and

David Begg
Professor of Economics
Birkbeck College
University of London

McGRAW-HILL BOOK COMPANY
London · New York · St Louis · San Francisco · Auckland · Bogotá · Caracas
Hamburg · Lisbon · Madrid · Mexico · Milan · Montreal · New Delhi · Panama
Paris · San Juan · São Paulo · Singapore · Sydney · Tokyo · Toronto

Economics
Workbook
Third Edition

Published by
McGRAW-HILL Book Company Europe
Shoppenhangers Road, Maidenhead, Berkshire, SL6 2QL, England
Telephone 0628 23432
Fax 0628 770224

British Library Cataloguing in Publication Data
Smith, Peter
  Economics Workbook. – 3rd ed.
  1. Economics. Questions and answers
  I. Title   II. Begg, David K. H.
  330

ISBN 0-07-707404-1

34 TL 932

Typeset by Paston Press, Loddon, Norfolk
and printed and bound in Great Britain by
M & A Thomson Litho, East Kilbride, Scotland

ECONOMICS WORKBOOK

Third Edition

For Ashley and Eliot

Contents

Preface

Economics is a lively and fascinating subject, dealing with many of the issues that affect our everyday lives. The book ECONOMICS by David Begg, Stanley Fischer and Rudiger Dornbusch introduces students to a wide range of such issues in a vibrant and interesting way.

Economics is not a subject that can be learnt only by reading. This workbook is designed to be used in conjunction with ECONOMICS (the 'main text') and allows the reader to go beyond reading to apply the techniques and ideas which comprise modern economics.

TO THE STUDENT

Whatever your reason for studying economics, you will find that the subject comes alive as you begin to see it in action for yourself. The workbook enables this.

The opening section of each chapter reviews in words the material covered in the main text. *Important Concepts and Technical Terms* provides a valuable checklist of key definitions, helping you to think carefully about important ideas and pieces of economic jargon. Many of the definitions echo the wording of the main text.

The *Exercises* put economics into action in a variety of formats, whenever possible using 'real-world' data and allowing you to carry out economic analysis of many day-to-day issues. Multiple-choice questions (many taken from A-level examination papers) help to focus on contentious topics in a thought-provoking way.

Ready revision is facilitated by the *True/False* section, which includes commentary on many common fallacies of economic life.

Questions for Thought provides topics for further discussion—perhaps in the classroom context. Some exercises in this section extend the concepts of the chapter and introduce new ideas and applications.

A vital part of the workbook is the *Answers and Comments* section which is part of each chapter. The emphasis is upon clear explanation of answers, especially in areas where students often encounter difficulty. In many cases, you may well wish to tackle the exercises step-by-step *with* the commentary, which can be a valuable learning process. Where appropriate, the commentary refers you to appropriate sections of the main text. This is especially stressed in the *True/False* section to aid revision.

ACKNOWLEDGEMENTS

We are grateful to the following examination boards for permission to reproduce questions from recent GCE and Scottish CE examination papers:

The Associated Examining Board
Northern Ireland Schools Examination Council
Oxford and Cambridge Schools Examination Board
Southern Universities' Joint Board
University of Cambridge Local Examinations Syndicate
University of London School of Examinations Board
University of Oxford Delegacy of Local Examinations
Welsh Joint Education Committee

In cases where answers or hints are given for these questions, the authors are solely responsible: neither answers nor commentary were provided by the examination boards.

Our special thanks go to Mrs Rosalyn Kriteman for her most helpful comments and suggestions and to those students who kindly agreed to test drive individual chapters of the workbook. No small debt is owed to Mrs Maureen Smith for typing and encouragement.

Peter Smith
and
David Begg
with
Susie Symes

Preface to the Second Edition

This is a new edition of the ECONOMICS WORKBOOK which reinforces the second edition of ECONOMICS by David Begg, Stanley Fischer and Rudiger Dornbusch. Each workbook chapter corresponds to one in the main text and features a lucid commentary section with illustrations and definitions of technical terms. Many of the chapters and exercises have been substantially revised and updated in the second edition, bringing the study of economics into the 1990s.

Preface to the Third Edition

As with earlier editions of this ECONOMICS WORKBOOK, our intention is to take the reader beyond just reading about economics, and to provide a way in which the ideas presented in the third edition of ECONOMICS by David Begg, Stanley Fischer and Rudiger Dornbusch can be applied. The chapters and exercises have been much revised and updated in this new edition, reflecting the changes that take place in economics and in the real-life economy.

1 An Introduction to Economics and the Economy

Most people setting off on a journey do so knowing where they want to go, why they want to go there, and the approximate route they intend to take. As we begin to study economics, it is helpful to look at what economics is about and why we wish to study it—and also to see something of the route to be travelled. These are the issues which are the concern of this opening chapter.

A feature of the world about us which leads to the study of economics is the existence of scarcity. The people who belong to society have needs and desires for goods and services which exceed the availability of resources. As a result, decisions must be made, either by society or by individuals, on three central economic questions. These involve *what* goods and services are to be produced, *how* these goods and services are to be produced, and *for whom* they are to be produced. Economics is about these three questions and the decisions surrounding them, which are so vital to the functioning of any society.

In a market economy, many of these decisions are affected by *prices*. This was well illustrated by the oil price shocks of 1973–74 and 1979–80, which had wide-ranging repercussions for our three issues of *what*, *how*, and *for whom*. Smaller cars and gas-fired central heating became more popular; firms looked for techniques of production which were less reliant on oil; the oil-producing countries became relatively better off. All this was in response to price changes. We may view prices as a key element in reconciling the demand for goods and services with the available supply, and as reflecting economic scarcity.

One of the most striking economic issues of our day is the pronounced inequality in the distribution of income, both *between* nations and between individuals *within* nations. Discussion of this subject again involves our three basic questions. The *what* is produced and *for whom* questions are dominated by the fact that the 15 per cent of the world's population living in the rich industrial countries receive almost two-thirds of world income. This in part reflects the *how* question, with the poorer countries having access to much less machinery per worker with which to produce.

One way of summarizing information on *what* may be produced is the *production possibility frontier*, which for an economy producing just two goods depicts points of efficient production. That is, for each level of output of one good, the production possibility frontier shows the maximum amount of the other good that can be produced. The production possibility frontier is usually drawn concave to the origin, reflecting the assumption of *diminishing returns*, which states that, as more resources are devoted to the production of a commodity, their productivity declines.

A society producing at a point on the frontier is operating efficiently, in the sense that more output of one good can be achieved only by sacrificing output of the other good. We can thus regard the cost of producing a good in terms of opportunities forgone. This concept is known as *opportunity cost*, which we will encounter again in Chapter 7. A society producing at a point *within* the frontier is inefficient in the sense that some resources are not being used to the full. No point beyond the frontier can be attained without the acquisition of additional resources via 'economic growth' or technical progress.

In some economies, the government takes a very active role in economic activity. In a *command economy*, all decisions about production and consumption are taken by a government planning office. In a completely *free market economy*, the government would not intervene but would allow individuals to act for themselves. Resources are then allocated within society through the medium of the market, with prices playing a key role in the process. In reality, examples of neither extreme exist, and economic issues are determined by the interaction of private and governmental decisions within the so-called *mixed economy*.

Statements about economic issues can take two differing forms; it is very important to distinguish carefully between them. On the one hand, the economist may try to describe some aspect of the economy, or to explain how part of the economy operates. This involves *positive* statements, which offer objective analysis of the issues involved. On the other hand, the economist may at times go beyond such objective analysis and offer prescriptive advice—for instance, concerning a particular policy which should be adopted. He or she then makes *normative* statements which are no longer objective, but rest upon value judgements. Throughout our economic journey, we must maintain an awareness of this distinction between the positive (what *is*) and the normative (what *ought to be*).

Economics is often regarded as being divided into two major branches: *microeconomics* and *macroeconomics*. In fact, the difference is largely that of focus, many of the techniques, topics, and lines of argument being common to both branches. In considering an economic problem, we may choose to focus upon the detailed aspects—for instance, by analysing the decisions taken by individual agents about particular commodities. Such analysis falls within the province of microeconomics. Alternatively, we may choose to gain a broader perspective by focusing upon the interactions in the economy at large—which takes us into macroeconomics. As our journey continues, we look first at the decisions made by individuals (microeconomics) before broadening the perspective to refocus upon macroeconomics.

IMPORTANT CONCEPTS AND TECHNICAL TERMS

Match each lettered concept with the appropriate numbered phrase:

(a)	Scarce resource	(i)	Production
(b)	Law of diminishing		possibility frontier
	returns	(j)	Unemployment rate
(c)	Market	(k)	Opportunity cost
(d)	Gross national	(l)	Macroeconomics
	product	(m)	Mixed economy
(e)	Distribution of	(n)	Aggregate price
	income		level
(f)	Positive economics	(o)	Normative
(g)	Free markets		economics
(h)	Microeconomics	(p)	Command economy

1   The branch of economics offering a detailed treatment of individual decisions about particular commodities.
2   Economic statements offering prescriptions or recommendations based on personal value judgements.
3   An economy in which the government and private sector interact in solving economic problems.
4   The way in which income (in a country or in the world) is divided between different groups or individuals.
5   The process by which households' decisions about consumption of alternative goods, firms' decisions about what and how to produce, and workers' decisions about how much and for whom to work are all reconciled by adjustments of prices.
6   The quantity of other goods that must be sacrificed in order to obtain another unit of a particular good.
7   Markets in which governments do not intervene.
8   A resource for which the demand at a zero price would exceed the available supply.
9   The branch of economics emphasizing the interactions in the economy as a whole.
10 The value of all goods and services produced in the economy in a given period such as a year.

11 The percentage of the labour force without a job.
12 A measure of the average level of prices of goods and services in the economy, relative to their prices at some fixed date in the past.
13 A curve which shows, for each level of the output of one good, the maximum amount of the other good that can be produced.
14 The situation in which, as more workers are employed in an industry, each additional worker adds less to total industry output than the previous additional worker added.
15 A society where the government makes all decisions about production and consumption.
16 Economic statements dealing with objective or scientific explanations of the working of the economy.

EXERCISES

1   A tribe living on a tropical island includes five workers whose time is devoted either to gathering coconuts or to collecting turtle eggs. Regardless of how many other workers are engaged in the same occupation, a worker may gather either 20 coconuts or 10 turtle eggs in a day.
    (a) Draw the production possibility frontier for coconuts and turtle eggs.
    (b) Suppose that a new climbing technique is invented making the harvesting of coconuts easier. Each worker can now gather 28 coconuts in a day. Draw the new production possibility frontier.
2   Figure 1.1 shows a society's production possibility frontier for cameras and watches.
    (a) Identify each of the following combinations of the two goods as being either efficient, inefficient, or unattainable:

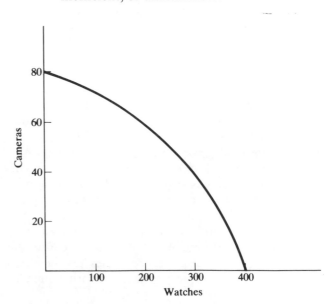

FIGURE 1.1   The production possibility frontier

(i) 60 cameras and 200 watches.
(ii) 60 watches and 80 cameras.
(iii) 300 watches and 35 cameras.
(iv) 300 watches and 40 cameras.
(v) 58 cameras and 250 watches.

(b) Suppose the society is producing 300 watches and 40 cameras, but wishes to produce an additional 20 cameras. How much output of watches must be sacrificed to enable these extra cameras to be made?

(c) How much output of watches would need to be given up to enable a further 20 cameras (i.e., 80 in all) to be produced?

(d) Explain the difference in the shape of the frontier in Figure 1.1 as compared with the ones you drew in exercise 1.

3 Figure 1.2 illustrates a production possibility boundary for an economy. If the economy is in recession, which of the four combinations of goods (A, B, C, or D) would be produced?

(Associated Examining Board GCE A level Economics Paper 1, June 1988)

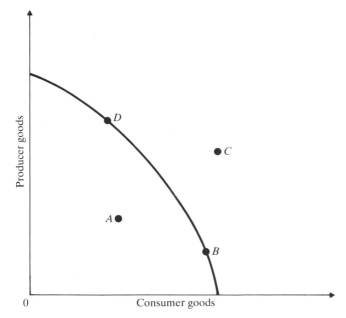

FIGURE 1.2

4 Which of the following statements are *normative*, and which are *positive*?

(a) The price of oil more than tripled between 1973 and 1974.

(b) In 1984, the poor countries of the world received less than their fair share of world income.

(c) The world distribution of income is too unjust, with poor countries having 61 per cent of the world's population, but receiving only 6 per cent of world income.

(d) In the early 1980s, most Western economies faced sharp rises in the aggregate unemployment rate.

(e) The UK government ought to introduce policies to reduce the unemployment rate.

(f) Smoking is antisocial and should be discouraged.

(g) The imposition of higher taxes on tobacco will discourage smoking.

(h) The economy of Hong Kong is closer to a free market system than that of Albania.

5 Which of the following statements are the concern of microeconomics and which of macroeconomics?

(a) Along with other Western economies, the UK faced a sharp rise in the unemployment rate in the early 1980s.

(b) The imposition of higher taxes on tobacco will discourage smoking.

(c) Unemployment among building labourers rose sharply in the early 1980s.

(d) An increase in a society's aggregate income is likely to be reflected in higher consumer spending.

(e) A worker who has received a pay rise is likely to buy more luxury goods.

(f) A firm will invest in a machine if the expected rate of return is sufficiently high.

(g) High interest rates in an economy may be expected to discourage aggregate investment.

(h) The level of gross national product in the UK is higher this year than in 1981.

6 Figure 1.3 shows society's choice between social

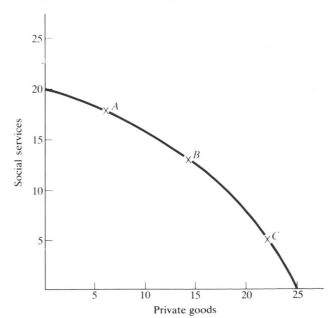

FIGURE 1.3 Society's choice between social services and private goods

services and private goods, in the form of a production possibility frontier. The three points A, B, and C represent economies in which the government plays a more or less active role. Match each of the points with the most appropriate of the following descriptions of hypothetical economies:

(a) An economy in which the government intervenes as little as possible, providing only the minimum necessary amounts of essential services.

(b) An economy in which the government takes a great deal of responsibility, taxing at a high level and providing considerable social services.

(c) An economy in which the government provides more than the minimum necessary amounts of social services, but leaves room for a buoyant private sector.

7 Which of the following statements would *not* be true for a pure 'command economy'?
(a) Firms choose how much labour to employ.
(b) The distribution of income is government-controlled.
(c) The government decides what should be produced.
(d) Production techniques are not determined by firms.
(e) A government planning office decides what will be produced, how it will be produced, and for whom it will be produced.

8 A jungle tribe catches fish and gathers mangoes. The tribe's production possibility frontier is shown in Figure 1.4. Which of the following bundles of the goods can be reached with present resources?

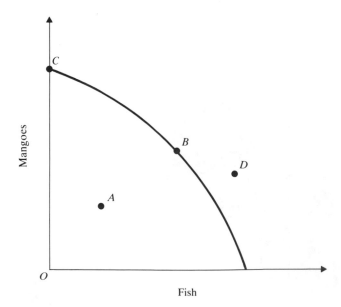

FIGURE 1.4 Fish or mangoes?

(a) Only A.
(b) Only B.
(c) Only A and B.
(d) Only A, B, and C.
(e) Only D.

TRUE/FALSE

1 _____ Economics is about human behaviour, so cannot be a 'science'.

2 _____ The oil price shocks of 1973–74 and 1979–80 had no effect on what was produced in the UK.

3 _____ An expansion of an economy's capacity to produce would be reflected in an 'outwards' movement of the production possibility frontier.

4 _____ An economy in which there is unemployment is not producing on the production possibility frontier.

5 _____ Adam Smith argued that individuals pursuing their self-interest would be led 'as by an invisible hand' to do things that are in the interests of society as a whole.

6 _____ The Soviet Union is an example of a command economy in which private markets play no part.

7 _____ The government should subsidize the health bills of the aged.

8 _____ Gross national product is the value of all goods produced in the economy during a period.

9 _____ Many propositions in positive economics would command widespread agreement among professional economists.

QUESTIONS FOR THOUGHT

1 We have seen that economics is concerned with three fundamental questions: *what* is produced, *how* it is produced, and *for whom* it is produced. For each of the following economic events, think about which of the three fundamental questions are of relevance:
(a) The discovery of substantial reserves of natural gas in a readily accessible site.
(b) A change in the structure of income tax, such that income is redistributed from 'rich' to 'poor'.
(c) The privatization of a major industry.
(d) The invention of the microcomputer.
(e) An increase in the price of imported goods.

2 An economy can choose between producing goods to be consumed now and producing *investment goods* which have an effect on the future

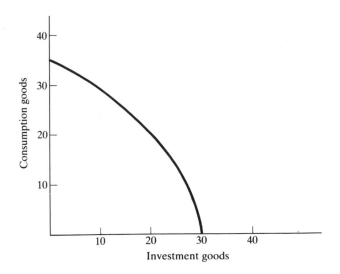

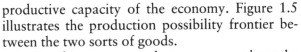

FIGURE 1.5   The choice between consumption and investment goods

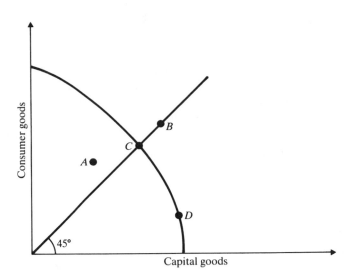

FIGURE 1.6

productive capacity of the economy. Figure 1.5 illustrates the production possibility frontier between the two sorts of goods.

(a)   For this economy, what can we say about the position of the frontier in subsequent periods?

(b)   How is your answer to (a) affected by the particular choice point selected in a given period?

3   This question is based on the production possibility curve in Figure 1.6. Which of the points (A, B, C, or D) would be most likely to lead to the fastest rate of economic growth in the next time period?

(Associated Examining Board GCE A level Economics Paper 1, November 1988)

ANSWERS AND COMMENTS FOR CHAPTER 1

Please note   Where questions are reproduced from A level examinations, the examination boards bear no responsibility for the answers provided in this volume, which are the sole responsibility of the authors.

Important Concepts and Technical Terms

1	*h*	7	*g*	12	*n*
2	*o*	8	*a*	13	*i*
3	*m*	9	*l*	14	*b*
4	*e*	10	*d*	15	*p*
5	*c*	11	*j*	16	*f*
6	*k*				

Exercises

1 (*a*)   The straight line PPF_a in Figure A1.1 represents the production possibility frontier for this society.

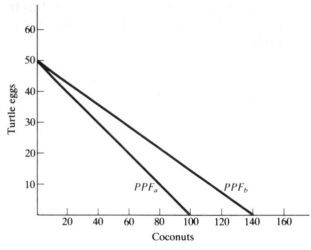

FIGURE A1.1   The effect of technical change

  (*b*) PPF_b is the new production possibility frontier. The change in technology enables more coconuts to be 'produced' than before, without any reduction in output of turtle eggs.

2 (*a*)   Combinations (*i*) and (*iv*) lie on the production possibility frontier and thus represent points of *efficient* production. Combinations (*ii*) and (*v*) lie outside the frontier and are thus *unattainable* with the resources available. Combination (*iii*) lies within the frontier, and is a point of *inefficient* production. Not all the available resources are being fully or effectively used.

  (*b*)   100 watches must be given up for the 20 cameras when the society begins at (300, 40).

  (*c*)   200 watches must be given up for the 20 cameras when the society begins at (200, 60).

  (*d*)   The difference in shape results from the law of diminishing returns. On the tropical island, the amounts produced by a worker did not vary according to whether other workers were engaged in the same activity. In the cameras and watches case, this is not so: as more workers are used to produce cameras, the additional output produced falls. This is explained in Section 1–2 of the main text.

3   *A.*

4   (*a*), (*d*), (*g*), and (*h*) are positive statements, containing objective descriptions of economies and the way they work. (*b*), (*e*), and (*f*) are normative statements which rely upon value judgements for their validity. Statement (*c*) contains elements of both: it includes a (positive) statement of fact about the distribution of world population and income but also rests on a (normative) value judgement that this was 'too unjust'.

5   (*a*), (*d*), (*g*), and (*h*) deal with economy-wide issues, and are thus the concern of macroeconomics. (*b*), (*c*), (*e*), and (*f*) are devoted to more detailed microeconomic issues.

6   (*a*) C. (*b*) A. (*c*) B.

7   Only (*a*) would be untrue for a *pure* command economy. Remember, though, that no such 'pure' command economy actually exists.

8   (*d*).

True/False

1   False: the claim of economics to be a science rests not on its subject matter, but upon its methods of analysis.

2   False: see Section 1–1 of the main text.

3   True.

4   True.

5   True.

6   False: while being closer to a command economy than many others, the Soviet Union tolerates the existence of some private markets, for instance in agriculture.

7   Sorry, this was a trick question! This is another example of a normative statement, which rests on a subjective value judgement. As a result, it can never be proven to be either true or false.

8   False: don't forget services! The production of services may be more difficult to measure than that of goods, but is important none the less.

9   True: many disagreements between economists reflect differences in beliefs and values (normative statements), rather than differences of opinion about objective analysis.

Questions for Thought

1   *Hint*   It is rare that an economic issue involves only one of the three basic questions.

2   *Hint*   So far, we have only considered an economy in a single time period. Here, the production of one of the goods directly affects what can be produced in the future.

3   *D.*

2

The
Tools
of Economic
Analysis

In Chapter 1 we embarked on an economic journey. What sort of 'map' might we use to guide our thinking? A geographical map begins from observation of the world and presents relevant facts in a schematic way that is easily understood and interpreted. Economists also need a way of summarizing relevant economic facts so that they can be usefully interpreted. This entails both *data* and *models*.

A model is a deliberate simplification of reality designed to isolate the relevant aspects of economic behaviour. Much of the skill of the economist lies in being able to focus upon *relevant* facts. Just as a cartographer may check the accuracy of his map, the economist may wish to evaluate his model in terms of economic data. This chapter looks in turn at economic data, at economic models, and at ways in which the two interact.

As a budding economist, it is important for you to develop skills in the interpretation and handling of data, as data are our link with the 'real world'. Don't confine your practice to the problems in this workbook, but watch for other opportunities to read data and sharpen your awareness and your skills. One way of doing this is by reading a 'serious' newspaper regularly. However, first we need to explore the sorts of data that economists use.

Many data series, especially those used in macroeconomics, take the form of *time series*. For instance, we might observe aggregate consumers' expenditure at different points in time. Observations on some variables may be collected on a daily, weekly, or monthly frequency. If we are interested in the underlying consistency of economic behaviour through time, we may prefer to use annual, or perhaps quarterly, data which dampen the effects of short-term fluctuations in behaviour. In other situations, especially in microeconomics, we may be more interested in how different individuals behave at a single moment in time. In this case, we use *cross-section* data such as the General Household Survey or the Census.

Index numbers are frequently used by economists. We sometimes need to compare the levels of variables measured in different units, or to combine such variables into an aggregate measure. Index numbers enable this to be done. Well-known and widely publicized indices include the retail price index (RPI) and the index of industrial production. The RPI is an aggregate price index measuring the cost of a given bundle of goods in different periods. It is commonly used to measure inflation. The index of industrial production is designed to reflect changes in the amounts produced by a range of industries.

Inflation complicates the measurement of economic variables. Suppose we wish to compare the value of this year's consumers' expenditure with the 1985 value. If we simply measure money expenditure, we neglect the fact that prices have changed since 1985. An alternative measurement would take this year's quantities but use the prices which prevailed in 1985. By this method, we measure consumers' expenditure 'at constant 1985 prices', often referred to as *real* consumers' expenditure. The measurement 'at current prices' is known as the *nominal* value.

Similarly, when we wish to examine the price of a commodity, we may be interested in the price *relative* to the prices of other goods. If the price of a commodity has increased, but by less than that of other goods, we will want to say that its *real price* has fallen. We might perhaps define the real price as the ratio of the price index of a good to the RPI.

Data may be presented in the form of tables of numbers, but economists often find it more convenient and revealing to 'plot' data on charts. This can often highlight important stories hidden in the data. Variables are plotted against time to show changes between periods, or against each other to suggest how two variables interact—this is known as a *scatter diagram*. All such charts must be used with care. It is all too easy to misuse statistical information—for instance, by manipulating the *scale* of the diagram to conceal or overemphasize particular features. Sensible interpretation of data relies crucially on the models produced by the economist.

The process of devising an economic model may be conducted independently of the data, although sometimes it may be a response to the data. The economist may typically begin by identifying the relevant elements of an economic issue, perhaps writing them down in the formal statement $y = f(a, b)$, where this is no more than a shorthand way of saying that a variable y is a function of (depends upon) two other variables, a and b. This is often a useful device for focusing the mind and ensuring that important influences are not neglected.

The evaluation of models is rarely straightforward in economics: unlike in many physical sciences, the economist cannot set up laboratory experiments to test theories, but must rely on sifting the available empirical evidence. The economist can never *prove* that a theory is correct, but can allow evidence to build up in support of or in contradiction to it.

Econometrics brings together economics, mathematics, and statistics to assist this sifting of evidence.

Economists often find it helpful to focus upon the relationships between two variables, holding 'other things equal'. This allows the use of two-dimensional charts and analytical diagrams. Econometrics (among other things) provides techniques for fitting a line to a scatter diagram. Our economic model helps to explain the scatter and serves to remind us of which other things are being held equal.

The association we observe between two variables may be 'upward'-sloping (*positive* relationship) or 'downward'-sloping (*negative* relationship); it may be in the form of a straight line (*linear*) or a curve (*nonlinear*). The 'slope' or gradient of the line is often of interest; the slope of a linear relationship is constant throughout its length, that of a nonlinear relationship varies. The position of the relationship will be affected by changes in the background 'other things equal' factors.

The importance of the economic model in interpreting data cannot be too strongly emphasized. We may observe a close association between two variables, but, unless we can provide an economic explanation, it is always possible that the association is spurious. Only in the context of the model can we come to an understanding of the significance of observed relationships.

IMPORTANT CONCEPTS AND TECHNICAL TERMS

Match each lettered concept with the appropriate numbered phrase:

(*a*)	Data	(*k*)	Retail price index
(*b*)	Growth rate	(*l*)	Other things equal
(*c*)	Index number	(*m*)	Cross section
(*d*)	Model	(*n*)	Scatter diagram
(*e*)	Function	(*o*)	Econometrics
(*f*)	Nominal variable	(*p*)	Negative relationship
(*g*)	Purchasing power of money	(*q*)	Index of industrial production
(*h*)	Real price	(*r*)	Real variable
(*i*)	Time series		
(*j*)	Positive relationship		

1 A sequence of measurements of a variable at different points in time.

2 A situation in which higher values of one variable are associated with lower values of another variable.

3 The price of a commodity relative to the general price level for goods.

4 A simplifying assumption which enables the economist to focus on key economic relationships.

5 A deliberate simplification of reality based on a series of simplifying assumptions from which it may be deduced how people will behave.

6 An index of the prices of goods purchased by a typical household.

7 A variable measured in money terms at current prices.

8 The percentage change in a variable per period (typically per year).

9 Measurements of an economic variable at a point in time for different individuals or groups of individuals.

10 An index of the quantity of goods that can be bought for £1.

11 A way of expressing data relative to a given base value.

12 A graphical device to show how two variables are related.

13 A situation in which higher values of one variable are associated with higher values of another variable.

14 Pieces of information pertaining to economic variables.

15 Relationship between economic variables, in which one variable *depends upon* one or more other variables: abbreviated to $f(\ )$.

16 A weighted average of the quantity of goods produced by British industry.

17 A variable measured at constant prices, or after adjustment has been made for inflation.

18 The branch of economics devoted to measuring relationships using economic data.

EXERCISES

1 Which of the following data sets would be *time series* and which would relate to a *cross section*?
   (*a*) Consumers' expenditure on durable goods, annually 1980–91.
   (*b*) Households' expenditure on housing in urban areas in 1990.
   (*c*) Monthly price index for potatoes for 1990.
   (*d*) Gross national product of the UK for each quarter of 1991.
   (*e*) Average weekly earnings for a sample of 350 individuals first interviewed in 1980 and re-interviewed in 1982, 1984, 1986, and 1988.
   (*f*) Unemployment categorized by industry of last occupation, 10 May 1987.

2 Table 2.1 presents information about agricultural employment in six European countries in the two years 1976 and 1986.
   (*a*) From observation of the figures (i.e. without reaching for your calculator), comment

TABLE 2.1 Agricultural employment in six European countries (thousands)

Country	1976	1986	Index (1976 = 100)
Belgium	128	103	
Denmark	191	154	
West Germany	803	702	
France	2082	1536	
Netherlands	261	248	
United Kingdom	685	603	

Source: OECD Labour Force Statistics 1966–86, OECD, Paris, 1988.

on the trend in agricultural employment in the six countries. In which countries was the trend *most* and *least* strong?

(b) For each country, calculate an index for 1986, using 1976 as a base.

(c) Reassess your response to part (a). Did you correctly identify the countries in which the trend was most and least strong?

3 On average, 12 per cent of expenditure by households is on alcohol and tobacco, the remaining 88 per cent is on 'other goods and services'. (These proportions are 'close to' those used in construction of the UK retail price index, as are other data in this exercise.) Price indices for these goods are given in Table 2.2.

(a) Construct an aggregate price index for the economy based on weights of 0.12 for alcohol and tobacco and 0.88 for other goods and services.

(b) Using this aggregate price index, calculate the annual rate of inflation for the economy in the years 1982–86.

(c) Although this gives a general view of inflation in the economy, individuals may view inflation differently if their pattern of expenditure differs from that of society at large. Calculate the rate of inflation for an individual whose expenditure pattern conforms to the norm *except* for the fact that she is a non-smoking teetotaller.

TABLE 2.2 Price indices, 1981–86 (15 Jan. 1974 = 100)

Year	Price index, alcohol and tobacco	Price index, other goods and services	Aggregate price index	'Inflation'	Inflation for non-smoking teetotaller
1981	322.4	291.3			
1982	366.1	314.2			
1983	391.3	327.4			
1984	420.6	342.4			
1985	451.9	362.5			
1986	481.2	372.9			

(d) Using graph paper, draw two charts, one showing the three price indices, the second showing your two calculated inflation series.

4 (a) Using the data of Table 2.3, draw a scatter diagram with real imports on the vertical axis and real income on the horizontal axis.

(b) Does your diagram suggest a *positive* or a *negative* association between these variables?

(c) Does this conform to your economic intuition concerning imports and income?

(d) Can you think of variables likely to be covered by the 'other things equal' clause for this relationship?

TABLE 2.3 Imports and income, UK, 1982–88

Year	Imports of goods and services	Real personal disposable income
	(at constant 1985 prices in £m)	
1982	82 721	222 857
1983	88 116	227 887
1984	96 735	232 945
1985	99 165	239 581
1986	105 829	248 434
1987	113 905	257 309
1988	127 833	269 867

Source: Monthly Digest of Statistics.

5 Figure 2.1 shows scatter diagrams for different types of association between variables. Match

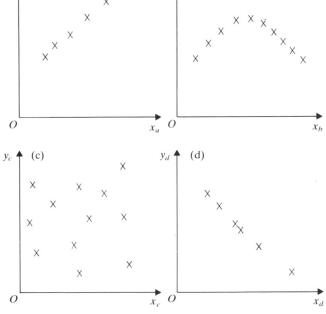

FIGURE 2.1 Patterns of association

each with the most appropriate description from the following:

(i)   A negative linear relationship.
(ii) A positive linear relationship.
(iii) A nonlinear relationship.
(iv) No apparent pattern of relationship.

To which of these associations would you *not* attempt to fit a straight line?

6 The retail price index for clothing and footwear in 1983–86 based on 15 January 1974 = 100 took values as follows:

1983	1984	1985	1986
214.8	214.6	222.9	229.2

(*Source: Employment Gazette, June 1987*)

(a) What additional information would you require to gauge whether the *real* price of clothing was rising or falling in this period?

(b) Use the data you calculated as the aggregate price index in question 3 to calculate a real price index for clothing and footwear.

(c) Comment upon the meaning of your results.

7 Consider the following simple economic model, which relates to the demand for chocolate bars:

$$\begin{array}{c} \text{Quantity of} \\ \text{chocolate bars} \\ \text{demanded} \end{array} = f \left(\begin{array}{c} \text{price of} \\ \text{chocolate} \\ \text{bars} \end{array} , \begin{array}{c} \text{consumer} \\ \text{incomes} \end{array} \right)$$

(a) Using only words, explain this statement.

(b) Assuming consumer incomes to be held constant, would you expect quantity demanded and price of chocolate bars to be positively or negatively associated?

(c) Assuming the price of chocolate bars to be held constant, what sort of association would you expect to observe between the quantity of chocolate bars demanded and the level of consumer incomes?

(d) Do you consider this model to be complete, or are there other economic variables which you would have included?

8 The following information relates to components of a retail price index for 1990:

Item	Weight	Price index (1981 = 100)
Food, catering, and alcohol	3	170
Housing, fuel, and light	2	186
Other goods and services	5	173

What is the value of the aggregate price index?
(a) 172. (b) 173. (c) 174.7, (d) 176.3. (e) 178.

TABLE 2.4   Household expenditure on food, UK 1988, in £ million

1988	Quarter 1	Quarter 2	Quarter 3	Quarter 4
At current prices	8772	9137	9342	9436
At constant 1985 prices	7839	7914	8069	8089

Source: Monthly Digest of Statistics.

9 (a) Calculate total real expenditure on food in 1988.

(b) Calculate total money expenditure on food in 1988.

(c) Calculate for each quarter the ratio of current price to constant price expenditure and multiply by 100. How might you interpret the results?

10 Figure 2.2 shows UK personal savings as a percentage of disposable income for the postwar period. Describe the general trend of the series and comment on the pattern displayed over time.

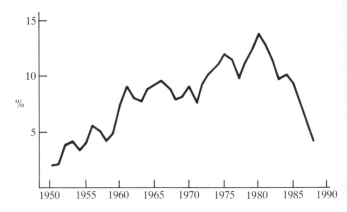

FIGURE 2.2   UK savings ratio, 1950–88 (*Source: Economic Trends Annual Supplement* and *Monthly Digest of Statistics.*

TRUE/FALSE

1 _____ Economics cannot claim to be a science since it is incapable of controlled laboratory experiments.

2 _____ We may accumulate evidence in support of an economic theory, but we can never prove beyond doubt that it is 'true'.

3 _____ Charts are a useful way of highlighting the important features of a data series.

4 _____ When we observe a strong association between two variables we know that one depends causally upon the other.

5 _____ Cross-section data are more often used in microeconomics because they deal with individuals.

6 _____ Invoking 'other things equal' enables us to ignore the complicated parts of an economic model.

7 _____ Economic models deal with straight-line relationships between variables.

8 _____ If you look hard enough at the facts, you will inevitably discover the correct theory.

9 _____ Index numbers are an invaluable device if we wish to compare two variables measured in different units.

10 _____ A positive economic relationship is one that supports our model.

11 _____ The retail price index provides a measure of the cost of living, obtained as the weighted average of different commodity prices.

12 _____ Inflation is measured by the price level.

13 _____ Real wage rates are calculated by adjusting nominal wage rates for changes in the cost of living.

14 _____ Empirical evidence suggests that, on average, high real tube fares on the London Underground are associated with lower passenger use.

QUESTIONS FOR THOUGHT

1 From Table 2.5, deduce the weighted index number of prices for year Y
(a) 94.6 (b) 105.7 (c) 113.3 (d) 131
(e) Cannot be determined from the above, because one needs to know the total expenditure on each item.

TABLE 2.5

Commodity	Price in base year	Price in year Y	Weights
1	10p	12p	2
2	100p	80p	5
3	50p	70p	3
			—
			10

2 Devise a simple economic model to analyse the demand for school lunches.

ANSWERS AND COMMENTS FOR CHAPTER 2

Please note   Where questions are reproduced from A level examinations, the examination boards bear no responsibility for the answers provided in this volume, which are the sole responsibility of the authors.

Important Concepts and Technical Terms

1 *i*	4 *l*	7 *f*	10 *g*	13 *j*	16 *q*
2 *p*	5 *d*	8 *b*	11 *c*	14 *a*	17 *r*
3 *h*	6 *k*	9 *m*	12 *n*	15 *e*	18 *o*

Exercises

1   (*a*), (*c*), and (*d*) comprise information for the same variables at different points in time: they are thus *time series*. (*b*) and (*f*) are straightforward *cross-section* data series, observing different individuals or groups of individuals at an instant in time. (*e*) is a different sort of data set: it is a cross section repeated at different points in time. It thus combines features of both cross-section and time series. Often known as *panel data*, such series are rare because of the expense of collecting the information and the difficulty in recontacting the same individuals in different periods.

2   (*a*)   Simple observation of the figures does not take us very far. It is clear that agricultural employment decreased in this ten-year period for all the countries in the table, but the differences in the size of employment in the six countries is substantial. Employment in France fell by a large number, but to assess the proportional change, we need to carry out some calculations.

(*b*)   **TABLE A2.1**   Agricultural employment in six European countries (thousands)

Country	1976	1986	Index (1976 = 100)
Belgium	128	103	80.5
Denmark	191	154	80.6
West Germany	803	702	87.4
France	2082	1536	73.8
Netherlands	261	248	95.0
United Kingdom	685	603	88.0

(*c*)   The index numbers enable much more ready comparison of the countries. We can now see clearly that the proportional decrease was at its greatest in France—a fall of 26.2 per cent over the decade. The smallest relative change was in the Netherlands, with only a 5 per cent decrease.

3   (*a*), (*b*)   See Table A2.2.

(*c*)   Inflation for the non-smoking teetotaller is calculated directly from the price index for 'other goods and services'. In general, it seems that the non-smoking teetotaller fares relatively well here, in the sense that in each of the 8 years prices of alcohol and tobacco rose more rapidly than those of other goods and services—e.g. by 6.3 per cent

TABLE A2.2   Price indices, 1981–86 (15 Jan. 1974 = 100) and inflation

Year	Price index, alcohol and tobacco	Price index, other goods and services	Aggregate price index	Inflation	Inflation for non-smoking teetotaller
1981	322.4	291.3	295.0		
1982	366.1	314.2	320.4	8.6	7.9
1983	391.3	327.4	335.1	4.6	4.2
1984	420.6	342.4	351.8	5.0	4.6
1985	451.9	362.5	373.2	6.1	5.9
1986	481.2	372.9	385.9	3.4	2.9

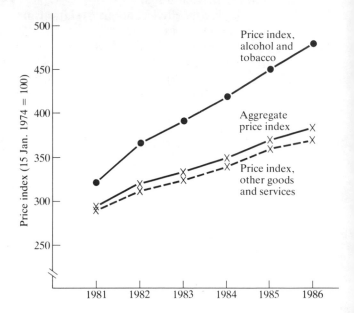

FIGURE A2.1   Price indices for 1981–86

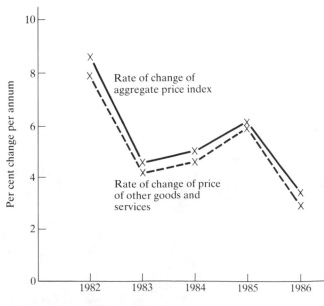

FIGURE A2.2   Inflation, 1982–86

in 1986, compared with 3.4 per cent on average (2.9 per cent for 'other goods and services').

(d) The chart (see Figure A2.1) underlines the fact that the price level for alcohol and tobacco is higher (relative to the 1974 base) than that for other goods and services.

Notice that in the first chart (Figure A2.1), the scale on the vertical axis has been chosen to draw out the difference between the series. Had the diagram been drawn with the scale starting at zero, the three series would have been indistinguishable (unless you have a very large piece of graph paper!). Remember also that both axes should be clearly labelled.

4 (a) See Figure A2.3.

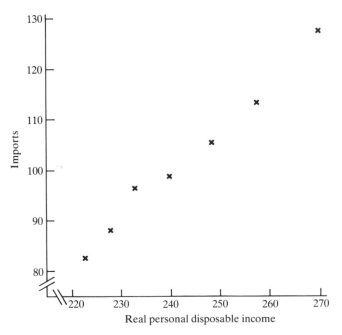

FIGURE A2.3 Imports and income at 1985 prices (£b)

(b)–(d) There seems to be a positive association between real imports and household income. We might perhaps expect households to buy more imported goods at higher levels of real income, but this is not likely to be the only variable affecting imports. For instance, changes in the relative price of UK and foreign goods or changes in demand by UK firms for imported raw materials also influence the overall level of real imports. Indeed, we would expect that as real incomes increase firms will need to import increased amounts of materials and machinery. You may have thought of other factors. When we focus upon this simple association, these elements are all covered by our assumption that 'other things are equal'.

5 (a) ii. (b) iii. (c) iv. (d) i.

If we are considering just these simple relationships the fitting of a straight line would not be appropriate for (b) or (c).

6 (a) An aggregate price index is required as a basis for comparison: we need the price of clothing *relative to* that of other goods.

(b) Real price index for clothing and footwear:

1983	1984	1985	1986
64.1	61.0	59.7	59.4

Method:

$$\text{1983 figure is } \frac{\text{Price of clothing}}{\text{Aggregate price index}} \times 100.$$

(c) Prices for clothing have increased much less than other prices, so their *real price* has fallen since 1974, and continues to do so.

7 The model states that the quantity of chocolate bars demanded depends upon their price, and upon the level of consumer incomes. You will find that this question is answered in Chapter 3 of the main text, where this example is used as an illustration.

8 We calculate $3 \times 170 + 2 \times 186 + 5 \times 173 = 1747$. Then we must divide by the sum of the weights ($2 + 3 + 5 = 10$), giving answer (c). 174.7.

9 (a) $7839 + 7914 + 8069 + 8089 = 31\,911$.
   (b) $8772 + 9137 + 9342 + 9436 = 36\,687$.
   (c)

Quarter 1	Quarter 2	Quarter 3	Quarter 4
111.9	115.5	115.8	116.7

The results of this calculation look very much like an index of some kind—and that is exactly what they *do* represent. In fact, this calculation provides us with a price index based on 1985 = 100, known as the 'implicit deflator' of consumers' expenditure, or sometimes as the 'consumer price index'. It is always the case that

$$\begin{array}{c}\text{Variable at} \\ \text{current prices}\end{array} = \begin{array}{c}\text{Variable at} \\ \text{constant prices}\end{array} \times \frac{\text{Price index}}{100}.$$

10 When asked to 'describe a trend', it is always tempting to go into great detail about all the ups and downs of the series. However, as economists it is more important for us to be able to filter the data and identify the salient features. It sometimes helps to lay a pencil on to the diagram so that it follows the overall trend of the line. For this graph, we see that the savings ratio increased steadily through the period until 1980, after which it declined. 1980 seems to have been the key turning-point of the series. We can also see that a surge around 1960 was followed by a decade of virtual stability: this interrupted the steady increase.

True/False

1 False: admittedly economists cannot easily carry out laboratory experiments. This does not prevent us from applying scientific methods to economic problems, and making the best we can of available information. There are other non-experimental sciences—astronomy, parts of biology, etc.

2 True: see Section 2–9 in the main text.

3 True: but we must be careful not to manipulate our charts to distort the picture so as to prove a point.

4 False: the association may be spurious—perhaps both variables depend upon a third one, or both happen to be growing over time.

5   True: but not invariably.
6   False: 'other things equal' is an assumption enabling us
     to simplify and to focus upon particular aspects of our
     model. However, we cannot *ignore* these other factors
     which affect the position of our curves and contribute
     to our explanation.
7   False: we may often assume a linear function for
     simplicity, but there are also many economic relation-
     ships which are nonlinear.
8   False: facts cannot speak for themselves and can be
     interpreted only in the light of careful and informed
     reasoning.
9   True: of course they have other uses also.
10   False: 'positive' refers to the direction of association
     between two variables.
11   True.
12   False: inflation measures the *rate of change* of the price
     level.
13   True.
14   True: see the discussion and evidence presented in
     Chapter 2 of the main text, especially Sections 2–6 and
     2–8.

Questions for Thought

1   This question requires careful treatment. The preferred
     calculation uses the ratio of the weighted sum of the
     prices in year Y to that in the base year; that is,

$$\frac{(2 \times 12) + (5 \times 80) + (3 \times 70)}{(2 \times 10) + (5 \times 100) + (3 \times 50)} \times 100 = 94.6.$$

     Notice that, if we first calculate the index for each
     commodity and then take a weighted average—as if
     calculating a retail price index—we do *not* get the same
     answer. In this instance, we would get 106. This serves
     to illustrate that the retail price index calculation is not
     an exact one.
2   Quantity of school lunches demanded = $f(?)$.
     What items would you put in brackets? An obvious one
     is the price of school lunches—but what else would you
     include? Perhaps the price of competing 'goods' . . .
     individual preferences . . . the time of year . . . income . . .
     no doubt you can think of more.

3

Demand, Supply, and the Market

In this chapter, we meet one of the most important concepts in all of economics—the *market*—together with the associated ideas of *demand* and *supply*. In so doing, we begin to tackle the key questions of how society decides what, how, and for whom to produce.

All members of society are either 'buyers' or 'sellers'. Households buy food and other goods and services and may sell their labour; firms may sell goods and buy labour; other agents may buy or sell foreign currency or stocks and shares. A 'market' is a set of arrangements which allows buyers and sellers to exchange goods and services. A market thus need not be a specific physical location, although it may be.

To see how this exchange takes place, we must examine the behaviour of both buyers and sellers. For instance, how do potential buyers of skimmed milk make a decision on how much to buy? Almost certainly, they will check the price of skimmed milk. They may also consider their income and preferences or check the price of other goods. If we take as given these other 'background' factors, we define the *demand* for a good as the amount of that good which buyers are prepared to purchase at each conceivable price, holding these 'other things equal'. We would normally expect the *quantity demanded* to be higher when the price of skimmed milk is relatively low than when price is relatively high. The *demand curve* illustrates this relation graphically; its position depends upon the background factors which we assumed constant.

How about the sellers of skimmed milk? In deciding how much to supply, they will consider such factors as the possible selling price of their produce, the price of inputs used in its production, and the technology required to produce it. If we again focus on the part played by the price of the product, holding other things equal, we define the *supply* of a good as the amount that suppliers are prepared to sell at each potential price. We would expect that the *quantity supplied* will be relatively high when price is high, and relatively low when price is low. The *supply curve* is a graphical illustration of this relation; its position again depends on the other things which we have assumed given.

If price is at a high level, sellers may wish to supply more than buyers wish to purchase. If exchange is voluntary, we describe this situation as one of *excess*

supply. Conversely, if we find that price is at such a low level that buyers are demanding more than sellers wish to supply at that price, we then have *excess demand*. However, if price is such that buyers demand just the quantities which sellers supply at the going price, then the market is said to be in *equilibrium*.

If there is excess supply, sellers will find their stocks building up, and so may reduce price and quantity supplied. When there is excess demand, sellers will see the run-down of stocks and may respond by raising both price and quantity supplied. The market will thus tend to move towards equilibrium. The speed of this adjustment may be rapid or gradual, depending upon the particular market.

The equilibrium price and quantity will be affected by the position of the demand and supply curves. Using *comparative-static* analysis, we can examine the effect of changing our background factors. For example, changes in buyers' incomes may shift the demand curve and influence the equilibrium price and quantity. If an increase in income leads to a decrease in demand for a commodity, that commodity is known as an *inferior good*. If demand increases in response to an increase in income, the commodity is known as a *normal good*.

The demand curve will also move in response to a change in buyers' preferences or in the price of other goods. In the latter case, the direction of response will depend upon whether the goods are *substitutes* or *complements*. A fall in the price of unskimmed milk may decrease the demand for skimmed milk (they are substitutes). A fall in the price of coffee may lead to an increase in the demand for skimmed milk (they are complements).

Similarly, changes in technology or in the costs of inputs may induce movements of the supply curve. New efficient techniques of production may mean that sellers will be prepared to supply more at any given price. Higher production costs might have the reverse effect.

The distinction between movements of a curve and movements *along* a curve is an important one. A typical comparative static exercise will involve both. For instance, a change in incomes will lead to a movement *of* the demand curve, which in turn will induce a movement *along* the supply curve. (See Box 3–1 of the main text for a fuller explanation.)

Sometimes governments may consider that the free market equilibrium is not in the best interests of society at large. They may thus intervene, perhaps to protect sellers by holding price above its equilibrium level (e.g., agricultural commodity prices, minimum wage legislation) or perhaps to protect buyers by holding price below its equilibrium level (e.g., rent controls). In practice, such intervention may have unintended effects on income or welfare.

Analysis of market equilibrium tells us the quantity of a good that will be produced, and at what price. It tells us for whom it is produced (those who are willing and able to pay the going price). Some goods may not be produced at all, if the price required to induce supply is above that which buyers are prepared to pay. We thus take the first steps towards examining our key economic questions.

IMPORTANT CONCEPTS AND TECHNICAL TERMS

Match each lettered concept with the appropriate numbered phrase:

(a) Market   (g) Demand
(b) Equilibrium price   (h) Inferior good
(c) Normal good   (i) Free market
(d) Excess supply   (j) Excess demand
(e) Comparative-static   (k) Supply
     analysis   (l) Price controls
(f) Market price

1 The price at which the quantity supplied equals the quantity demanded.
2 A good for which demand falls when incomes rise.
3 The price prevailing in a market.
4 The study of the effect (on equilibrium price and quantity) of a change in one of the other-things-equal factors.
5 A set of arrangements by which buyers and sellers are in contact to exchange goods or services.
6 Government rules or laws that forbid the adjustment of prices to clear markets.
7 A good for which demand increases when incomes rise.
8 The situation in which quantity supplied exceeds quantity demanded at a particular price.
9 The quantity of a good that sellers wish to sell at each conceivable price.
10 The situation in which quantity demanded exceeds quantity supplied at a particular price.
11 A market in which price is determined purely by the forces of supply and demand.
12 The quantity of a good that buyers wish to purchase at each conceivable price.

EXERCISES

1 Suppose that the data of Table 3.1 represent the market demand and supply schedules for baked beans over a range of prices.
   (a) Using graph paper, plot on a single diagram the demand curve and supply curve, remembering to label the axes carefully.

TABLE 3.1 Demand and supply of baked beans

Price (pence)	Quantity demanded (million tins/year)	Quantity supplied (million tins/year)
8	70	10
16	60	30
24	50	50
32	40	70
40	30	90

   (b) What would be the excess demand or supply if price were set at 8p?
   (c) What would be the excess demand or supply if price were set at 32p?
   (d) Find the equilibrium price and quantity.
   (e) Suppose that, following an increase in consumer's incomes, the demand for baked beans rises by 15 million tins/year at each price level. Find the new equilibrium price and quantity.

2 The distinction between shifts of the demand and supply curves and movements along them is an important one. Place ticks in the appropriate columns of Table 3.2 to show the effects of changes in the other-things-equal categories detailed in the first column. (Two ticks are required for each item.)

TABLE 3.2

Change in other-things-equal category	Shift of demand curve	Movement along demand curve	Shift of supply curve	Movement along supply curve
Change in price of competing good				
Introduction of new technique of production				
A craze for the good				
A change in incomes				
A change in price of a material input				

[*Please note that in questions 3–8 more than one answer is possible.*]

3 In Figure 3.1 the demand curve for pens has moved from D_0 to D_1. Which of the following could have brought about this move?
   (a) A fall in the price of a substitute for pens.
   (b) A fall in the price of a complement to pens.
   (c) A fall in the price of a raw material used to produce pens.
   (d) A decrease in consumers' incomes (assume that a pen is an inferior good).
   (e) A decrease in the rate of value added tax.
   (f) A decrease in consumers' incomes (assume that a pen is a normal good).
   (g) An advertising campaign for pens.

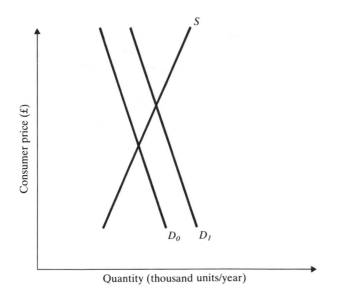

FIGURE 3.1   The demand for pens

4   Which of the following would probably lead to a shift in the demand curve for cameras?
  (a)   A decrease in the price of cameras.
  (b)   An increase in real incomes.
  (c)   A decrease in the price of film.

5   In Figure 3.2 the supply curve for tents has moved from S_0 to S_1. Which of the following could have brought about this move?
  (a)   The introduction of a new improved method of producing tents.
  (b)   A fall in the price of a complement to tents.
  (c)   An increase in the wage rate paid to tent workers.
  (d)   An increase in consumers' incomes (assume that a tent is a normal good).
  (e)   A fall in the price of a tent component.

6   Which of these goods would you expect to be 'normal' goods, and which 'inferior'?
  (a)   Colour television.
  (b)   Coffee.
  (c)   Rice.
  (d)   Monochrome television.
  (e)   Remould tyres.

7   Which of these goods might be regarded as 'substitutes' for strawberries, and which 'complements'?
  (a)   Raspberries.
  (b)   Fresh cream.
  (c)   Petrol.
  (d)   Ice cream.
  (e)   Roast beef.
  (f)   Bus journey.
  (g)   Microcomputer.

8   Which of the following could cause a rise in house prices?
  (a)   A decline in housebuilding.
  (b)   An increase in lending by building societies.
  (c)   A rise in mortgage interest rates.
  (d)   An increase in the willingness of local authorities to sell council houses to tenants.

9   Suppose that Figure 3.3 depicts the market for eggs, and that the government decides to safeguard egg production by guaranteeing producers a minimum price for eggs. Thus, if eggs are left unsold to households, the government promises to buy up the surplus at the set price.
  (a)   What would be the equilibrium price and quantity in the absence of intervention?
  (b)   What would be the market price if the government were to guarantee a price of P_1?

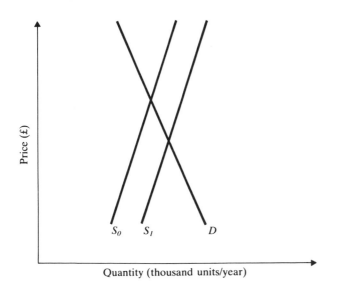

FIGURE 3.2   The supply of tents

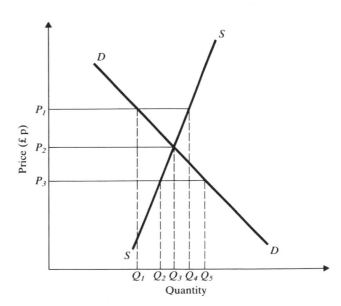

FIGURE 3.3   The market for eggs

(c) What would be the quantity demanded by households at this market price?

(d) How many eggs would need to be purchased by the government at this price?

(e) What would be the market price if the government were to guarantee a price of P_3?

(f) What would be the quantity demanded by households at this market price?

(g) How many eggs would need to be purchased by the government at this price?

10 Suppose that the data of Table 3.3 represent the (linear) market demand and supply schedules for commodity X over a range of prices.

TABLE 3.3 Demand and supply of good X

Price (pence)	Quantity demanded units/year	Quantity supplied units/year
15	50	35
16	48	38
17	46	41
18	44	44
19	42	47
20	40	50
21	38	53
22	36	56

(a) Using graph paper, plot the demand curve and supply curve.

(b) Find the equilibrium price and quantity.

Suppose that a tax of 5p per unit is imposed on firms supplying this commodity. Thus, if a firm charges 20p per unit to buyers, the government takes 5 pence, and the firm receives 15 pence.

(c) Draw the supply curve after tax is imposed—i.e., the relation between quantity supplied and the price paid by consumers.

(d) Find the equilibrium price and quantity.

TRUE/FALSE

1 _____ A change in the price of a good will cause a shift in its demand curve.

2 _____ An increase in consumers' incomes will cause an expansion in the demand for all goods.

3 _____ A poor potato harvest will result in higher prices for chips, other things being equal.

4 _____ The price charged for a good is the equilibrium price.

5 _____ An inferior good is one that has been badly produced.

6 _____ If the demand for a good rises following an increase in consumers' incomes (other things being equal), that good is known as 'normal'.

7 _____ The imposition of a minimum legal wage will lead to an increase in employment.

8 _____ In everyday parlance, two goods X and Y are known as complements if an increase in the price of X, other things being equal, leads to a fall in demand for good Y.

9 _____ The imposition of a £1 per unit tax on a good will lead to a £1 increase in the price of the good.

10 _____ When the Pope gave permission for Catholics to eat meat on Fridays, the equilibrium price and quantity of fish fell.

QUESTIONS FOR THOUGHT

1 How would you expect the market for coffee to react to a sudden reduction in supply, perhaps caused by a poor harvest? Would you expect the revenue received by coffee-growers to fall or rise as a result?

2 Discuss some of the ways in which a change in the demand or supply conditions in a market may spill over and affect conditions in another market. Provide some examples of such spillover effects.

3 Suppose you are trying to observe the demand curve for a commodity. When you collect price and quantity data for a sequence of years, you find that they suggest a *positive* relationship. What line of reasoning and additional information would you need to use in order to make an interpretation of the data?

ANSWERS AND COMMENTS FOR CHAPTER 3

Please note Where questions are reproduced from A level examinations, the examination boards bear no responsibility for the answers provided in this volume, which are the sole responsibility of the authors.

Important Concepts and Technical Terms

1 *b*	4 *e*	7 *c*	10 *j*
2 *h*	5 *a*	8 *d*	11 *i*
3 *f*	6 *l*	9 *k*	12 *g*

Exercises

1 *(a)*

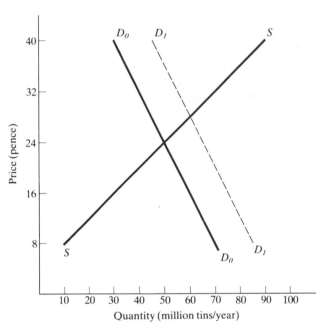

FIGURE A3.1   The market for baked beans

(b)   Excess demand of 60 million tins/year.
(c)   Excess supply of 30 million tins/year.
(d)   50 million tins/year at a price of 24p.
(e)   60 million tins/year at a price of 28p.

2   **TABLE A3.1**

Change in other-things-equal category	Shift of demand curve	Move-ment along demand curve	Shift of supply curve	Move-ment along supply curve
Change in price of competing good	√			√
Introduction of new technique of production		√	√	
A craze for the good	√			√
A change in incomes	√			√
A change in price of a material input		√	√	

3   The movement could have been caused by *(b)*, *(d)*, or *(g)*. Factors *(a)* and *(f)* would move the demand curve in the opposite direction; factors *(c)* and *(e)* would move the supply curve.

4   The shift could have been caused by *(b)* or *(c)*. *(a)* may have been a *response* to a change in demand but will not initiate a shift in the demand curve. If the change in price results from a shift in supply, the result will be a movement *along* the demand curve.

5   The movement could have been caused by *(a)* or *(e)*. Factor *(c)* would move the supply curve in the opposite direction; factors *(b)* and *(d)* would move the demand curve.

6   *(a)* and *(b)* are likely to be normal goods. *(c)* and *(e)* are likely to be inferior goods—as incomes rise, we might expect the demand for these commodities to fall, as consumers find they can afford other alternatives. In the case of *(d)* there may be arguments both ways. As incomes rise, more people may afford televisions, tending to increase demand. However, if more people switch to colour televisions, the demand for old-fashioned monochrome televisions may decline. In the UK now it is likely that monochrome televisions are inferior goods.

7   The answer here depends very much upon individual preferences! Most would regard strawberries and fresh cream as being complements. Others may like raspberries and/or ice cream with their strawberries. However, in the final analysis, most goods will turn out to be substitutes—if you spend more on strawberries, you must spend less on other goods.

8   *(a)* or *(b)* could cause a rise in house prices. Factors *(a)* and *(d)* will lead to movements of the supply curve, whereas *(b)* and *(c)* affect the demand curve. Try drawing a diagram to see the effects of these movements.

9   *(a)* P_2, Q_3.
    (b) P_1.
    (c) Q_1.
    (d) $(Q_4 - Q_1)$.
    (e) P_2. A minimum price will be effective only if set above the equilibrium level.
    (f) Q_3.
    (g)   None.

10 *(a)*   See Figure A3.2.
    (b)   Price 18p, quantity 44 units. So far, so good. It's the next bit that's tricky: the key is to think through the supplier's decision process. Suppose the market price is 20p: 5 pence of this goes in tax to the government and the supplier receives 15 pence—at which price we know he is prepared to supply 35 units per year. Using this sort of argument, we can construct a new supply schedule showing how much will be supplied at each (gross of tax) price.
    (c)   The new supply curve is given by S^*S^* in Figure A3.2; the vertical distance between SS and S^*S^* is 5 pence.
    (d)   Price 21p, quantity 38 units. Notice that price does not rise by the full amount of the tax.

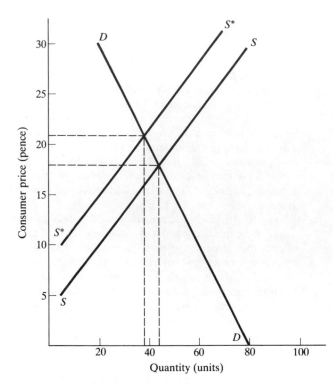

FIGURE A3.2   A tax on good *X*

True/False

1   False: the demand curve itself shows how buyers respond to price changes.
2   False: some goods may be 'inferior'.
3   True.
4   False: there may be periods when markets adjust sluggishly towards equilibrium. Government intervention may prevent adjustment to equilibrium.
5   False: an inferior good is one for which demand falls as incomes rise.
6   True.
7   False: if effective, such legislation may lead to a fall in employment (see Section 3–9 of the main text).
8   True: but a more precise economist's view of complementarity awaits in Chapter 6.
9   False: see exercise 10.
10 True: see Section 3–8 of the main text.

Questions for Thought

1   The result depends crucially on the steepness of the demand curve: this example is discussed in Chapter 5.
2   There are many such examples: in particular, we may consider whether a pair of goods are complements or substitutes.
3   *Hint*   See Box 3–2 in the main text.

4

Government in the Mixed Economy

Although much stress has recently been laid on the importance of the 'free market' in allocating resources, governments fulfil an important economic role, even in the mixed economies of the West. In this chapter, we introduce three questions about the role of the government in the economy. We look first of all at what economic activities are carried out by governments. Secondly, we explore the rationales offered by economic theory to justify such activities. Finally, we consider the way in which government decisions are taken.

In terms of expenditure, the share of government activity in national income has been rising in many market economies, including Britain, where there has been a revival of belief in the free market system, and attempts by the public sector to disengage from economic involvement, for instance through privatization (discussed in Chapter 18).

An important role for government in all societies is to establish the rules by which economic activity will be conducted, in particular the rules regarding the ownership of property and the operation of markets. A distinguishing characteristic of *socialist economies* is that the private ownership of businesses is prohibited by law, whereas in *capitalist economies* individuals may own businesses and may be motivated by the aim of making profits. However, neither extreme exists in reality. In most 'socialist' economies there have been moves towards granting more economic freedom to individuals (the process known as *perestroika*). Equally, in the 'capitalist' economies, economic freedom may be limited or regulated; for example, there may be limitations on the right to carry fire-arms, or regulations concerning the sale of drugs.

In mixed economies, the government acts also as a direct participant in the market by buying and selling goods and services. In addition, governments may act to redistribute income by making *transfer payments*. These payments are made on welfare grounds and not in return for any direct economic service provided by the recipient. Clearly, this excludes such payments as salaries paid to government employees.

These various expenditure items must of course be financed. Governments raise funds in two main ways: by *taxation* and by *borrowing*. Taxes may be levied both at national level (income tax, VAT) and at local level (the community charge). As the scale of government activity has risen over time, there has been a reluctance to keep increasing the tax burden. This encourages governments to borrow in order to finance their spending through running a *budget deficit*. As a result of this, there has been an increase in the burden of government debt in many countries. The UK was unusual in achieving a reduction in the ratio of government debt to national income during the 1980s.

Another way in which governments have intervened has been in attempting to stabilize the economy, that is, trying to counteract the fluctuations in economic activity manifested in the *business cycle*. This issue will be studied more carefully in the macroeconomics section of the book.

Another way of looking at all this is to see the government as an influence on the three central economic questions that were introduced in Chapter 1. As a producer and consumer, the government influences *what* is produced (e.g. defence, the arts); it affects *how* goods and services are produced (through health, safety and other regulations); finally, it influences *for whom* goods and services are produced (through taxes and transfers).

Notice that taxes on particular goods like alcohol and tobacco may also affect *what* is produced: a high rate of excise tax on cigarettes may reduce the quantity demanded as well as raising revenues for the government. Whether the brunt of the tax falls on the consumer or the producer is determined by the elasticity of demand and supply.

Given Adam Smith's 'Invisible Hand', we must ask why it should be necessary for governments to intervene in these various ways. The fundamental economic justification is in cases of *market failure*, which may reveal areas in which theory suggests that government action may be able to improve resource allocation. Of course, whether it *will* improve is quite a different question.

How can we justify government spending on goods and services? Some goods by their nature are *public goods*: goods which, even if consumed by one person, can still be consumed by others, an obvious example being defence. A feature of such public goods is that they involve strong *externalities* and give rise to the *free-rider problem*. There is thus a case for government intervention to ensure the socially efficient level of production of such goods. This is not to say that public goods must always be government-produced; the production of some public goods may well be subcontracted to private firms—but paid for from government sources. It may also be sometimes appropriate for government agencies to produce *private* goods, although experience suggests that this does not guarantee efficiency in production.

In the case of *merit goods*, the argument for government involvement may be strengthened by an awareness that social efficiency may demand that individuals consume a commodity whether they want to or not. For instance, compulsory vaccination may be necessary to safeguard the interest of individuals or society at large.

Other justifications may relate to situations in which the government may have access to better information than the general public, for instance in regulating the preparation of food: it is not possible for each diner at a restaurant to check the cleanliness of the kitchen. Further, the government may wish to protect the consumer from the potential misuse of market power by a *monopolist*. Finally, society may view some redistribution of income as being desirable, perhaps in the form of welfare programmes to protect the unemployed, elderly, disabled or other disadvantaged groups.

In looking at how economic 'agents' take decisions, the economist almost always begins with an assumption about motivations. In Chapter 6 we will assume that a consumer tries to 'maximize utility'—to choose combinations of commodities to provide as much satisfaction as possible. In Chapter 9 we will assume that firms set out to maximize profits. But what about governments? In a democratic society, governments are elected by voters and are ultimately accountable to the electorate. Individual citizens make their preferences known in elections and through pressure groups. The *paradox of voting* shows that there is no guarantee that majority voting will lead to consistent decision-making, unless each voter has *single-peaked preferences*. The *median voter* result suggests that there will be a tendency to avoid extreme outcomes. In practice, the process of decision-making may be influenced by vote-trading among politicians (e.g. *logrolling*) or by civil servants.

IMPORTANT CONCEPTS AND TECHNICAL TERMS

Match each lettered concept with the appropriate numbered phrase:

(a)	Public good	(j)	Transfer payments
(b)	Monopolist	(k)	Median voter
(c)	Private good	(l)	Capitalist economy
(d)	Socialist economy	(m)	Single-peaked preferences
(e)	Budget deficit		
(f)	Business cycle	(n)	Log-rolling
(g)	Externality	(o)	Paradox of voting
(h)	Free-rider	(p)	Merit good
(i)	Regulation		

1   Payments for which no current direct economic service is provided in return.

2   An economy in which the legal framework outlaws the private ownership of businesses.

3   Fluctuations in total production or GNP, accompanied by fluctuations in the level of unemployment and the rate of inflation.

4   A situation in which government expenditure exceeds government revenue such that borrowing is undertaken, and government debt increases.

5   An economy in which businesses are owned by individuals and operated for private profit.

6   A good that, even if it is consumed by one person, is still available for consumption by others.

7   The single seller of a good or service.

8   A good that society thinks people should consume or receive, no matter what their incomes are.

9   Exists when the production or consumption of a good directly affects businesses or consumers not involved in buying and selling it but when those spillover effects are not fully reflected in market prices.

10   A good that, if consumed by one person, cannot be consumed by another.

11   Description of a situation where an individual is happier with an outcome the closer it is to the preferred level as judged by that individual.

12   A description of voting behaviour in which the majority outcome turns out to be that favoured by the voter in the middle.

13   Someone who gets to consume a good that is costly to produce without paying for it.

14   An argument demonstrating that majority voting does not necessarily permit consistent decision-making.

15   An example of how politicians may trade votes so that an individual gets a preferred package.

16   Rules imposed by governments to control the operation of markets.

EXERCISES

1   Figure 4.1 shows UK general government revenue and expenditure as a percentage of gross domestic product (GDP at market prices) for the period 1965–88.

   (a)   In which years was the government *not* operating with a budget deficit?

   (b)   Government debt fell in the UK as a percentage of national income (see main text, Table 4.3). Can you explain this by studying Figure 4.1? If not, what additional factors do you think might be important?

   (c)   Mrs Thatcher was first elected in 1979 and pursued a 'disengagement' strategy. How-

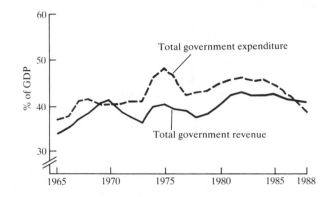

FIGURE 4.1 UK government revenue and expenditure, 1965–88 (*Source*: CSO, *United Kingdom National Accounts* (1989) and *Economic Trends* Annual Supplement.)

ever, you can see in Figure 4.1 that government expenditure did not begin to fall relative to GDP until about 1983. Why might it be difficult for a government to find ways of reducing its level of involvement in the economy?

(d) See if you can find data on the level of activity of the government in the UK economy for a more recent year. Have the trends shown in Figure 4.1 continued?

2 This exercise echoes and extends some analysis first introduced in Chapter 3 (exercise 10). Figure 4.2 shows the market for a good before and after the imposition of a unit tax on the sales of the good.

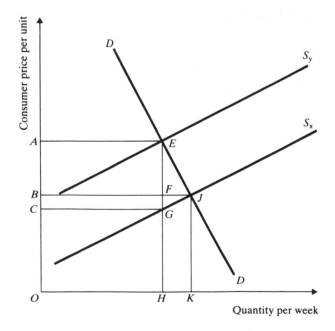

FIGURE 4.2 A commodity tax

(a) Which supply curve represents the 'with-tax' market?

(b) Which area represents the revenue received by the government from this tax?

(c) Identify the area representing the incidence of the tax on
   (i) buyers of the good.
   (ii) sellers of the good.

(d) Given your answer to (c), which group bears the main burden of the tax? How would you expect your answer to differ if the demand curve were relatively elastic and the supply curve relatively inelastic?

3 The incidence of an expenditure tax will fall entirely on the consumer when the
   (a) producer's supply curve is perfectly inelastic
   (b) good has a high income elasticity
   (c) good is imported
   (d) consumers' demand for the good is perfectly elastic
   (e) consumers' demand for the good is perfectly inelastic
                     (University of London GCE A level Economics 3, January 1987)

4 Which of the following are *not* examples of transfer payments?
   (a) Unemployment benefit.
   (b) Payment of the Community Charge.
   (c) Old-age pension.
   (d) Supplementary benefit.
   (e) Nurses' pay.

5 Which of the following is nearest to being a 'pure' public good?
   (a) Defence.
   (b) Education.
   (c) Water supply.
   (d) Health services.
   (e) Postal services.

6 Which of the following are merit goods?
   (a) Any good that cannot be provided by private enterprise because non-payers cannot be excluded from enjoying its benefits.
   (b) Any good that is made available to consumers on merit.
   (c) Any good that the government believes consumers will buy too little of if it is provided by private enterprise at market prices.
   (d) Any good provided free of charge to consumers by the government.
   (e) Any good where the private benefits of consuming the good exceed its social benefits.
   (f) Any good that society thinks people should receive regardless of income.

7 All of the factors below, relating to an extension to

the London Underground system, are externalities, with the exception of

(a) savings in time expected to result through faster travel

(b) reductions in congestion resulting in inner London

(c) health effects of traffic pollution in inner London

(d) wage costs of the line during construction

(Associated Examining Board GCE A level Economics Paper 1, November 1988)

8 Table 4.1 shows the ranking of 5 possible outcomes by 5 voters.

TABLE 4.1 Each voter's ranking of outcomes *A, B, C, D,* and *E*

Voter	A	B	C	D	E
1	1	3	5	2	4
2	3	5	2	4	1
3	5	2	4	1	3
4	2	4	1	3	5
5	4	1	3	5	2

(a) How many voters would vote for outcome *A* as against *B*?

(b) How many would vote for *B* as against *C*?

(c) For *C* as against *D*?

(d) For *D* as against *C*?

(e) And for *E* as against *A*?

(f) Comment on the significance of this sequence of results for decision-making.

(g) What sort of voters' preferences could allow this problem to be evaded?

9 Which of the following would be classified as public goods?

(a) Lighthouses.

(b) International football matches.

(c) Council houses.

(d) The telephone service.

(e) Flood control.

(f) The London Underground.

(g) Street lighting.

(h) Police force.

TRUE/FALSE

1 _____ A socialist economy is one in which the private ownership of property is prohibited by law.

2 _____ A capitalist economy is one in which the free market is given free rein.

3 _____ In the mid-1980s, government spending relative to national income in the UK was the lowest among the industrial market economies.

4 _____ In the late-1980s, government debt relative to national income in the UK was low compared to most industrial market economies.

5 _____ When demand for a commodity is highly elastic, the main burden of a sales tax will fall on the consumer.

6 _____ Transfer payments are a means by which governments influence *for whom* goods and services are produced.

7 _____ The free market is the best way of allocating resources, so governments should never intervene in the working of the economy.

8 _____ The function of government intervention is less to tell people what they ought to like than to allow them better to achieve what they already like.

9 _____ The paradox of voting states that, even when people disagree, majority voting produces consistent decision-making.

10 _____ The median voter result implies that extreme outcomes will be avoided.

QUESTIONS FOR THOUGHT

1 In what senses could the market system 'fail'? To what extent could your arguments be used to justify the production and distribution of goods and services by the public sector?

(University of Oxford Delegacy of Local Examinations, GCE A level Economics Paper 1, June 1989)

2 Assess the economic arguments for and against providing a health service free of charge to everyone in the community.

(Associated Examining Board GCE A level Economics Paper 3, November 1988)

ANSWERS AND COMMENTS FOR CHAPTER 4

Please note Where questions are reproduced from GCE examinations, the examining boards bear no responsibility for the answers provided in this volume, which are the sole responsibility of the authors.

Important Concepts and Technical Terms

1	*j*	5	*l*	9	*g*	13	*h*
2	*d*	6	*a*	10	*c*	14	*o*
3	*f*	7	*b*	11	*m*	15	*n*
4	*e*	8	*p*	12	*k*	16	*i*

Exercises

1 (a) The only years in which government revenue exceeded expenditure were 1970 and 1988. In 1987 the two were almost equal. For the rest of the period there was a budget deficit.

   (b) We do not really have enough information in Figure 4.1 to explain the fall in government debt between 1980 and 1989. It seems unlikely that the budget surplus of 1988 is a sufficient explanation. However, we should be aware that the government's borrowing requirement during the 1980s was tempered by receipts from privatization.

   (c) There are a number of reasons why a government might not be able to make rapid adjustments to its involvement in the economy. Many long-term capital projects commit funds for particular uses over a long time horizon (e.g. the Channel Tunnel), so that some expenditure items cannot be rapidly reduced. The recession of the early 1980s aggravated the situation, requiring an increase in the funds devoted to the payment of unemployment and other welfare benefits.

   (d) We cannot comment here, as we do not know when you will be tackling this question. Make sure that you have data on total government expenditure and revenue (including capital transactions). Notice that we used GDP at current market prices as our measurement of 'national income'.

2 (a) S_y.

   (b) *AEGC*.

   (c) (i) *AEFB*.

      (ii) *BFGC*.

3 (e).

4 (b) is a tax contributing to local authority revenues; (e) is a payment for nursing services rendered.

5 (a) Defence is the closest here to being a 'pure' public good, in the sense that all citizens of a country 'consume' nearly equal amounts of defence: this is not true of any of the other goods mentioned. Of course, different individuals may obtain differing amounts of utility from their consumption of defence.

6 The correct answers here are (c) and (f): the key feature of merit goods is that the government wishes to make sure that they are consumed by individuals. The 'merit' lies in the good, not in the consumer; thus response (b) is incorrect. Notice that answer (a) refers to a public good.

7 An externality is a cost or benefit which is *not* reflected in market prices. The wage costs (item (d)) clearly do have a market price, so are not an externality.

8 (a)–(e) 3, i.e. a majority.

   (f) This is one illustration of the 'paradox of voting', by which we see that voters' preferences may fail to allow consistent decision-making. Further discussion of some of these issues may be found in an article by Alan Hamlin in the *Economic Review*, March 1989.

   (g) Single-peaked (see Section 4–3 of the main text).

9 (a), (e), (g), and (h).

True/False

1 True: but with *perestroika* such restrictions have been much relaxed (see Section 4–1 of the main text).

2 Not really true: in most capitalist economies the government regulates markets in one way or another (see Section 4–1 of the main text).

3 False: UK government spending was lower than France or Sweden, but higher than other economies such as Germany, Japan or the USA (see Table 4–1 of the main text).

4 True: see Table 4–3 of the main text.

5 True: see Box 4–1 of the main text.

6 True.

7 False: there are situations in which governments may be justified in intervening. These situations reflect the presence of some form of *market failure* (see Section 4–2 of the main text).

8 True: but in the case of merit goods (bads), the government may intervene because it believes it has a clearer view of what is in society's best interests.

9 False: see Section 4–3 of the main text.

10 True.

Questions for Thought

It may be much to expect for you to be able to tackle A level essay questions after reading only four chapters. However, the fundamental issues underlying both of these questions have been outlined in Section 4–2 of the main text, and this discussion should provide the foundation for thinking about the questions. More detailed analysis of market failure and of government activity will appear in a later chapter.

5

The Effect of Price and Income on Demand Quantities

Chapter 3 served to introduce you to the notion of market equilibrium between demand and supply. In the following chapters, we focus more closely upon these important concepts, beginning in Chapters 5 and 6 with a look at the factors influencing demand and at applications of demand analysis.

From the supplier's point of view, an issue of great moment concerns the likely degree of responsiveness of demand to a change in price. If price is increased by 50 pence, by how much will the quantity demanded alter? When considering different goods, it is more helpful to consider *percentage* changes than the absolute changes. The ratio of the percentage change in quantity demanded of a good to the percentage change in price that brought it about is known as the *own price elasticity of demand*, often referred to as the price elasticity of demand or simply the demand elasticity.

For a linear demand curve (and many nonlinear ones), the demand elasticity is not constant throughout its length, but differs according to the point at which it is measured. For nonlinear demand curves the elasticity should be measured by examining *small* percentage changes in price. For conventional downward-sloping demand curves, the own price elasticity of demand is negative—reflecting the fact that as price falls, quantity rises.

When the percentage change in demand is greater than the percentage change in price (i.e., if the demand elasticity is more negative than −1) then demand is said to be *elastic*. If elasticity is between 0 and −1, demand is said to be *inelastic*. The size of the elasticity depends crucially on the availability of substitutes: if there are ready substitutes for a particular good, then demand is likely to be extremely sensitive to price changes—i.e., demand is elastic. For instance, if the price of raspberry jam increases (other things being equal), buyers will tend to switch to strawberry or other flavoured jams—and the demand for raspberry jam will fall substantially. However, if there are no ready substitutes, demand will tend to be rather unresponsive to price changes.

In general, if we measure elasticity for a narrowly defined commodity—a particular flavour of jam, or a single brand of toothpaste—then elasticity will tend to be 'high', whereas the demand elasticity for a broadly defined commodity group (e.g., food) will tend to be 'low', as the possibilities for substitution are restricted. If households respond sluggishly to price changes, then elasticity will tend to be greater in the long run than in the short run. Indeed, in this context we define the long run as the time that elapses until consumers have adjusted fully to price changes.

The value of the elasticity provides valuable information about how *expenditure* will alter following a price change. When demand is elastic, a price fall will increase expenditure; if demand is inelastic, then expenditure will fall as price falls. This may be vital information for suppliers, for whom expenditure by consumers represents *revenue*. Revenue is maximized at the threshold between elastic and inelastic demand. This situation, where elasticity is equal to −1, is known as *unit elasticity*.

The uses of the demand elasticity are myriad and may sometimes produce surprising results. For example, how will a disastrous harvest affect farmers producing a particular crop? If the demand for their produce is inelastic, then the price increase initiated by the contraction in supply will lead to an *increase* in revenue. Collusion between farmers to restrict output would have a similar effect, but this is difficult to organize, as individual producers stand to gain by cheating on such a collusive agreement—as we shall see in a later chapter.

The cross price elasticity of demand measures the responsiveness of the demand for a commodity to a change in the price of some other good. If the two goods are complements, the cross price elasticity will tend to be negative; if they are substitutes, the cross price elasticity will tend to be positive. The cross price elasticity is likely to be smaller in magnitude than the own price elasticity.

The income elasticity of demand measures the sensitivity of the demand for a commodity to a change in income of consumers. A normal good has a positive income elasticity of demand; an inferior good has a negative income elasticity. A good having an income elasticity of demand greater than one is a *luxury good*; a good having an income elasticity of less than one is a *necessity*.

The *budget share* of a good indicates the proportion of total expenditure on that good. An increase in income causes the budget share of luxury goods to rise and that of necessities (whether normal or inferior goods) to fall. Knowledge of income elasticities can be important if we wish to predict the pattern of consumer spending as income in an economy rises.

When we draw a demand curve, we focus on the relationship between the demand for a good and its price, holding 'other things equal', where the 'other things' include income and other prices. The position of the demand curve is determined by these and other background factors. Knowledge of income and cross price elasticities also tells us how the demand curve for a good will shift as either incomes or other prices change. The sign of the elasticity (positive or negative) tells us the direction of movement of the demand curve; the magnitude tells us the extent of the shift.

The 'other things equal' condition also explains why knowledge of the elasticity measures does not tell us how the pattern of demand will react to inflation. Indeed, if inflation is general throughout an economy, affecting all prices equally (including wages and other incomes), then we have no reason to believe that the pattern of demand will change at all unless households misperceive the price changes. The elasticity measures do not help because they rest upon the 'other things equal' assumption—which is not valid when all prices and incomes are changing at once.

IMPORTANT CONCEPTS AND TECHNICAL TERMS

Match each lettered concept with the appropriate numbered phrase:

(a) Cross price elasticity of demand
(b) Inelastic demand
(c) Long run
(d) Budget share
(e) Normal good
(f) Necessity
(g) Substitutes
(h) Unit elastic demand
(i) Short run
(j) Income elasticity of demand
(k) Elastic demand
(l) Inferior good
(m) Total spending on a good
(n) Complements
(o) Luxury good
(p) Own price elasticity of demand

1 The percentage change in quantity demanded divided by the corresponding percentage change in income.
2 Expenditure on a good as a proportion of total spending.
3 The quantity demanded is insensitive to price changes: elasticity is between 0 and −1.
4 A good with a positive income elasticity of demand.
5 A good with a negative income elasticity of demand.
6 A measure of the responsiveness of demand for a good to a change in the price of another good.
7 A good having an income elasticity of demand less than 1.
8 The percentage change in the quantity of a good demanded divided by the corresponding change in its price.
9 Two goods are described thus if a rise in the price of one is generally associated with an increase in demand for the other.
10 A good having an income elasticity of demand greater than 1.
11 Quantity demanded of a good multiplied by its price.
12 The quantity demanded is highly responsive to price changes: elasticity is more negative than −1.
13 Expenditure is unchanged when price falls: elasticity is equal to −1.
14 The period necessary for complete adjustment to a price change.
15 Two goods are described thus when an increase in the price of one is generally associated with a fall in demand for the other.
16 The period during which consumers are still in the process of adjusting to a price change.

EXERCISES

1 Table 5.1 presents the quantity of rice popsicles demanded at various alternative prices:

TABLE 5.1 The demand for rice popsicles

Price per packet (£p)	Quantity demanded (thousands)	Total spending (revenue) (£ thousands)	Own price elasticity of demand
2.10	10		
1.80	20		
1.50	30		
1.20	40		
0.90	50		
0.60	60		
0.30	70		

(a) Draw the demand curve on graph paper, plotting price on the vertical axis and quantity on the horizontal axis.
(b) Suppose price were £1.20. What would be the change in quantity demanded if price were to be reduced by 30 pence? Would your answer be different if you started at any other price?
(c) Calculate total spending on rice popsicles at each price shown.
(d) Calculate the own price elasticity of demand for prices between 60p and £2.10.
(e) Draw a graph showing total revenue against sales. Plot revenue on the vertical axis and quantity demanded on the horizontal.
(f) At what price is revenue at its greatest?
(g) At what price is the demand elasticity equal to −1?
(h) Within what ranges of prices is demand
(i) elastic?
(ii) inelastic?

2   **TABLE 5.2** Cross price and own price elasticities of demand in Mythuania

Percentage change in quantity demanded of:	In response to a 1% price change in		
	Food	Wine	Beer
Food	−0.25	0.06	0.01
Wine	−0.13	−1.20	0.27
Beer	0.07	0.41	−0.85

Answer the following questions using the estimated elasticities presented in Table 5.2.
(a) Comment on the own price demand elasticities of the three goods, identifying for which goods demand is elastic and for which it is inelastic.
(b) What is the effect of a change in the price of food on the consumption of wine and of beer? What does this suggest about the relationship between food and the other commodities?
(c) Figure 5.1 shows the demand curve for wine (D_w).
Sketch in the effect on the demand curve of an increase in the price of
   (i) food.
   (ii) beer.

3   Which of the demand curves DD and dd in Figure 5.2 would you expect to represent the long-run demand for electricity? Explain your answer.

4   Table 5.3 presents the total spending and income of a household in two years.
(a) Calculate the budget shares in each year for each good.
(b) Calculate the income elasticity of demand for each good.
(c) Classify each of the goods as either 'normal' or 'inferior'.
(d) Classify each of the goods as either a 'luxury' or a 'necessity'.

5   Sketch the effect of a *fall* in income upon the demand curve for each of the three goods whose income elasticities are given in Table 5.4.

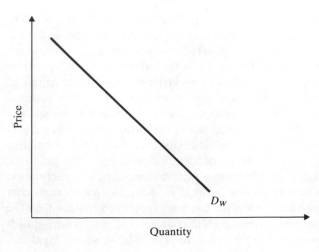

FIGURE 5.1 The demand for wine in Mythuania

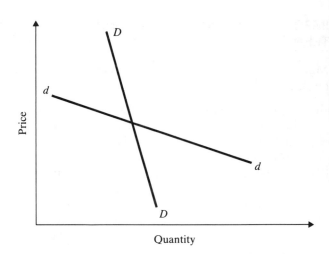

FIGURE 5.2 Short- and long-run demand curves for electricity

TABLE 5.4 Income elasticity of demand for three goods

Good X	1.7
Good Y	−0.8
Good Z	0

TABLE 5.3

Income	Year 1 £100	Year 2 £200	Budget share (year 1)	Budget share (year 2)	Income elasticity of demand	Normal (No) or inferior good (I)	Luxury (L) or necessity (Ne)
Good A	£30	£50					
Good B	£30	£70					
Good C	£25	£20					
Good D	£15	£60					

6   A manufacturer of washing machines reduces his price by 5% and, as a result, the volume of sales of washing machines rises by 4%. The price elasticity of demand for his good is
    (a)   greater than unity
    (b)   equal to unity
    (c)   less than unity
    (d)   indeterminate from available information
    (Associated Examining board GCE A-level Economics Paper 1, November 1988)

7   An economist would classify a consumer product as inferior if its
    (a)   income elasticity of demand were −0.5
    (b)   price elasticity of demand were −1.3
    (c)   cross-elasticity of demand were −0.7
    (d)   income elasticity of demand were 1.3
    (e)   cross-elasticity of demand were 0.1
    (University of London A level Economics 3, June 1989)

8   If butter and margarine have a cross elasticity of demand of 2 and the price of butter rises from 20p per lb to 30p per lb, the percentage change in the demand for margarine will be
    (a)   20%
    (b)   25%
    (c)   75%
    (d)   100%
    (e)   150%
    (University of London A level Economics 3, June 1987)

9   For which of the following commodities would you expect demand to be *elastic*, and which *inelastic*?

Good	Elastic	Inelastic
Bread		
Theatre tickets		
Foreign holidays		
Fuel and light		
Catering		
Dairy produce		
Clothing		

10 A household's income and consumption pattern were observed at various points in time. Table 5.5 shows income and quantities of bacon purchased.

TABLE 5.5

Real income (£ p.a.)	Quantity of bacon (lb/month)
2000	2
3000	3
4000	3.5
5000	4
6000	4.3
7000	4.4
8000	4.5

(a)   Construct a scatter diagram showing bacon consumption on the vertical axis and income on the horizontal.
(b)   Does your diagram show a positive or a negative relationship between these variables?
(c)   Does this suggest that bacon is a normal or an inferior good?
(d)   What might your diagram look like for an inferior good?

TRUE/FALSE

1   _____ Price elasticities measure the response of quantity demanded to changes in the relative price of goods.

2   _____ The own price elasticity of demand is constant throughout the length of a straight-line demand curve.

3   _____ Price cuts will increase total spending on a good if demand is inelastic.

4   _____ Demand will tend to be more elastic in the long run than in the short run.

5   _____ Total spending by consumers generates total revenue for sellers.

6   _____ Total revenue is maximized when the demand elasticity is equal to −1.

7   _____ Broadly defined commodity groups such as food are likely to have more elastic demand than narrowly defined commodities such as rump steak.

8   _____ If two goods are complements, the cross price elasticity of demand is likely to be positive.

9   _____ Income elasticities measure the response of quantity demanded to changes in the real value or purchasing power of income.

10 _____ The budget share of a normal good will always rise following an increase in income.

11 _____ If two goods are substitutes, the cross price elasticity of demand is likely to be negative.

12 _____ A general inflation will have substantial effects on the pattern of demand.

13 _____ A poor harvest may be disastrous for farmers by reducing the revenue received from sale of their produce.

14 _____ What is true for the individual is not necessarily true for everyone together, and what is true for everyone together does not necessarily hold for the individual.

15 _____ Higher levels of consumer income must be good news for producers.

16 _____ For price changes, we say that demand is more elastic in the long run than in the

short run. The same arguments suggest that income elasticities of demand should be higher once consumers have had time to adjust to the increase in their incomes. The reason economists emphasize the long-run/short-run distinction for price elasticity, but not for income elasticity of demand, is that changes in income are usually small.

QUESTIONS FOR THOUGHT

1 The prices of some goods are seen to be more volatile than others. Why might the price elasticity of demand be an important influence on fluctuations in the prices of different products?

2 The price elasticity of demand provides information about the shape of the demand curve. How would you interpret a price elasticity of +0.3?

3 Flora Teak likes a nice cup of tea but is equally content to accept a cup of coffee. She takes two teaspoons of sugar in coffee, but none in tea. What signs would you expect to observe for her cross price elasticities between the three commodities?

4 An economy is prospering; the real incomes of its citizens are expected to grow at a rapid rate during the next five years. Four of the commodities produced in the economy have income elasticities as follows:

Good	Income elasticity of demand
Milples	0.46
Nohoes	−1.73
Bechans	2.31
Zegroes	0.0

Assess the prospects for the four industries.

ANSWERS AND COMMENTS FOR CHAPTER 5

Please note Where questions are reproduced from A level examinations, the examination boards bear no responsibility for the answers provided in this volume, which are the sole responsibility of the authors.

Important Concepts and Technical Terms

1	*j*	5	*l*	9	*g*	13	*h*
2	*d*	6	*a*	10	*o*	14	*c*
3	*b*	7	*f*	11	*m*	15	*n*
4	*e*	8	*p*	12	*k*	16	*i*

Exercises

1 (*a*)

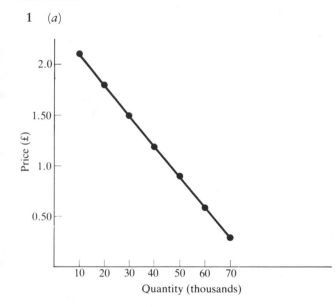

FIGURE A5.1 The demand curve for rice popsicles

(*b*) The demand curve being a straight line, the response to a 30 pence reduction in price will always be an increase of 10 000 in the quantity demanded—at least within the range of prices shown.

(*c*) and (*d*)

TABLE A5.1 The demand for rice popsicles

Price per packet (£ p)	Quantity demanded (thousands)	Total spending (revenue) (£ thousands)	Own price elasticity of demand
2.10	10	21	−7
1.80	20	36	−3
1.50	30	45	−1⅔
1.20	40	48	−1
0.90	50	45	−0.6
0.60	60	36	−0.3
0.30	70	21	

Notice that we cannot calculate the elasticity for a reduction in price at a price of 30p, as we are not told what happens to demand if price falls below this level. We could of course calculate elasticities for price *increases* instead.

(*e*)

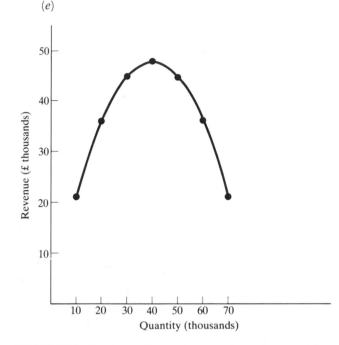

FIGURE A5.2 Total spending on (revenue from) rice popsicles

(*f*) At a price of £1.20.

(*g*) At a price of £1.20. Expenditure is always greatest at the point of unit elasticity.

(*h*) (i) At prices above £1.20.
     (ii) At prices below £1.20.

2 (*a*) For the own price elasticities we need to use the figures in the top left–bottom right diagonal of Table 5.2. For instance, the response of the demand for food to a 1 per cent change in the price of food is −0.25. The demand for food is thus inelastic, as we might expect. The demand for beer is also inelastic, although the response is stronger than for food. The demand for wine is elastic (−1.20).

(*b*) Using the cross price elasticities in the first column of the table, we see that an increase (say) in the price of food will lead to a fall in the quantity of wine demanded but an increase in the quantity of beer demanded. This implies that, in response to the change in the price of food, food and wine may well be complements, but food and beer seem more likely to be substitutes.

(*c*) An increase in the price of food causes a contraction in the demand for wine, shifting the demand curve to D_F in Figure A5.3 (food and wine are complements). The cross price elasticity of demand for wine with respect to the price of beer is positive, indicating that these goods are substitutes. The demand curve moves to D_B.

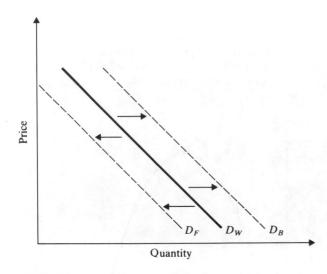

FIGURE A5.3   The demand for wine in Mythuania

3   If the price of electricity increases, other things being equal, we would expect households to switch to alternative energy sources—perhaps installing gas central heating or using gas for cooking. However, such changes will not take place immediately, so in the short run the demand for electricity will be relatively inelastic (*DD*). The long-run demand curve is thus represented by *dd*, the more elastic of the two.

4

TABLE A5.2

Income	Year 1 £100	Year 2 £200	Budget share (year 1)	Budget share (year 2)	Income elasticity of demand	Normal (No) or inferior good (I)	Luxury (L) or necessity (Ne)
Good A	£30	£50	30%	25%	2/3	No	Ne
Good B	£30	£70	30%	35%	4/3	No	L
Good C	£25	£20	25%	10%	−1/5	I	Ne
Good D	£15	£60	15%	30%	3	No	L

5

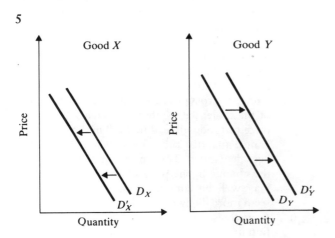

FIGURE A5.4   The effect of income on demand

The demand curve for good *Z* would remain static: with an income elasticity of demand of zero, a change in income has no effect upon demand.

6   (*c*).

7   (*a*).

8   (*d*).

9

Good	Elastic	Inelastic
Bread		✓
Theatre tickets	✓	
Foreign holidays	✓	
Fuel and light		✓
Catering	✓	
Dairy produce		✓
Clothing		✓

Estimates of own price elasticities for commodities close in definition to those in the table may be found in Section 5–1 of the main text.

10   (*a*)   See Figure A5.5.
   (*b*)   A positive relationship.
   (*c*)   Bacon seems to be a normal good, with consumption increasing with income. However, the *rate* at which consumption increases slackens off at higher incomes: this is very clear in the diagram.
   (*d*)   See Figure A5.6.
   Such a curve showing the relationship between the consumption (quantity) of a good and income is sometimes known as an *Engel curve*.

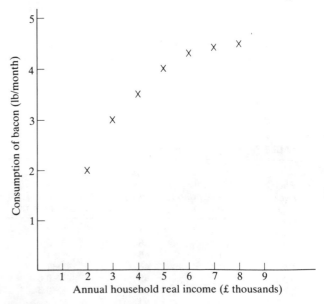

FIGURE A5.5   The relationship between consumption of bacon and income

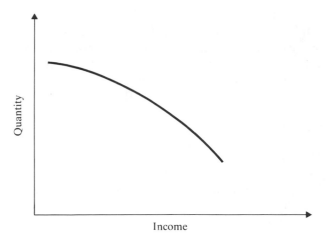

FIGURE A5.6   The relationship between consumption and income for an inferior good

True/False

1   True: see Section 5–7 of the main text.
2   False: if in doubt, see your answers to exercise 1 of this chapter.
3   False.
4   True: in the long run consumers have more opportunity to adjust their expenditure patterns.
5   True.
6   True: see main text Section 5–2 and also exercise 1 of this chapter.

7   False: the more narrowly defined the commodity, the more likely it is that there are readily available substitutes. Demand will thus tend to be highly sensitive to price.
8   False.
9   True: see Section 5–7 of the main text.
10   False: only if the income elasticity is greater than 1—see your answers to exercise 4 of this chapter.
11   False.
12   False: if relative prices are unchanged, and incomes increase at the same rate as prices, the *pattern* of expenditure will not change.
13   False: see main text Section 5–3.
14   True: again see main text Section 5–3.
15   False: somebody somewhere must be producing 'inferior' goods.
16   True.

Questions for Thought

1   Price volatility will be discussed much later on (Chapter 35).
    Hint   Think about the main factors influencing elasticity and sketch some diagrams to assess the effect on price of a supply shift under alternative assumptions about the demand elasticity.
2   A positive elasticity implies a very unusual demand curve. This *curiosum* will be encountered in Chapter 6.
4   If you require a hint, see Section 5–6 of the main text.

The Theory of Consumer Choice

6

In Chapter 5 we discussed some of the factors which determine the shape and position of the demand curve for a good. Such a demand curve is the result of decisions made by the whole host of individual potential buyers of the good. This chapter attempts to analyse these individual decisions more carefully and to show how they come together to form the demand curve faced by the sellers of the good.

In choosing what commodities to buy, an individual consumer does not have complete freedom of choice. We may reasonably assume that he will try to gain as much satisfaction as possible, but he will be constrained by the amount of income he has to spend and by the prices he must pay for the goods. Given these, his decision will be determined by his tastes or preferences. The model which we construct to explain his choice must formalize these four basic elements: motivation, income, prices, and preferences. For much of the discussion, we choose to simplify matters by considering an individual's choice between just two goods.

We begin by considering the various combinations of the goods which our individual can afford, expressed by the *budget constraint*, which separates the affordable from the unattainable. In a two-good world, we represent this by the *budget line*, whose slope depends upon the relative price of the two goods and whose position depends upon the consumer's available income.

Consumer preferences may be represented by a family of *indifference curves*. Each curve shows the consumption bundles yielding the same amounts of satisfaction—or *utility*—to the individual. These are constructed on the assumption that individuals can rank alternative bundles of goods in consistent fashion. We also normally assume that individuals prefer more of a good to less.

The slope of an indifference curve is the *marginal rate of substitution* of one good for another—that is, the quantity of one good which the individual must sacrifice in order to increase the quantity of the other good by one unit while maintaining the total level of utility. We assume that consumer tastes show a diminishing marginal rate of substitution, implying that each indifference curve will become flatter as we move along it to the right. This reflects the notion that another unit of one of the goods will confer more utility when that good constitutes a small part of the

commodity bundle than when it is relatively plentiful.

If consumers are consistent in preferences, indifference curves cannot intersect. Different individuals will have differently shaped indifference curves depending on their own personal preferences for the goods.

An individual trying to do the best he can (to maximize his utility) will strive to reach an indifference curve as far from the origin as possible. This will be achieved where an indifference curve just touches (is tangent to) the budget line. At this unique choice point, the slope of the indifference curve (the marginal rate of substitution) is equal to the slope of the budget line (the ratio of the relative prices of the goods).

We can readily analyse the effect of changing one of the background factors. For instance, holding prices and preferences constant, we can examine the effect on the choice point of a change in money income, which alters the position (but not the slope) of the budget line. From this analysis, we can derive the *income expansion path* showing how consumption of the goods varies as money income changes, other things being equal. We can also distinguish between *normal* and *inferior* goods.

Similarly, we can investigate the effect on the choice point of varying one of the prices, other things being equal. In this case, it is the *slope* of the budget line which changes. This important piece of economic analysis leads to a number of interesting results. For instance, by varying the price of a good and observing the effect upon consumption of that good, we obtain the information needed to construct an individual's demand curve for the good.

An individual's reaction to a price change can be thought of as the combination of two effects. Firstly, the *relative* price of the two goods changes, and there will tend to be a *substitution effect* in response. Secondly, the change in price has an effect on the real income or purchasing power of the individual, so there will be a *real income effect*. For a *normal good*, the two effects work in the same direction, confirming our belief that the demand curve will slope downwards. For an *inferior good*, the effects work against each other. Suppose that the price of a good falls. By the substitution effect, demand for that good will rise. However, real income has risen with the fall in price, so that the income effect causes demand to fall (for this inferior good). For all usual cases, the substitution effect will be the larger, so on balance a price fall will lead to an increase in demand—i.e., the demand curve will be downward-sloping. In the unlikely event that the income effect dominates, an inferior good would have an upward-sloping demand curve (a Giffen good). This is so rare that we can ignore it in future analysis.

By looking at the effects of changes in one price upon consumption of the other good, we can examine cross-price effects. The direction of the cross-price effect depends upon the relative strength of the income and substitution effects.

Our two-good world gives clarity and simplicity to our analysis, but we must recognize that the 'real world' is a more complex place. When there are more than two goods, there is the possibility that some goods will be *complements*; that is, they will be jointly consumed—like bread and jam, for example. Thus, an increase in the price of jam could lead to a decrease in the demand for bread.

This kind of analysis has other applications, for instance in assessing the merits of relieving poverty by transfers in cash or in kind.

It is important to see the link between individual decisions about demand and the market demand curve for a good. If individuals take demand decisions in isolation from the decisions taken by other consumers, then market demand is obtained by horizontal addition of the individual demand curves—that is, by asking how much each person demands at each price.

If we could make the assumption that utility was measurable, then we could show that an individual will choose to buy a combination of goods such that the ratio of marginal utility to price is the same for each good consumed. This approach is a simple alternative to indifference curve analysis, but is not popular because of the strength of its assumptions. It is discussed in the Appendix to Chapter 6 of the main text.

IMPORTANT CONCEPTS AND TECHNICAL TERMS

Match each lettered concept with the appropriate numbered phrase:

(a) Consumption bundle
(b) Utility
(c) Income expansion path
(d) Point of consumer choice
(e) Budget constraint
(f) Indifference curve
(g) Substitution effect
(h) Individual demand curve

(i) Marginal rate of substitution
(j) Budget line
(k) Transfers in kind
(l) Utility maximization
(m) Income effect
(n) Market demand curve
(o) Complementarity
(p) Giffen good

1 A curve showing how the chosen bundle of goods varies with consumer income levels.
2 Any particular combination of goods considered for purchase by an individual consumer.
3 The sum of the demand curves of all individuals in that market.
4 The quantity of one good that the consumer must sacrifice to increase the quantity of the other good by one unit without changing total utility.
5 A situation where goods are necessarily consumed jointly.
6 A line representing the maximum combination of two goods that a consumer can afford to purchase.
7 The point at which the consumer maximizes utility, where the marginal rate of substitution between two goods is equal to the ratio of their prices.
8 An inferior good where the income effect outweighs the substitution effect, causing the demand curve to slope upwards to the right.
9 That part of a consumer's response to a price change arising from the change in the consumer's purchasing power.
10 That part of a consumer's response to a price change arising from the change in relative prices.
11 A curve showing all the consumption bundles that yield the same utility to the consumer.
12 A transfer payment made in some form other than cash.
13 The assumption that the consumer chooses the affordable bundle that yields the most satisfaction.
14 The set of different consumption bundles that the consumer can afford, given income and prices.
15 The satisfaction a consumer derives from a particular bundle of goods.
16 A curve showing the amount demanded by a consumer at each price.

EXERCISES

1 Ashley, a student living at home, has a weekly allowance of £20 which he spends on two goods: food and entertainment. Draw Ashley's budget line for each of the following situations, using the vertical axis for food and the horizontal axis for entertainment:
   (a) The price of food (P_F) is 50p per unit; the price of entertainment (P_E) is 50p per unit.
   (b) P_F is 50p; P_E is £1.
   (c) P_F is £1; P_E is 50p.
   (d) P_F is 40p; P_E is 40p.
   (e) P_F is 50p; P_E is 50p, but Ashley's allowance is increased to £25 per week.
   Comment on the budget lines of (d) and (e) compared with (a).

2 Table 6.1 summarizes part of Ashley's preferences for food (F) and entertainment (E), by showing various combinations of the two goods between which he is indifferent. Each of the three sets of bundles represents a different utility level.

TABLE 6.1 Ashley's preferences for food and entertainment

Set 1 utility IC_1		Set 2 utility IC_2		Set 3 utility IC_3	
E	F	E	F	E	F
2	40	10	40	12	45
4	34	12	35	14	40
8	26	14	30	16	35
12	21	17	25	18	30
17	16	20	20	21	25
22	12	25	16	27	20
29	9	30	14	33	17
34	7	37	12	38	15
40	5	43	10	44	13
45	4	50	8	50	12

(a) Using graph paper, use the information from the table to sketch three indifference curves, plotting food on the vertical axis and entertainment on the horizontal axis.

(b) Which of the three indifference curves represents the highest level of utility?

(c) Which of the three indifference curves represents the lowest level of utility?

(d) Consider the following bundles of goods:
   A: 50(E), 8(F).
   B: 45(E), 4(F).
   C: 12(E), 45(F).
   D: 25(E), 16(F).
   E: 21(E), 11(F).
   Rank the five bundles in descending order of satisfaction.

(e) Can the information in this exercise be used to find Ashley's optimal choice point?

(f) Superimpose on your graph the budget line from part (a) of exercise 1. Can you now find the consumption bundle that maximizes Ashley's utility?

3 Barbara is choosing how to allocate her spending between records and clothes. Figure 6.1 shows her budget line and an indifference curve. Match each lettered point on the diagram with the appropriate numbered phrase:

(1) The point at which Barbara maximizes her utility.

(2) The point at which Barbara buys only records and no clothes.

(3) A consumption bundle which would not exhaust Barbara's budget for these goods.

(4) A point yielding the same satisfaction as at *d* but which Barbara cannot afford.

(5) The point at which Barbara buys only clothes, and no records.

(6) A consumption bundle preferred to point *d* but which Barbara cannot afford.

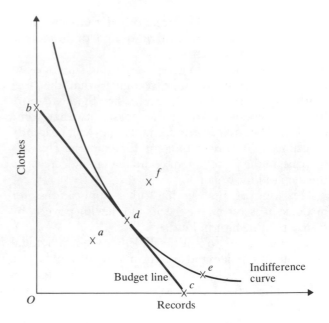

FIGURE 6.1 Barbara's choice between records and clothes

4 Christopher is choosing between two goods X and Y. Figure 6.2 shows some of his indifference curves between these goods. BL_1 represents his budget line, given his income and the prices of the goods.

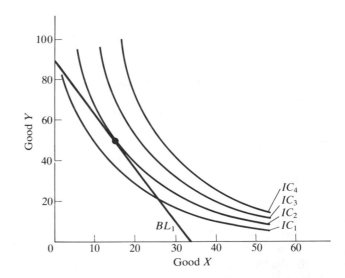

FIGURE 6.2 Christopher's preferences between goods X and Y

(a) Suppose that Christopher's tastes and the prices of X and Y remain constant, but his income varies. Plot the income expansion path.

(b) Classify the two goods as being either 'normal' or 'inferior'.

(c) What form would the income expansion

path take if both X and Y were normal goods?

(d) Is it possible to draw an income expansion path to depict the case where both X and Y are inferior goods?

5 Christopher is still choosing between goods X and Y. Figure 6.3 is the same as Figure 6.2.

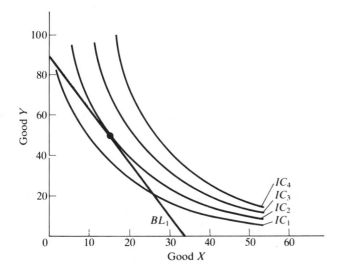

FIGURE 6.3 Christopher's preferences between goods X and Y

Suppose that Christopher's tastes, income, and the price of good Y remain fixed, but the price of good X varies.

(a) Show on the diagram the way in which Christopher's demand for X varies as the price of X varies.

(b) Is it possible to derive Christopher's demand curve for X from this analysis?

(c) Comment on the cross-price effect—that is, the way in which the demand for good Y changes as the price of X varies.

6 Which of the following statements is *not* valid? A utility-maximizing consumer chooses to be at a point at a tangent between his budget line and an indifference curve because

(a) this is the highest indifference curve that can be attained.

(b) at any point to the left of the budget line some income would be unused.

(c) all combinations of goods that lie to the right of his budget line are unreachable, given money income.

(d) this point represents the most favourable relative prices.

(e) at any other point on the budget line he will gain less utility.

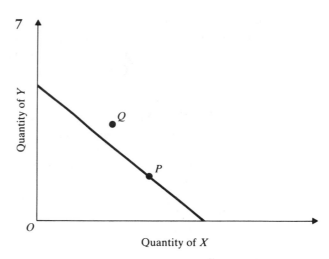

FIGURE 6.4 A change in a consumer's choice point

A consumer begins at point P in Figure 6.4 with the budget line as depicted. Which of the following could have transpired if the consumer later chooses to be at Q?

(a) A change in tastes.

(b) A small increase in the price of X and a larger percentage decrease in the price of Y.

(c) An increase in the price of X and a smaller percentage increase in the price of Y.

(d) A fall in real income.

(e) Equal percentage increases in money income and both prices.

8 Figure 6.5 shows how Debbie reacts to a fall in the price of beefburgers, in her choice between beefburgers and pork chops.

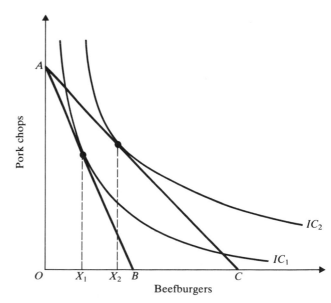

FIGURE 6.5 Debbie's choice between beefburgers and pork chops

AB represents the original budget line and OX_1 the quantity of beefburgers bought by Debbie. After the price fall, the budget line moves to *AC*, and Debbie now consumes OX_2 beefburgers.

(a) Illustrate the real income and substitution effects involved in Debbie's reaction to the price fall. (*Hint* You will need to be careful, because the discussion of this topic in the main text (Section 6–3) is in terms of a price *increase*. A price fall must be treated a little differently.)

(b) Does your analysis reveal beefburgers to be a normal or an inferior good?

(c) Do the income and substitution effects reinforce each other or work in opposite directions?

(d) Under what circumstances would the opposite be the case?

9 In reality, we cannot observe indifference curves. However, we can observe prices and income, and in some situations we can make inferences about consumer preferences. Suppose we observe Eliot in two different circumstances. He is choosing between goods *X* and *Y* and has constant money income, but faces different prices in two situations. His budget lines are shown in Figure 6.6.

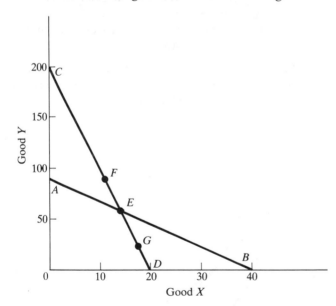

FIGURE 6.6 Eliot's preferences

AB is his initial budget line and *CD* the new one after an increase in the price of *X* and a fall in the price of *Y*. His initial choice point was at *E*. All questions relate to his subsequent choice.

(a) If Eliot's tastes do *not* change, is it possible

that he would choose to be at point *F*? Explain your answer.

(b) If Eliot's tastes do *not* change, is it possible that he would choose to be at point *G*? Explain your answer.

(c) If Eliot's tastes do *not* change, in what section of the budget line *CD* would you expect his new choice to lie?

(d) What would you infer about Eliot's tastes if he does choose point *G*?

10 *Please notice that this exercise is based on material in the Appendix to Chapter 6 in the main text, and assumes that utility can be measured.*
Fred reads magazines and listens to cassettes. Table 6.2 shows the utility he derives from consuming different quantities of the two commodities, given consumption of other goods. The price of magazines is £1.50 and the price of cassettes is £7.50. Suppose that Fred is currently buying 2 cassettes and 10 magazines. The issue to consider is whether he is maximizing his utility for a given expenditure.

TABLE 6.2 Fred's utility from magazines and cassettes

| | Magazines | | | Cassettes | | |
| | (1) | (2) | (3) | (4) | (5) | (6) |
Number consumed	Utility (utils)	Marginal utility	$\dfrac{MU_m}{P_m}$	Utility (utils)	Marginal utility	$\dfrac{MU_c}{P_c}$
1	60			360		
2	111			630		
3	156			810		
4	196			945		
5	232			1050		
6	265			1140		
7	295			1215		
8	322			1275		
9	347			1320		
10	371			1350		

(a) How much is Fred spending on these two goods in total?

(b) How much utility does Fred receive from this combination of goods?

(c) Calculate the *marginal* utility that Fred derives from magazines and cassettes.

(d) Sketch Fred's marginal utility schedule for cassettes.

(e) Can we yet pronounce on whether Fred is maximizing utility?

(f) What is Fred's utility if he spends his entire budget on cassettes?

(g) Calculate the ratios of marginal utility to price for each of the commodities.

(h) What combination of the two commodities maximizes Fred's utility?

TRUE/FALSE

1 _____ Indifference curves always slope downwards to the right if the consumer prefers more to less.

2 _____ Indifference curves never intersect if the consumer has consistent preferences.

3 _____ The slope of the budget line depends only upon the relative prices of the two goods.

4 _____ The budget constraint shows the maximum affordable quantity of one good given the quantity of the other good that is being purchased.

5 _____ An individual maximizes utility where his budget line cuts an indifference curve.

6 _____ A change in money income alters the slope and position of the budget line.

7 _____ All Giffen goods are inferior goods.

8 _____ All inferior goods are Giffen goods.

9 _____ The income expansion path slopes upwards to the right if both goods are normal goods.

10 _____ The substitution effect of an increase in the price of a good unambiguously reduces the quantity demanded of that good.

11 _____ If, following an increase in the price of X, the substitution effect is exactly balanced by the income effect, then X is neither a normal nor an inferior good.

12 _____ The theory of consumer choice demonstrates that consumers prefer to receive transfers in kind rather than transfers in cash.

QUESTIONS FOR THOUGHT

1 So far, we have always assumed that indifference curves are downward-sloping: this follows from the assumptions we made about consumer preferences. For instance, we assumed that there is always a diminishing marginal rate of substitution between the goods and that more is always better. If an individual has preferences which do not fit these rules, then the indifference curves can turn out to have quite a different pattern. In Figure 6.7 are some indifference curves reflecting different assumptions about preferences.

In each case, utility increases from IC_1 to IC_2 to IC_3. For each set of indifference curves, think about and explain the nature of the underlying consumer preferences and suggest examples of pairs of commodities which might illustrate these preferences.

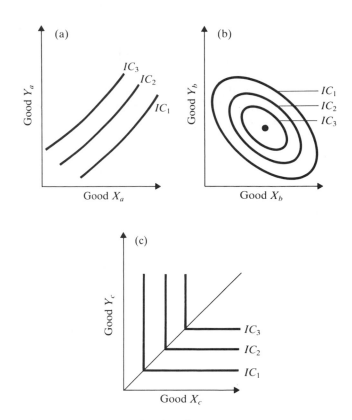

FIGURE 6.7 Unconventional preferences

2 The market demand curve has been portrayed as the horizontal sum of the individual demand curves, under the assumption that individual preferences are independent. However, suppose this assumption is not valid; for instance, it might be that consumers will demand more of a good if they think that 'everyone is buying it'—or they may demand more if they think it is exclusive because few can afford it. How would these interdependencies affect the relationship between the individual and market demand curves?

3 Will an increase in the hourly wage rate induce an individual worker to work longer or shorter hours? On the face of it, this seems an alien concept in the context of this chapter. However, an individual has preferences about other things than goods—for instance, between income and leisure (that is, hours not working). We can thus draw indifference curves between income (on the vertical axis) and hours of leisure (on the horizontal axis). If the individual gives up an hour of leisure, he receives an income, dependent upon the wage rate; so we can draw a budget line whose slope depends upon the wage rate. The higher the wage rate, the steeper the budget line. Use this framework to think about the question posed.

4 Felicity gains utility from listening to CDs and from watching videos. If she wishes to maximize her utility, which one of the following conditions must be met?

(a) The marginal utility from CDs must be equated with the marginal utility from videos.

(b) She must receive the same total utility from each of the two commodities.

(c) The price of CDs multiplied by the marginal utility obtained from CDs must be equal to the product of price and marginal utility of videos.

(d) The ratio of the marginal utility of CDs to the price of CDs must be equated to the ratio of marginal utility of videos to the price of videos.

(e) The ratio of the total utility of CDs to the price of CDs must be equated to the ratio of total utility of videos to the price of videos.

ANSWERS AND COMMENTS FOR CHAPTER 6

Please note   Where questions are reproduced from A level examinations, the examination boards bear no responsibility for the answers provided in this volume, which are the sole responsibility of the authors.

Important Concepts and Technical Terms

1	*c*	5	*o*	9	*m*	13	*l*
2	*a*	6	*j*	10	*g*	14	*e*
3	*n*	7	*d*	11	*f*	15	*b*
4	*i*	8	*p*	12	*k*	16	*h*

Exercises

1   If you are doubtful about how to draw a budget line, the simplest way to go about it is to calculate how much of each good Ashley could buy if he were to spend his entire allowance on it. Mark these two points on the graph (one on each axis) and join them.

This exercise should reveal that a change in one price alters the *slope* of the budget line, leaving the other intercept unchanged. An equal proportional change in both prices, e.g., (*d*) compared with (*a*), has the same effect as a change in income, e.g., (*e*) compared with (*a*)—namely, the budget line changes in position but not in slope.

2   (*a*)

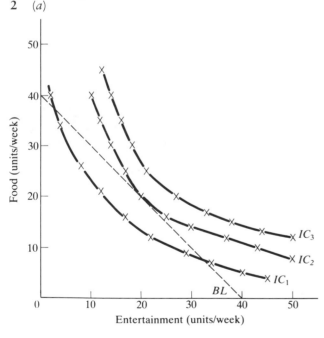

FIGURE A6.1   Ashley's indifference curves

(*b*) IC_3.
(*c*) IC_1.
(*d*)   Bundle C confers most utility, being on IC_3. Bundles A and D are both on IC_2 and would be ranked equally.

Bundle B confers less utility, being on IC_1.
Bundle E is below IC_1 and confers least utility.
(*e*)   No, we need to know Ashley's budget constraint.
(*f*)   *BL* in Figure A6.1 is the relevant budget line: it just touches indifference curve IC_2 at (20E, 20F). This point represents the highest level of satisfaction that Ashley can reach given his budget constraint.

3   (1)   *d*   (4)   *e*
    (2)   *c*   (5)   *b*
    (3)   *a*   (6)   *f*
4   (*a*)

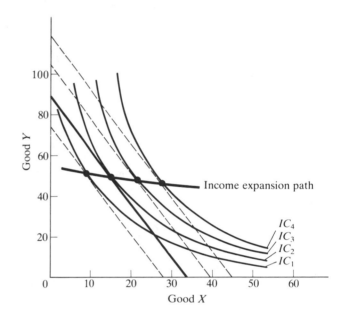

FIGURE A6.2   The income expansion path

(*b*)   As income expands, consumption of good X increases (X is a normal good) but consumption of good Y decreases (Y is an inferior good).
(*c*)   Upward-sloping to the right.
(*d*)   No. In a two-good world, it is not feasible for both goods to be inferior. For instance, suppose income falls with prices constant—clearly, the consumer could not consume more of both goods, as would be the case if both were inferior!
5   (*a*)   As the price of good X varies, the budget line changes its slope, while still cutting the Y axis at the same point: we can draw a series of budget lines, each tangent to an indifference curve on the diagram. This is done in Figure A6.3.
    (*b*)   Yes. If we know Christopher's money income, we can calculate the price of X corresponding to each budget line and we can read off the demand for X at each price. Indeed, we can get a rough idea of the demand curve by reference to the intercepts of the budget lines on the X-axis. If we call the original price '1', then the relative price for budget line BL_2 is approximately 33/14 = 2.36. (33 is the BL_1 intercept and 14 the BL_2 intercept.)

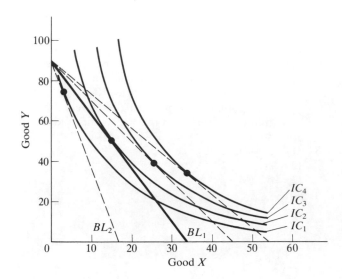

FIGURE A6.3 The effect on purchasing pattern of a change in the price of X

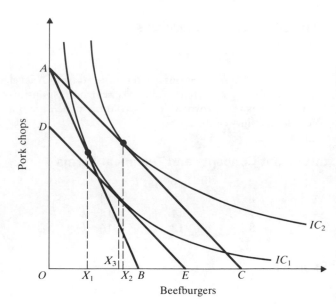

FIGURE A6.4 The effect of a price fall

Reading off the X quantities, we get the following:

Price	Quantity
2.36	2
1	15
0.75	24
0.59	32

You might like to plot these on a diagram. This analysis provides the theoretical underpinning of the demand curve. We see that its position and shape will depend upon income and upon preferences.

   (c) The demand for good Y increases as the price of X increases, indicating a strong substitution effect.

6 (d).

7 If only tastes change, Q remains unattainable, so the answer cannot be (a). Options (c) and (d) both move the budget line closer to the origin: (e) leaves the budget line unchanged. Hence, the answer is (b). Try sketching in the budget lines.

8 (a) See Figure A6.4.
        For a price *fall* we need to discover the resulting *increase* in real income. We do this by drawing in a new budget line (*DE*) which is parallel to the new budget line *AC* and tangent to the 'old' indifference curve IC_1. The substitution effect is from X_1 to X_3 and the real income effect from X_3 to X_2. This way of analysing the real income effect is sometimes known as the 'compensating income variation method'. It entails answering the question, 'What level of money income at the *new* relative prices would just allow Debbie to attain the original utility level?' If you are sure you have understood this, read on—otherwise, be warned that we are about to confuse you! We *could* have asked an alternative question—namely, 'What level of money income at the *old* relative prices would be equivalent to Debbie's

new utility level? We would analyse this by drawing another 'ghost' budget line parallel to *AB* at a tangent to IC_2—try it on your diagram if you like. This is sometimes known as the 'equivalent income variation method'.

  (b) As drawn, beefburgers are a normal good, although the income effect is relatively small.

  (c) They work together.

  (d) If beefburgers were an inferior good.

9 (a) Yes, it is quite consistent for him to choose to be at point *F*: it merely requires that his indifference curves are sufficiently steep that *F* (previously unattainable) lies on a higher indifference curve than *E*.

  (b) If Eliot is consistent in his preferences, there is no way he would choose to be at *G*. Both *E* and *G* were available options in the initial period; indeed, initially Eliot could have chosen a point to the north-east of *G*, with more of both goods—but yet he chose to be at *E*. If he now chooses *G*, it must be because of a change in tastes. You can confirm this by drawing indifference curves tangential to points *E* and *G*: you will find that they *must* intersect, indicating inconsistency.

  (c) CE.

  (d) They have changed—see comment on 9(b).

10 (a) 2 × £7.50 + 10 × £1.50 = £30.

  (b) 2 cassettes give Fred 630 utils, and 10 magazines give him 371, a total of 1001 utils.

  (c) See columns (2) and (5) of Table A6.1.

  (d) See Figure A6.5.

  (e) No, because we have not taken into account the relative prices of the two goods.

  (f) He could afford just 4 cassettes, which would give him 945 utils—less than his original choice.

  (g) See columns (3) and (6) of Table A6.1.

  (h) Fred maximizes utility by adjusting his expenditure such that MU_m/P_m is equal to MU_c/P_c. You will see from Table A6.1 that this occurs when he

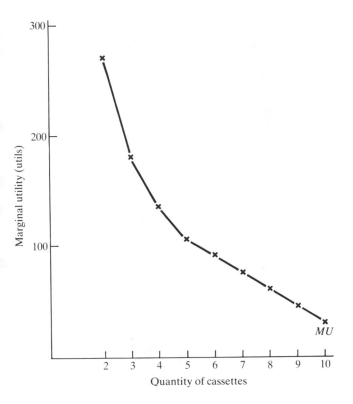

FIGURE A6.5 Fred's MU schedule for cassettes

TABLE A6.1 Fred's utility from magazines and cassettes

Number consumed	Magazines			Cassettes		
	(1) Utility (utils)	(2) Marginal utility	(3) $\frac{MU_m}{P_m}$	(4) Utility (utils)	(5) Marginal utility	(6) $\frac{MU_c}{P_c}$
1	60			360		
2	111	51	34	630	270	36
3	156	45	30	810	180	24
4	196	40	26.7	945	135	18
5	232	36	24	1050	105	14
6	265	33	22	1140	90	12
7	295	30	20	1215	75	10
8	322	27	18	1275	60	8
9	347	25	16.7	1320	45	6
10	371	24	16	1350	30	4

buys 3 cassettes and 5 magazines. His total expenditure is unchanged, but he now receives 1042 utils.

True/False

1 True: see Section 6–1 of the main text.
2 True.
3 True.
4 True: see section 6–1 of the main text.
5 False: the individual can always improve on such a point.
6 False: the slope depends only on the prices.
7 True.
8 False: see Section 6–3 of the main text.
9 True.
10 True: see Section 6–3 of the main text.

11 False: if the income effect is working against the substitution effect, then X must be an inferior good.
12 False: in general, consumers potentially gain by freedom to choose (see Section 6–6 of the main text).

Questions for Thought

1 Some hints:
  (a) What happens as you move along an indifference curve? What happens to utility if the quantity of Y_a stays constant but quantity of 'good' X_a increases? Possible example: medicine and sweets?
  (b) Even if you like cream doughnuts, or chocolate éclairs, how would you feel about eating 50 of each—or more?
  (c) What would be the substitution effect of a price change?
  Possible example: right and left shoes?
2 *Hint* These effects are sometimes referred to as the 'bandwagon' and 'snob' effects. The slope of the market demand curve will be affected.
3 The situation may be depicted as in Figure A6.6.

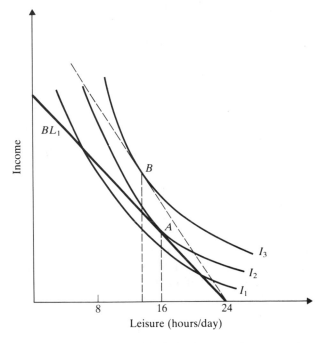

FIGURE A6.6 An individual's choice between income and leisure

The shape of the indifference curves reflects our individual's preferences between income and leisure. At the wage rate represented by BL_1 the choice point is at A: 16 hours of leisure are chosen and hence 8 hours of work. The dotted budget line shows a higher wage rate. As we have drawn it, our individual chooses less leisure, more work. This topic will be examined again later on, when we find that the reaction to an increase in the wage rate could be to work more or fewer hours (see Section 11–4 of the main text).
4 The answer is (d); this is explained in the Appendix to Chapter 6 in the main text.

7

Business Organization and Behaviour

We have now looked in some detail at the way in which individuals decide which goods to purchase and in what quantities, and also at how the market demand for a commodity is determined. Of course, this is only half of the story, and we now turn our attention towards *producers*. How is the *supply* of a commodity decided? Who takes the decisions about how much of a good to produce and at what price it should be sold? By what criteria are such decisions made?

First, we consider *who* produces. In the UK there are three typical ways in which businesses are organized. Most numerous are the *sole traders*, individuals running small businesses on their own account. Larger concerns may become *partnerships*, in which the business is jointly owned and run by two or more people. Finally, there are *companies*, in which ownership is distributed among the shareholders. Companies are the principal form of organization of large businesses. We shall refer to all such organizations as *firms*.

The viability of a firm depends upon its *profitability* and upon its *cash flow* position. We may think of a firm's profit as being the excess of its *revenue* over its *costs*. Cash flow refers to the timing of these revenue and cost items. Costs include expenditure on wages, rent, office expenses, and so on, but will also include an allowance for *depreciation* of capital equipment, which represents the cost of using that capital equipment during a period. The performance of a company may be judged with reference to its *income statement* or *balance sheet*.

A very important concept in economics is that of *opportunity cost*. This reflects the notion that the true, or economic, cost of using a resource is the amount forgone by not using that resource in its best alternative use. For instance, the cost of using part of profits to buy machinery might be represented by the return which could have been earned by using the funds in some other way.

A common assumption invoked in economics is that firms act in such a way as to maximize profits. For instance, a firm will choose to produce that amount of output which will yield the highest possible profit, given that both revenue and costs will vary according to the level of output. In large companies where the business is run by managers, it could be argued that

profit maximization may not be the sole criterion used in decision-making. However, such companies may well be aware that competing firms could take advantage of the potential for profit in the market. Profit maximization is thus a reasonable working assumption for us to make.

In analysing the firm's production decision, we assume that firms will attempt to minimize costs at their chosen level of output. In other words, having decided how much output to produce, firms will try to produce it as efficiently as possible in cost terms. The decision on how much to produce will be taken with reference to the way in which both revenue and costs vary with the level of output, remembering that profits may be seen as the difference between *total revenue* and *total cost*.

Total cost will normally increase as output rises: more labour must be hired, more inputs used, and so on, although some (fixed) costs may be incurred regardless of the output level. As higher output levels are considered, total cost need not vary smoothly. Very small levels of output may be costly to produce, but as output grows there may be efficiency gains such that the cost of producing additional units of output (the *marginal cost*) will fall. If there comes a point beyond which production becomes relatively less efficient, then the marginal cost will increase. This concept of marginal cost is a vital one: we will often want to ask whether a small (marginal) change in a decision will bring its rewards.

Total revenue will also change as output changes. The way in which revenue changes depends upon the demand curve faced by the firm. This is not necessarily the same as the market demand curve: a small firm among many in an industry may find that it has no influence over price, but can sell as much as desired at the going price. In this particular case of the competitive firm, *marginal revenue* (the amount by which total revenue increases when output is increased by one unit) is equal to price, as that represents the extra revenue from selling each additional unit. Where firms face a downward-sloping demand curve, marginal revenue will decline as output increases, as the firm must lower price in order to sell more output. Thus, the firm receives less revenue from the last unit sold than from the previous unit *and* less per unit on *all* sales, as all output is sold at the same price.

It can be seen that the profit-maximizing level of output is that at which marginal cost equals marginal revenue ($MC = MR$). If marginal revenue is greater than marginal cost, then it will pay the firm to increase output, for this will add to total profits. Similarly, if marginal revenue is less than marginal cost, profits would be increased by a reduction in output. This method of finding the profit-maximizing level of output is exactly equivalent to looking for the level of output where total revenue most exceeds total cost. In many ways, it is more useful to look at *marginal* revenue and cost, rather than *total* revenue and cost. Nevertheless, some checks on the totals should be carried out: if total revenue nowhere exceeds total cost, using $MC = MR$ will ensure that losses are minimized for any positive level of output, but the firm will do well to check also whether shutting down and producing nothing might be preferable. This and other important issues will be examined in Chapter 8.

IMPORTANT CONCEPTS AND TECHNICAL TERMS

Match each lettered concept with the appropriate numbered phrase:

(a)	Total revenue	(l)	Physical capital
(b)	Assets	(m)	Partnership
(c)	Profits	(n)	Liabilities
(d)	Retained earnings	(o)	Depreciation
(e)	Sole trader	(p)	Limited liability
(f)	Balance sheet	(q)	Marginal revenue
(g)	Income statement	(r)	Inventories
(h)	Total cost	(s)	Company
(i)	Marginal cost	(t)	Dividends
(j)	Opportunity cost	(u)	Supernormal profits
(k)	Accounting cost	(v)	Cash flow

1 A business owned by a single individual who is fully entitled to the income of the business and is fully responsible for any losses the business suffers.

2 An organization legally empowered to produce and trade with ownership divided among shareholders.

3 A business arrangement in which two or more people jointly own the business, sharing the profits and being jointly responsible for any losses.

4 That part of profits that the firm does not wish to re-invest and is thus paid to shareholders.

5 The profit over and above the return which the owners could have earned by lending their money elsewhere at the market rate of interest.

6 The *net* amount of money actually received by a firm during a period.

7 Goods held in stock by the firm for future sales.

8 The amount lost by not using a resource in its best alternative use.

9 The increase in total revenue when output is increased by 1 unit.

10 The loss in value resulting from the use of machinery during the period.

11 The increase in total cost when output is increased by 1 unit.

12 What the firm owns.

13 A listing sheet of the assets a firm owns and the liabilities for which it is responsible.

14 The situation whereby owners of a firm are not liable for more money than they paid for shares in the firm.

15 The part of after-tax profits that is ploughed back into the business rather than paid out to shareholders as dividends.

16 An account of the revenue received and expenses incurred during a particular period.

17 All expenses of production including both fixed costs and those costs which vary with the level of output.

18 What the firm owes.

19 The machinery, equipment, and buildings used in production.

20 The receipts of a business from sale of its output, equal to total expenditure by consumers on the firm's product.

21 The excess of total revenue over total cost.

22 The actual payments made by a firm in a period.

EXERCISES

1 Set out below are descriptions of four hypothetical firms. Identify each as being either a sole trader, a partnership, or a company.

(a) Count & Balance is a firm of chartered accountants. The five qualified accountants who work for the firm share the profits between them and are jointly responsible for any losses, as the firm does not have limited liability.

(b) Will Mendit & Son is a small family business. Will does electrical repair work while his son helps with the paperwork and assists with some repairs; they each take their share of the earnings. If the firm were to go bankrupt, Will would have to sell his car, and his son his motorbike.

(c) D. Harbinger Limited supplies communication equipment to the military. Profits are distributed among the shareholders, who have limited liability. The original founder of the firm has now retired, leaving management in the hands of the board of directors.

(d) Connie Fection runs a sweet shop, living in a flat over the premises with her daughter, who is paid to work the till on four afternoons a week. Connie does not have limited liability and in case of difficulty would have to sell her possessions.

2 The following items represent the expenditures and receipts of Lex Pretend & Sons Limited during 1991. Prepare the income statement for the firm

and calculate profits before and after tax on the assumption that the firm is liable only for corportion tax of 30 per cent on its profits.

(a) Rent £25 000.
(b) Proceeds from sale of 5000 units of good X at £40 each.
(c) Travel expenses £19 000.
(d) Stationery and other office expenses £15 000.
(e) Wages £335 000.
(f) Telephone £8000.
(g) Proceeds from sale of 4000 units of good Y at £75 each.
(h) Advertising £28 000.

3 Fiona Trimble is a sole trader operating in the textile industry. During the past year, revenue received amounted to £55 000 and she incurred direct costs of £27 000. Fiona had £25 000 of financial capital tied up in the business during the whole year. Had she chosen to work for the large company round the corner, she could have earned £21 000. Calculate the following items (you will need to know that the going market rate of interest was 10 per cent):

(a) Accounting cost.
(b) Accounting profit.
(c) Opportunity cost of Fiona's time.
(d) Opportunity cost of financial capital.
(e) Total economic cost.
(f) Economic profit (supernormal).

4 The following items comprise the assets and liabilities of GSC Limited (the Great Spon Company) as at 31 March 1990. Incorporate them into a balance sheet for the firm and calculate the net worth of the company. Note that the company has been in operation for just one year, and that buildings and other physical capital are assumed to depreciate at the rate of 20 per cent per annum.

(a) Wages payable £25 000.
(b) Inventories held £80 000.
(c) Bank loan payable £50 000.
(d) Buildings, original value £300 000.
(e) Cash in hand £30 000.
(f) Accounts receivable £55 000.
(g) Accounts payable £40 000.
(h) Mortgage £180 000.
(i) Salaries due to be paid £30 000.
(j) Physical capital other than buildings, original value £250 000.

5 Table 7.1 contains data which represent the cost and revenue situation of a firm.
(a) Calculate marginal cost as output rises.
(b) Calculate marginal revenue as output rises.

TABLE 7.1

Total production (units/week)	Price received (£)	Total costs
1	25	10
2	23	23
3	20	38
4	18	55
5	15	75
6	$12\frac{1}{2}$	98

(Hint You will need first to calculate total revenue.)
(c) At what level of output would profits be maximized?
(d) Calculate profit at each level of output.

6 In a fish and rabbit eating community, a man is able to catch either four fish or one rabbit in any six hours of activity.
This statement is an illustration of
(a) equi-marginal utility
(b) time preference
(c) diminishing returns
(d) opportunity cost
(e) double coincidence of wants
(University of London GCE A level Economics 3, January 1989)

7 A man bought a bicycle for £80, but never uses it. A similar bicycle would now cost £95 new, but his would fetch only £35 second-hand. The present opportunity cost of owning a bicycle is
(a) £15
(b) £35
(c) £60
(d) £80
(Associated Examining board, GCE A level Economics Paper 1, November 1988)

8 Mr Smith owns a small factory and every Thursday one of his lorry drivers spends the morning driving Mrs Jones round the shops. The lorry driver is, of course, paid his normal wage and Mrs Jones gives him an extra £5.
The opportunity cost to Mr Smith of the lorry driver's chauffeuring is
(a) the £5 plus the wage he would normally earn
(b) the work he would have done if not taken away
(c) the wage he would normally earn
(d) the £5 Mrs Jones pays him
(Associated Examining board, GCE A level Economics Paper 1, November 1986)

9 Table 7.2 summarizes marginal revenue and marginal cost for a firm:

TABLE 7.2

Total production (units/week)	Marginal revenue (£)	Marginal cost (£)
0		
	72	17
1		
	56	15
2		
	40	25
3		
	24	40
4		
	8	60
5		

(a) Use graph paper to plot both marginal revenue and marginal cost schedules, associating each marginal value with the mid-point of the appropriate quantity interval. (In other words, place the marginal cost of the first unit midway between 0 and 1, etc.)

(b) At what (approximate) level of output would the firm choose to operate if it wanted to maximize profits?

(c) At what (approximate) level of output would the firm choose to operate if it wanted to maximize *revenue*? (*Hint* You will need to extend your *MR* line a little.)

(d) If marginal cost were to increase by £30 at each level of output, at what point would the firm now maximize profits?

(e) Given the original level of marginal cost, at what level of output would the firm maximize profits if marginal revenue were to increase by £34 at each level of output?

TRUE/FALSE

1 _____ Small traders are the most numerous form of business organization in the UK, but companies are, on average, the most profitable.

2 _____ The balance sheet of a firm summarizes information concerning the flow of receipts and expenditures during a given year.

3 _____ To avoid the possibility of having to sell their possessions, shareholders should be careful to buy shares in thriving firms.

4 _____ Firms that show an accounting profit must be thriving.

5 _____ Opportunity cost plus accounting cost equals economic cost.

6 _____ The net worth of a firm as revealed by the balance sheet does not necessarily reflect the true worth, which should take notice of 'goodwill' factors.

7 _____ Firms maximize profits by selling as much output as they can.

8 _____ When a firm's demand curve slopes down, marginal revenue will fall as output rises.

9 _____ Long-term profitability is all that matters; cash flow is unimportant.

10 _____ Any firm wanting to maximize profits will minimize cost for any given level of output.

11 _____ A fall in marginal revenue will cause profits to be maximized at a lower output level.

12 _____ A profit-maximizing firm always does best by producing where $MC = MR$: this will either maximize profits or minimize losses.

13 _____ Inventories are produced by mad scientists.

14 _____ When the firm's demand curve slopes down, marginal revenue must be less than the price for which the last unit is sold.

QUESTIONS FOR THOUGHT

1 Why might marginal cost be falling at low levels of output? What might cause marginal cost to rise?

2 Opportunity cost is a widely applicable concept. What do you consider to be the opportunity cost that you are incurring by thinking about this question?

ANSWERS AND COMMENTS FOR CHAPTER 7

Please note   Where questions are reproduced from A level examinations, the examination boards bear no responsibility for the answers provided in this volume, which are the sole responsibility of the authors.

Important Concepts and Technical Terms

1	*e*	5	*u*	9	*q*	13	*f*	17	*h*	21 *c*
2	*s*	6	*v*	10	*o*	14	*p*	18	*n*	22 *k*
3	*m*	7	*r*	11	*i*	15	*d*	19	*l*	
4	*t*	8	*j*	12	*b*	16	*g*	20	*a*	

Exercises

1 (*a*) Partnership.   (*c*) Company.
   (*b*) Partnership.   (*d*) Sole trader.

2

Lex Pretend and Sons Limited
Income Statement
For the year ending 31 December 1991

Revenue: 5000 units of good *X* sold at £40 each	£200 000	
4000 units of good *Y* sold at £75 each	300 000	
		£500 000
Deduct expenditures:		
Wages	335 000	
Rent	25 000	
Travel expenses	19 000	
Advertising	28 000	
Telephone	8 000	
Stationery and other office expenses	15 000	
		430 000
Net income (profits) before tax		70 000
Corporation tax at 30%		21 000
Net income (profits) after tax		£49 000

3 (*a*) £27 000.   (*d*) £2500.
   (*b*) £28 000.   (*e*) £50 500.
   (*c*) £21 000.   (*f*) £4500.

4

GSC Limited
Balance Sheet
31 March 1990

Assets		Liabilities		
Cash in hand	£30 000	Accounts payable		£40 000
Accounts receivable	55 000	Wages payable		25 000
Inventories	80 000	Salaries payable		30 000
Buildings		Mortgage		180 000
(Original value £300 000)	240 000	Bank loan		50 000
Other equipment				
(Original value £250 000)	200 000		Total	325 000
			Net worth	280 000
Total assets	£605 000			£605 000

5   **TABLE A7.1**

Total production (units/week)	Price received (£)	Total revenue	Total costs	Profit	Marginal revenue	Marginal cost
1	25	25	10	15		
					21	13
2	23	46	23	23		
					14	15
3	20	60	38	22		
					12	17
4	18	72	55	17		
					3	20
5	15	75	75	0		
					0	23
6	$12\frac{1}{2}$	75	98	−23		

Profits are maximized at an output level of 2 units per week.

6   (d).
7   (b).
8   (b).
9   (a)

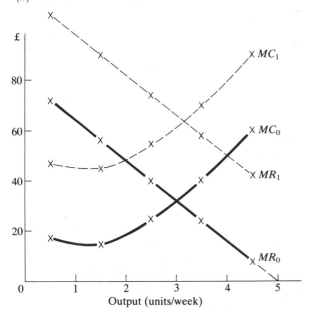

FIGURE A7.1   Marginal cost and marginal revenue

(b)   Marginal cost (MC_0) intersects marginal revenue (MR_0) at an output level of about 3 units per week.

(c)   Total revenue continues to increase while marginal revenue is positive. After an output level of about 5 units per week, marginal revenue would become negative. Total revenue is thus maximized at 5 units per week.

(d) MC_1 in Figure A7.1 represents the new marginal cost schedule. $MC_1 = MR_0$ at an output level of about 2 units per week: a cost increase thus causes output to fall.

(e) MR_1 in Figure A7.1 represents the new marginal

revenue schedule. $MC_0 = MR_1$ at an output level of about 4 units per week: i.e., output has increased.

True/False

1   True: see Section 7–1 of the main text.
2   False: the balance sheet sets out assets and liabilities of a firm at a particular date.
3   False: of course, nobody wants to end up with worthless shares, but shareholders are only liable for the amount they put into the firm and no more.
4   False: opportunity cost must also be considered.
5   True.
6   True: see Section 7–2 of the main text.
7   False.
8   True: see Section 7–5 of the main text.
9   False: unless you can convince your bank manager that all will be well, the long term may never come! Most new businesses (and many old ones) need to borrow to help them through periods of low cash flow.
10 True: see Section 7–4 of the main text.
11 True: remember exercise 9?
12 False: there may be times when it is better to close down and produce nothing.
13 False!
14 True: see Section 7–5 of the main text.

Questions for Thought

1   Some hints may be found in Section 7–5 of the main text: it will also be discussed again in Chapter 8.
2   If you are reading this, you have decided that the opportunity cost is not excessive—or you would have hurried on to the next chapter! Opportunity cost is involved every time we make a choice between alternatives: spending money in one way precludes us from buying other items; taking time to do something prevents us from doing something else.

8

Developing the Theory of Supply: Costs and Production

In Chapter 7 we began to look at how an individual firm decides how much to produce in order to maximize profits. We now look more carefully at this decision and introduce a number of important concepts and technical terms. A casual inspection of the corresponding Chapter 8 in the main text may suggest that it is confusingly packed with all sorts of similar but differently labelled curves. However, you should not be intimidated by this: if you can grasp the principles underlying the firm's decisions, the curves will then fall into place.

Production is a process by which a firm combines inputs to produce output. Inputs include labour and capital services as well as raw materials; often we will focus upon just two (labour and capital) for simplicity. For any particular good, there may be many alternative *techniques* by which inputs may be combined. The choice of technique is partly an 'engineering' problem but also an economic one, in the sense that we assume the firm will wish to choose the most cost-effective technique for a particular level of output, given the relative prices of the inputs. For instance, if labour is expensive relative to capital, then firms may consider capital-intensive production techniques. If relative prices change, firms may decide to substitute some inputs for others: if the cost of labour rises, a firm may use more capital-intensive techniques.

The choice of technique may also depend upon how much output the firm wishes to produce: a technique suitable for producing small quantities of a good may be inappropriate for large-scale production. The *production function* summarizes information about technically efficient methods of producing different output levels. In conjunction with the prices of the inputs, the production function reveals how costs vary with output.

A firm must make decisions with reference to two time horizons. Suppose a firm wishes to alter the scale of its operations by producing more output. The production function shows the most efficient means of producing the new level of output. However, this is a *long-run* decision, which the firm may not be able to implement immediately. For instance, the new scale of operations may require new capital equipment—new

machines or buildings—which are not instantly available. The firm will also therefore have to make *short-run* decisions to cover the transitional period. The long run is defined as the period sufficiently long that the firm can adjust all inputs as desired. The short run is the period in which only partial adjustment is possible.

Long-run total costs need not vary smoothly with the output level: a useful way of examining how they do vary is to look at long-run *average cost*: the cost per unit of producing a given output level. At relatively low levels of output, we may expect there to be *economies of scale*: these may result either because *fixed costs* can be spread across more units of output, or because larger-scale production enables specialization in the use of labour, or simply because it permits the use of better machinery. In such a situation of *increasing returns to scale*, long-run average costs will be falling. As the scale of operations continues to rise, *diseconomies of scale* may set in, perhaps because the management of production becomes more difficult. Such a situation of *decreasing returns to scale* will exhibit rising long-run average cost. *Constant returns to scale* describes the situation where long-run average cost is constant as output varies.

The extent of economies and diseconomies of scale will naturally vary from industry to industry. Empirical studies suggest that for some industries (especially in manufacturing), firms do not reach the point at which decreasing returns to scale set in, producing where long-run average cost is either falling or steady. The importance of this is considered in a later chapter, but for now we assume that firms face U-shaped average cost curves.

The point at which long-run average costs cease to fall is known as the *minimum efficient scale*. We will see later that the size of this relative to market demand is an important influence on the number of firms that can profitably operate in the market.

If we calculate marginal cost for *any* U-shaped average cost curve, the marginal curve will pass through the minimum point of the average cost curve. This property results from the mathematical nature of the curves and is *always* the case.

The firm's long-run supply decision is taken in two stages. Firstly, the firm finds the profit-maximizing level of output by equating marginal revenue with long-run marginal cost—the *marginal condition*. Secondly, the firm checks the *average condition*: will average revenue (that is, price) cover long-run average cost? If not, the firm would do better to close down.

As already mentioned, the firm has less flexibility in the short run. Typically, we might expect the firm to be able to vary labour input but not capital. The *marginal product of labour* is defined as the increase in output obtained by adding one unit of labour with other inputs fixed. The *law of diminishing returns* states that, after some level of input, further increases in one variable input (in this case, labour) will lead to a diminishing marginal product of that input.

One consequence of this inflexibility is that the firm will face some fixed costs in the short run which will be incurred whether or not the firm chooses to produce in the coming period. For purposes of the short-run decision, these fixed costs can be ignored: what is important is the level of variable costs. As with the long-run decision, the short-run choice is taken in two stages. The firm sets short-run marginal cost equal to marginal revenue to find the profit-maximizing level of output, and then checks whether average revenue will suffice to cover short-run average variable cost.

Finally, if we recall that the long-run average cost curve represents all the most efficient points of production, it should be clear that short-run average cost can never be below long-run average cost, and will be higher whenever the firm moves away from the level of output for which the quantity of the fixed factor was intended.

IMPORTANT CONCEPTS AND TECHNICAL TERMS

Match each lettered concept with the appropriate numbered phrase:

(a) Input
(b) Short-run average variable cost (SAVC)
(c) U-shaped average cost curve
(d) Capital-intensive
(e) Production function
(f) Short-run average fixed cost (SAFC)
(g) Fixed costs
(h) Constant returns to scale
(i) Long-run average cost
(j) Law of diminishing returns
(k) Short-run marginal cost
(l) Marginal product of capital
(m) Economies of (increasing returns to) scale
(n) Long run
(o) Short-run average total cost (SATC)
(p) Variable costs
(q) Long-run marginal cost
(r) Short run
(s) Labour-intensive
(t) Long-run total cost
(u) Minimum efficient scale
(v) Fixed factor of production
(w) Marginal product of labour
(x) Diseconomies of (decreasing returns to) scale

1 The specification of the maximum output that can be produced from any given amount of inputs.
2 The total cost of producing a given output level when the firm is able to adjust all inputs optimally.
3 The period long enough for the firm to adjust *all* its inputs to a change in conditions.
4 A factor of production: any good or service used to produce output.
5 The output level at which further economies of scale become unimportant for the individual firm and the average cost curve first becomes horizontal.
6 The increase in output obtained by adding one unit of labour, holding constant the input of all other factors.
7 The situation in which long-run average costs increase as output rises.
8 A production technique using a lot of labour but relatively little capital.
9 The increase in short-run total costs (and in short-run variable costs) as output is increased by one unit.
10 The cost per unit of producing a given output level when the firm is able to adjust all inputs optimally.
11 Costs that change as output changes.
12 The situation where, beyond some level of the variable input, further increases in the variable input lead to a steadily decreasing marginal product of that input.
13 Short-run variable cost per unit of output.
14 Short-run fixed cost per unit of output.
15 The increase in long-run total costs if output is permanently raised by one unit.
16 A production technique using a lot of capital but relatively little labour.
17 Costs that do not vary with output levels.
18 The situation when long-run average costs are constant as output rises.
19 Short-run total cost per unit of output.
20 The situation when long-run average costs decrease as output rises.
21 A long-run average cost curve faced by a firm confronted with first increasing and then decreasing returns to scale.
22 A factor whose input level cannot be varied in the short run.
23 The increase in output obtained by adding one unit of capital, holding constant the input of all other factors.
24 The period in which the firm can make only partial adjustment of its inputs to a change in conditions.

EXERCISES

1 A firm making toffees has a choice between three production techniques, each using different combinations of labour input and capital input, as shown in Table 8.1.

TABLE 8.1 Production techniques for toffees

Output	Technique A L	K	Technique B L	K	Technique C L	K
1	9	2	6	4	4	6
2	19	3	10	8	8	10
3	29	4	14	12	12	14
4	41	5	18	16	16	19
5	59	6	24	22	20	25
6	85	7	33	29	24	32
7	120	8	45	38	29	40

Note: L denotes labour; K denotes capital. All measured in units per week.

Suppose that labour costs £200 per unit/week and capital input costs £400 per unit/week.
(a) For each level of output, state which production technique should be adopted by the firm.
(b) Calculate total cost for each level of output.
(c) Suppose that the price of labour input increases to £300 per unit/week, but the price of capital remains constant. In what way would you expect the firm's choice of technique to be affected by this change in relative prices?
(d) With the new labour cost, state which production technique should be adopted for each output level and calculate total cost.

2 A firm faces long-run total cost conditions as given in Table 8.2.

TABLE 8.2 Output and long-run total cost

Output (units/week)	Total cost (£)	Long-run average cost	Long-run marginal cost
0	0		
1	32		
2	48		
3	82		
4	140		
5	228		
6	352		

(a) Calculate long-run average cost and long-run marginal cost.
(b) Using graph paper, plot long-run average cost and long-run marginal cost curves. (*Hint* Remember to plot LMC at points half-way between the corresponding output levels.)
(c) At what output level is long-run average cost at a minimum?
(d) At what output level does long-run marginal cost equal long-run average cost?

3 Look at the diagram you drew in exercise 2.
(a) Within what range of output does this firm experience economies of scale (increasing returns to scale)?
(b) Within what range of output does the firm experience diseconomies of scale (decreasing returns to scale)?
(c) What is the minimum efficient scale for this firm?
(d) Suppose that you could measure returns to scale at a particular *point* on the LAC curve: what would characterize the point where LAC is at a minimum?

4 A firm faces fixed costs of £45 and short-run average variable costs as shown in Table 8.3.

TABLE 8.3 Short-run costs of production

Output (units/week)	SAVC Short-run average variable cost
1	17
2	15
3	14
4	15
5	19
6	29

(a) From the figures in Table 8.3, calculate short-run average fixed cost, short-run average total cost, short-run total cost, and short-run marginal cost.
(b) Using graph paper, plot SAVC, SATC, and SMC; check that SMC goes through the minimum points of the other two curves.
(c) If the firm were to increase production from 5 to 6 units/week, the short-run marginal cost would be high. Explain why this should be so, being sure to describe the role played by the marginal product of labour.

5 In the short run, a firm can vary labour input flexibly but cannot change the level of capital input. Table 8.4 shows how output changes as only labour input is varied.
(a) Calculate the marginal product of labour (MPL) and the average product of labour (APL).
(b) Using graph paper, plot MPL and APL.
(c) At *approximately* what level of labour input do diminishing returns set in?

TABLE 8.4 Output and labour input

Labour input (workers/ week)	Output (goods/ week)	Marginal product of labour	Average product of labour
0	0		
1	35		
2	80		
3	122		
4	156		
5	177		
6	180		

(d) At *approximately* what level of labour input does *MPL* cut *APL*?

(e) How would you expect the *MPL* curve to be affected by a change in the level of capital input?

6 Which of the following statements describes the law of diminishing returns? Suppose in each case that labour is a variable factor, but capital is fixed. As more labour is used:

(a) total output will fall because the extra units of labour will be of poorer quality than those previously employed.

(b) the relative shortage of capital will eventually cause increases in total product to become progressively smaller.

(c) the cost of the product will eventually be forced up because the wage rate will rise as labour becomes more scarce.

(d) after a while, fewer units of labour will be needed in order to produce more output.

(e) the marginal revenue obtained from each additional unit produced will decline.

7 Which of the following conditions is (are) regarded as necessary before the law of diminishing returns to a factor can be said to operate?

1 Other factors are held constant.

2 The state of technical knowledge does not change.

3 All units of the variable factor are homogeneous.

Choose one of the following:

(a) 1, 2, 3 are correct

(b) 1, 2 only are correct

(c) 2, 3 only are correct

(d) 1 only is correct

(e) 3 only is correct

(University of London GCE A level Economics 3, January 1989)

8 Which of the following statements about the short-run marginal cost curve are *not* true?

(a) Marginal cost equals average cost when average cost is at a minimum.

(b) When average cost is falling, marginal cost will be below average cost.

(c) Marginal cost is greater than average cost when the number of units produced is greater than the optimum technical output.

(d) Marginal cost will be rising under conditions of diminishing returns.

(e) Marginal cost is unaffected by changes in factor prices.

(f) Marginal cost depends in part upon fixed costs.

9 Each of the four separate short-run average total cost curves in Figure 8.1 represents a different scale of operation of a firm.

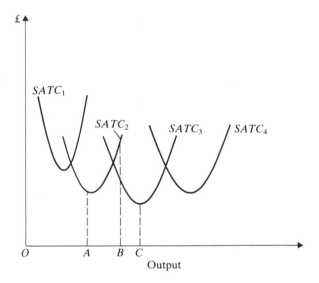

FIGURE 8.1 Short-run average cost

(a) On the basis of Figure 8.1, what would be the most efficient level of output for the firm to produce?

(b) If the firm were to expand its scale of operation beyond this point, what would be the nature of the returns to scale?

(c) Which of the four scales of operation would be appropriate if the firm wished to produce *OA* output?

(d) If the firm then wanted to expand to produce *OB* output, what would be the chosen scale of operation in the short run and in the long run?

(e) Sketch in the long-run average cost curve for the firm.

10 A firm has selected the output level at which it wishes to produce. Having checked the marginal condition, the firm is now considering the average condition as it applies in the short run and the long run. Cost conditions are as follows:

	£
Long-run average cost	12
Short-run average fixed cost	6
Short-run average variable cost	11
Short-run average total cost	17

In the following table, tick the appropriate short- and long-run decisions for the firm at each stated market price:

	Short-run decision			Long-run decision		
Price (£)	Produce at a profit	Produce at a loss	Close down	Produce at a profit	Produce at a loss	Close down
18						
5						
7						
13						
11.50						

11 In the short run a profit-maximising firm will stop producing if
   (a) price is less than minimum average total cost
   (b) normal profit is less than the average for the industry
   (c) total revenue is less than total cost
   (d) total revenue is less than total variable cost
   (e) average variable cost is less than price
          (University of London GCE A level Economics 3, June 1988)

12 Figure 8.2 shows the long-run average cost curve of a firm. From the diagram it can be concluded that
   1 up to a level of output OQ_1 the firm enjoys long-run increasing returns
   2 at levels of output greater than OQ_1 the firm suffers diseconomies of scale
   3 OQ_1 is the profit-maximising output for this firm
   Choose one of the following:
   (a) 1, 2, 3 are correct
   (b) 1, 2 only are correct
   (c) 2, 3 only are correct
   (d) 1 only is correct
          (Associated Examining Board, GCE A level Economics Paper 1, June 1988)

TRUE/FALSE

1 _____ Capital and labour are the only two factors of production which the firm needs to consider when making its output decision.

2 _____ The typical U-shape often assumed for the long-run average cost curve is valid only for a firm facing economies of scale at low levels of output, changing to diseconomies as output expands.

3 _____ Specialization (the division of labour) can lead to economies of scale.

4 _____ Small firms are always less efficient than large ones.

5 _____ Firms who make losses are lame ducks who should be closed down at once.

6 _____ A firm will close down in the short run if price is less than average revenue.

7 _____ The long-run supply decision is determined by finding the level of output at which long-run marginal cost is equal to marginal revenue.

8 _____ Holding labour constant while increasing capital input will lead to diminishing returns.

9 _____ LAC is falling when LMC is less than LAC and rising when LMC is greater than LAC; LAC is at a minimum at the output level at which LAC and LMC cross.

10 _____ Empirical evidence suggests that, if there were more than one refrigerator manufacturer in the UK, it would be impossible for every firm in that industry to be producing at minimum efficient scale.

11 _____ The decision whether to continue to produce should be taken regardless of how much money has been devoted to the project in the past.

12 _____ The long-run average cost curve passes through the lowest point of each short-run average cost curve.

QUESTIONS FOR THOUGHT

1 Explain why large firms can produce at lower cost than small firms. Under what circumstances might the reverse be true? Illustrate your answer with examples.
   (University of London GCE A level Economics Paper 1, June 1987)

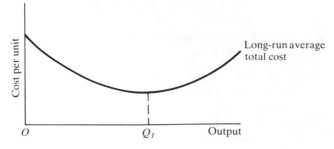

FIGURE 8.2

2 Is it possible for an industry to experience economies of scale and diminishing returns to labour
   simultaneously?

3 It might be suggested that in practice firms do not
   know all the details of the various cost curves that
   we have discussed. If this is so, how relevant is all
   this analysis?

ANSWERS AND COMMENTS FOR CHAPTER 8

Please note Where questions are reproduced from A level examinations, the examination boards bear no responsibility for the answers provided in this volume, which are the sole responsibility of the authors.

Important Concepts and Technical Terms

1 *e*	7 *x*	13 *b*	19 *o*
2 *t*	8 *s*	14 *f*	20 *m*
3 *n*	9 *k*	15 *q*	21 *c*
4 *a*	10 *i*	16 *d*	22 *v*
5 *u*	11 *p*	17 *g*	23 *l*
6 *w*	12 *j*	18 *h*	24 *r*

Exercises

1 (a) and (b). In fact, the calculations for (b) have to be carried out before (a) can be answered. Total costs for each technique are set out in Table A8.1; the preferred technique for each output level has been indicated by lines of enclosure.

TABLE A8.1 Total cost and the choice of technique

Output (units/week)	Total cost technique A	Total cost technique B	Total cost technique C
1	2 600	2 800	3 200
2	5 000	5 200	5 600
3	7 400	7 600	8 000
4	10 200	10 000	10 800
5	14 200	13 600	14 000
6	19 800	18 200	17 600
7	27 200	24 200	21 800

At low levels of output, technique A provides the least-cost method of production—notice that this technique is relatively labour-intensive, using more labour but less capital than the alternatives. However, as output levels increase, technique B becomes more efficient, and then technique C takes over when output reaches 6 units/week, this being the most capital-intensive technique.

(c) If labour becomes more expensive relative to capital, we expect the firm to move towards more capital-intensive techniques. In particular, we expect a move away from technique A in this exercise—and this is what happens, as you can see in Table A8.2.

(d) See Table A8.2.

2 (a) See Table A8.3.
(b) See Figure A8.1.
(c) At 2 units/week.
(d) It is always the case that *LMC = LAC* at the minimum point of *LAC*—thus the intersection is at 2 units/week of output.

3 (a) Up to 2 units/week.
(b) In excess of 2 units/week.

TABLE A8.2 Total cost and the choice of technique after the change in labour cost

Output (units/week)	Total cost technique A	Total cost technique B	Total cost technique C
1	3 500	3 400	3 600
2	6 900	6 200	6 400
3	10 300	9 000	9 200
4	14 300	11 800	12 400
5	20 100	16 000	16 000
6	28 300	21 500	20 000
7	39 200	28 700	24 700

TABLE A8.3 Output and long-run total cost

Output (units/week)	Total cost (£)	Long-run average cost	Long-run marginal cost
0	0		
			32
1	32	32	
			16
2	48	24	
			34
3	82	27.3	
			58
4	140	35	
			88
5	228	45.6	
			124
6	352	58.7	

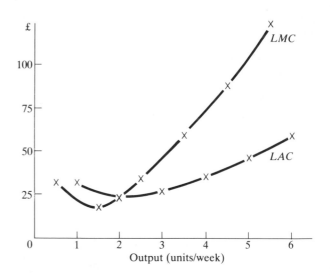

FIGURE A8.1 Long-run average cost and long-run marginal cost

(c) 2 units/week.
(d) This point represents the switch-over from falling *LAC* to rising *LAC*, from increasing to decreasing returns to scale. *At that point*, the firm has constant returns to scale.

4 (a) **TABLE A8.4** Short-run costs of production

Output (units/week)	SAVC Short-run average variable cost	SAFC Short-run average fixed cost	SATC Short-run average total cost	STC Short-run total cost	SMC Short-run marginal cost
					17
1	17	45	62	62	
					13
2	15	22.5	37.5	75	
					12
3	14	15	29	87	
					18
4	15	11.25	26.25	105	
					35
5	19	9	28	140	
					79
6	29	7.5	36.5	219	

$SAFC$ = £45 divided by output
$SATC$ = $SAVC$ + $SAFC$
STC = $SATC$ multiplied by output

(b)

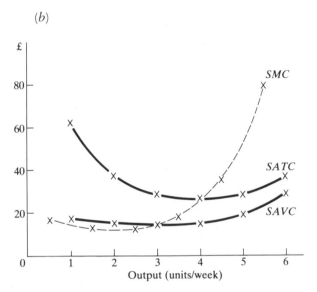

FIGURE A8.2 Short-run average total cost, short-run average variable cost, and short-run marginal cost

(c) In the short run, the firm cannot adjust its capital input. If it wishes to change the level of output, it must do so by altering labour input. However with capital input fixed, diminishing returns to labour set in rapidly, such that the marginal product of labour falls. For this reason, the marginal cost of producing more output may be very high in the short run.

5 (a) Table A8.5.
   (b) Figure A8.3.
   (c) MPL turns down close to $1\frac{1}{2}$ workers/week: this is the point at which diminishing returns set in.
   (d) MPL must cut APL at its maximum point—i.e. just below 3 workers/week.
   (e) A change in the level of capital input affects the *position* of MPL and APL. An increase in capital would move these curves upwards.

TABLE 8.5 Output and labour input

Labour input (workers/week)	Output (goods/week)	Marginal product of labour	Average product of labour
0	0		
		35	
1	35		35
		45	
2	80		40
		42	
3	122		40.6
		34	
4	156		39
		21	
5	177		35.4
		3	
6	180		30

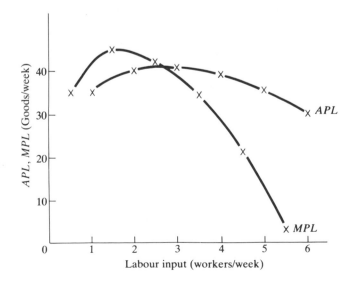

FIGURE A8.3 Average and marginal product of labour

6 (*a*) is a tempting response, but incorrect: diminishing returns to a factor do not require that the extra units used diminish in quality; nor need total product fall—it is *marginal* product that diminishes. Response (*c*) is an interesting observation (in jargon, this describes a 'pecuniary external diseconomy of scale'), but it is not pertinent to diminishing returns. If you think about it you will realize that (*d*) described *increasing* returns to a factor. (*e*) is concerned with revenue rather than costs. This leaves us with (*b*) as the correct response: diminishing returns are indeed concerned with the returns to the variable factor.

7 (*a*)

8 (*e*), (*f*).

9 (*a*) OC can be produced at minimum average cost.
  (*b*) Decreasing returns to scale.
  (*c*) That corresponding to $SATC_2$.
  (*d*) The firm would have no choice in the short run but to produce using $SATC_2$. In the long run, it would pay to expand to $SATC_3$.
  (*e*)

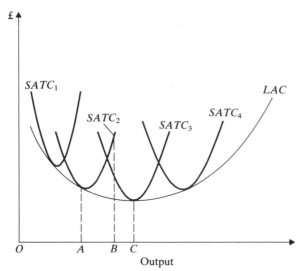

FIGURE A8.4 Short-run (and long-run) average cost

10

Price (£)	Short-run decision			Long-run decision		
	Produce at a profit	Produce at a loss	Close down	Produce at a profit	Produce at a loss	Close down
18	✓			✓		
5		✓				✓
7		✓				✓
13	✓			✓		
11.50	✓					✓

Notice that firms will never choose to produce at a loss in the *long run*.

11 The firm's decision to close-down in the short run depends upon its ability to cover variable costs. If price falls below average cost, then the firm minimizes losses by ceasing to produce. In this list, this condition appears in slightly different guise as (*c*).

12 (*b*). OQ_1 would be the profit-maximizing output only for a firm in long-run equilibrium under perfect competition.

True/False

1 False: it may seem like that sometimes, for economists often assume for simplicity that there are only these two factors. In reality, there may be others: managerial input, raw materials, energy—even bandages for the rest room! (See Section 8–1 of the main text.)

2 True: of course, the economies of scale may persist to quite high output levels (see Section 8–4 of the main text).

3 True: this was discussed in the writings of Adam Smith in the eighteenth century.

4 False: not all industries experience significant economies of scale.

5 False: remember exercise 10?

6 False: price and average revenue are the same if all output is sold at the same price.

7 False: reference must also be made to the *average* condition, to see whether the firm should close down (see Section 8–6 of the main text).

8 True: see Section 8–7 of the main text.

9 True: see Section 8–5 of the main text.

10 True: see Section 8–4 of the main text.

11 True: sunk costs are sunk: what is important is the level of variable costs (see Box 8–1 in the main text).

12 False: the *LAC* curve touches each *SATC* curve but never *cuts* one.

Questions for Thought

1 You should realize that economies and diseconomies of scale will be an important element in your discussion of this question. The construction of examples is a valuable way of confirming your understanding of the issues.

2 *Hint* Remember the long-run/short-run distinction.

3 There was some brief discussion of this at the end of Chapter 7 in the main text.

9 Perfect Competition and Pure Monopoly: The Limiting Cases of Market Structure

When we looked at demand, we drew a distinction between an individual's demand for a good and the market demand. The same distinction is important in considering the supply decision. We have considered how an individual profit-maximizing firm might choose its output level: now we must focus upon the market or industry as a whole. The determination of an industry's output and price is greatly influenced by *market structure*—in particular, by the number of firms in the industry and how they interact. This chapter considers two extreme 'benchmark' cases, between which other forms of market structure fall. These are *perfect competition* and *monopoly*.

Throughout this chapter, we assume that there are many buyers of a good, and that the *market* demand curve is downward-sloping. The case of *monopsony* (where there is a single buyer of a good) is deferred to a later chapter.

In a perfectly competitive market, there are many buyers and sellers of a good, none of whom believe that they have any influence on market price. Consequently, each firm is a *price-taker*—each must accept the going market price. Thus, the firm faces a horizontal demand curve. Four characteristics are essential if this is to be reasonable. Firstly, there must be a large number of firms. Secondly, they must be producing a homogeneous (standardized) product which is sold by all at the same price. Thirdly, buyers must have perfect information about the price and quality of the goods for sale. Fourthly, firms must be free to enter or leave the industry.

Because the firm under perfect competition faces a horizontal demand curve, marginal revenue is equal to price, and we can readily analyse the short-run and long-run supply decisions using the method discussed in Chapter 8. The firm will select that output at which marginal revenue equals marginal cost, and then will check that it is more profitable to continue to produce than to close down. In the short run, if price exceeds short-run average variable cost, then the firm will choose to produce. The quantity produced at each price above this *shutdown price* represents the firm's short-run supply curve—given by the short-run marginal cost curve. For the industry, the short-run supply curve is obtained by adding together the individual firms' supply curves.

In the long-run, the firm's supply curve is the portion of the long-run marginal cost curve which lies above the long-run average cost curve. The price just equal to the minimum point of long-run average cost is known as the *entry* or *exit* price. When price is below this point, the firm will choose to leave the industry. When price is at the entry price, the firm will just break even after paying all economic costs, including the opportunity cost of the owner's money and time. If price were to settle and remain at a point above the entry price, then the firm would make *supernormal profits* in the long run.

However, considering the whole industry, such a price is likely to persist only if the firm has a cost advantage over other firms. If *all* firms in the industry were in the happy position of making supernormal profits, then in the long run other new firms would be encouraged to enter the industry, causing industry supply to increase. The result would be a fall in price, as the industry as a whole faces the downward-sloping market demand curve. Price would fall towards the entry/exit price. Indeed, if all firms in the industry face identical cost conditions, then in the long run price will fall inexorably to this point, at which all firms would make only normal profits, and there would be no further incentive for more firms to enter. In this situation, the industry's long-run supply curve is horizontal. If there are cost differences between firms, then long-run equilibrium would have the least efficient or *marginal firm* just making normal profits. Thus, the long-run industry supply curve is flatter than the short-run partly because of firms' increased flexibility to vary input structure and partly because of the tendency for firms to leave and join the industry.

When there is international trade in a commodity, it is not sufficient to consider only the domestic market. In the absence of obstacles to trade and transport costs, the *Law of One Price* suggests that the price of a commodity would be the same anywhere in the world. The existence of a world market has two important effects. Firstly, changes in world conditions may affect the domestic market. Secondly, the impact of domestic changes may be lessened by the existence of world trade.

The other extreme form of market structure is pure monopoly, where there is a single seller of a good, perhaps because the firm is a sole patent holder or because it can exploit a significant cost advantage. Analysis in this chapter is confined to the behaviour of a profit-maximizing monopolist, although this excludes many 'real-world' monopolies.

Being the sole seller of a good, the monopolist directly faces the downward-sloping market demand curve. In contrast to the firm under perfect competition, the monopolist's marginal revenue curve slopes downwards; indeed, marginal revenue falls more rapidly than average revenue as output rises. The monopolist can ignore the behaviour of other firms—because there aren't any! The firm determines the profit-maximizing position by the usual two-stage procedure, and makes a joint decision about price and output in the knowledge of demand conditions. Unlike the perfectly competitive firm, the monopolist is a *price-setter*.

A comparison of a competitive industry with a multi-plant monopolist reveals that the monopolist will tend to produce less output and to sell at a higher price. The fact that a monopolist sets a price above marginal cost, whereas price equals marginal cost under perfect competition, has led to the argument that monopoly carries a social cost. This will be examined in a later chapter. There may be cases where substantial economies of scale make it unlikely and undesirable for there to be more than one producer of a good.

There is no unique supply curve for the monopolist, because the supply decision depends crucially upon demand conditions. In some situations, it may be possible for a monopolist to charge different prices to different customers. This can happen when a market is divided or the commodity is such that it cannot be resold. In the case of perfect price discrimination (where the monopolist can charge a different price to each customer), the monopolist can be induced to produce considerably more output—in return for substantial profits!

Monopolies have been defended on the grounds that only large firms can afford to undertake the large-scale research and development which can reduce costs of production in the long run and lead to the introduction of new products.

IMPORTANT CONCEPTS AND TECHNICAL TERMS

Match each lettered concept with the appropriate numbered phrase:

(a) Perfectly competitive market
(b) Industry supply curve
(c) Discriminating monopoly
(d) Market structure
(e) Natural monopoly
(f) Shutdown price
(g) Law of One Price
(h) Monopoly
(i) The social cost of monopoly
(j) Marginal firm
(k) Short-run equilibrium
(l) Normal profit
(m) Supernormal profits
(n) Long-run equilibrium
(o) Firm's supply curve
(p) Monopsony
(q) Comparative statics
(r) Free entry or exit

1   A description of the behaviour of buyers and sellers in a market.
2   A market in which both buyers and sellers believe that their own buying or selling decisions have no effect on the market price.
3   The curve showing the quantity that the firm wants to produce at each price.
4   The least efficient firm in a perfectly competitive industry, just making normal profits.
5   The analysis of how equilibrium changes when there is a change, for example, in demand or cost conditions.
6   In perfect competition, a situation in which the market price equates the quantity demanded to the total quantity supplied by the given number of firms in the industry when each firm produces on its short-run supply curve.
7   A market structure in which there is only one buyer or potential buyer of the good in that industry.
8   A situation in which firms can leave or join an industry without hindrance.
9   In perfect competition, a situation in which the market price equates the quantity demanded to the total supplied by the number of firms in the industry when each firm produces on its long-run supply curve; the marginal firm makes only normal profits.
10 A market structure in which there is only one seller or potential seller of the good in that industry.
11 A situation in which the price of a given commodity would be the same all over the world if there were no obstacles to trade and no transport costs.
12 An industry in which the firm faces such substantial economies of scale that long-run average cost falls over the entire range of output, making it difficult for more than one firm to operate.
13 A market structure in which a monopolist can charge different prices to different customers.
14 The price below which the firm reduces its losses by choosing not to produce at all.
15 That level of profits which just pays the opportunity cost of the owners' money and time.
16 An excess of total revenue over total cost.
17 The curve showing the total quantity that firms in (or potentially in) an industry want to supply at each price.
18 The cost borne by society as a result of a monopolist who sets price above marginal cost.

EXERCISES

1 A firm operating in a perfectly competitive industry faces the cost curves shown in Figure 9.1. OP is the going market price.

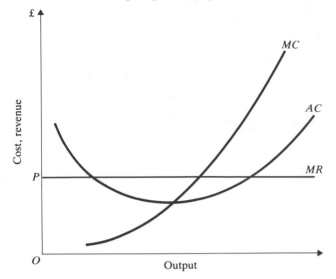

FIGURE 9.1 A firm under perfect competition

(a) Mark on the diagram the profit-maximizing level of output.

(b) Mark on the diagram the area representing the profits made by the firm at this level of price and output.

(c) If you were told that this industry was in equilibrium, would you judge it to be a short-run or a long-run equilibrium? Justify your answer.

(d) How would you expect the firm to be affected by a decrease in the market demand for the commodity produced by this industry?

2 Figure 9.2 shows the short-run cost curves for a perfectly competitive firm.

(a) What is the shutdown price for the firm?

(b) At what price would the firm just make normal profits?

(c) What area would represent total fixed cost at this price?

(d) Within what range of prices would the firm choose to operate at a loss in the short run?

(e) Identify the firm's short-run supply curve.

(f) Within what range of prices would the firm be able to make short-run supernormal profits?

3 A monopolist faces the cost and revenue conditions shown in Figure 9.3.

(a) Mark on the diagram the profit-maximizing level of output.

(b) Mark on the diagram the price at which the

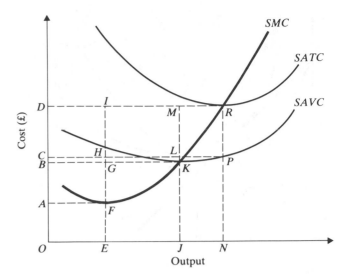

FIGURE 9.2 Short-run cost curves for a perfectly competitive firm

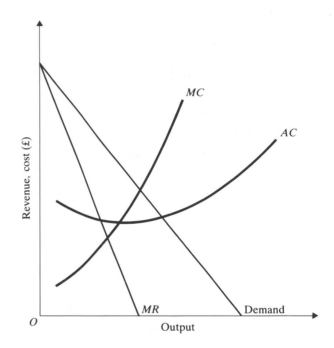

FIGURE 9.3 A monopolist's cost and revenue conditions

monopolist would choose to sell this output.

(c) Identify the area representing the level of monopoly profits at this price and output.

(d) How would you expect the monopolist to be affected by a decrease in the market demand for his commodity?

4 Figure 9.4 shows the long-run cost and revenue situation facing a monopolist.

(a) What is the profit-maximizing level of output?

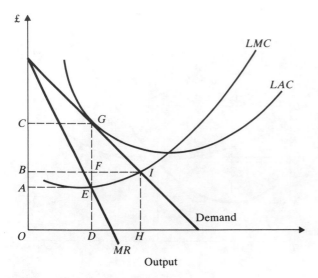

FIGURE 9.4   The long-run position of a monopolist

(b)   At what price would the monopolist choose to sell the good?
(c)   What level of supernormal profits would be made in this situation?
(d)   How much output (and at what price) would the monopolist produce if forced to set price equal to marginal cost?

5   Table 9.1 represents the demand curve faced by a monopolist.

TABLE 9.1   A monopolist's demand curve

Demand (thousands/week)	Price (£)	Total revenue	Marginal revenue
0	40		
1	35		
2	30		
3	25		
4	20		
5	15		
6	10		
7	5		

(a)   Calculate total revenue and marginal revenue.
(b)   Using graph paper, plot average revenue and marginal revenue.
(c)   On a separate graph, plot total revenue.
(d)   At what level of demand is total revenue at a maximum?
(e)   At what level of demand is marginal revenue equal to zero?
(f)   At what level of demand is there unit own price elasticity of demand?

6   Figure 9.5 shows a firm's cost and revenue position.
    At which output level would the firm be
(a)   maximizing profits?
(b)   maximizing total revenue?

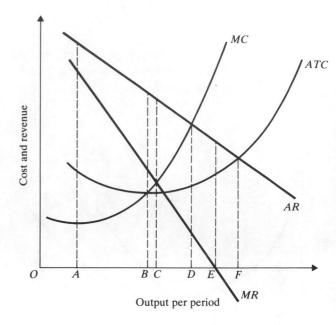

FIGURE 9.5   Cost and revenue for a firm

(c)   producing the technically optimum output?
(d)   making only normal profits?

7   Under which of the following conditions will a profit-maximizing, perfectly competitive firm close down in the short run?
(a)   Price is less than marginal cost.
(b)   Average revenue is less than average cost.
(c)   Average fixed cost is greater than price.
(d)   Average revenue is less than average variable cost.
(e)   Total cost is greater than total revenue.

8   Which of the following would indicate that a firm is *not* producing under conditions of perfect competition?
(a)   The equilibrium output is where marginal revenue equals marginal cost.
(b)   The marginal cost curve cuts the average cost curve at its lowest point.
(c)   The marginal revenue curve is downward-sloping to the right.
(d)   The average and marginal cost curves are U-shaped.
(e)   The technically optimum output is where the average cost curve is at its lowest point.
        (University of London GCE A level Economics 3, January 1989)

9   Which of the following corresponds most closely to the economists' notion of 'normal profit'?
(a)   The level of profits a firm makes by setting MC = MR.
(b)   The level of profits made by the typical firm in an industry.
(c)   The level of profits that firms would tend to

make under normal conditions of trade.
(d)   The level of profits needed to persuade a firm to stay in its present line of business.
(e)   The rate of profits that ensures a comfortable standard of living for the entrepreneur.

10   A profit-maximising monopolist would be likely to cut the price of his product if
(a)   average total costs fall
(b)   advertising costs increase
(c)   marginal revenue is greater than marginal costs
(d)   marginal revenue is equal to variable costs
(Associated Examining Board, GCE A level Economics Paper 1, November 1986)

11   A perfectly competitive industry is taken over by a monopolist who intends to run it as a multi-plant concern. Consequently, the long-run supply curve of the competitive industry ($LRSS$) becomes the monopolist's long-run marginal cost curve (LMC_m); in the short-run the $SRSS$ curve becomes the monopolist's SMC_m. The position is shown in Figure 9.6.
(a)   What was the equilibrium price and industry output under perfect competition?
(b)   At what price and output would the monopolist choose to operate in the short run?

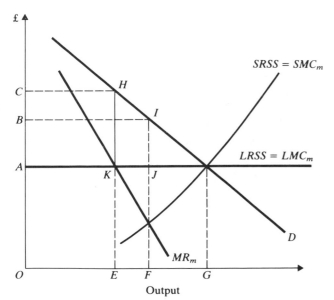

FIGURE 9.6   The monopolization of a perfectly competitive industry

(a)   What was the equilibrium price and industry output under perfect competition?
(b)   At what price and output would the monopolist choose to operate in the short run?
(c)   At what price and output would the monopolist maximize profits in the long run?

(d)   What would be the size of these long-run profits?

TRUE/FALSE

1   _____ Price is equal to marginal revenue for a firm under perfect competition.
2   _____ The short-run supply curve for a perfectly competitive firm is flatter than the long-run supply curve.
3   _____ A firm making economic profits is said to be making normal profits.
4   _____ An industry in which long-run average costs fall throughout the relevant range of output is ideally suited for a perfectly competitive market.
5   _____ The supply curve of an industry is obtained by a horizontal aggregation of the quantities supplied by firms in the industry at each price.
6   _____ A monopolist will always produce on the inelastic part of the demand curve.
7   _____ Other things being equal, an increase in variable costs will cause a monopolist to increase output and reduce price.
8   _____ A monopolist makes supernormal profits because it is more efficient than a competitive industry.
9   _____ For a given demand curve, marginal revenue falls increasingly below price the higher the output level from which we begin.
10   _____ Total revenue is maximized when average revenue is at a maximum.
11   _____ A monopolist may increase total profits by charging different prices in different markets.
12   _____ A vertical supply curve has zero price elasticity.
13   _____ A perfectly competitive firm will be selling at a price equal to marginal cost, but a monopolist can set a price above marginal cost.
14   _____ Very small firms typically do little research and development, whereas many larger firms have excellent research departments.

QUESTIONS FOR THOUGHT

1   We have seen that a monopolist wishing to maximize profits will tend to restrict output and increase price. Can you think of circumstances in which a monopolist might choose not to take full advantage of these potential profits?
2   Explain why it is said that the firm under perfect

competition operates at the technically optimum point of production in the long run. Can any conclusions be drawn about the efficient allocation of resources in the industry?

3   The monopoly producer of a commodity supplies two separate markets. The commodity is one that cannot be resold—in other words, it is not possible for a consumer to buy in market 2 and resell in market 1. Figure 9.7 shows the demand and marginal revenue curves in the two markets and in the combined market. Notice that the MR curve for the combined market has a 'jump' in it at the point where price falls sufficiently for the monopolist to make sales in market 2.

This question extends the analysis of Section 9–9: you may wish to tackle it slowly, with the help of the comments provided in the 'Answer and Comments' section. Throughout the analysis, the monopolist's output level is decided by reference to marginal cost and revenue in the *combined* market. You can draw lines across to the submarket diagrams to find MR and AR.

(a)   What level of output will the monopolist produce to maximize profits?

(b)   If the monopolist sets a common price to all customers, what would that price be?

(c)   How much will the monopolist sell in each of the two submarkets?

(d)   At this selling price, what is marginal revenue in each of the two markets?

(e)   If the monopolist now finds that price discrimination is possible, how could profits be increased? (*Hint*   Your answer to part (d) is important here.)

(f)   With price discrimination, what prices would the monopolist set in each market, and how much would be sold?

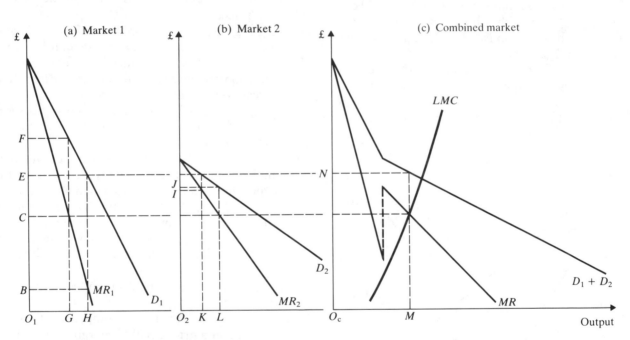

FIGURE 9.7   A discriminating monopolist

ANSWERS AND COMMENTS FOR CHAPTER 9

Please note   Where questions are reproduced from A level examinations, the examination boards bear no responsibility for the answers provided in this volume, which are the sole responsibility of the authors.

Important Concepts and Technical Terms

1	d	7	p	13	c
2	a	8	r	14	f
3	o	9	n	15	l
4	j	10	h	16	m
5	q	11	g	17	b
6	k	12	e	18	i

Exercises

1

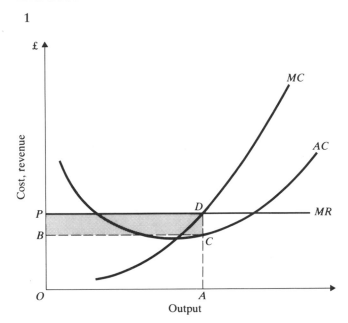

FIGURE A9.1   A firm under perfect competition

(a) Profits would be maximized at output *OA* where *MC* = *MR*.

(b) Profits would be calculated by the excess of average revenue over average cost, multiplied by output—on the diagram, this is the area *PBCD*.

(c) This firm is making profits over and above 'normal profits', which are included in average cost. It is thus probable that this diagram represents short-run equilibrium, as we would expect other firms to be encouraged to enter the industry by the lure of these supernormal profits. However, it could be a long-run equilibrium if this firm enjoys a cost advantage—perhaps a better geographical location. In this case, further entry would depend upon the marginal firm's performance.

(d) A decrease in demand would lead initially to a fall in price of the good, and firms such as the one

represented in the diagram would experience a reduction in profits. In the long run, firms would be able to adjust their input structures to the new conditions, so that price would drift up again. (See Section 9–4 of the main text for a similar analysis of an *increase* in demand.)

2 (a) *OB*: the price at which the firm just covers its variable costs.

(b) *OD*.

(c) *CDRP*: total cost less variable cost.

(d) Between *OB* and *OD*.

(e) The supply curve in the short run is the portion of the *SMC* curve above point *K*.

(f) Above *OD*.

3

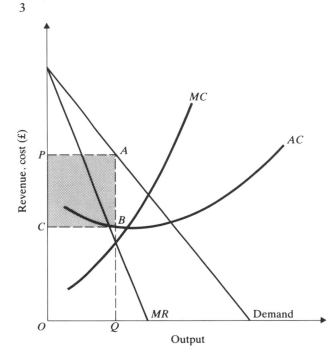

FIGURE A9.2   A monopolist's conditions

(a) Profit would be maximized at output *OQ*, where *MR* = *MC*.

(b) The demand curve shows that the monopolist could sell *OQ* output at a price *OP*.

(c) Profits would be calculated, as before, as the excess of average revenue over average cost, multiplied by output—this is the area *PABC*.

(d) A decrease in demand would affect both 'Demand' and *MR* curves on the diagram, moving them to the left. *MC* and *MR* will now intersect at a lower level of output, so the monopolist will produce less.

4 (a) *MR* = *LMC* at the output level *OD*.

(b) *OC*.

(c) *LAC* is just tangent to the demand curve at this point, so the monopolist makes only normal profits: supernormal profits are zero.

(d) If the monopolist were forced to charge a price equal to marginal cost, then an output of *OH* is indicated, with price *OB*. However, notice that in this situation LAC exceeds average revenue and the monopolist would close down, unless the authorities were prepared to offer a subsidy.

5   (a)

TABLE A9.1   A monopolist's revenue curves

Demand (thousands/week)	Price (£) (average revenue)	Total revenue	Marginal revenue
0	40	0	
			35
1	35	35	
			25
2	30	60	
			15
3	25	75	
			5
4	20	80	
			−5
5	15	75	
			−15
6	10	60	
			−25
7	5	35	

(b)   and (c)

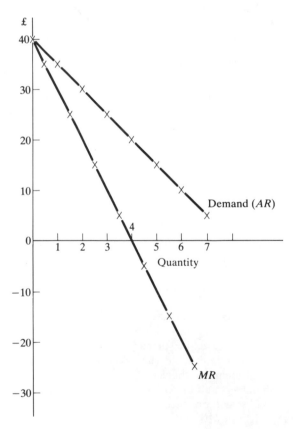

FIGURE A9.3   A monopolist's revenue curves

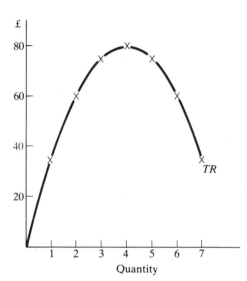

(d)   4.
(e)   4.
(f)   4.

6   (a)   OC.
    (b)   OE.
    (c)   OB.
    (d)   OF.
7   (d).
8   Option (a) would hold for any firm choosing output to maximize profits, whether operating under perfect competition or not. Similarly, (b) is a condition that *always* holds true. We very often assume that average and marginal cost curves are U-shaped in a variety of circumstances—and the analysis of perfect competition requires this assumption. We define the technically optimum output level as being at the minimum point of long-run average cost. This reasoning eliminates all except option (c). As every firm under perfect competition is assumed to be a price-taker, the marginal revenue curve must be horizontal at the market price.

9   (d).
10 (c). Check this on a standard monopoly diagram: if marginal revenue is greater than marginal cost, the monopolist is operating to the left of the profit-maximizing output level.
11 (a)   Under perfect competition, industry equilibrium would be where demand (D) equals supply ($LRSS$)—that is, at price OA and output OG.
    (b)   In the short run the monopolist will set marginal revenue (MR_m) equal to short-run marginal cost (SMC_m). Output is reduced to OF and price increased to OB.
    (c)   In the long run, the monopolist will close down some plants and equate MR_m with long-run marginal cost (LMC_m). Output is reduced further to OE and price raised to OC.

(*d*)   The monopolist will still operate each individual plant at its minimum *LAC*. *LAC* is thus given by *OA*—and profits by the area *ACHK*.

True/False

1   True.

2   False: the increased flexibility in the long run makes the long-run supply curve *flatter* than in the short run.

3   False: the firm is said to be making just normal profits when economic profits are zero (see Section 9–2 of the main text).

4   False: such an industry is a natural monopoly (see Section 9–8 of the main text).

5   False: we must also consider the quantity that would be supplied by firms who are not currently operating in the market, but who would enter if market price were at a higher level.

6   False: a monopolist will *never* produce on the inelastic part of the demand curve (see Section 9–7 of the main text).

7   False: draw the diagram to check.

8   False: even where efficiency is the same, the monopolist has influence on price and can use this market power to make supernormal profits.

9   True: see Section 9–7 of the main text.

10   False.

11   True.

12   True: see Box 9–1 in the main text.

13   True.

14   True: see Section 9–10 of the main text.

Questions for Thought

1   *Hint*   What could threaten the monopolist's long-term position?

2   No hints offered.

3   (*a*) O_cM: the output at which $LMC = MR$ in the combined market.

(*b*) O_cN (= O_1E), this being the price to clear the combined market.

(*c*)   At the price of O_1E demand in market 1 would be O_1H, and demand in market 2 would be O_2K. Notice, of course, that the scales of the three diagrams are common, and that $O_1H + O_2K = O_cM$.

(*d*)   Marginal revenue is O_1B in market 1 and O_2I in market 2. This large difference has important implications for profits.

(*e*)   In part (*d*), it was clear that marginal revenue in market 2 was much higher than in market 1. If the monopolist can increase sales in market 2 and reduce sales in market 1, the additional revenue from the former will more than offset the lost revenue from the latter, and profits will increase. It will pay to continue this switching until marginal revenue is equal in the two markets.

(*f*)   To equalize marginal revenue in the two submarkets, the monopolist would sell in market 1 at a price of O_1F and in market 2 at a price of O_2J; sales would be O_1G and O_2L, respectively. Again, $O_1G + O_2L = O_cM$.

Notice that this analysis depends upon the nature of the commodity (cannot be resold), the separation of the market, and the differing elasticities of demand in the two markets.

It is also worth noticing that if LMC cut MR much further to the left in Figure 9.7c, it could be that without discrimination no sales at all are made in market 2.

Market Structure and Imperfect Competition

In Chapter 9 we analysed two polar forms of market structure: perfect competition and monopoly. Between these extremes lies a variety of intermediate market situations, differing from the former in various characteristics. These are all forms of *imperfect competition*, and are the basis for this chapter; in particular, we examine *oligopoly* and *monopolistic competition*.

One characteristic shared by firms under all forms of imperfect competition is that they face downward-sloping demand curves for their products: an increase in sales must be accompanied by a reduction in price.

What is it that predisposes an industry towards a particular form of market structure? An important factor concerns the cost conditions faced by a firm relative to the extent of market demand. In the previous chapter we saw that, if there are substantial economies of scale relative to market size, then an industry may be a natural monopoly. It would then not be feasible for the industry to be a competitive market. If economies of scale are limited relative to market size, conditions may favour a competitive situation, with large numbers of small firms. It is no accident that many examples of competitive industries are service sectors with little, if any, scope for scale economies. Equally, it is possible that the available economies of scale are such that only a few firms are encouraged. The extent to which an industry is dominated by a few large firms can be measured by the *concentration ratio*.

Monopolistic competition describes a market situation with a large number of firms, producing similar but not identical products ('*product differentiation*'). In the long run, entry or exit of firms ensures that each firm makes only normal profits at the profit-maximizing level of output, but not at minimum average cost. Price charged is above marginal cost. Unlike a perfectly competitive firm, a monopolistic competitor would be keen to sell more at the going price.

Where economies of scale are such that only a few firms are encouraged, we see the emergence of oligopoly: a market characterized by few sellers.

A key feature of oligopolistic markets is that the firms within the market must consider the likely behaviour of other firms when making their own decisions. This interaction may take the form of either collusion or competition. *Collusion*, or co-operation, may carry the market towards the 'monopoly end' of the market spectrum. By co-operating, the firms in an industry may be able to increase total industry profits by restricting output and raising price as if the industry were a monopoly. However, such collusion may be fragile, as an individual firm always stands to gain by reducing price a little and thus increasing its market share. This behaviour can rapidly lead to general non-cooperation, carrying the industry towards the 'competitive end' of the market spectrum.

Firms may collude by forming a *cartel*. These are outlawed in many countries as they are seen to act against the public interest. OPEC is one famous and current example of an operating cartel.

The *kinked oligopoly demand curve* model is probably the most famous of non-cooperative models. Here the fundamental idea is that a firm's perceptions of its demand curve are different for a price increase than for a price decrease. The firm believes that, if it lowers price, competing firms will follow suit to protect their own interests, whereas they would not be threatened by a price rise, and would not feel the need to follow. Consequently, the firm perceives its demand curve to be more elastic for a price rise than for a price reduction. This model suggests that price may be stable even in the face of changes in demand or cost conditions. However, it does not explain how price is set in the first place.

Game theory is one approach that has been adopted to analyse the way in which firms behave. Firms are seen as players in a game situation, choosing their moves according to perceptions about the likely moves of the other players (firms), and according to their assessments of the consequences of possible combinations of moves. An equilibrium situation in which all firms in a market choose their strategies in the light of the strategies adopted by the other firms is known as a *Nash equilibrium*. Occasionally, a firm may have a *dominant strategy*, in which its optimal strategy is independent of the strategies adopted by other firms.

Tensions are inherent in a cartel: firms gain by collusion, but the incentive for an individual firm to cheat is ever-present. Game theory sheds light on possible resolutions of these tensions. A firm may announce its strategy through *pre-commitment* to a course of action, knowing that this will affect the strategic decisions of other firms. A firm may announce a *punishment strategy* to be adopted if there is cheating by other cartel members. This constitutes a *credible threat* only if the punishment strategy is seen to be optimal for the firm to adopt should cheating occur.

In the discussion of market structure and behaviour, a key market characteristic is the degree of *freedom of entry*. We have already seen how free entry erodes supernormal profits in long-run equilibrium in both perfect competition and monopolistic competition. (A market in which there is complete freedom of entry and exit is known as a *contestable market*.) In monopoly, the behaviour of the firm is conditioned by complete barriers to entry. However, in oligopoly firms must take account of the behaviour not only of existing firms, but also of *potential* competitors.

Barriers to entry may be *innocent* or *strategic*. Substantial scale economies may confer natural protection on incumbent firms in an industry. Thus, a market may not be able to support more than a few firms because of innocent entry barriers.

However, we may find that existing firms take strategic decisions designed to discourage further entry. Tactics such as predatory pricing, product proliferation, defensive advertising, or operating with surplus capacity all make it more difficult for potential entrants to join a market.

This way of thinking about firms' behaviour is sometimes known as the *New Industrial Economics*. It represents an attempt to move away from the stark unreality (but clean simplicity) of the models of Chapter 9 and towards an analysis that informs us more directly about the way in which markets operate in practice.

IMPORTANT CONCEPTS AND TECHNICAL TERMS

Match each lettered concept with the appropriate numbered phrase:

(a) Oligopoly
(b) Cartel
(c) Imperfect competition
(d) Contestable market
(e) Credible threat
(f) Dominant strategy
(g) Product differentiation
(h) N-firm concentration ratio
(i) New Industrial Economics
(j) Collusion
(k) Pre-commitment
(l) Tangency equilibrium
(m) Monopolistic competition
(n) Predatory pricing
(o) Game theory
(p) Kinked demand curve
(q) Strategic move
(r) Prisoners' Dilemma
(s) Minimum efficient scale
(t) Innocent entry barrier
(u) Nash equilibrium
(v) Strategy

1 A market structure in which firms recognize that their demand curves slope downwards and that output price will depend on the quantity of goods produced and sold.

2 An industry with only a few producers, each recognizing that its own price depends not merely on its own output but also on the actions of its important competitors in the industry.

3 A tactic adopted by existing firms when faced by a new entrant, involving deliberately increasing output and forcing down the price, causing all firms to make losses.

4 The output at which a firm's long-run average cost curve stops falling.

5 The analysis of the principles behind intelligent interdependent decision-making.

6 An explicit or implicit agreement between existing firms to avoid competition with each other.

7 A game plan describing how a player will act or move in every conceivable situation.

8 The demand curve perceived by an oligopolist who believes that competitors will respond to a decrease in his price but not to an increase.

9 An industry having many sellers producing products that are close substitutes for one another, and in which each firm has only a limited ability to affect its output price.

10 Actual or perceived differences in a good compared with its substitutes, designed to affect the behaviour of potential buyers.

11 A situation in which a player's best strategy is independent of that adopted by other players.

12 An arrangement entered into voluntarily which restricts one's future options.

13 A description of the long-run situation under monopolistic competition in which each firm maximizes profits but just breaks even, with AR and AC curves just touching.

14 A game between two players, each of whom has a dominant strategy.

15 An explicit agreement among firms to determine prices and/or market shares.

16 The market share of the largest N firms in the industry.

17 A barrier to entry not deliberately erected by firms.

18 The threat of a punishment strategy which, after the fact, a firm would then find it optimal to carry out.

19 A situation in which each player chooses the best strategy, given the strategies being followed by the other players.

20 Recent developments (game theory in general and notions such as pre-commitment, credibility, and deterrence) which have allowed economists to analyse many of the practical concerns of big business.

21 A market characterized by free entry and free exit.

22 A move that influences the other person's choice, in a manner favourable to one's self, by affecting the other person's expectations of how one's self will behave.

EXERCISES

1 For each of the situations listed below, select the market form in the list which offers the best description.

Market forms
A   Perfect competition
B   Monopoly
C   Oligopoly
D   Monopolistic competition
E   Monopsony

(a) A fairly large number of firms, each supplying branded footwear at very similar prices.
(b) A sole supplier of telecommunication services.
(c) A large number of farmers supplying carrots at identical prices.
(d) A few giant firms supplying the whole of the market for car tyres.
(e) A single buyer of coal-cutting equipment.
(f) A sole supplier of rail transport.

2 Table 10.1 presents some hypothetical concentration ratios and information about scale economies in a number of industries.

TABLE 10.1   Concentration and scale economies in Hypothetica

Industry	3-firm concentration ratio (CR)	Number of plants at min. efficient scale allowed by market size (NP)
A	100	1
B	11	221
C	81	3
D	49	5
E	21	195

(a) Which industry is *most* likely to be operated as a monopoly.
(b) Which industry(ies) would you expect to find operating under conditions of perfect competition?
(c) In which industry(ies) would conditions be conducive to oligopoly?
(d) In which industry(ies) would oligopoly be *unlikely* to arise? Explain your answer.

3 Which of the following characteristics are typical of an industry operating under monopolistic competition in long-run equilibrium? (*Note:* there may be more than one valid response.)
(a) Individual firms in the industry make only small monopoly profits.
(b) Individual firms in the industry would be keen to sell more output at the existing market price.
(c) There is product differentiation.
(d) Each firm faces a downward-sloping demand curve.
(e) Firms operate below full capacity output.
(f) Firms maximize profits where marginal cost equals marginal revenue.
(g) There is collusion among firms in the industry.
(h) The profits accruing to firms are just sufficient to cover the opportunity cost of capital employed.

4 Oligopoly is best described as a market situation where
(a) there is a large number of competing firms with similar products
(b) there is a large number of competing firms whose products differ slightly
(c) there is a small number of competing firms
(d) there are only two competing firms
(e) the market is dominated by one firm only
(University of London GCE A level Economics 3, January 1989)

5 In industry X, the four largest firms produce 50% of the industry's total output. In industry Y, the four largest firms produce 70% of the industry's output. It can be concluded from the information that
(a) firms are larger in industry Y than in industry X
(b) there are more economies of scale in industry Y than in industry X
(c) the concentration ratio is higher in industry Y than in industry X
(d) small firms have more chance of survival in industry X than in industry Y
(Associated Examining Board GCE A level Economics Paper 1, June 1988)

6 Figure 10.1 shows a profit-maximizing firm in monopolistic competition.
(a) How much output will be produced by the firm?
(b) At what price will the output be sold?
(c) Will the firm make supernormal profits in this situation? If so, identify the extent of supernormal profits.
(d) Would you consider this to be a long-run or short-run equilibrium for the firm?
(e) Explain your answer to (d) and describe

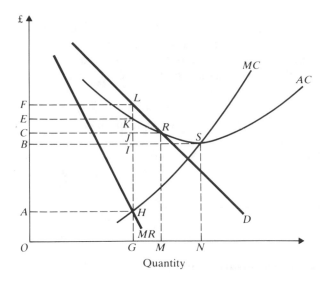

FIGURE 10.1   A firm in monopolistic competition

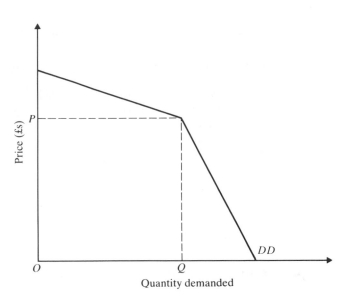

FIGURE 10.2   A firm's perceived demand curve

how the situation might differ in the 'other run' (i.e., the one you haven't plumped for).

7   In an oligopolistic market, which of the following conditions tend to favour collusion and which are more likely to encourage non-cooperation?

Influence	Encourages collusion	Favours non-cooperation
	(Tick one column)	
Barriers to entry		
Product is non-standard		
Demand and costs are stable		
Collusion is legal		
Secrecy about price and output		
Collusion is illegal		
Easy communication of price and output		
Standard product		

8   Figure 10.2 shows the demand curve (*DD*) for the output of an individual firm, as perceived by that firm. The firm is currently producing the amount *OQ* at a price *OP*. Assess the likely validity of each of the following inferences that may be drawn concerning conditions in the industry of which this firm is a part:

(*a*)   The firm may be slow to change price, even if faced by a change in cost conditions.

(*b*)   The firm is a discriminating monopolist, charging different prices in two separated markets.

(*c*)   The industry is a non-cooperative oligopoly in which the individual firm must take into consideration the likely behaviour of the few rival firms.

(*d*)   The firm faces production difficulties at

levels of output above *OQ*, perhaps as a result of labour shortages.

9

		Firm Y chooses:			
		Low output		High output	
	Profits	X	Y	X	Y
Firm X chooses	Low output	15	15	2	20
	High output	20	2	8	8

FIGURE 10.3   The Prisoners' Dilemma game

Suppose that there are two firms (X and Y) operating in a market, each of which can choose to produce either 'high' or 'low' output. Figure 10.3 summarizes the range of possible outcomes of the firms' decisions in a single time period. Imagine that you are taking the decisions for firm X.

(*a*)   If firm Y produces 'low', what level of output would maximize your profit in the current time period?

(*b*)   If you (X) produce 'high', what level of output would maximize profits for firm Y?

(*c*)   If firm Y produces 'high', what level of output would maximize your profit in the current time period?

(*d*)   Under what circumstances would you decide to produce 'low'?

(*e*)   Suppose you enter into an agreement with firm Y that you both will produce 'low': what measures could you adopt to ensure that Y keeps to the agreement?

(*f*)   What measures could you adopt to convince Y that you will keep to the agreement?

10 Which of the following entry barriers are 'innocent', and which are strategic?
  (a) Exploiting the benefits of large-scale production.
  (b) Undertaking a large research and development (R&D) project to develop new techniques and products.
  (c) Holding a patent on a particular product.
  (d) Producing a range of similar products under different brand-names.
  (e) Extensive multi-media advertising.
  (f) Installing more machinery than is required for normal (or current) levels of production.
  (g) Holding an absolute cost advantage.

TRUE/FALSE

1 _____ The firm under imperfect competition has some influence over price, evidenced by the downward-sloping demand curve for its product.

2 _____ A key aspect of an oligopolistic market is that firms cannot act independently of each other.

3 _____ An industry in which diseconomies of scale set in at a relatively low level of output is likely to be a monopoly.

4 _____ A firm in long-run equilibrium under monopolistic competition produces at an output below the technically optimum point of production.

5 _____ A feature of the kinked oligopoly demand curve model is that price may be stable when costs for a single firm change, but prices may change rapidly when the whole industry is faced with a change in cost conditions.

6 _____ Firms under oligopoly face kinked demand curves.

7 _____ A player holding a dominant strategy always wins.

8 _____ Cartels may be made workable if their members are prepared to enter into binding pre-commitments.

9 _____ A cartel member's announcement of intent to adopt a punishment strategy will maintain a cartel.

10 _____ A monopolist always maximizes profits by setting marginal cost equal to marginal revenue.

11 _____ Free exit from a market implies that there are no sunk or irrecoverable costs.

12 _____ Fixed costs may artificially increase scale economies and help to deter entry by firms new to the industry.

13 _____ Firms would not advertise unless they expected it to increase sales.

QUESTIONS FOR THOUGHT

1 British Telecom operated as a legally protected monopoly until 1981. Discuss the extent to which you would expect to have seen changes in market structure and efficiency when this legal protection was withdrawn.

2 Exercise 10 listed various sorts of entry barriers. Can you think of examples of British industries in which they appear to be operative?

3 Think about some of the firms that operate in your own neighbourhood. Try to classify them according to market structure—that is, think whether they are operating in conditions of perfect competition, monopoly, oligopoly, or monopolistic competition.

ANSWERS AND COMMENTS FOR CHAPTER 10

Please note Where questions are reproduced from A level examinations, the examination boards bear no responsibility for the answers provided in this volume, which are the sole responsibility of the authors.

Important Concepts and Technical Terms

1	c	7	v	13	l	19	u
2	a	8	p	14	r	20	i
3	n	9	m	15	b	21	d
4	s	10	g	16	h	22	q
5	o	11	f	17	t		
6	j	12	k	18	e		

Exercises

1 (a) D.
  (b) B.
  (c) A.
  (d) C.
  (e) E: we haven't talked about monopsony yet, but it was defined in Chapter 9.
  (f) B/C: although a monopolist in the supply of rail transport, the supplier would doubtless be aware of potential competition from other forms of transport, and would thus perhaps behave more like an oligopolist than a monopolist.

2 (a) A, because of the existence of substantial economies of scale relative to market size.
  (b) B, E: in both industries, the biggest three firms supply a small proportion of the market. In addition, it is clear that no great scale economies exist, in that the minimum efficient size is very small relative to market size.
  (c) C, D seem capable of supporting just a handful of firms.
  (d) Oligopoly is unlikely to arise in either B or E, with the large number of firms likely to be present in these industries. Could A be an oligopoly? It is perhaps not impossible: we cannot know for sure, as we only have the *three*-firm concentration ratio; nor do we know whether the firm(s) is (are) actually operating at minimum efficient scale. The monopolist may be prevented by law from exploiting his position—or may have other 'industries' with which to compete (see example (f) in exercise 1). The steepness of the average cost curve below minimum efficient scale is also important. For more details, see Section 10–1 in the main text.

3 (b), (c), (d), (e), (f) and (h) are all typical characteristics of such an industry—see Section 10–6 of the main text. As for the other factors:
  (a) In long-run equilibrium, firms find themselves in tangency equilibrium with average revenue just covering average costs—so *no* monopoly profits are to be reaped in the long run. If this were not

so, then there would be an incentive for more firms to enter the market.
  (g) Monopolistic competition is typified by a large number of firms, so the opportunities for collusion are limited.

4 The options presented in the question carry us through the spectrum of alternative market structures. Oligopoly involves a *few* firms, so the appropriate response is (c).

5 The information presented in the question is simply the four-firm concentration ratio, so we can see straight away that the appropriate response is option (c). The statements in the other options *could* be correct, but need not be.

6 (a) $MR = MC$ at output OG.
  (b) OF.
  (c) Yes: the area $EFLK$.
  (d) This must be a short-run equilibrium. The presence of supernormal profits will attract new entrants into the industry, causing our firm's demand curve to become more elastic at any price and to shift to the left. This is because of the increased availability of substitutes and because the firm loses some customers to the new entrants. The process continues until the typical firm is in tangency equilibrium, with its demand curve just touching the long-run average cost curve, so that only normal profits are made.

Influence	Encourages collusion	Favours non-cooperation
	(Tick one column)	
Barriers to entry	✓	
Product is non-standard		✓
Demand and costs are stable	✓	
Collusion is legal	✓	
Secrecy about price and output		✓
Collusion is illegal		✓
Easy communication of price and output	✓	
Standard product	✓	

8 The figure shows the typical shape of the famous 'kinked demand curve'. A feature of this model is the stability of prices, so we can accept statement (a). The price discrimination model can also produce a demand curve with a kink in it—but in that case, the kink faces the other way (see Figure 9.7). We thus reject (b). As this is an oligopoly model, and the 'kink' occurs because the firm is aware of its rivals' actions, statement (c) is likely to be acceptable. Statement (d) has no foundation.

9 (a) Given that Y produces 'low', you (X) can make profits of 15 by also producing 'low' or 20 by producing 'high'. For this period, you maximize profits by producing 'high'—but notice that, in so doing, you reduce the profit made by Y.
  (b) With you producing 'high', firm Y must also produce 'high' to maximize profits.

(c)   Given the answer to (b), it seems probable that Y will indeed produce 'high', in which case your only option is also to produce 'high'. In actual fact, your dominant strategy is to produce 'high'—it pays you to do this whatever Y does if we are concerned only with the single time period.

(d)   If we start thinking in terms of a sequence of time periods, it should be clear that both firms could be better off if both agree to produce 'low'. If you can be sure that firm Y will produce 'low' and will continue to do so, then it will pay you to decide to produce 'low' also.

(e)   One possibility is to announce a punishment strategy. You threaten to produce 'high' in all future periods if Y cheats on the agreement. The threat is credible only if Y believes that you would actually find it in your best interests to carry it out.

(f)   One possibility is that you enter into a pre-commitment to produce 'low', restricting your own future options.

10   (a) is an innocent barrier: if the minimum efficient scale is high relative to market demand, then we are heading towards a natural monopoly situation. (b) may well be strategic: potential entrants will perceive that staying in this market will require R&D expenditure and may thus be deterred. Also, R&D expenditure may lead to the generating of patents (c) for the future, further preventing entry. Items (d), (e), and (f) are other ways in which the incumbent firm(s) may deter potential entrants; you will find more detailed discussion in Section 10–6 of the main text. The final item (g) could be either innocent or strategic. Existing firms may have 'innocent' advantages in locations or experience which make it difficult for new entrants to compete. On the other hand, the advantage may be another offspring of past R&D effort, and thus partly strategic.

True/False

1   True: the possible exception, however, is the firm in the competitive fringe of a dominant firm oligopoly, which must accept the price set.

2   True.

3   False: in these conditions a monopoly would be unlikely (see Section 10–1 of the main text).

4   True: see Section 10–6 of the main text.

5   True: a firm's behaviour is determined by its *perceptions* about the actions of other firms. Thus, firms will be prepared to raise price if it is known that all firms face an increase in costs.

6   False: the kinked demand curve may be the most famous of oligopoly models, but, as this chapter has shown, it is by no means the only way in which economists have tried to analyse such markets.

7   False: 'dominant' has nothing to do with winning; the question is whether the strategy dominates other possible strategies the firm can adopt, given what other firms may do. See Section 10–4 of the main text.

8   True: this is also discussed in Section 10–4 of the main text.

9   Not necessarily true: for this tactic to be successful, it must be apparent that the threat of a punishment strategy is a credible one.

10 This may be 'true' in the short run, but it could be 'false' in the long run: if there is a threat of new entry into the industry, it may pay to use limit pricing to deter potential entrants.

11 True: see Section 10–5 of the main text.

12 True: see Section 10–6 of the main text.

13 False: advertising may be intended to maintain sales by being 'defensive' or by acting as a barrier to entry.

Questions for Thought

1   Key issues are whether British Telecom is a natural monopoly, and whether competition would cause an increase in efficiency. Government regulation is discussed more fully in Chapter 18. British Telecom is discussed by James Foreman-Peck in the *Economic Review*, September 1986.

2, 3   No hints are offered for these questions: think about it!

11

The Analysis of Factor Markets: Labour

In the last two chapters, we have seen how the firm's decisions about price and output are affected by its economic environment. In taking those decisions, the firm is also making other decisions about the employment of factors of production. As ever in economics, these decisions cannot be taken in isolation: the firm cannot demand labour without taking account of the potential supply of labour—which is determined by the individual decisions of households. In this chapter we look at the labour market from both sides. Among the topics considered are a number of important issues: Why are some occupations paid more than others? Why do some individuals in the same occupation receive more than others? Why are different production techniques adopted in different countries in the same industry? How may unemployment arise?

The demand for labour is a *derived demand*: a firm demands labour not for its own sake, but for the output produced. In Chapter 8 we saw that factor prices were important in the choice of cost-minimizing production techniques: for instance, an increase in labour cost could in the long run lead to a switch to more capital-intensive methods of production. This story is complicated by the fact that a change in factor prices also causes a change in the pattern of costs faced by the firm, and leads to a change in the profit-maximizing level of output itself. The overall effect on factor demand is thus not obvious. If wage rates rise, there may be a *substitution effect* in favour of capital, but as costs have risen there is also likely to be an *output effect*, tending to reduce the demand for capital.

This can be studied by using *isoquants* and *isocost lines*, a piece of analysis which echoes the indifference curve analysis of Chapter 6. Whether the substitution effect or the output effect dominates depends upon the ease with which labour and capital are substitutable and upon the elasticity of demand for the product.

We can study the firm's short-run demand for labour on the assumption that capital input is fixed. The question for the firm is whether the marginal benefit of hiring an additional worker exceeds the marginal cost. For a perfectly competitive firm facing perfect competition in the labour market (i.e.,

accepting the wage as given), the marginal benefit is measured as the value of the marginal product of labour, and the marginal cost is simply the wage rate. Under these conditions, it pays the firm to employ labour up to the point where the wage rate equals the *marginal value product of labour (MVPL)*.

In the presence of some monopsony or monopoly power, the firm finds that it faces an upward-sloping labour supply curve, so that the marginal cost of labour increases as labour use increases—the firm must pay higher wages to attract new workers. In addition, as demand for labour increases and output supply increases, the firm must lower the selling price of the product. The marginal revenue created by an additional worker is thus less than the *MVPL*. The employment rule is now to equate the marginal cost of labour with the *marginal revenue product of labour*. This is sometimes known as 'marginal productivity theory'. Comparative-static analysis reveals how the firm's demand for labour responds to changes in conditions.

For a competitive industry, the industry demand curve is not a simple aggregation of the firm's demand (*MVPL*) curves, because account must be taken of the change in price resulting at different levels of industry output. The industry demand curve will be steeper than that for the firm. The steepness of the *MVPL* curve depends upon the speed with which the marginal product of labour diminishes as output rises: the industry demand curve depends upon the steepness of the *MVPL* curves and upon the elasticity of demand for the product.

The supply of labour may be analysed using the theory of consumer choice. The labour supply decision may be viewed in two parts—the decision to work at all, and the decision on how many hours to work, given the decision to participate. The hours an individual chooses to work will depend upon the *real wage*. We regard an individual as making a choice between income (obtained by working) and leisure (hours spent not working). A higher real wage rate offers the possibility of more income but also the opportunity of increased leisure time. The result of this trade-off is uncertain: an increase in real wage may induce some individuals to work longer hours and others to work less and enjoy more leisure. This is another instance of the income and substitution effects encountered in Chapter 6.

Participation rates also depend upon the real wage, and upon the fixed costs of working, the availability of income from non-labour sources, and the individual's preferences for work and leisure. Other things being equal, it is likely that an increase in the real wage will induce more workers to enter the *labour force*.

The supply curve of labour faced by most industries will be upward-sloping: to encourage a higher level of employment will require higher wages, although it is possible that some industries are 'wage-takers' for some types of labour. The industry supply curve tends to be flatter in the long run than in the short run.

The wage rate and employment level in an industry will be determined by the equilibrium of demand and supply, but the existence of *labour mobility* may mean that there are spillover effects between industries when conditions change.

An important distinction may be drawn between *transfer earnings* and *economic rent*. Transfer earnings are the payment necessary to attract a factor into an industry. However, given an upward-sloping supply curve, at higher levels of demand transfer earnings will also be higher. If all workers are paid the same wage rate, then all but the marginal unit of labour are being paid a higher wage than would have been necessary to attract them into the industry. This surplus is known as *economic rent* (and must not be confused with payment for accommodation). An employer may be able to reduce labour costs if he can 'wage-discriminate' by paying some workers at different rates.

A vital question is whether we can validly assume that wage rates are sufficiently flexible for labour markets always to be in equilibrium. If for any reason the wage rate in a market is higher than that necessary for equilibrium, there will be *involuntary unemployment*. Such inflexibility may be the result of minimum wage agreements, trade union power, scale economies, insider–outsider distinctions, or efficiency wages. The possible existence and persistence of labour market disequilibrium will be re-examined in a later part of the book.

IMPORTANT CONCEPTS AND TECHNICAL TERMS

Match each lettered concept with the appropriate numbered phrase:

(a) Insider–outsider distinctions
(b) Efficiency wage theory
(c) Economic rent
(d) Derived demand
(e) Labour force
(f) Isocost line
(g) Isoquant
(h) Marginal value product of labour
(i) Poverty trap
(j) Real wage
(k) Minimum wage
(l) Marginal revenue product of labour
(m) Participation rate
(n) Involuntary unemployment
(o) Equalizing wage differential
(p) Transfer earnings
(q) Marginal cost of labour
(r) Labour mobility

1 The demand for a factor of production—not for its own sake, but for the output produced by the factor.
2 A condition that may result in effective barriers to entering employment in existing firms.
3 The monetary compensation for differential non-monetary characteristics of the same job in different industries, so that workers with a particular skill have no incentive to move between industries.
4 The nominal or money wage divided by the firm's output price.
5 The cost of an additional unit of labour: when the firm has some monopsony power, this cost will be greater than the price of labour.
6 A legal constraint imposed on firms establishing the lowest wage payable to workers.
7 The minimum payments required to induce a factor to work in a particular job.
8 The ability of workers to leave low-paying jobs and join other industries where rates of pay are higher.
9 A condition that occurs when workers are prepared to work at the going wage rate but cannot find jobs.
10 The marginal physical product of labour multiplied by the output price.
11 A curve showing the different minimum combinations of inputs to produce a given level of output.
12 All individuals in work or seeking employment.
13 The extra payment a factor receives over and above that required to induce the factor to supply its services in that use.
14 A line showing different input combinations with the same total cost.
15 The marginal physical product of labour multiplied by the change in the firm's total revenue when it sells these extra goods.
16 The percentage of a given group of the population of working age who decide to enter the labour force.
17 A theory which argues that firms may pay existing workers a wage which on average exceeds the wage for which workers as a whole are prepared to work.
18 A situation in which unskilled workers are offered such a low wage that they lose out by working.

EXERCISES

1 Table 11.1 reproduces some information used (and calculated) in Exercise 5 of Chapter 8: we are now in a position to carry the analysis further.

TABLE 11.1 Output and labour input, etc.

Labour input (workers/week)	Output (goods/week)	Marginal physical product of labour (MPL)	Price (£)	Total revenue	Marginal revenue per unit output	Marginal value product of labour (MVPL)	Marginal revenue product of labour (MRPL)
0	0						
		35					
1	35		12				
		45					
2	80		10				
		42					
3	122		8				
		34					
4	156		6				
		21					
5	177		4				
		3					
6	180		2				

A new column in the table shows the price which must be charged by the firm to sell the output produced. The firm is a 'wage-taker', and must pay £280 per unit of labour input however much labour is hired. The only other cost to the firm is capital, for which the firm incurs a fixed cost of £200.

(a) Calculate the marginal value product of labour (*MVPL*).
(b) Calculate the marginal revenue product of labour (*MRPL*).
(c) Using graph paper, plot *MVPL* and *MRPL* curves.
(d) At what level of labour input will profits be maximized in the short run?
(e) Calculate the level of short-run profits.

2 Figure 11.1 shows marginal cost, marginal product of labour curves, and the wage rate for a firm. Identify the profit-maximizing level of output for each of the following firms:

(a) A perfectly competitive firm facing a perfectly competitive situation in the labour market.
(b) A firm having no influence on the price of its output but acting as a monopsonist in the labour market.
(c) A firm facing a downward-sloping demand curve for its product and acting as a monopsonist in the labour market.
(d) A firm facing a downward-sloping demand curve for its product but a perfectly competitive labour market.
(e) What is the effect of monopoly and monopsony power on the firm's labour demand?

3 Figure 11.2 shows George's indifference curves between income and leisure.

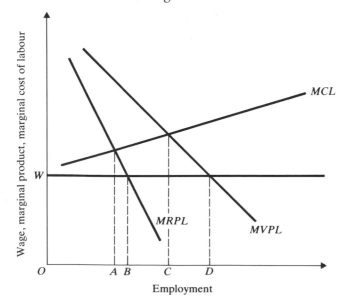

FIGURE 11.1 The effect of monopoly and monopsony power

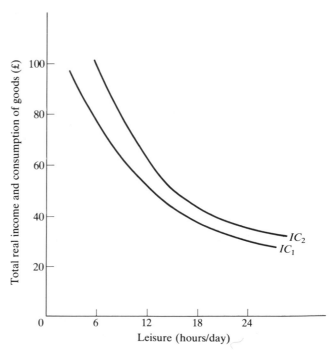

FIGURE 11.2 An individual's supply of labour

Suppose that George faces no fixed costs of working and receives £20 unearned income whether or not he chooses to work.

(a) Add to the diagram his budget line if he can work at the rate of £2.50 per hour.

(b) How many hours will George choose to work?

(c) Suppose the wage rate increases to £3.33: show how this affects the budget line.

(d) How many hours will George now choose to work?

(e) Does George regard leisure as a normal or an inferior good?

4   An industry's demand curve for typists is shown in Figure 11.3, together with the supply curve it faces.

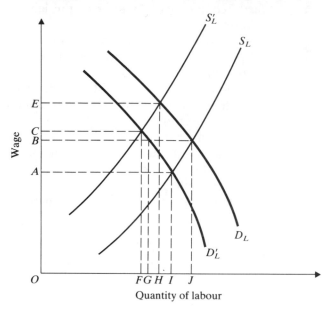

FIGURE 11.3   Equilibrium in an industry labour market

(a) Initially the industry demand curve is D_L and it faces the supply curve S_L. What is the equilibrium wage and employment level?

(b) Suppose the industry faces a decline in the demand for its output: what would be the new equilibrium wage and employment level? Explain your answer.

(c) Beginning again at D_L, S_L, the industry now finds that an increase in the demand for typists in another industry has affected typists' wages elsewhere. How would the equilibrium wage and employment level be affected for this industry?

(d) From D_L, S_L the industry demand for labour moves to D'_L, but the clerical workers' trade union resists a wage cut, maintaining the wage rate at its original

level. Identify the nature and extent of the disequilibrium.

5   Figure 11.4 represents a monopsonistic labour market in which employees are *not* organised into a union.

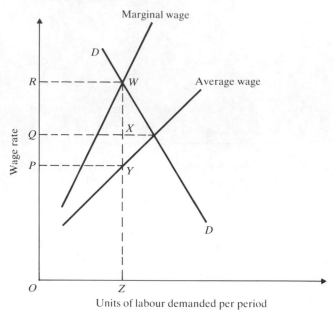

FIGURE 11.4

The surplus which accrues to the employer is represented by the area

(a) $OQXZ$

(b) $PQXY$

(c) $ORWZ$

(d) $PRWY$

(e) $OPYZ$

(University of London GCE A level Economics 3, June 1988)

6   Figure 11.5 illustrates the demand and supply situation in a particular labour market.

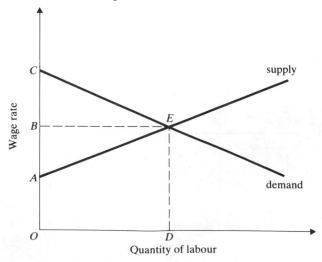

FIGURE 11.5

Suppose the market to be in equilibrium:
(a) Which area represents the amount of transfer earnings?
(b) Identify the amount of economic rent.
(c) How would the *relative* size of economic rent and transfer earnings differ if the supply of labour were more inelastic?

7 Figure 11.6 shows the amount of labour supplied by an individual at different wage rates.

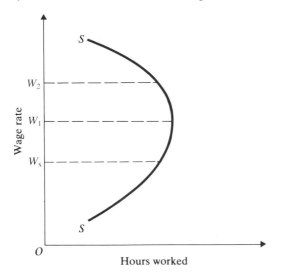

FIGURE 11.6

Which of the following statements concerning the reaction to a move from W_1 to W_2 is *not* valid?
(a) The individual's employer fails to induce an increase in hours worked by this move.
(b) The firm substitutes capital for labour.
(c) The employer could have induced the same amount of hours worked by offering a wage rate W_x.
(d) The individual demands more leisure.
(e) In the choice between income and leisure, the 'income effect' dominates the 'substitution effect'.

8 A firm is seeking the cost-minimizing method of producing a good. Various combinations of labour and capital can be used to produce a particular level of output, as shown in Table 11.2.
(a) Draw the isoquants for these three levels of output, using graph paper.
(b) Draw the isocost line showing the combinations of capital and labour input which the firm could purchase for £1000 if capital costs £20 per unit and labour costs £2 per unit.

TABLE 11.2 Production techniques available to a firm

To produce					
10 units of output		20 units of output		30 units of output	
Capital	Labour	Capital	Labour	Capital	Labour
35	80	42	100	45	170
28	100	30	150	35	200
20	140	25	175	30	230
16	160	20	200	27	250
13	200	16	250	21	290
10	250	12	300	18	350
7	300	10	350	16	400
5	350	8	400	14	450
3	400				

(c) What is the maximum amount of output which the firm could produce in these conditions? How much capital and labour is used in producing this output?
(d) Draw the isocost line if the firm still spends £1000, but the cost of labour increases to £3 per unit.
(e) What is the maximum output which could now be produced? How much capital and labour would now be used?
(f) Calculate the percentage change in the use of capital and labour in (e) compared with (c). Is this what you would expect to happen?
(g) How much output could be produced by the firm if it spends only £800? (Capital still costs £20 per unit, and labour £3 per unit.)

9 Which of the following may cause involuntary unemployment by impeding labour market adjustment?
(a) Minimum wage legislation intended to protect the lower-paid.
(b) The payment of higher-than-average wage rates by employers wishing to discourage quits.
(c) Economies of scale.
(d) Entry barriers confronting outsiders being implemented by insiders.
(e) Action taken by a strong trade union to increase rates of pay for its members.

10 Figure 11.7 shows the various combinations of labour and capital which could be employed to produce 1000 units of output. A movement from X to Y on the curve would be caused by
(a) an increase in the cost of labour
(b) an increase in the cost of capital
(c) an increase in labour productivity
(d) technical innovation

(Associated Examining Board GCE A level Economics Paper 1, November 1986)

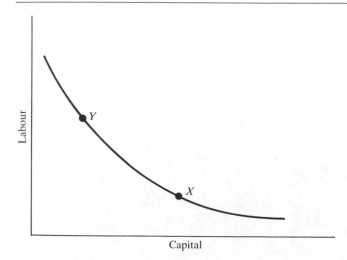

FIGURE 11.7

TRUE/FALSE

1 _____ The labour market ensures that a helicopter pilot is paid the same money wage in whatever industry he is employed.

2 _____ Following an increase in labour cost, a firm will employ more capital input.

3 _____ For a firm operating under perfect competition in both output and labour markets, profits are maximized by employing labour up to the point where the marginal value product of labour equals the money wage rate.

4 _____ For a firm operating under perfect competition in both output and labour markets, profits are maximized by employing labour up to the point where the marginal physical product of labour equals the real wage rate.

5 _____ A firm with monopsony power is not a price-taker in its input markets.

6 _____ For a firm with a downward-sloping demand curve, the marginal revenue product of labour is greater than the marginal value product of labour.

7 _____ For a competitive industry, the industry labour demand curve is the horizontal aggregation of the firms' $MVPL$ curves.

8 _____ An individual's labour supply curve is always upward-sloping—a higher real wage induces the individual to work longer hours.

9 _____ The participation rate is higher for unmarried than for married women.

10 _____ Labour mobility provides a crucial link between industry labour markets.

11 _____ Economic rent reflects differences in individuals' supply decisions, not in their productivity.

12 _____ Involuntary unemployment arises from inflexibility of adjustment in the labour market.

QUESTIONS FOR THOUGHT

1 In an earlier chapter, we saw that a firm operating under perfect competition would maximize profits in the short run by producing at the point where $SMC = MR$. Now it transpires that the firm should employ labour up to the point where $W = MVPL$. Can you reconcile these two methods?

2 Figure 11.8 shows Helen's indifference curves between income and leisure. Helen receives £10 per day unearned income only if she does not work. She never chooses to work more than 12 hours per day, so the diagram focuses on only the relevant 12 hours.

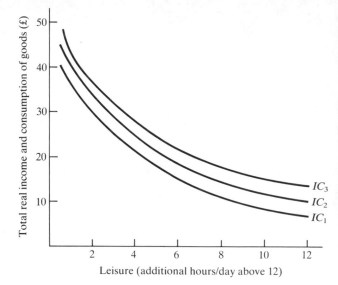

FIGURE 11.8 Labour supply with overtime

(a) Mark on the diagram the point where Helen would be if she chooses not to work.

(b) Add to the diagram Helen's budget line if she can work at £2.50 per hour.

(c) Assuming Helen has complete flexibility on hours of work, how many hours will she choose to work at that rate of pay?

(d) Amend the budget line to conform to a situation in which Helen earns 'treble time' for hours worked in excess of 8 hours a day.

(e) How many hours will Helen now choose to work?

3 Discuss theories which have been advanced to explain inflexibility in a labour market. Which of them do you find plausible in relation to the current UK situation?

4 Why are the wages and salaries paid for some occupations greater than those paid for others? Do real wages differ between countries for similar reasons?

(University of Oxford Delegacy of Local Examinations, GCE A level Economics Paper 1, June 1988)

ANSWERS AND COMMENTS FOR CHAPTER 11

Please note Where questions are reproduced from A level examinations, the examination boards bear no responsibility for the answers provided in this volume, which are the sole responsibility of the authors.

Important Concepts and Technical Terms

1	d	4	j	7	p	10	h	13	c	16	m
2	a	5	q	8	r	11	g	14	f	17	b
3	o	6	k	9	n	12	e	15	l	18	i

Exercises

1 (*a*), (*b*), (*c*).

TABLE A11.1 Output and labour input, etc.

Labour input (*workers/week*)	Output (*goods/week*)	Marginal physical product of labour (MPL)	Price (£)	Total revenue	Marginal revenue per unit output	Marginal value product of labour (MVPL)	Marginal revenue product of labour (MRPL)
0	0			0			
		35			12	420	420
1	35		12	420			
		45			8.44	450	378
2	80		10	800			
		42			4.19	336	176
3	122		8	976			
		34			−1.18	204	−40.12
4	156		6	936			
		21			−10.86	84	−228
5	177		4	708			
		3			−116	6	−348
6	180		2	360			

(*d*) Adding the wage cost line to Figure A11.1 shows that profit will be maximized at 2 units of labour input—the firm will continue to hire labour as long as the *MRPL* exceeds the wage.

(*e*) With 2 units of labour input, total revenue is $80 \times 10 = 800$; capital cost is 200; wage cost is $280 \times 2 = 560$. Profits are $800 - 200 - 560 = £40$.

2 (*a*) OD.
(*b*) OC.
(*c*) OA.
(*d*) OB.
(*e*) Both tend to reduce labour demand.

3

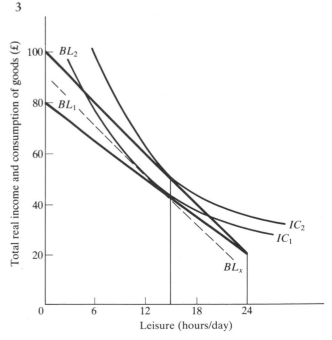

FIGURE A11.1 *MVPL, MRPL*

FIGURE A11.2 An individual's supply of labour

(a) With the wage rate at £2.50, and with £20 unearned income, the maximum earnings for 24 hours would be $20 + 24 \times 2.5 = £80$ (but wouldn't George be tired!) The budget line is thus BL_1.

(b) BL_1 is at a tangent to IC_1 at 15 hours' leisure—so George works 9 hours.

(c) The budget line moves to BL_2.

(d) As it happens, George still chooses to work 9 hours: this is because the 'income' and 'substitution' effects exactly balance—and would not normally happen.

(e) The 'income' effect can be seen by adding a new budget line parallel to BL_2, tangent to $IC_1 - BL_x$ in the diagram. This shows leisure to be a normal good for George.

4 (a) Wage would be OB and employment OJ.

(b) As demand for its product declines, the industry must reduce prices: this will affect the marginal revenue product of labour and reduce labour demand. In the diagram, this could be represented by a move to D'_L with a new equilibrium at wage OA and employment OI. The supply curve is not affected.

(c) As wages increase elsewhere, typists will prefer to leave in quest of better pay, so the supply of labour to our industry falls to S'_L. In the new equilibrium, wage is OE and employment OH. The demand curve is not affected.

(d) With demand D'_L, supply S_L, and wage OB there is excess supply of labour—i.e., unemployment. There are GJ workers who would like to obtain work in the industry, but cannot at that wage rate.

5 The employer will employ labour up to OZ, paying a wage of OP. The area $OPYZ$ represents payment of wages, leaving the employer with a surplus of $PRWY$, which is option (d).

6 (a) $OAED$.

(b) ABE.

(c) Economic rent would be higher, transfer earnings correspondingly lower.

7 (b).

8 Figure A11.3.

(a) The isoquants are labelled $I10$, $I20$, and $I30$ on the diagram. (If you are unfamiliar with these concepts, you should consult the Appendix to Chapter 11 of the main text.)

(b) The isocost line is given by the line $L1\ K1$.

(c) The isocost line is tangent to the $I30$ isoquant, so the maximum possible output is 30 units, for which the firm uses 290 units of labour and 21 units of capital.

(d) The new isocost is $L2\ K1$.

(e) 20 units of output, using 200 units of labour and 20 units of capital.

(f) Labour use is reduced by 31 per cent and capital use by only 4.8 per cent. This is as we would expect—the 'output effect' leads to a reduction in both inputs, but the change in relative factor

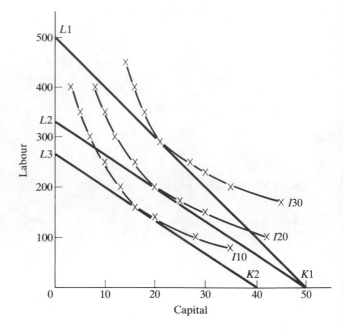

FIGURE A11.3   Cost minimization for a firm

prices leads to a substitution effect towards capital.

(g) Adding the isocost line $L3\ K2$ shows that the firm produces only 10 units of output, employing 160 units of labour and 16 of capital.

9 All of them: these are discussed in Section 11–7 of the main text.

10 The curve on the diagram is of course an *isoquant* (see the Appendix to Chapter 11 in the main text). Options (c) and (d) would cause a movement *of* the isoquant, so can be eliminated. A movement from X to Y is a move towards the use of more labour and less capital, suggesting that option (b) has occurred—i.e., there has been an increase in the cost of capital leading the firm to substitute labour for capital in the production process.

True/False

1 False: non-monetary differences in working conditions will give rise to an equalizing wage differential (see the introduction to Chapter 11 in the main text).

2 False: the firm will tend to employ *relatively* more capital, but will probably employ less of both (see exercise 9 of this chapter).

3 True.

4 True: statements 3 and 4 are equivalent (see Section 11–2 of the main text).

5 True.

6 False: $MRPL < MVPL$.

7 False: this ignores the effect of changing industry supply upon output price (see Section 11–3 of the main text).

8 False: an individual may choose to enjoy more leisure and work fewer hours (see Section 11–4 of the main text).

9   True.
10 True: see Section 11–5 of the main text.
11 True: see Section 11–6 of the main text.
12 True: see Section 11–7 of the main text.

Questions for Thought

1   The methods are equivalent: think about the nature of short-run marginal cost.
2   (a) Point A.
    (b) The budget line is given by the line BC in Figure A11.4.
    (c) If Helen were to work, then she would choose to be at point X, where the budget line is at a tangent to IC_1. Here she would be working 6 hours per day. However, she will not in fact do this, as she obtains more utility by not working and being at point A on indifference curve IC_2.
    (d) The effect of overtime, paid at a premium rate, is to kink the budget line after 8 hours' work, as shown by the line CDE in Figure A11.4.
    (e) Helen can now reach a tangency point with IC_3 and will work $(12 - L_0)$ hours.
3   No hints, but see the discussion in Section 11–7 of the main text.

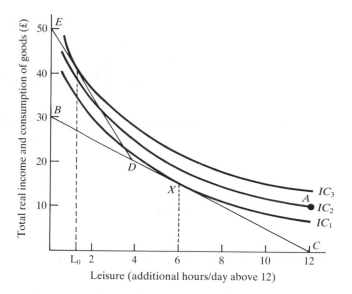

FIGURE A11.4 Labour supply with overtime

4   You should be able to tackle the first part of this essay question on the basis of the material we have explored so far, but for the second part you may need to think a bit more.

12 Human Capital, Discrimination, and Trade Unions

In Chapter 11 we looked at some of the influences which make some occupations more highly paid than others. This tackles only some of the questions we might ask about labour markets. It is also the case that different workers in the same occupation may be paid at differing rates, or that some groups of workers tend to be more lowly paid in whatever occupation they are employed. This chapter examines these questions and suggests some possible explanations.

The groups of workers we might wish to consider are many and diverse, reflecting the fact that workers themselves are heterogeneous, differing in sex, race, age, experience, training, trade union membership, or innate ability. If we wish to say anything about the possibility of *discrimination* in a labour market, we must sift through these different characteristics.

Some of the characteristics mentioned are 'natural' ones, over which the individual worker has no control; others are the result of choices made by the individual. We begin by analysing one of these latter—namely, training or education. Empirical evidence shows that education has two effects on workers' earnings. Firstly, workers with relatively high levels of training tend to enjoy higher earnings than the less skilled. Secondly, the pattern of earnings through a worker's lifetime (the *age–earnings profile*) is affected by the level of education. Thus, not only do the highly trained workers earn more than the unskilled, but also, the disparity grows as the workers grow older.

How does a worker view the training he may receive? (We refer to the worker as 'he', but this is not intended to be discriminatory!) Training may be seen as an investment in *human capital*, undertaken for the benefits expected in the future from higher earnings, and undertaken despite the costs incurred. The balancing of these items is an exercise in *cost–benefit analysis*. At the same time he decides whether or not to undertake training, the worker must evaluate the *present value* of the future expected gains (which may include any expected enjoyment from student life, etc.) and compare them with the opportunity cost of the training—taking into account earnings forgone.

Demand and supply analysis illustrates the effects of an increase in demand for educated workers. In the short run supply is fixed, so an increase in demand for educated workers will lead to an increase in the *wage differential*. This will have an effect on the perceived benefits of education, and in the long run we would expect to see some increase in the supply of such workers, as more are enticed into education.

Much training takes place 'on the job', and here we may draw an important distinction between firm-specific and general skills. This may affect the age–earnings profile that a firm is prepared to offer to the workers. A trainee typist or accountant may find that earnings during training are relatively low, as the acquisition of skill enhances potential mobility between firms; a trainee telephone engineer may be seen quite differently, as the skills acquired reduce mobility.

An underlying assumption of this approach is that training increases the workers' productivity—but how would this explain the demand for graduates to work in areas remote from their degree specialism? An alternative argument is that educational achievement acts as a *signalling* device: an indicator of innate ability, and thus an indirect promise of high productivity. However, education would not contribute directly to the high productivity of able people. If this were so, then there might be important implications for society as a whole in choosing to allocate resources to education.

So how about discrimination? Average weekly earnings for women are only about two-thirds of earnings for men. Does this imply discrimination? The difference partly reflects differences in employment patterns between men and women, but it also reflects differences in pay *within* occupations. The latter need not be the result of discrimination: it could reflect differences in educational choices made earlier, such that men tend to undertake more training and therefore land the higher paid jobs. From the firm's point of view, an important factor in the hiring decision is the expected stream of future benefits. If a firm perceives women as potential mothers, then the evaluation of future productivity will be lower for women than for men, whose role as potential fathers would not be expected to affect their future productivity. This is because the firm expects women to work for a shorter period than men, so that training costs are spread less thinly. It would then be rational for the firm to offer lower wages to women in line with marginal productivity theory.

Racial discrimination may be handled in similar fashion. Again, it may be that access to education may be a pertinent factor. None of this is to deny that discrimination may happen: what it perhaps does suggest is that the root may lie in the misperceptions of firms concerning the productivity of particular workers, now or in the future.

Trade union members in the UK earn about 7.7 per cent more than other workers, even making allowance for differences in sex, education, and so on. Trade unions were originally formed to defend the interests of their members. Since then, they have also become concerned with rates of pay. This is not necessarily to say that trade unions gain higher wages by exploiting monopoly power—that is, by restricting labour supply and thus forcing up wages. The extent to which this can be done depends upon the elasticity of demand for labour. It could also be argued that the higher wages reflect the result of negotiated productivity deals with firms. Unions may attempt to consolidate their position by arguing for a *closed shop*—an agreement whereby all workers in a firm must join the union, the rationale being that all workers will benefit equally from any negotiated agreement. Strikes are much publicized, but are not as significant in terms of working days lost as might be thought. In most situations, both firms and workers stand to lose by a strike, and those that do occur may result from misperceptions on either side of the bargaining process, or from a breakdown in long-run credibility.

IMPORTANT CONCEPTS AND TECHNICAL TERMS

Match each lettered concept with the appropriate numbered phrase:

(a) Human capital
(b) Cost–benefit analysis
(c) Trade union
(d) Firm-specific human capital
(e) Signalling
(f) Compensating wage differentials
(g) Age–earnings profile
(h) General human capital
(i) Discrimination
(j) Closed shop

1 A procedure for making long-run decisions by comparing the present value of the costs with the present value of the benefits.
2 The stock of expertise accumulated by a worker, valued for its income-earning potential in the future.
3 A situation in which a group of workers is treated differently from other groups because of the personal characteristics of that group, regardless of qualifications.
4 Differences in wage rates reflecting non-monetary aspects of working conditions.
5 An agreement that all a firm's workers will be members of a trade union.
6 The skills which a worker acquires that can be transferred to work for another firm.
7 The theory that educational qualifications indicate a worker's worth even when not directly relevant to his or her productivity.
8 The skills which a worker acquires that cannot be transferred to work for another firm.
9 A schedule showing how the earnings of a worker or group of workers vary with age.
10 A worker organization designed to affect pay and working conditions.

EXERCISES

1 Ian, a teenager, is considering whether or not to undertake further education. Having studied A level Economics, he decides to apply cost–benefit analysis to evaluate his decision. After applying appropriate discount rates, he arrives at the following valuations (the units are notional):

	Present value
Books, fees	3000
Benefits (non-monetary) of student life	2500
Income forgone (net)	7000
Additional future expected income due to qualification	9000

(a) Given these valuations, would Ian decide upon further education?
(b) How would Ian's calculations be affected if he were not confident of passing his examinations at the end of his course?
(c) Ian's friend Joanne shares Ian's views about the economic value of education, but is much less keen on the idea of university life. How would her calculations differ?
(d) Keith subscribes to the 'eat, drink, and be merry, for tomorrow we die' philosophy, and is keen to enjoy life in the present. How would his calculations differ from Ian's?

2 Below are figures showing how pre-tax earnings vary with age for three groups of male workers in full-time employment in the economy of Hypothetica. Average gross weekly earnings are measured in Hypothetical dollars.

Group	A	B	C
Age			
20–29	236	180	200
30–39	310	200	250
40–49	370	195	280
50–64	425	185	235

(a) Using graph paper, plot the age–earnings profile for each group of workers.
(b) The distinguishing characteristic of each group is the level of highest educational attainment. Using your knowledge of similar groups in the UK, associate each of the following with the appropriate age–earnings profile:

(i)   Workers with GCE A levels or their equivalent.
(ii)   Workers with no formal qualifications.
(iii) Workers with a university degree or equivalent.

3   In the economy of Elsewhere, the following observations are made. Which of them would provide strong evidence of discrimination?
(a)   Women earn less than men.
(b)   Female trainee accountants earn less than male trainee accountants.
(c)   Black workers earn less than white workers.
(d)   Black machine tool fitters earn less than white machine tool fitters.

4   Figure 12.1 shows the position in a labour market. OA represents the economy-wide wage rate. DD is the initial demand curve for labour.

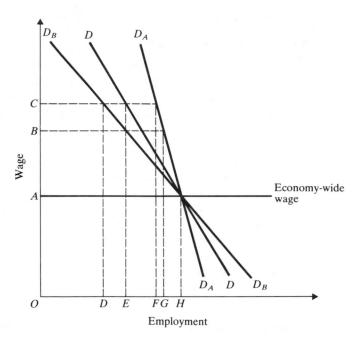

FIGURE 12.1   Unions, wages, and employment

(a)   Identify the initial equilibrium for the industry.
(b)   Suppose a trade union restricts the supply of labour to OE. What is the equilibrium wage in the industry?
(c)   In the long run, this industry faces increased competition from overseas suppliers, who face lower labour costs. Which of the demand curves in the diagram might represent the industry's new (derived) demand for labour?
(d)   What is the new equilibrium for the industry?
(e)   What wage rate would the union need to accept to maintain employment at OE?

5   Trade unions within a given industry are likely to be in a weak bargaining position when
1   the demand for labour is greater than its supply
2   a 'closed shop' policy operates
3   the marginal revenue product is less than wages
(a)   1, 2, 3 correct
(b)   1, 2 only are correct
(c)   2, 3 only are correct
(d)   1 only is correct
(e)   3 only is correct
(University of London GCE A level Economics 3, June 1989)

6   Figure 12.2 represents two different earnings profiles. The diagram shows that
1   lifetime earnings of graduate employees are higher.
2   the earnings of graduates are less over the ten years after compulsory school leaving age.
3   the opportunity cost of university education is represented by the shaded area Z.

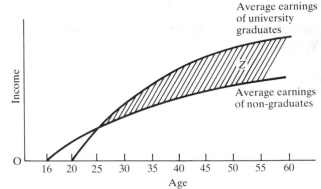

FIGURE 12.2

(a)   1, 2, 3 all correct
(b)   1, 2 only are correct
(c)   2, 3 only are correct
(d)   1 only is correct
(Associated Examining Board GCE A level Economics Paper 1, June 1988)

TRUE/FALSE

1   _____ The human capital approach assumes that wage differentials reflect differences in the productivity of different workers.
2   _____ Workers in firms receiving general training will be offered high but shallow age–earnings profiles.
3   _____ Reading Classics at university does nothing to improve productivity; it is more

profitable to leave school and go straight into industry.

4 _____ Free schooling between 16 and 18 means that children from poor families can stay on in education as easily as children from wealthy families.

5 _____ The perceived return from higher education is less for women than for men, so fewer women than men decide to invest in higher education.

6 _____ Black workers earn less than white workers; therefore employers are racist.

7 _____ Differences in the occupational structure of the employment of men and women do not suffice to explain differences in earnings.

8 _____ By 1980, more than two-thirds of the civilian labour force in the UK belonged to trade unions.

9 _____ Since many low-paid workers belong to a trade union, this proves that unions have little effect on improving pay and conditions for their members.

10 _____ The largest rise in wages would be achieved by restricting labour supply in the industry where the demand for labour is most inelastic.

11 _____ The UK is the most strike-prone economy in the world.

QUESTIONS FOR THOUGHT

1 Would society find it worth while to invest in a higher education system if degree training provides only a signalling device and has no effect on the productivity of workers?

2 If strikes benefit neither employers nor employees, why do they ever happen?

3 A firm that has been operating without trade unions becomes unionized. Is it necessarily the case that employment in that firm will fall?

ANSWERS AND COMMENTS FOR CHAPTER 12

Please note   Where questions are reproduced from A level examinations, the examination boards bear no responsibility for the answers provided in this volume, which are the sole responsibility of the authors.

Important Concepts and Technical Terms

1	*b*	6	*h*
2	*a*	7	*e*
3	*i*	8	*d*
4	*f*	9	*g*
5	*j*	10	*c*

Exercises

1 (a) Total benefits amount to $2500 + 9000 = 11\,500$. Total costs amount to $3000 + 7000 = 10\,000$ (both in 'present value' terms). Ian would thus choose to undertake further education, as the benefits outweigh the costs.

  (b) If Ian were to fail to obtain the qualification, then the additional future income would not be forthcoming. In the calculations, Ian would reduce his valuation of this item.

  (c) Joanne would place a lower valuation on the non-monetary benefits of student life. Whether or not she decides to continue in education depends upon how little she expects to enjoy herself.

  (d) Keith is likely to use a different discount rate when assessing the present value of future costs and benefits. On the other hand, he could place a high valuation on 'student life', so again his decision could go either way.

2 (a) Figure A12.1.

  (b) (i) Group *C*.
  (ii) Group *B*.
  (iii) Group *A*.
  Profiles based upon authentic UK information may be seen in Section 12–1 of the main text.

3 (a) and (c) could be explained in terms of differences in occupational structure, and of themselves do not provide evidence of discrimination. It is possible that differences in occupational choice may reflect earlier discrimination in educational opportunities, but that is a separate issue. Observation (b) avoids the occupational explanation, but differences in pay here may reflect employers' different evaluation of the future productivity of men and women rather than overt discrimination. Observation (d) offers the strongest evidence of discrimination, as here we have a closely defined skill level and presumably similar marginal products of black and white workers, and yet we observe differences in earnings. For more discussion see Section 12–2 of the main text.

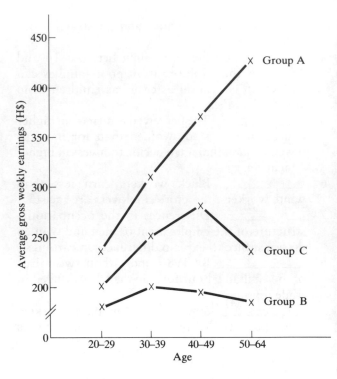

FIGURE A12.1   Age–earnings profiles for three groups of workers

4 (a) Wage *OA*, employment *OH*.
  (b) *OC*.
  (c) $D_B D_B$: the demand curve becomes more elastic.
  (d) Wage *OC*, employment *OD*.
  (e) *OB*.
5 (e).
6 (b). Notice that the area *Z* in Figure 12.2 represents the extent to which average earnings are higher for graduates than for non-graduates.

True/False

1 True.
2 False: workers with general training are highly mobile between firms, so it pays the firm to offer low pay during training but relatively high pay to the qualified worker (see Section 12–1 of the main text).
3 False: degree training may act as a signalling device.
4 False: this statement ignores the opportunity cost of further schooling and the different marginal utilities of income of rich and poor families.
5 True: and notice it is the *perception* that is important, not the actuality (see Section 12–2 of the main text).
6 False: the difference in pay may reflect other factors, such as occupational choice, educational training, and so on. This is not to say that there may not be discrimination in some covert or overt form in some parts of the economy.
7 True: see discussion in Section 12–2 of the main text.
8 False: the true figure is just over one-half (see Section 12–3 of the main text).

9 False: we should not compare these low-paid workers with other groups of workers, but rather should ask what rates of pay they would have received in the absence of the union.

10 True.

11 False: see the evidence presented in Section 12–3 of the main text.

Questions for Thought

1 This issue is tackled towards the end of Section 12–1 of the main text and will be reconsidered in a later chapter. It is one example where there may be a divergence between the interests of the individual and those of society at large.

2 This issue is discussed towards the end of Section 12–3 of the main text.

3 We would normally expect that a trade union will bargain for higher wages, and that this would be at the cost of accepting a lower employment level. There is one exception to this, however. Consider Figure A12.2. Suppose a firm operating with perfect competition in the product market is a monopsonist in the labour market. S_L represents the supply curve of labour and MCL the marginal cost of labour as faced by the firm; $MVPL$ constitutes the demand curve for labour. Before the trade union appears on the scene, the firms employs N_1 at a wage of W_1. When the firm is unionized, it is possible to negotiate with the firm to be at any position

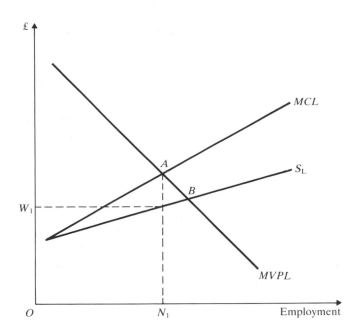

FIGURE A12.2

along the $MVPL$. At any point along the section AB it is possible for the union to negotiate both an increase in wages *and* an increase in employment. This is a very special case, which is why this question appears in the 'Questions for Thought' section of the chapter.

13

Capital and Land: Completing the Analysis of Factor Markets

The last two chapters have examined aspects of the market for labour. Attention is now focused on the other important factors of production: capital and land. *Capital* is taken to refer to physical capital—the stock of produced goods used in the production of other goods. This includes machinery, buildings, and vehicles. *Land* is a factor of production which is not produced, but is provided by nature. Capital and land together comprise the *tangible wealth* of an economy. The facts suggest that the UK is tending to become more capital-intensive, in the sense that tangible wealth per worker has increased in recent years.

Important distinctions are drawn between stocks and flows and between asset prices and rental payments. The *stock* of a capital asset is the amount in existence at a particular time. However, in considering the input of capital as a factor of production, we are concerned with the *flow* of services obtained from the stock of assets during a particular period. In parallel with this, we can think of the *asset price* of a capital good as being the 'stock' price, whereas the cost of using the 'flow' of capital services is known as the *rental payment*. This distinction was not important in the case of labour input, as the abolition of slavery did away with the labour equivalent of the asset price. However, we may think of the wage rate as the rental payment for labour.

The asset price of a capital good requires careful interpretation. The purchase of a capital asset entitles the buyer to the future stream of services produced by the asset. However, at the time of purchase, it is the *present value* of the future stream of services which is of relevance. If the purchaser had chosen instead to lend his money, then the return received would depend upon the rate of interest at which the money was lent and upon the rules of compound interest. In assessing the future stream of capital services, it is thus important to apply an appropriate *discount rate* to calculate the present value. We may regard the interest rate as the opportunity cost of the money to be used in buying the asset.

Which interest rate should be used? We may wish to take account of the effect of changing prices upon the calculations, by using the inflation-adjusted, or *real interest rate*, rather than the *nominal interest rate*. The real interest rate may be approximated by the difference between the nominal interest rate and the rate of inflation.

The demand for capital services can be analysed in similar fashion to the former analysis of the demand for labour. It will pay firms to employ capital services up to the point where the marginal value product of capital ($MVPK$) is equal to the rental rate. The $MVPK$ is expected to decline as the capital:labour ratio rises. The position of a firm's $MVPK$ curve depends upon the price of output produced, the level of input of other factors, and technical progress. The industry's demand curve for capital services will be steeper than the horizontal sum of the firms' $MVPK$ curves. All this parallels the earlier discussion of labour.

On the supply side, the main difference between the analysis of capital and of labour is that for the firm or industry capital is less flexible in the short run: by its very nature, it takes time to install capital, whereas labour input may be varied more quickly. However, capital may be varied in the long run.

The *required rental* is that rate which just allows the owner of capital to cover the opportunity cost of owning it. The required rental depends upon the price of capital, the real interest rate, and the depreciation rate.

Bringing together the demand and supply of capital services, it is possible to analyse short-run and long-run equilibrium positions for an industry, and to examine how that equilibrium changes in response to background factors. For instance, an increase in the wage rate will have both substitution and output effects influencing the capital market. There will be a substitution effect towards more capital-intensive means of production, but an output effect tending to reduce the demand for all factors. In the short run, the rental rate is likely to fall; in the long run, the quantity of capital services will be allowed to fall via depreciation until the long-run equilibrium rental rate is reached.

The treatment of land as a factor differs because land is in fixed supply even in the long run (except in countries where reclamation is feasible). The issue here is to analyse the way in which a fixed amount of land is to be allocated between alternative uses. Equilibrium occurs when the rental rate is the same for all uses of the land.

Labour, capital, and land receive similar treatment from economists, being the most commonly encountered *factors of production*. The main difference that arises between them lies in the speed of adjustment of supply. The increasing significance of *energy* as an input has led economists to treat it as a fourth factor of production in some analysis.

The move towards more capital-intensive

production techniques seen in many Western economies in recent years partly reflects the increase in the wage:rental ratio, leading to substitution of capital for labour. It also reflects the rate of technical change, leading firms to install new capital embodying new techniques.

The *functional income distribution* shows how national income is shared between the factors. In the UK, this showed relatively little change between 1960 and 1987. The share of earnings from employment in national income fell a little and the shares of profits, self-employment income, and property rents increased correspondingly.

If we wish to consider issues like poverty and inequality, it is the *personal income distribution* which must be considered. The unevenness of this distribution in the UK reflects not only the factor shares revealed by the functional income distribution, but also the uneven distribution of wealth. For instance, the most wealthy 1 per cent of the population in 1985 owned some 20 per cent of the country's marketable wealth. Making allowance for pension rights reduces but by no means eliminates this uneven distribution.

IMPORTANT CONCEPTS AND TECHNICAL TERMS

Match each lettered concept with the appropriate numbered phrase:

(a)	Land	(l)	Marginal value product of capital
(b)	Personal income distribution	(m)	Financial capital
(c)	Rental rate	(n)	Flow
(d)	Physical capital	(o)	Net investment
(e)	Capital:labour ratio	(p)	Real rate of interest
(f)	Asset price	(q)	Present value
(g)	Gross investment	(r)	Tangible wealth
(h)	Wage:rental ratio	(s)	Opportunity cost of capital
(i)	Stock		
(j)	Required rental	(t)	Functional income distribution
(k)	Nominal rate of interest		

1　The stock of produced goods that contribute to the production of other goods and services.
2　The factor of production that nature supplies.
3　The value today of a sum of money due at some time in the future.
4　The increase in the value of the firm's output when one more unit of capital services is employed.
5　Wealth in the form of physical items, comprising capital and land.
6　The rate of return available on funds in their best alternative use: may be represented by the real interest rate.

7　Shows the division of national income between the different factors of production.
8　The return on a loan measured as the increase in goods that can be purchased, not as the increase in the money value of the loan fund.
9　A measure of relative factor prices: the price of labour relative to the price of capital.
10　A stream of services that an asset provides during a given interval.
11　Shows how national income is divided between different individuals, regardless of the factor services from which these individuals earn their income.
12　Describes the relative importance of inputs of capital and labour in the production process.
13　The payment due for the use of the services provided by capital or land.
14　The sum for which a capital asset can be purchased outright.
15　The production of new capital goods.
16　The return on a loan measured in money terms.
17　The quantity of an asset at a point in time: the accumulation of a flow at a particular moment.
18　Assets such as money or bank deposits which may be used to buy factors of production.
19　The rental rate that just allows the owner of capital to cover the opportunity cost of owning the capital.
20　The production of new capital goods and the improvement of existing capital goods minus the depreciation of the existing capital stock.

EXERCISES

1　Identify each of the following as being either a 'stock' or a 'flow':
　　(a)　Vans owned by Rent-a-Van Limited.
　　(b)　Land available for planting wheat.
　　(c)　Use of truck for delivery.
　　(d)　Railway lines.
　　(e)　TV programme as viewed by consumer.
　　(f)　Use of office space.

2　A 10 per cent government bond with a nominal value of £100 sells on the stock exchange for £62.50.
　　(a)　What is the prevailing rate of interest?
　　(b)　What would the rate of interest be if the price of the bond were £75?
　　(c)　If the rate of interest fell to 8 per cent, for what price would you expect the bond to sell?

3　Linda has £100 to save or spend. If she loans out the money she will receive £112 in a year's time. Inflation is proceeding at 14 per cent per annum.

(a) What is the nominal rate of interest which Linda faces?
(b) What is the real rate of interest?
(c) Financially, would Linda be advised to save or spend?
(d) How would your answer be affected if the inflation rate were 10 per cent, with the nominal interest rate at the same level?

4 A machine is expected to be productive for three years, bringing earnings of £2000 in each year and being worth £6000 as scrap at the end of the third year. Using present value calculations, what would be the 'break-even' price for the machine if
(a) the interest rate is 8 per cent?
(b) the interest rate is 10 per cent?
(c) the interest rate is 8 per cent and it is realized that no account has been taken of inflation which is expected to be 7 per cent per annum?

5 A firm is considering the purchase of a piece of capital equipment, to be funded by a bank loan. (For simplicity, assume that both capital good and loan last for ever.) The cost of the equipment is £25 000 and the interest on the bank loan is fixed at 10 per cent per annum. Maintenance and depreciation amount to 12 per cent of the cost of the machine each year. Inflation is occurring at an annual rate of 8 per cent.
(a) What is the required rental on the capital equipment?
(b) What would be the required rental if inflation increased to 10 per cent per annum?

6 An economy has two sectors: agriculture and industry. Figure 13.1 shows their demand schedules for land (D_A^1 and D_I, respectively). SS represents the total fixed supply of land.

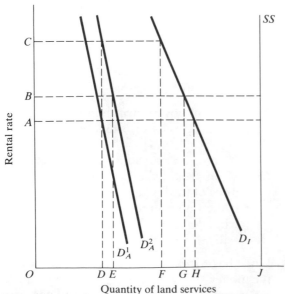

FIGURE 13.1 Allocating land between alternative uses

(a) Identify the equilibrium rental rate, and each sector's demand for land.
Suppose that the government is concerned about the level of food imported into the economy and decides to encourage domestic food production by subsidizing agricultural land. This has the effect of shifting the demand curve for agricultural land to D_A^2.
(b) How will land be allocated between agriculture and industry in the short run?
(c) What will be the rental rates in the two sectors in the short run?
(d) What will be the equilibrium position in the long run?

7 What do economists mean by 'fixed capital'?
(a) Debenture stock secured on a company's assets
(b) The combination of land, labour and equipment used in the productive process
(c) The buildings, equipment and machines used in the productive process
(d) The buildings, equipment, machines and power to operate these machines used in the productive process
(Associated Examining Board GCE A level Economics Paper 1, June 1987)

8 The demand for a factor of production will be more price-inelastic,
1 the more price-inelastic the demand for the final good
2 the larger the proportion of total cost attributable to the factor
3 the more price-elastic the supply of the other factors of production
(a) 1, 2, 3 all correct
(b) 1 and 2 only are correct
(c) 2 and 3 only are correct
(d) 1 only is correct
(Associated Examining Board GCE A level Economics Paper 1, June 1988)

9 Which of the following statements could validly be applied to the UK? (More than one response may be appropriate.)
(a) There has been little change in the shares of factors of production in pre-tax earnings during the last three decades.
(b) Labour receives the greatest portion of national income.
(c) Wealth is less equally distributed than income.
(d) Capital stock grew much more rapidly than the labour force between 1960 and 1987.
(e) Inequality in the distribution of wealth contributes to inequality in the distribution of income.

10 **TABLE 13.1** UK income distribution

(1) Proportion of households %	(2) Original income	(3) Final income	(4) Cumulative households	(5) Percentages original income	(6) Final income
Bottom 20	0.3	6.3	20		
Next 20	6	11	40		
Next 20	16	17	60		
Next 20	27	24	80		
Top 20	51	42	100		

Source: Economic Trends, December 1988.

Table 13.1 shows information concerning the distribution of 'original' and 'final' household income in the UK in 1986. Original income represents income before account is taken of any taxes, benefits, etc. Final income does take account of such redistribution. Copy the table and complete columns (5) and (6) to show amounts of income accruing to the bottom 20, 40, 60, etc., per cent of households.

Economists sometimes try to illustrate such data on distribution using 'Lorenz curves'. Using graph paper, construct a diagram plotting the figures from column (4) on the horizontal axis and those from column (5) on the vertical axis. If you join the points, the result is a Lorenz curve. The closer the curve to a straight line joining (0, 0) to (100, 100), the more even is the distribution. Draw a second Lorenz curve on the same diagram using the figures in column (6): the difference between the two should help to give an impression of the redistributive effect of UK taxation and benefits.

In 1977 in Mexico, the poorest 20 per cent of the population received 2.9 per cent of income, the next 20 per cent received 7.0 per cent, the next 20 per cent, 12.0 per cent, the next 20 per cent, 20.4 per cent, and the richest 20 per cent received 57.7 per cent of total income. Construct a Lorenz curve showing this distribution and compare it with that for the UK. (Data are taken from the *World Development Report* 1989.)

TRUE/FALSE

1 _____ Tangible wealth includes land, machinery, factory buildings, vehicles, and government bonds.

2 _____ Since people cannot be bought and sold, there can be no asset price for labour.

3 _____ The present value of a capital asset is the sum of future rental payments which that asset will provide.

4 _____ Inflation makes nominal interest rates go up. This must reduce the present value of future income.

5 _____ The inflation-adjusted interest rate can be precisely calculated as the difference between the nominal interest rate and the inflation rate.

6 _____ The real interest rate can be negative.

7 _____ The flow of capital services can be varied only in the long run and is rigidly fixed in the short run.

8 _____ Differences in rental rates can lead to the transfer of capital between industries or even between nations.

9 _____ Equilibrium in the market for land demands that rents be equal in all sectors.

10 _____ The main feature distinguishing between the three factors of production (land, capital, and labour) is the speed of adjustment of their supply.

11 _____ The wage-rental ratio increased in the UK between 1977 and 1987.

12 _____ Labour's share in UK national income increased markedly between 1960 and 1987.

QUESTIONS FOR THOUGHT

1 Distinguish between economic rent and transfer earnings.

(20)

With reference to examples, explain what determines the economic rent received by factors of production.

(80)

(University of London A level Economics Paper 1, June 1989)

2 Examine the extent to which it is helpful to treat energy as a fourth factor of production.

ANSWERS AND COMMENTS FOR CHAPTER 13

Please note Where questions are reproduced from A level examinations, the examination boards bear no responsibility for the answers provided in this volume, which are the sole responsibility of the authors.

Important Concepts and Technical Terms

1	*d*	6	*s*	11	*b*	16	*k*
2	*a*	7	*t*	12	*e*	17	*i*
3	*q*	8	*p*	13	*c*	18	*m*
4	*l*	9	*h*	14	*f*	19	*j*
5	*r*	10	*n*	15	*g*	20	*o*

Exercises

1. (a) Stock.
   (b) Stock.
   (c) Flow.
   (d) Stock.
   (e) Flow.
   (f) Flow.
2. (a) The rate of interest may be calculated as the constant annual coupon payment (£10) divided by the bond price (£62.50), i.e., $10/62.5 = 0.16$, or 16 per cent.
   (b) $13\frac{1}{3}$ per cent.
   (c) Price of bond = present value = coupon value/interest rate; i.e., price = $10/0.08 = £125$.
3. (a) 12 per cent.
   (b) $12 - 14 = -2$ per cent (approximately).
   (c) With a negative real rate of interest, Linda would do better to spend the money now, as the return on money saved is not sufficient to compensate for changing goods prices.
   (d) The real rate of interest would then be +2 per cent, and Linda might be encouraged to save the money and spend later—unless she is impatient for the goods!
4. To calculate the 'break-even' price for the machine, we simply sum the present value rows of Table A13.1, with the following results:
   (a) $£1851.85 + £1714.68 + £6350.66 = £9917.19$.
   (b) £9841.59.
   (c) £11 705.51.
5. (a) Annual cost of the machine is calculated as the real interest cost plus the cost of maintenance and depreciation; i.e.,
   $25\,000 \times (0.10 - 0.08 + 0.12) = £3500$
   This is the required rental—the proceeds necessary for the firm to cover the opportunity cost of buying the equipment.
   (b) An increase in the inflation rate reduces the real interest cost of the loan, so the required rental falls to £3000.

TABLE A13.1 Present value calculations

	Year 1	Year 2	Year 3
Stream of earnings	2000	2000	2000
Scrap value			6000
Present value (a) $r = 8\%$	1851.85*	1714.68*	6350.66
Present value (b) $r = 10\%$	1818.18	1652.89	6010.52
Present value (c) $r = 8\%$ inflation = 7%	1980.20	1960.59	7764.72

* The present value of £2000 in one year when the rate of interest is 8 per cent is calculated as

$$\frac{2000}{(1.08)} = 1851.85.$$

After two years, the calculation is

$$\frac{2000}{(1.08)^2}.$$

The present value calculations for (c) are based on a real interest rate of 1 per cent—i.e., after 1 year:

$$\frac{2000}{(1.01)} = 1980.20.$$

(See the Appendix to Chapter 13 of the main text for details.)

6. (a) Equilibrium will occur when the rental rate is the same in the two sectors, and when their joint demand exhausts the supply of land. This happens when the rental is *OA*, at which level, *OD* land is used for agriculture and *OH* for industry. (Note that $OD = HJ$.)
   (b) In the short run, land use cannot change, so *OD* is used for agriculture and *OH* for industry.
   (c) The rental rate in agriculture increases to *OC*, but the rental in industry remains at *OA*.
   (d) In the long run, the high rental rate in agriculture relative to that on industrial land encourages the transfer of land from industry to agriculture. This continues until the rental is the same for both sectors. This occurs at rental *OB*, with *OE* land in agricultural use and *OG* in industry. $OE + OG = OJ$.
7. Fixed (or 'physical') capital refers to the stock of produced goods that are used in the productive process—so (c) is the appropriate response.
8. If the demand for the final good is price-inelastic, then the demand for a factor of production used in producing it will also tend to be inelastic. If the factor constitutes a high proportion of total cost, then a firm will tend to be more sensitive to changes in the factor's price. Similarly, if the other factors of production display price-elastic supply, the firm will tend to show more elastic demand for the factor. Hence (d) is the appropriate response.
9. All statements are valid: see Section 13–10 of the main text.
10. The straight line *OA* would represent a perfectly equal distribution of income. *LC1* represents the distribution of original income in the UK and *LC2* the distribution

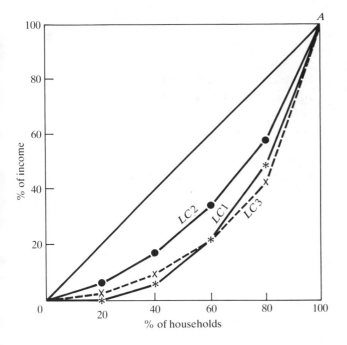

FIGURE A13.1 Lorenz curves

of final income—noticeably nearer to the straight line. *LC3* shows that the distribution of income in Mexico in 1977 was very skewed. For further discussion, see *Economic Review*, March 1988.

True/False

1 False: not government bonds: see Section 13–1 of the main text.
2 True.
3 False: the rental payments must be discounted to give the present value.
4 False: it is the *real* interest rate that matters.
5 False: this is a reasonable approximation which is sufficient for most purposes, but it is not precise: see Section 13–2 of the main text.
6 True.
7 False: even in the short run, capital services can be varied to some extent by overtime working, shift adjustment, etc. (see Section 13–4 of the main text).
8 True.
9 True to an extent: but, as with labour, all land is not the same and some land may in practice command relatively high rentals because of its characteristics.
10 True: see Box 13–1 of the main text.
11 True: see Section 13–9 of the main text.
12 False: declined from 69.1 to 64.4 per cent (see Section 13–10 of the main text).

Questions for Thought

1 The distinction between economic rent and transfer earnings was discussed in Section 11–6 of the main text.

14 Coping with Risk in Economic Life

An inescapable aspect of life is *uncertainty*. This is especially true of our economic life, where decisions must be taken in conditions of uncertainty: we do not know for sure the results of our decisions or what the future holds. This chapter discusses some of the ways in which people come to terms with risk in their economic actions.

Two characteristics of risk are important. Firstly, there is the question of the most likely outcome of an action. Secondly, there is the range and variability of the possible outcomes. Individuals differ in their attitude to risk, which we classify by recording the reaction to an offer of a *fair gamble*. An individual who requires favourable odds to induce acceptance of a bet is said to be *risk-averse*. An individual who will bet except at unfavourable odds is said to be *risk-neutral*. Those who so enjoy the thrill of risk that they will bet even when the odds are unfavourable are described as *risk-lovers*. An assumption often made by economists when considering risk is that individuals face diminishing marginal utility of wealth. An implication of this is that risk aversion is prevalent.

Risk-pooling allows individuals facing independent risks to reduce their joint risk. For instance, a farmer and an actress agreeing to pool their incomes can achieve some stability of their joint income even if one of them hits hard times. (For the full story of the farmer and the actress, see Section 14–2 of the main text!) The existence of the insurance market is a formalization of risk-pooling, in which the independent risks faced by large numbers of individuals are pooled through the purchase of insurance.

Sometimes, risk is shared not among individuals facing risk, but among the companies offering insurance. This typically happens when the cost of an adverse outcome is too high to be borne by a single firm. This is known as *risk-sharing*.

Insurance may lead to problems of *moral hazard*, where the very existence of insurance may lead to an increase in risk. For instance, an individual may take less pains to maintain or secure a consumer durable that is heavily insured. This may be reflected in insurance premia.

Further problems of *adverse selection* may arise. The risk faced by an individual may depend upon certain personal characteristics—whether he/she smokes, drinks, etc. If information on these characteristics is not available to the insurance companies, then premia are set by 'national averages', and those wishing to insure will be those most at risk. There may also be instances where price discrimination to reflect differing risk may not be implemented because of a sense of social fairness.

Riskiness has especial importance in determining the return on financial assets. The return on Treasury bills is relatively certain: it depends upon the (known) nominal rate of return and the rate of inflation. The return on company shares is more uncertain: not only does it depend upon the dividend payments (and inflation), but there is also the possibility of capital gains (or losses). Observation of the postwar period in the UK indicates that the return on company shares is subject to considerable variation, whereas that on Treasury bills is remarkably stable. However, the average return on Treasury bills is close to zero, whereas that on company shares was about 10 per cent in real terms. This suggests that the return on company shares is offered as compensation for the risk of holding them.

In choosing how to hold their wealth, individuals thus face a choice between risk and return. In practice, agents tend to hold a *portfolio* of assets, rarely holding their wealth in a single form of asset. This reflects the fact that *diversification* reduces risk without too much sacrifice of return. The riskiness of a portfolio declines with the number of independent assets held, but the rate of decline diminishes as more assets are added. Diversification is successful if the assets held are independent. If all share prices moved together through time, then the gains from diversification would be small. Shares which tend to move against the general trend are thus a valuable part of any portfolio. *Beta* measures the extent to which a particular share's return moves independently of the rest of the market. A share with a high beta offers high returns when the market booms, but plummets when the market is depressed. A low-beta share moves with the market, but sluggishly. A share with negative beta moves against the market. Share prices reflect beta characteristics in equilibrium, so, for instance, high-beta shares will command relatively low prices.

The stock market has been viewed in two ways. One view is that it is a casino, in which fluctuations in prices occur randomly, implying that funds are allocated to firms in random fashion. An alternative view is that it represents an *efficient market*, where fluctuations in share prices are an appropriate response to new information; i.e., prices at all times reflect all available and relevant information about the economy and about individual firms. In this scenario, investors cannot hope to 'make a killing' in the market because net returns are equalized across assets by movements in prices. The only hope of a better-than-average return is to have better information than the market or to react more quickly to news.

Clearly, the expectations of agents in the market are vital in determining share prices. At times this has led to *speculative bubbles*, in which some share prices have been borne up by expectations, with agents buying purely in the hope of selling at a later higher price and taking the capital gain. Famous examples in the past include the South Sea Bubble of 1720.

Forward markets allow agents to contract to buy or sell commodities at a date in the future at a price agreed now, but reflecting the expected price at the future date. Such markets are only feasible with standardized commodities, such as copper, US dollars, etc.

IMPORTANT CONCEPTS AND TECHNICAL TERMS

Match each lettered concept with the appropriate numbered phrase.

(a)	Risk-pooling	(l)	Diversification
(b)	Risk-neutral	(m)	Risk-averse
(c)	Fair gamble	(n)	Forward market
(d)	Beta	(o)	Correlated stock
(e)	Portfolio		returns
(f)	Speculative bubble	(p)	Risk-sharing
(g)	Hedgers	(q)	Compensating
(h)	Moral hazard		differentials
(i)	Spot price	(r)	Theory of efficient
(j)	Adverse selection		markets
(k)	Diminishing	(s)	Risk-lover
	marginal utility of	(t)	Speculators
	wealth		

1 A measurement of the extent to which a particular share's return moves with the return on the whole stock market.

2 The reduction of uncertainty about the average outcome by spreading the risk across many individuals who independently face that risk.

3 The difference in wage rates paid to workers in high-risk occupations.

4 The strategy of reducing risk by risk-pooling across several assets whose individual returns behave differently from one another.

5 A view of a market as a sensitive processor of information, quickly responding to new information to adjust prices correctly.

6 A person who will accept a bet even when a strict mathematical calculation reveals that the odds are unfavourable.

7 A trader in a forward market who expects to earn profits by taking risks.

8 The spreading of risk among insurance companies, thus reducing the stake of each individual company.

9 A situation where the act of insuring increases the likelihood of the occurrence of the event against which insurance is taken out.

10 A market dealing in contracts made today for delivery of goods at a specified future date at a price agreed today.

11 A person who pays no attention to the degree of dispersion of possible outcomes, but is concerned with the average outcome.

12 The collection of financial and real assets in which a financial investor's wealth is held.

13 A gamble which on average will make exactly zero monetary profit.

14 A market in which everyone believes the price will rise tomorrow, even if the price has already risen a lot.

15 Traders who use a forward market to reduce their risk by making contracts about future transactions.

16 The assumption that successive increases of equal monetary value add less and less to total utility.

17 The price for immediate delivery of a commodity.

18 A person who will refuse a fair gamble, requiring sufficiently favourable odds that the probable monetary profit outweighs the risk.

19 The situation faced by insurance companies in which the people wishing to insure against a particular outcome are also those most likely to require a payoff.

20 A situation in which asset returns move closely together over time.

EXERCISES

1 Maureen, Nora, and Olga are each offered the opportunity of buying a sketch, allegedly by a famous artist, for £500. If genuine, the value of the sketch would be £1000; if phoney it would be totally worthless. There is a 50–50 chance of each alternative. Maureen rejects the idea outright, Nora jumps at the chance, and Olga flips a coin to decide.
   (a) Characterize each attitude to risk.
   (b) Would *you* buy the sketch?
   (c) What does this imply about your own attitude to risk?
   (d) Would your attitude differ if you had recently won £1 million on the pools?

2 In which of the following circumstances are risks being pooled?
   (a) Insurance for Miss World's legs.
   (b) Car insurance.
   (c) Insurance for contents of a freezer.

(d)   Insurance against an accident at a nuclear power station.

(e)   Medical insurance for a holiday abroad.

3   Which of the following situations illustrate moral hazard, and which adverse selection?

(a)   Paula never locks her car, knowing it is adequately insured.

(b)   Having taken out life insurance in favour of his family, Quentin continues to smoke heavily.

(c)   Rosemary takes out life insurance, knowing that her heavy smoking has given her terminal lung cancer.

(d)   Having insured against rain, Simon makes advance payments to cricket stars for his Easter single-wicket competition.

(e)   Tessa takes out extra health insurance shortly before going on a skiing holiday.

4   Suppose you wish to invest £200 in shares. Two industries, chemicals and computers, have shares on offer at £100 each. The returns expected from the two industries are independent. In each case, there is a 50 per cent chance that returns will be good (£12) and a 50 per cent chance that returns will be poor (£6).

(a)   If you buy only chemicals shares, and times are good, what return will you earn?

(b)   If you buy only computers shares, and times are bad, what return will you earn?

(c)   If you put all your funds in one industry, what is your average expected return?

(d)   If you put all your funds in one industry, what is the chance of a poor return?

(e)   What is your average return if you diversify?

(f)   If you diversify, what is the chance of a poor return (i.e., the same level as part (b))?

5   Match each lettered definition with the numbered term (suppose that contracts are established for one year hence and that today's date is 1 July 1991):

(a)   The price of gold on 1 July 1991 for delivery and payment on 1 July 1991.

(b)   The price in the forward market on 1 July 1991 at which gold is being traded for delivery and payment on 1 July 1992.

(c)   Today's best guess about what the spot price will be on 1 July 1992.

(d)   The price of gold being traded in the spot market on 1 July 1991.

(e)   The difference between the expected future spot price and the current forward price.

(1)   Risk premium.

(2)   Future spot price.

(3)   Today's spot price.

(4)   Forward price.

(5)   Expected future spot price.

6   Which of the following offers the best chance of a better-than-average return in the stock market?

(a)   Careful reading of the financial press.

(b)   Sticking a pin into the financial pages of the newspaper.

(c)   Employing a financial adviser.

(d)   Computer analysis of past share price movements.

(e)   Being the first agent to react to news.

7   Which of the following statements is/are correct?

(a)   A share with beta = 1 moves independently of the rest of the market.

(b)   A share with a high beta moves with the market, but more sluggishly.

(c)   A share with a negative beta decreases the riskiness of a portfolio.

(d)   A share with a negative beta increases the riskiness of a portfolio.

(e)   Most shares have a beta close to 1.

8   Which of the following statements concerning unit trusts is/are true?

(a)   They allow small savers to diversify their risks.

(b)   They normally give a fixed rate of interest and re-invest surpluses so as to give unit trust holders capital appreciation.

(c)   Their price remains constant so that unit trust holders can never lose their savings in monetary terms.

(d)   They are especially attractive to risk-lovers.

TRUE/FALSE

1   _____ A risk-lover is indifferent to risk.

2   _____ The principle of diminishing marginal utility of wealth makes most people risk-averse.

3   _____ Insurance companies often do not insure against acts of God because these risks cannot be pooled.

4   _____ In purely economic terms, life insurance premia should be lower for women than for men because women live longer than men on average.

5   _____ Treasury bills are more risky than company shares.

6   _____ A risk-averse financial investor prefers higher average return on a portfolio but dislikes higher risk.

7   _____ Diversification means not putting all your eggs in one basket.

8 _____ Diversification fails when share returns are negatively correlated.

9 _____ In equilibrium, low beta shares will have below average prices.

10 _____ Speculative bubbles are less likely the larger the share of the total return that comes in the form of dividends rather than capital gains.

11 _____ A forward market in cars would help to stabilize prices.

12 _____ A trader buying forward in the hope of a higher future spot price is hedging.

QUESTIONS FOR THOUGHT

1 Explain why the occurrence of large positive or negative returns on shares in particular years was probably unanticipated.

2 Discuss whether the stock market most resembles a casino or an efficient market. What sort of evidence helps your decision?

3 Regardless of how you believe the stock market *does* work, which is the more desirable method if we are concerned that funds are appropriately allocated between firms?

4 Discuss whether moral hazard or adverse selection might influence the markets for insurance against unemployment or bad health in a situation where there is no state provision of such insurance.

ANSWERS AND COMMENTS FOR CHAPTER 14

Please note   Where questions are reproduced from A level examinations, the examination boards bear no responsibility for the answers provided in this volume, which are the sole responsibility of the authors.

Important Concepts and Technical Terms

1	d	6	s	11	b	16	k
2	a	7	t	12	e	17	i
3	q	8	p	13	c	18	m
4	l	9	h	14	f	19	j
5	r	10	n	15	g	20	o

Exercises

1 (a) Maureen is risk-averse.
Nora is a risk-lover.
Olga is risk-neutral.

(d) You may well have been risk-averse like Maureen in choosing not to buy in (b). However, Maureen tells us that if she had lots of money, she might accept the deal. This, of course, reflects the diminishing marginal utility of wealth (see Section 14–1 of the main text).

2 Risk-pooling occurs in situations (b), (c), and (e), where relatively large numbers of people face the risk, each with a relatively small likelihood of needing to claim.

3 Moral hazard is present in cases (a), (b), and (d). In case (d), the probability of rain is unaffected by the insurance, but the size of the bills is not. (c) and (e) are concerned with adverse selection.

4 (a) £24.
(b) £12.
(c) £18.
(d) 50 per cent.
(e) Still £18.
(f) The chance that both industries hit bad times together is now only 25 per cent, so you have reduced the risk by diversifying.

5 (a) 3.
(b) 4.
(c) 5. See Box 14–1 of the main text.
(d) 2.
(e) 1.

6 If the Efficient Markets theory of the stock market is correct, then any method relying on past information is doomed to failure, as current share prices already incorporate the effects of past information. The best hope is to be the first trader to respond to new relevant information—i.e., option (e). If the market were a casino, then option (b) might be as effective as anything else (see Section 14–5 of the main text).

7 (c) and (e) are correct: a share with negative beta tends to move against the market, and thus reduces the risk of a portfolio. Most shares move with the market, and thus have a beta close to 1.

8 (a).

True/False

1 False: on the contrary, the risk-lover gains utility from risk (see Section 14–1 of the main text).
2 True.
3 True: see Section 14–2 of the main text.
4 True.
5 False: see Section 14–3 of the main text.
6 True: see Section 14–4 of the main text.
7 True: this was James Tobin's characterization.
8 False: it is precisely when share returns are negatively correlated that diversification is most successful.
9 False: low-beta shares will be highly valued (see Section 14–4 of the main text).
10 True: see Section 14–5 of the main text.
11 False: whether or not prices would be stabilized is irrelevant: the point is that a forward market in cars is not a viable proposition (see Section 14–6 of the main text).
12 False: he or she would be speculating.

Questions for Thought

1 See Section 14–3 of the main text.
2 and 3   See Section 14–5 of the main text.
4 Moral hazard may be thought to be a potential problem in the case of unemployment insurance. In the case of health insurance, adverse selection is a possibility. See an interesting article by John Hey in *Economic Review*, March 1987.

15 Introduction to Welfare Economics

A major bone of contention between the two main political parties in the UK is the extent to which the *free market* should be important in the allocation of resources within the economy. The Conservative Party might argue that free enterprise should be encouraged; the Labour Party might instead suggest that legal safeguards are necessary to protect individuals in society. This chapter begins to look at how an economist might shed light on these issues.

Welfare economics is a branch of economics which does not *describe* how the economy operates, but attempts to *assess* how the economy is working. Two important aspects of such an assessment are examined. Firstly, we may wish to see whether the economy is *efficiently* organized: could resources be reallocated more productively? Secondly, we may be concerned about the fair distribution of resources between individuals or groups within society. These two issues: *allocative efficiency* and *equity*—are seen to be related but yet distinct.

Many people would tend to be in agreement on the principle of *horizontal equity*—the idea that identical people should receive identical treatment. However, the extent to which we should aim at *vertical equity* is more contentious. To what extent should interpersonal differences be reduced by the different treatment of different people—for instance, by taking from the rich to give to the poor?

The efficiency of the allocation of resources may be assessed by the *Pareto criterion*. By this, an allocation will be judged to be efficient if no reallocation can make some people better off without making others worse off. This enables us to assess efficiency, but does not say anything about equity. For any economy, there are a number of efficient allocations, some of which will involve more equity in distribution between individuals in the society than others. The Pareto criterion does not allow us to distinguish between these.

A key issue is whether the free market allows an economy to attain a Pareto-efficient allocation of resources without the need for intervention. It turns out that, with some qualifications, the answer is 'yes'. In particular, if perfect competition is prevalent in all markets in an economy, then it can be shown that a Pareto-efficient outcome will be obtained, guided by movements in prices. Competitive equilibrium ensures that there is no way of making all consumers better off simply by transferring resources between industries.

What, then, is the role of government in this process? It could be suggested that the free market should be allowed to take the economy to an efficient resource allocation and that the government should intervene only if redistribution proves to be necessary. Problems may arise with this partly because individuals will differ in their opinion as to how much redistribution is needed, and partly because of the 'qualifications' mentioned, which are essentially concerned with circumstances in which the free market may fail to operate effectively.

For the free market solution to work, it is important that competitive equilibrium is achieved in *all* markets. The problem here is that there may be occasions where individual markets do not even exist. The full competitive equilibrium will not be reached whenever a *distortion* exists, a distortion being anything which causes social marginal cost and social marginal benefit to diverge. Such a distortion can be introduced, for example, if a government tries to redistribute resources by using a commodity tax. The *Theory of the Second Best* shows that, if some distortion cannot be avoided, then the best strategy may be not to concentrate that distortion in one sector and allow freedom in other sectors, but to introduce offsetting distortions elsewhere—i.e., to spread the distortion thinly across many sectors.

Distortions arise because of *market failure*. In the remainder of this chapter, we concentrate on two kinds of market failure, arising from the existence of externalities and from the absence of some markets involving time and risk.

Externalities occur when an activity involves costs or benefits which are not reflected in the working of the price system, thus causing a divergence between private and social costs or benefits. Examples of external costs include pollution, noise, and congestion. Thus, if a firm produces pollutants as a by-product of its production process, it imposes a cost upon the environment, which is not incorporated in any price mechanism. The absence of a market for pollutants causes their over-production. Analysis suggests that it may not be optimal to eliminate pollution altogether, but rather to reduce it just to the point where marginal social costs and benefits are equalized.

The granting of *property rights* may allow the 'internalization' of externalities, by making explicit who should be compensated by whom and forcing the implicit market into existence. In the case of pollution, this may not be a viable solution, as it will be difficult to co-ordinate the efforts of those bearing the cost of the pollution because of the *free-rider* problem.

It is no easy matter to judge whether past measures to control pollution have been successful—especially remembering that the best strategy is not necessarily the total elimination of pollution. Some economists believe that it is better to try to control pollution by prices rather than by quantity restrictions. Although desirable in some ways, there may be difficulty in calculating the level of prices needed to produce the desired results. It must also be remembered that monitoring and enforcement themselves use up scarce resources.

In Chapter 14, we have already seen that some forward markets would not be workable in practice and that moral hazard and adverse selection may prevent the perfect working of the insurance market. These are further examples of distortions which prevent the achievement of the overall competitive equilibrium.

In some instances, a problem arises because information is not freely available to agents. This may lead to the need for the authorities either to ensure the provision of information or to impose health and safety standards.

IMPORTANT CONCEPTS AND TECHNICAL TERMS

Match each lettered concept with the appropriate numbered phrase:

(a) Horizontal equity   (g) Market failure
(b) Resource allocation (h) Allocative efficiency
(c) Property rights   (i) Externality
(d) Welfare economics   (j) Pareto-efficient
(e) Second-best   (k) Vertical equity
(f) Free-rider problem   (l) Distortion

1 The branch of economics dealing with normative issues, its purpose being not to describe how the economy works but to assess how well it works.
2 The identical treatment of identical people.
3 A list or complete description of who does what and who gets what.
4 Circumstances in which equilibrium in free unregulated markets will fail to achieve an efficient allocation.
5 The different treatment of different people in order to reduce the consequences of these innate differences.
6 A situation causing society's marginal cost of producing a good to diverge from society's marginal benefit from consuming that good.
7 A situation in which an individual has no incentive to pay for a good which is costly to produce, as he or she can consume it anyway.
8 A theory by which the government may increase the overall efficiency of the whole economy by introducing new distortions to offset distortions that already exist.

9 A situation occurring when an economy is getting the most out of its scarce resources and not squandering them.
10 A situation arising whenever an individual's production or consumption decision directly affects the production or consumption of others, other than through market prices.
11 An allocation of resources such that, given the set of consumer tastes, resources, and technology, it is impossible to move to another allocation which would make some people better off and nobody worse off.
12 The legal right to compensation for infringement of vested rights.

EXERCISES

1 Suppose that Ursula and Vince judge their utility in terms of the goods they receive. Figure 15.1 shows a number of alternative allocations of goods between the two of them.

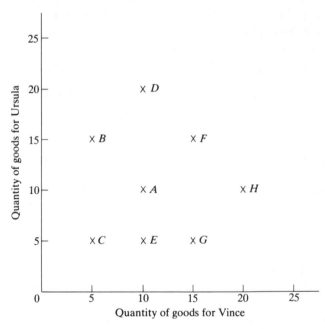

FIGURE 15.1 Allocation of goods between Ursula and Vince

In the following questions, the Pareto criterion should be used to assess alternative allocations:
(a) Which allocations are superior to A?
(b) Which allocations are inferior to A?
(c) Are there any allocations which you have not mentioned in your answers to (a) and (b)? If so, explain why you have not been able to judge them either superior or inferior to A. Is society indifferent between such points?

Suppose that the quantity of goods available is 20:

(d) Which allocations are inefficient?
(e) Which allocations are efficient?
(f) Which allocations are infeasible?

2 Suppose that an economy has many producers and consumers, but only two goods, food and books. Both markets are unregulated and perfectly competitive. The equilibrium price of food is £20 and that of books is £10. Labour is the variable factor of production, and workers gain equal job satisfaction from working in each of the two sectors. The economy is in equilibrium.

(a) How much additional utility (in money value) did consumers obtain from the last book produced?
(b) How many books would consumers exchange for one unit of food if their utility were to remain constant.
(c) What was the marginal cost of the last book and last unit of food produced? Justify your answer.
(d) What can be said about relative wage rates in the two sectors?
(e) What is the ratio of the marginal physical product of labour in production of books to that in production of food?
(f) How many additional books could be produced if one less unit of food is produced?
(g) Bearing in mind your answers to parts (b) and (f), what can be said about the allocation of resources in this economy?

3 Panel (a) of Figure 15.2 shows the demand curve for books (DD) in the economy of exercise 2. SS shows the supply curve for books.

(a) Identify equilibrium price and quantity.
(b) Suppose the authorities impose a tax on books: identify the tax-inclusive supply curve and the new equilibrium consumer price and quantity. What is the amount of the tax?
(c) At this equilibrium, what is the marginal social cost of books? What is the marginal consumer benefit?

Given that the books tax is imposed as in part (b), now consider the market for food, shown in panel (b) of Figure 15.2. D represents the demand curve, MPC the marginal private cost of food, and MSC the marginal social cost of producing food.

(d) Identify equilibrium price and quantity in market for food.
(e) Does this equilibrium ensure a satisfactory resource allocation? Explain your answer.
(f) Explain the divergence between MPC and MSC.
(g) Given that the tax on books must remain, what is the preferred output of the food industry? How could the authorities bring about this production level?

4 Which of the following would be indicative of market failure? (Note: more than one response may be appropriate.)

(a) Traffic congestion.
(b) The existence of a collusive oligopoly.
(c) The absence of a forward market for cars.
(d) The presence of a market in which marginal social benefit exceeds marginal private benefit.
(e) A situation in which a firm is free to pollute the atmosphere around its factory (a residential area) without cost.

5 Two neighbouring factories in a remote rural area operate independently. One is a branch of a

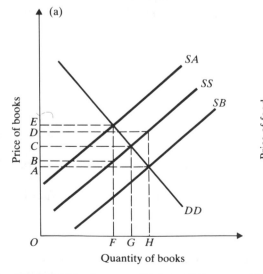

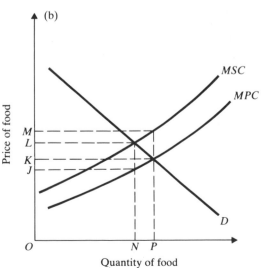

FIGURE 15.2 A commodity tax and the second best

large company (XYZ plc) which spends substantial sums of money in improving and maintaining the main road linking the two factories with the motorway. The other factory makes no contribution towards the road, but shares its advantages. Figure 15.3 illustrates the position facing XYZ plc. *DD* is the demand curve, and *MPC* represents the marginal private cost faced by XYZ plc.

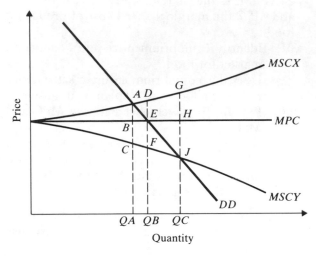

FIGURE 15.3   The effect of a production externality

(a)   At what point will the firm produce?
(b)   Taking account of the externality of the road, identify the marginal social cost curve (*MSCX* or *MSCY*). Explain your answer.
(c)   What would be the socially efficient point of production? Why?
(d)   What is the social cost of producing at (a) rather than at (c)?

6   A dog-owner daily allows his dog to foul the pavement. In what sense is this an externality? In the absence of a realistic charge to dog-owners, would you expect there to be too many or too few dogs for social efficiency? Should the authorities tackle this problem by raising the dog licence fee or by restricting the number of licences issued— or should they leave things as they are?

7   Which of the following statements that refer to the price mechanism is *not* true?
(a)   High prices ration out scarce goods in accordance with effective demand of consumers
(b)   High prices and profits tend to attract resources from less remunerative activities
(c)   Immobility of factors makes the price mechanism less perfect as an allocative device
(d)   In a private enterprise economy the sovereignty of the consumer is absolute
(Associated Examining Board GCE A level Economics Paper 1, June 1988)

8   A factory emits smoke during the production process which imposes an external diseconomy upon the environment. The following data describe the situation:

Output (units)	Marginal private cost (£)	Marginal revenue (£)	Marginal social cost of air pollution (£)
1	12	24	4
2	12	22	6
3	12	20	8
4	12	18	10
5	12	16	12
6	12	14	14
7	12	12	16
8	12	10	18

Initially, the firm maximizes profits without regard to the social cost of air pollution. If, subsequently, the authorities levy pollution tax on the firm equal to the marginal social cost, which of the following describes what happens to output?
(a)   Falls by 4 units.
(b)   Falls by 2 units.
(c)   Falls by 1 unit.
(d)   Remains constant.
(e)   Rises by 1 unit.

9   Resource allocation is said to be efficient when
(a)   production processes use as little energy as possible.
(b)   no one can be made better off without someone else being made worse off.
(c)   there is no need to trade with other countries.
(d)   the balance of payments is in surplus.
(e)   the production of one commodity cannot be increased without reducing the production of another commodity.
(f)   all private companies within the economy are producing at an equilibrium level of output in order to maximize profits.
(g)   gross national income grows at a planned percentage rate every year.

10   A local government councillor said: 'The authority is short of revenue and the roads into the town centre are congested; therefore, we should double car parking charges.'
To achieve its objectives, this recommendation assumes
(1)   the elasticity of demand for car parking in the town centre is less than unity.
(2)   the social costs of driving to the town centre outweigh the social benefits.
(3)   the local authority has no substantial competition in the provision of car parking facilities in the town centre.

Select one of the following combinations:

(a) 1, 2, and 3 all correct
(b) 1, 2 only correct
(c) 2, 3 only correct
(d) 1 only correct
(e) 3 only correct

(University of London GCE A level Economics Paper 2, January 1985)

TRUE/FALSE

1 _____ Welfare economics deals with normative issues.

2 _____ An allocation of resources in which it is impossible to make any one individual better off without making somebody else worse off is Pareto-efficient.

3 _____ If every market in the economy but one is a perfectly competitive free market, the resulting equilibrium throughout the economy will be Pareto-efficient.

4 _____ If a distortion is unavoidable in a particular sector, the best action for the government to take is to ensure that the other sectors are distortion-free.

5 _____ Under imperfect competition, marginal revenue is different from average revenue: this causes market failure.

6 _____ A noisy transistor radio on a crowded beach is an example of an externality.

7 _____ The formal establishment of property rights can help to achieve the socially efficient allocation by internalizing externalities.

8 _____ River pollution represents a situation where private cost exceeds social cost.

9 _____ Private cost exceeds social cost whenever a firm fails to make a profit.

10 _____ Pollution still exists; therefore past pollution control has been ineffective.

11 _____ An important problem which inhibits the development of forward and contingent markets is the provision of information.

12 _____ In most countries, governments have accepted an increasing role in regulating health, safety, and quality standards because it has been recognized that this is a potentially important area of market failure.

13 _____ Human life is beyond economic calculation and must be given absolute priority, whatever the cost.

14 _____ Estimates for the implicit social marginal benefit from saving life in the UK range from £50 to £20 million.

15 _____ Acid rain is related to emissions from power stations that burn fossil fuels.

QUESTIONS FOR THOUGHT

1 Explain the sense in which some pollution might be socially desirable.

2 The nuclear accident at Chernobyl created widespread radioactive pollution. Discuss how you would assess the costs and benefits of nuclear energy.

3 Discuss how the granting of property rights could help to internalize externalities suffered by people living near football grounds or having noisy neighbours.

ANSWERS AND COMMENTS FOR CHAPTER 15

Please note Where questions are reproduced from A level examinations, the examination boards bear no responsibility for the answers provided in this volume, which are the sole responsibility of the authors.

Important Concepts and Technical Terms

1 *d*	5 *k*	9 *h*
2 *a*	6 *l*	10 *i*
3 *b*	7 *f*	11 *j*
4 *g*	8 *e*	12 *c*

Exercises

1 (a) *D, F*, and *H* each make at least one of our two subjects better off without making the other worse off. For instance, at *D* Ursula is better off, and Vince no worse off. Both are better off at *F*.
   (b) *C* and *E*.
   (c) *B* and *G* cannot be judged either superior or inferior to *A*: in each case one individual is better off, but at the expense of the other. This does not mean that 'society' is indifferent between *A, B*, and *G*. The three points represent different distributions of goods, between which the Pareto criterion cannot judge.
   (d) *C, E*.
   (e) *A, B, G*.
   (f) *D, F, H*.

2 (a) £10, this being the purchase price of books.
   (b) 2, reflecting the ratio of prices (marginal utility) of the two goods.
   (c) Marginal cost of the last book was £10, last unit of food, £20. Under perfect competition, equilibrium price = marginal cost (this was discussed in Chapter 9).
   (d) As 'job satisfaction' is equal in the two sectors, so also will be the wage rate in equilibrium—otherwise there would be movement of labour.
   (e) 2:1.
   (f) 2, reflecting the difference in the marginal physical product of labour.
   (g) The allocation is Pareto-efficient—there is no feasible reallocation of resources which will make society better off.
If you have had difficulty following the chain of arguments in this exercise, you should re-read Section 15–2 in the main text, where a similar exercise is discussed in more detail.

3 (a) Price *OC*, quantity *OG*.
   (b) The new supply curve is *SA*. Equilibrium price would be *OE*, quantity *OF*. Tax is *BE*.
   (c) Marginal social cost is *OB*. Marginal consumer benefit is *OE*. This allocation is socially inefficient, as too few books are being produced.
   (d) Price *OK*, quantity *OP*.

   (e) It is not a satisfactory allocation because marginal social cost (*OM*) is greater than marginal private benefit (*OK*) at this price: 'too much' food is being produced.
   (f) The books tax causes a distortion, such that *MSC* represents the true marginal social cost in terms of the utility forgone by using resources in food rather than books.
   (g) The preferred output would be *ON* at price *OL*, where the marginal social cost equals the marginal social benefit of food production. This could be achieved by a tax of size *JL*.
This topic is discussed in Section 15–3 of the main text.

4 (b), (c), and (e) all indicate that distortions exist which lead to market failure. (a)—traffic congestion—is not evidence of market failure. Just as the optimal level of pollution may not be zero, so there may be some 'optimal' level of congestion. It all depends how it has been handled in the economy. As far as (d) is concerned, it is not the divergence of marginal social and private benefit which matters: the issue is whether marginal social *cost* is equated to marginal benefit.

5 (a) *E*.
   (b) *MSCY*: the marginal social cost lies below the marginal private cost to the individual firm when production externalities are beneficial (see Section 15–5 of the main text).
   (c) *J*: this is the point where the marginal social cost equals the marginal social benefit.
   (d) The area *EHJ*.

6 Pavement-fouling imposes a cost on society in that it reduces the utility of other people or forces someone to bear the cost of clearing it. The absence of a charge for dog ownership would tend to lead to there being more dogs than is socially efficient. Many economists would argue that a price control (increasing the fee) is preferable to a quantity control.

7 (d).

8 (a): firm initially produces 7 units of output, where *MPC* = *MR*, and then restricts output to 3 units where (*MPC* + *MSC* of pollution) = *MR*.

9 (b) and (e): these options relate directly to the Pareto criterion.

10 Here, all the options are correct. If the local authority wants to increase revenue, it is vital that demand be inelastic (as we saw way back in Chapter 5). If the authority wishes to relieve congestion, as the wording implies, then this is tantamount to saying that option (2) holds. Option (3) is closely allied to (1), in that demand would not be likely to be inelastic if there were alternative car parking facilities in the town centre.

True/False

1 True.
2 True: see Section 15–1 of the main text.
3 False: one non-competitive market is sufficient distortion to prevent Pareto efficiency.
4 False: the second-best theory says it is better to spread

the distortion across all sectors (see Section 15–3 of the main text).

5 True: given our definition of market failure (see Section 15–4 of the main text).
6 True: see Section 15–5 of the main text.
7 True.
8 False: the reverse is so (see Section 15–6 of the main text).
9 False.
10 False: the optimal level of pollution need not be zero.
11 True: see Section 15–7 of the main text.
12 True: see Section 15–8 of the main text.
13 False: no economy could afford such priority.
14 True.

15 Many people do believe that power station emissions are a prime cause of acid rain, but this is not undisputed. See Box 15–1 in the main text for a more complete discussion.

Questions for Thought

1 Think of the costs entailed in the *total* elimination of pollution (see Section 15–6 of the main text).
3 The granting of property rights would entitle these suffering people to compensation—perhaps from the football club for damage and disruption, or from noisy neighbours (re-read Section 15–5 of the main text).

16

Taxes and Public Spending: The Government and Resource Allocation

During Chapter 15 we saw that attempts by the government to affect income distribution by commodity taxation could introduce distortion and hence market failure. In this chapter, we look more carefully at the role of government in a modern market economy, and at taxation and public spending.

The desirable level of government intervention was controversial in the 1980s, with politicians in many countries arguing for the reduction of government spending to allow a reduction in the level of taxation. In the UK this position was adopted by Mrs Thatcher and influenced economic policy from the moment she came into office. The UK has a *progressive income tax structure*: as individual income increases, people face higher *marginal* and *average* tax rates. An early action of the first Thatcher administration was to cut income tax rates, especially for those on high incomes.

In the UK in the early 1980s, total government expenditure amounted to more than 40 per cent of national income, much of it going on health, defence, and education, and on transfer payments. The distinction between spending on goods and services and on transfers is an important one: if the government spends on goods and services, it pre-empts scarce resources which cannot then be used in the private sector. Transfer payments do not pre-empt in this way, but redistribute income between groups in society. Such payments accounted for an increasing proportion of government spending as the rate of unemployment rose.

We saw back in Chapter 4 that there are situations in which government spending on goods and services may be justified—for instance in the case of *public goods*.

The difficult question concerning public goods is the issue of how much to produce. The socially efficient quantity is determined by equating marginal social cost and marginal social benefit, as we know from earlier analysis—but how can the marginal social benefit be evaluated? A crude way of canvassing public opinion is through the electoral process, whereby election manifestos present alternative choices for government spending, among all the other issues of the day.

On the other side of the coin is the question of *revenue*—what principles should guide the taxation system, and what options are available? There are three main forms of taxation: direct, indirect, and wealth taxes. *Direct taxes* comprise income taxes (paid on earnings from labour), rents, dividends, and interest. *Indirect taxes* comprise taxes on expenditure on goods and services—mainly VAT, but also taxes on tobacco, alcohol, cars, television, and imports. The most important form of *wealth tax* in the UK used to be that on property—the rates.

Income tax is based on the *ability to pay* principle and reflects a concern for vertical equity. In a progressive income tax structure, the amount paid by an individual depends upon the size of income and thus reflects ability to pay. An alternative guide is the *benefits principle*, which states that those who benefit from public expenditure should fund it. An example of this is car tax, whereby road-users contribute towards road maintenance. The benefits principle may sometimes conflict with the ability to pay principle; for example, those most likely to benefit from unemployment insurance may be those least able to pay for it. The pattern of consumption of some commodities (e.g., beer) may make some commodity taxes *regressive* in their effect.

The *incidence of a tax* measures the final tax burden including its indirect effects. The burden of a wage tax, for instance, may be shared by employer and employee. In general, the more inelastic the supply curve, and the more elastic the demand curve for a commodity, the more the final incidence will fall on the sellers of the commodity rather than the buyers.

In terms of the social efficiency of taxation, there will usually be some *deadweight burden* involved with taxation. This will be at its smallest when the supply curve or demand curve is very inelastic; in the UK context, this applies to goods like alcohol and tobacco (inelastic demand) and North Sea oil (inelastic supply). In some cases, the commodity tax may help in offsetting undesirable externalities—as in the case of cigarettes.

What, then, would be the effect of reducing the degree of government involvement in an economy? It might be argued that a reduction in spending by government would free more resources for use in the private sector—where some might suggest they would be more productive. Tax cuts might be seen to reduce the deadweight wastage of resources—for instance, cuts in income tax could lead to an increase in employment. Indeed, some have argued that the increase in labour employed would be so strong that a cut in income tax might actually *increase* tax revenues.

Local government may be responsible for providing a range of services from street-sweeping to schooling, and for administering certain forms of regulation, for instance to influence or control land use. Local government finance has been a contentious topic in the 1980s and 1990s. The *Tiebout model* suggests that efficient resource allocation may be achieved through competition between relatively small local government units. Economic analysis of externalities suggests that larger jurisdictions would enable greater efficiency through internalizing the externalities. The *community charge* or *poll tax*, introduced in the UK in 1990 (1989 in Scotland), is a move towards recognition of the Tiebout model, its main rationale being to increase the accountability of local authorities.

IMPORTANT CONCEPTS AND TECHNICAL TERMS

Match each lettered concept with the appropriate numbered phrase:

(a) VAT
(b) Transfer payment
(c) Private good
(d) Poll tax
(e) Progressive tax structure
(f) Public good
(g) Corporation tax
(h) Average rate of income tax
(i) Indirect tax
(j) Zoning laws
(k) Incidence of a tax
(l) Merit good
(m) Laffer curve
(n) Direct tax
(o) Marginal tax rate
(p) Tiebout model
(q) Benefits principle
(r) Rateable value
(s) Deadweight tax burden
(t) Wealth tax
(u) Regressive tax structure
(v) Ability to pay

1 A tax structure in which the average tax rate rises with an individual's income level.
2 The waste caused by a distortionary tax leading to a misallocation of resources.
3 A description of the relationship between tax rates and tax revenue.
4 A tax on asset holdings or transfers rather than the income from asset holding: examples in the UK are rates and capital transfer tax.
5 A tax structure in which the average tax rate falls as income level rises.
6 The principle underlying a tax structure in which the incidence of the tax falls most heavily on those who can pay.
7 Hypothetical prices for houses or other buildings, used under the former rating system as the basis for calculating an individual's or firm's liability for property tax.
8 Regulations that control the uses to which land may be put in a particular geographical area.
9 The principle underlying a tax structure in which people who receive more than their share of public spending pay more than their share of tax revenues.
10 The percentage taken by the government of the last pound that an individual earns.
11 A tax levied on expenditure on goods and services.
12 A method by which purchasing power is redistributed from one group of consumers to another.
13 A good that, even if consumed by one person, can still be consumed by others.
14 An important model of local government, sometimes called the model of the 'invisible foot'.
15 A flat rate tax levied on adults living in a local authority area, known in the UK as the community charge.
16 Tax paid by UK companies based on their taxable profits after allowance for interest payments and depreciation.
17 The percentage of total income that the government takes in income tax.
18 Tax levied directly on income.
19 A good that society thinks everyone ought to have regardless of whether it is wanted by each individual.
20 A sales tax collected at different stages of the production process.
21 A good that, if consumed by one person, cannot be consumed by another person.
22 A measure of the final tax burden on different people once we have allowed for the indirect as well as the direct effects of the tax.

EXERCISES

1 (a) Use the data of Table 16–3 of the main text to draw pie-charts showing the shares of the major categories of government expenditure and tax revenue.
   (b) The Thatcher administration pursued a philosophy based on freedom of individual choice. In part, this meant following policies which allow direct taxes to be reduced. How do you think this will have affected the pattern of revenue shares revealed by your pie-chart?
   (c) How would you expect the pattern of government expenditure to have been affected by the increase in unemployment in the early 1980s?

2 Assume that income tax is levied at a standard rate of 30 per cent on all income over £5000.
   (a) Calculate the marginal and average tax rates at the following income levels:

(i)   £3000.
(ii) £9000.
(iii) £12 000.
(iv) £20 000.

(b) Is the tax progressive or regressive?
Suppose the tax structure is revised so that income over £5000 is taxed at 30 per cent as before, but the rate increases to 50 per cent for income over £10 000.

(c) Calculate the marginal and average tax rates at the same income levels as in part (a).

(d) Is the tax more or less progressive than before?

3 This exercise is concerned with the market for a pure public good. In Figure 16.1, D1 and D2 represent the demand curves for the good of two individuals: we assume that for each individual the demand curve shows the marginal private benefit of the last unit of the public good. The line MC shows the private and social marginal cost of producing the public good.

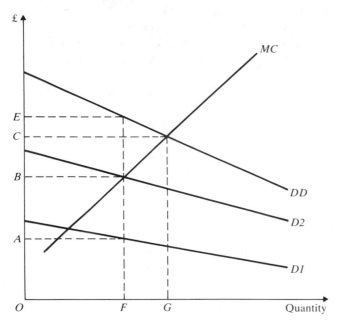

FIGURE 16.1

(a) If DD is to represent the marginal social benefit obtained from the good, what should be the relationship between DD and D1 and D2?

(b) If the quantity produced is given by OF, what valuation per unit is placed upon the good by individual 1?

(c) If individual 1 actually pays this amount for the provision of the good, what will individual 2 have to pay?

(d) What is the marginal *social* benefit of OF units of this good?

(e) How does marginal social benefit compare with marginal social cost in this situation?

(f) What is the socially efficient quantity of this good?

4 Figure 16.2 shows the market for a good in which there is a negative production externality such that marginal social cost (MSC) is above marginal private cost (MPC). MSB represents the marginal social benefit derived from consumption of the good.

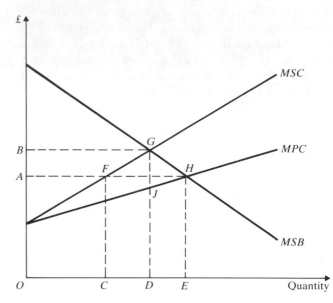

FIGURE 16.2

(a) If this market is unregulated, what quantity of this good will be produced?

(b) What is the socially efficient quantity?

(c) What is the amount of the deadweight loss to society if the free market quantity is produced?

(d) What level of tax on the good would ensure that the socially efficient quantity is produced?

(e) Suggest an example of a situation in which this analysis might be relevant.

5 Non-rivalry and non-excludability are characteristics of
(a) normal goods
(b) inferior goods
(c) demerit good
(d) public goods
(Associated Examining Board, GCE A level Economics Paper 1, June 1987)

6 A firm engaged in producing a certain good has private costs which are not equal to social costs. In order to increase economic welfare the government could

(a) tax the firm if social costs are less than its private costs

(b) subsidise the firm if social costs exceed its private costs

(c) tax the firm if social costs exceed its private costs

(d) subsidise other firms in the same industry if their private costs are less than social costs

(Associated Examining Board, GCE A level Economics Paper 1, November 1986)

7 Assuming a positively sloping supply curve for a product, an indirect tax levied on the product will be paid by

(1) suppliers only, if demand is perfectly elastic

(2) purchasers only, if demand is completely inelastic

(3) suppliers and purchasers, if elasticity of demand is greater than zero but less than infinity

(a) 1, 2, 3 correct

(b) 1, 2 only

(c) 2, 3 only

(d) 1 only

(e) 3 only

(University of London A level Economics 3, June 1988)

TRUE/FALSE

1 _____ Government spending on transfer payments has risen faster than national income since 1956, and continues to do so.

2 _____ Income tax is progressive because the marginal tax rate is greater than the average tax rate.

3 _____ The largest government revenue raiser in the UK in 1987 was taxes on goods.

4 _____ A football match is a public good.

5 _____ Social security payments damage social efficiency by pre-empting resources that would be more productively used in the private sector.

6 _____ The community charge is a tax on wealth.

7 _____ Public goods must be produced by the government.

8 _____ The underlying principle of income tax is the 'benefits principle'.

9 _____ The tax on tobacco tends to be regressive in its effect.

10 _____ The Laffer curve demonstrates that, for many 'big government–big tax' countries, a cut in tax rates would increase tax revenues.

11 _____ The community charge aims to make local authorities more responsible in their expenditure decisions.

12 _____ The theory of the 'invisible foot' suggests that efficiency is best achieved by having centralized decision-making for large local authority regions.

QUESTIONS FOR THOUGHT

1 Discuss the economic arguments for and against the imposition of high taxes to deter cigarette smoking.

(Associated Examining Board, GCE A level Economics Paper 3, June 1987)

2 Assess the case for the introduction of an annual community charge or poll tax upon adult residents, as a means of financing local government expenditure.

(Associated Examining Board, GCE A level Economics Paper 3, June 1988)

3 How would you expect a switch in policy from direct to indirect taxation to affect the distribution of income?

ANSWERS AND COMMENTS FOR CHAPTER 16

Please note Where questions are reproduced from GCE examinations, the examination boards bear no responsibility for the answers provided in this volume, which are the sole responsibility of the authors.

Important Concepts and Technical Terms

1	*e*	7	*r*	13	*f*	19	*l*
2	*s*	8	*j*	14	*p*	20	*a*
3	*m*	9	*q*	15	*d*	21	*c*
4	*t*	10	*o*	16	*g*	22	*k*
5	*u*	11	*i*	17	*h*		
6	*v*	12	*b*	18	*n*		

Exercises

1 (*a*)

(i)

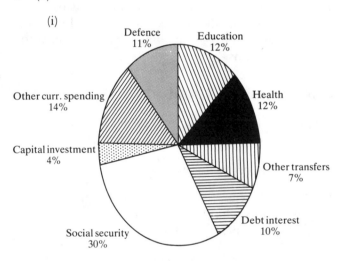

(ii)

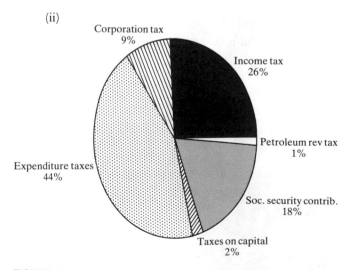

FIGURE A16.1 (*i*) Pattern of government expenditure; (*ii*) Sources of tax revenue

(*b*) We would expect to find an increase in the share of expenditure taxes, and a fall in the share of direct taxes—especially income tax. For instance, in the very first Budget of the first Thatcher government in 1979, the Chancellor reduced the rate of income tax, but introduced increases in VAT. If we were to see a pie-chart for 1978, we would expect to observe 'Income tax' with a larger slice, and 'Taxes on expenditure' with a smaller one.

(*c*) The increase in unemployment will have had a number of effects. On the expenditure side, we would expect in particular to see an increase in payments of social security benefits. On the revenue side, we would expect there to have been some fall in receipts from income tax.

2

TABLE A16.1 Marginal and average tax rates (All figures expressed in percentage terms)

Income level (£)	Scheme A (30% tax on income over £5000)		Scheme B (30% tax on income over £5000) (50% tax on income over £10 000)	
	Marginal rate (%)	Average rate (%)	Marginal rate (%)	Average rate (%)
3 000	0	0	0	0
9 000	30	13.3	30	13.3
12 000	30	17.5	50	20.8
20 000	30	22.5	50	32.5

Both schemes are progressive, with average tax rates rising with income: Scheme B is more progressive, as intuition suggests, with average rates rising more rapidly.

3 (*a*) As this good is a pure public good, one individual's consumption of the good does not prevent others from also consuming it; thus the marginal social benefit *DD* should be the vertical summation of *D*1 and *D*2—and we have of course drawn it that way.

(*b*) *OA*.

(*c*) If individual 1 actually pays *OA* for this good, then individual 2 need not pay at all in order to consume it. One of the characteristics of a public good is that individuals cannot be excluded from consuming it. This is at the heart of the 'free-rider' problem entailed with public goods.

(*d*) The marginal social benefit is given by the *DD* schedule—i.e. the amount *OE*.

(*e*) At this point marginal cost is at *OB*, which is well below marginal social benefit, suggesting that too little of the good is being produced.

(*f*) At *OG*, where marginal social benefit is equal to marginal cost.

4 (*a*) In a free market, equilibrium in the market is where marginal social benefit (demand) is equal to marginal private costs (supply) at *OE* quantity (and price *OA*).

(*b*) The socially efficient quantity is where *MSB* equals marginal *social* cost: the quantity *OD*.

(c) The triangle *GHJ*.

(d) The tax required is that which would induce producers to take decisions on the basis of *MSC* rather than *MPC*. A tax of the amount *GJ* would accomplish this.

(e) There are a number of possible examples. Perhaps the most obvious would be pollution, or traffic congestion.

5 (d).

6 In a situation where social costs are less than private costs, there will be a tendency for too *little* of the good to be produced, so a subsidy to firms might be appropriate. Option (a) would have the opposite effect. Conversely, if social costs are above private costs (as they were in exercise 4), then too much of the good will be produced in a free market, and a tax is the appropriate response. This eliminates option (b) and leads us to option (c) as being the correct answer.

7 The best way of tackling this question is to sketch a diagram to show the various options. This quickly reveals that all three statements are valid—option (a).

True/False

1 False: the decline in unemployment in the late 1980s brought with it a fall in the ratio of transfer payments to national income.

2 True.

3 True: see Section 16–1 of the main text.

4 False: in the case of a football match, there is the possibility of exclusion (see Section 16–3 of the main text).

5 False: this is an example of a transfer payment, which serves to redistribute income between groups in society (see Section 16–2 of the main text).

6 False: the community charge replaced a form of wealth tax (the tax on property known as the 'rates'), but it itself is not a wealth tax, but a simple flat-rate tax per person.

7 False: this is not necessarily so. The key feature of public goods is that the government should determine how much is produced, but this need not entail direct production.

8 False: see Section 16–3 of the main text.

9 True: this results from the typical consumption patterns of 'rich' and 'poor'.

10 False: the statement is too strong. It may be that this effect would be evident in some countries, but it has by no means been proved and many economists remain sceptical (see Section 16–4 of the main text).

11 True: see Box 16–1 in the main text.

12 False: it argues the very opposite (see Section 16–5 of the main text).

Questions for Thought

1 There are a number of issues to consider here. For instance, there is the question of *why* cigarette smoking is to be discouraged, perhaps because of the externalities produced or because cigarettes are a 'merit bad'. Another issue to be considered is whether high taxes are the best way of producing the socially desired outcome.

2 At the time the community charge was introduced in 1990, feelings ran very high. Try to cut through the emotion and analyse the *economic* arguments for and against the switch from the rates to the community charge.

3 *Hint* Is income tax a *progressive* or a *regressive* tax? How about expenditure taxes?

17

Competition Policy and Industrial Policy

We have seen that market failure leads to inefficiency in economic organization. Imperfect competition is one source of distortion which prevents the achievement of Pareto efficiency. However, there are industries where economies of scale encourage the growth of large—perhaps very large—firms. Unregulated, such firms would tend to produce at a point where marginal cost is less than marginal consumer benefit. The next two chapters examine such industries, beginning here with large firms in the private sector.

The extent to which price exceeds marginal cost in an imperfectly competitive market may be used as a measure of the *monopoly power* exerted by the firm. The *deadweight burden* or *social cost* of monopoly power has been variously estimated as being as low as less than 1 per cent of national income or as high as 7 per cent, the differences arising from alternative estimates of the elasticity of demand and also from other welfare costs included by some economists; for instance, it may be argued that firms operating under imperfect competition expend too many resources in advertising or in political lobbying to protect their market position.

In addition to the allocative inefficiency of monopoly, society may also be aware of the distributional aspects of monopoly—the fact that a monopoly is reaping large profits may be of concern. Some share of monopoly profits may eventually find its way into the pockets of the workers through the medium of insurance companies or pension funds. Taxing monopoly profits is a possible option for the authorities, but would do nothing to improve allocative efficiency.

How can the authorities attempt to regulate monopolies? One possibility is that monopolies could be ordered to be split into smaller independent firms. Alternatively, the authorities could allow the monopoly to continue but could monitor prices and profits to ensure that the firm was not abusing its market power. In the UK, regulation has tended to follow this latter course. This in part recognizes that the disadvantage of the deadweight burden may be offset by the lower average costs enabled by economies of scale.

The legal position in the UK is that a company can be referred to the *Monopolies and Mergers Commission* if it comes to control more than 25 per cent of the total market. The Monopolies and Mergers Commission and the *Restrictive Practices Court* are responsible for investigating the 'public interest'; these investigations have ranged widely in the past and have not been concerned solely with market share. This is probably sensible, given that UK firms must compete with other firms in the EC, so the share of the UK market alone may be a misleading indicator of monopoly power. There is also the danger that legislation could force collusion underground where it is less easily monitored. The open-minded stance of UK policy contrasts strongly with the attitude in the USA.

Firms may become large through *mergers* (the voluntary union of two companies) or through *takeover bids* (whereby one firm buys out the shareholders of another firm). *Horizontal mergers* allow firms to gain access to economies of scale. *Vertical mergers* allow improved co-ordination and planning. The gains from *conglomerate mergers* may be less obvious, but may allow increased financial security or economies of scale in marketing.

British industry has been becoming steadily more concentrated, especially with the merger boom of the 1960s, which continued into the 1970s. Evidence suggests that a new merger boom started in 1985. Mergers have been mainly horizontal, with an increasing number of conglomerate mergers in recent years. Mergers have been subject to scrutiny since 1965, but relatively few have actually been referred. As with monopoly, the issue to be considered is the balance of cost reductions against allocative inefficiency. There is some evidence that the cost reductions from mergers have not been substantial.

The regulation of natural monopolies poses especial problems. If the firm in such a market is permitted to set marginal revenue equal to marginal cost, there will be a large deadweight burden. However, setting price equal to marginal cost would put the firm into a loss-making situation because at this point marginal cost would be below average cost. One solution is *average cost pricing*—this may reduce but not eliminate the deadweight loss. An alternative is a *two-part tariff* system, whereby consumers pay a fixed charge which contributes towards fixed costs, and a charge per unit covering marginal cost.

A further alternative is to instruct the monopolist to produce at the social optimum, setting price equal to marginal cost, and to proffer a subsidy to cover the resulting loss. Where this solution is adopted, there is often pressure for *nationalization* (discussed in Chapter 18). A problem arises in maintaining productive efficiency, and *regulatory capture* may occur, in which the body set up as a watchdog of a monopoly ends up as its champion instead.

We have seen how *competition policy* attempts to combat the market failure resulting from scale economies and market power. There are other types of market failure which may encourage the authorities to introduce *industrial policy*.

The effects of such policy require careful analysis if they are to be successful. For instance, a *patent system* can be effective in preventing the stifling of invention by granting a firm a temporary legal monopoly. However, *pre-emptive patenting* to erect an entry barrier is an unintended misuse of such a system.

The social returns to large Research and Development (R & D) projects may be seen to exceed the expected private returns. Indeed, the riskiness of such projects may deter potential private investors. Hence the government has devoted more than 1 per cent of GDP each year to expenditure on R & D.

A national government may in some cases offer assistance to large companies (perhaps by way of pre-commitments) in order to enhance their strategic international position.

As time passes, structural change takes place: new industries gain in importance, old ones decline. Another form of market failure may be where new *sunrise* industries are unable to attract resources sufficiently readily to enable them to expand as rapidly as they could; or again, it may be that old *sunset* industries undergo a slow and painful demise. Industrial policy may be able to ease such problems, but it must be conducted with care.

IMPORTANT CONCEPTS AND TECHNICAL TERMS

Match each lettered concept with the appropriate numbered phrase:

(a) Monopolies and Mergers Commission
(b) Horizontal merger
(c) Industrial concentration
(d) Monopoly power
(e) Sunrise industries
(f) Natural monopoly
(g) Deadweight burden
(h) Vertical merger
(i) Regulatory capture
(j) Nationalized industries
(k) Takeover bid
(l) Sunset industries
(m) R & D
(n) Marginal cost pricing
(o) Conglomerate merger
(p) Competition policy
(q) Restrictive Practices Court
(r) Two-part tariff
(s) Patent system
(t) Industrial policy

1 Enjoyed by firms in an imperfectly competitive industry, enabling a firm to produce an output at which price exceeds marginal cost.
2 A governmental body set up to investigate whether or not a monopoly acts against the public interest, firms being referred to it by the Director-General of Fair Trading.
3 A voluntary union of two firms whose production activities are essentially unrelated.
4 The part of government production that covers the provision of private goods for sale through the market-place.
5 A governmental body set up in 1956 to examine agreements between firms supplying goods and services in the UK—for example, agreements on collusive pricing behaviour.
6 A situation in which one firm offers to buy out the shareholders of the second firm.
7 A part of government economic policy which aims to offset market failures arising from scale economies and market power.
8 A price system where users pay a fixed sum for access to the service and then pay a price per unit which reflects the marginal cost of production.
9 A price system where users pay a price equal to marginal production costs: a system infeasible for a private natural monopoly, as the firm would incur losses.
10 A union of two firms at different production stages in the same industry.
11 The loss to society resulting from the allocative inefficiency of imperfect competition.
12 Government economic policy designed to offset sources of market failure arising in the production process, other than those which result from scale economies and market power.
13 A situation in which activity in an industry becomes focused in a few firms.
14 An industry having enormous economies of scale such that only one firm can survive.
15 A policy instrument which confers a temporary legal monopoly on an inventor.
16 Activity undertaken by private and public sector organizations to discover and develop new products, processes, and technologies.
17 A union of two firms at the same production stage in the same industry.
18 A situation in which a regulator gradually comes to identify with the interests of the firm it regulates, eventually becoming its champion, rather than its watchdog.
19 The emerging new industries of the future, perhaps in hi-tech.
20 Industries in long-term decline.

EXERCISES

1 Identify each of the following as vertical, horizontal, or conglomerate mergers:
    (a) The union of a motor vehicle manufacturer with a tyre producer.
    (b) The union of a motor vehicle manufacturer with a retail car distributor.

(c) The union of a tobacco company with a cosmetic firm.

(d) The union of two firms producing man-made fibres.

2 In Figure 17.1, *DD* represents the market demand curve for a commodity. If organized as a competitive market, *BY* would represent the long-run marginal cost curve. However, a monopolist would face the long-run marginal (and average) cost curve *AX*.

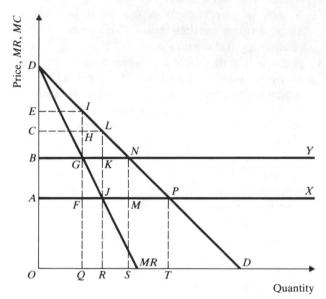

FIGURE 17.1 Monopoly and competition

(a) What would be the price and output of the competitive industry?

(b) What would be the price and output under monopoly?

(c) What is the deadweight loss to consumers from the monopoly as compared with the competitive industry?

(d) What area represents the cost savings of monopoly?

(e) What area represents monopoly profits?

(f) Explain why the monopolist and competitive industry might face different cost conditions.

3 Which is the 'odd one out' of the following companies?

(a) Pilkington Glass.

(b) Hoffman La Roche.

(c) Rank Xerox.

4 Conglomerate mergers are most likely to be embarked upon by a firm wishing to

(a) retain its share of the market for its main product

(b) gain control of its raw material supplies

(c) eliminate overseas competition

(d) diversify and extend its range of products

(e) reduce its dependence on supplies of skilled labour

(University of London GCE A level Economics 3, January 1989)

5 Motives for horizontal integration could include

(1) acquiring monopoly power.

(2) achieving external economies of scale.

(3) promoting product diversification.

(a) if 1, 2, and 3 are correct

(b) if 1 and 2 only are correct

(c) if 2 and 3 only are correct

(d) if 1 only is correct

(e) if 3 only is correct

(University of London GCE A level Economics 3, June 1989)

6 Figure 17.2 illustrates an industry which is a natural monopoly, with long-run average costs falling continuously over the relevant range of output.

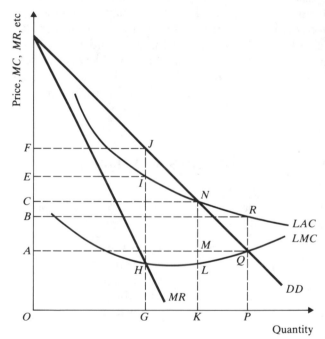

FIGURE 17.2 A natural monopoly

(a) If the industry is operated by an unregulated profit-maximizing monopolist, what price and output would be chosen?

(b) What would be the deadweight loss to society of this decision?

(c) What would be the level of monopoly profits?

(d) What would be the socially efficient levels of price and output?

(e) How would the monopolist act if allowed to produce only at the socially efficient point?

(f) If the industry has been nationalized and

produces at the socially efficient point, what subsidy is necessary?

(g) At what price and output would the industry break even?

(h) What would be the deadweight loss to society in this break-even position?

(i) Explain how a two-part tariff system might function in the industry.

7 Which of the following would tend to increase the degree of monopoly power of a firm?

(a) The concentration of production into a smaller number of industrial plants.

(b) The expiry of a patent.

(c) Diversification into a broader range of product lines.

(d) An increase in monopoly profits.

(e) A reduction in advertising expenditure.

(f) A fall in the cross price elasticity of demand for the firm's product.

8 Below are listed a number of policy actions. Identify each as belonging either to competition policy or to industrial policy:

(a) Referral to the Monopolies and Mergers Commission of a firm supplying more than 25 per cent of the total market for a particular commodity.

(b) The promotion of R & D.

(c) Assistance for a national firm involved in strategic international competition.

(d) Subsidization of an emerging hi-tech industry.

(e) A patent system.

(f) The restriction of excessive non-price competition (e.g. advertising).

(g) The subsidization of 'lame duck' industries in areas of high unemployment.

(h) The outlawing of explicit price-fixing agreements between firms in an industry.

(i) Nationalization.

TRUE/FALSE

1 _____ Each firm in an imperfectly competitive market enjoys a degree of monopoly power.

2 _____ The social cost of monopoly in the UK is probably equivalent to more than one-tenth of national income.

3 _____ UK policy towards monopolies is more liberal than that in the USA.

4 _____ Monopoly may allow social gain through the exploitation of economies of scale.

5 _____ One of the potential benefits of merger activity is that it allows an inspired management team to show its worth.

6 _____ We would expect that the law allowing mergers to be referred to the Monopolies and Mergers Commission would discourage mergers from taking place.

7 _____ The deadweight burden of a natural monopoly can be eliminated by forcing the firm to set price equal to long-run average cost.

8 _____ The experience with deregulation of airlines in the USA shows that the removal of legal barriers to entry encourages competition and leads to lower prices and higher usage.

9 _____ Pre-emptive patenting can be used as an effective strategic barrier to entry.

10 _____ Government expenditure on R & D in the UK is aimed mainly at the advancement of knowledge (via the universities) and at developing new products and processes in the industrial sector.

11 _____ An important part of industrial policy is to subsidize sunrise industies.

12 _____ It is silly to spend money on dole payments; a much better policy is to subsidize declining industries to protect employment.

QUESTIONS FOR THOUGHT

1 The UK economy is more open to international trade than that of the USA. To what extent does this justify the more liberal attitude adopted towards the regulation of monopolies in the UK?

2 It has often been suggested that here in Britain we are quite good at producing new ideas, but hopeless when it comes to exploiting them. Use the analysis presented in this chapter to explore why this state of affairs might arise.

3 Why do firms merge? Has recent United Kingdom experience shown that mergers are in the public interest?

(Associated Examining Board GCE A level Economics Paper 3, June 1988)

ANSWERS AND COMMENTS FOR CHAPTER 17

Please note Where questions are reproduced from GCE examinations, the examination boards bear no responsibility for the answers provided in this volume, which are the sole responsibility of the authors.

Important Concepts and Technical Terms

1	*d*	6	*k*	11	*g*	16	*m*
2	*a*	7	*p*	12	*t*	17	*b*
3	*o*	8	*r*	13	*c*	18	*i*
4	*j*	9	*n*	14	*f*	19	*e*
5	*q*	10	*h*	15	*s*	20	*l*

Exercises

1 (*a*) and (*b*) are examples of vertical mergers. If in (*a*) the vehicle manufacturer took over the tyre producer, this could be described as 'backward vertical integration'—the vehicle firm is expanding activity back down the production process. A vehicle firm expanding by buying car distributors would be indulging in 'forward vertical integration'.
   (*c*) represents a conglomerate merger—there is no direct production link between tobacco and cosmetics.
   (*d*) is an example of a horizontal merger where the firms presumably hope to benefit from economies of scale.

2 (*a*) Price *OB*, output *OS*.
   (*b*) Price *OC*, output *OR*.
   (*c*) The area *KLN*.
   (*d*) *ABKJ*.
   (*e*) *ACLJ*.
   (*f*) The most likely explanation is that the monopolist is able to exploit economies of scale.

3 (*b*): both Pilkington Glass and Rank Xerox were honourably acquitted by the Monopolies and Mergers Commission, in spite of huge market shares and healthy profits. Hoffmann La Roche received praise for its competence and product quality, but its profit rate was said to be unjustifiably high (see Section 17–2 of the main text).

4 (*d*).

5 (*b*).

6 (*a*) *LMC* = *MR* at output *OG*, price *OF*.
   (*b*) The area *HJQ*.
   (*c*) *EFJI*.
   (*d*) *P* = *LMC* at output *OP*, price *OA*.
   (*e*) At this point, long-run average costs (*OB*) exceed average revenue (*OA*), and a private monopolist would be forced out of business.
   (*f*) The necessary subsidy would be represented by the area *ABRQ*.
   (*g*) *LAC* = *AR* at output *OK*, price *OC*.
   (*h*) *NLQ*.

   (*i*) Under a two-part tariff system, customers would be charged a price per unit equal to marginal cost, plus a fixed charge to cover the loss (see answer (*f*)) that would otherwise be sustained.

7 (*f*): this is the only factor mentioned which leads to a reduction in competition. If you sketch a diagram, you will see that, if cross elasticity falls and thus the demand curve becomes steeper, the deadweight loss to society increases.

8 Policies (*a*), (*f*), and (*h*) are elements of competition policy. Item (*i*) can also be viewed in this way, being one way of tackling the 'natural monopoly' problem. The other policies would be regarded as belonging to industrial policy.

True/False

1 True: see Section 17–1 of the main text.

2 False: few estimates have been set so high, although Cowling and Mueller set it as high as 7 per cent.

3 True: see Section 17–2 of the main text.

4 True—but society may wish to take steps to ensure a just distribution of the monopoly profits.

5 This could be regarded as true or false—it depends upon your point of view. Most economists would tend to be sceptical.

6 True enough, but the extent to which this directly affects merger activity is not clear. A study by Pickering in the *Journal of Industrial Economics*, March 1983, suggests that 'about one-third of all merger proposals referred to the MMC have been abandoned on reference'. There may be several reasons for such abandonments.

7 False: the deadweight burden will be reduced but not eliminated.

8 False: the initial effects were encouraging to those who believe in free markets, but subsequently the establishment of strategic barriers to entry eroded these benefits. (See Box 17–1 in the main text.)

9 True: see Section 17–5 of the main text.

10 False: more than one-half of such expenditure in the UK is related to military defence. For a useful economist's eye view of R & D, see an article by Paul Stoneman in the *Economic Review*, March 1986.

11 Not necessarily true: it is important to approach this question carefully—see Section 17–5 of the main text again.

12 Often false: if structural change must take place, then it may be unwise to try to resist it; better to manage the adjustment. However, unless new industries can be developed to replace old ones, it may sometimes be desirable to ease the transition by temporarily subsidizing lame ducks.

Questions for Thought

No hints this chapter.

18 Nationalization and Privatization

A prominent economic issue of recent years has been the choice between public and private ownership of certain industries. Are there some industries which function better under state ownership? Are there some industries previously under public ownership which would operate more effectively if returned to the private sector?

As was noted in the previous chapter, one solution to the natural monopoly dilemma is to instruct the industry concerned to produce at the socially optimal price–output combination, and to subsidize the resulting loss. Some form of monitoring will be required to ensure technical efficiency in this situation.

Such a system may not be workable for all industries. In some cases, the solution may be to have marginal cost pricing plus a government subsidy, together with monitoring to ensure technical efficiency. The subsidy itself may impose a deadweight burden elsewhere because of the taxation required to finance it.

Nationalized industries are industries in which the government produces private goods for sale. They tend to be relatively capital-intensive industries. An industry may be nationalized because it is a natural monopoly, because of externalities, or because of distributional or equity considerations.

Investment decisions in nationalized industries should be taken with reference to the present value of social costs and benefits, using a lower discount rate than would be used by private firms. In the absence of distortions elsewhere, prices should be set equal to social marginal cost. *Peak load pricing* may allow overall gains in efficiency.

Official attitudes towards the nationalized industries in the UK have changed in recent years. In the immediate postwar period, the concern was mainly to ensure that nationalized industries broke even and enjoyed independent management. From 1967 onwards, emphasis switched towards attaining first-best Pareto efficiency through marginal cost pricing, the use of a social rate of discount below the prevailing private discount rate, and the recognition of a distinction between private and social costs. Since 1978 there has been a further switch of emphasis, with less concern expressed for marginal cost pricing and with the imposition of *cash limits*, intended to reduce the social cost of distortionary taxes elsewhere in the economy. This policy has been further pursued by the recent moves to 'privatize' industries (or parts of industries) formerly under public control.

Difficulties arise when we try to devise some means of assessing the performance of nationalized industries. The earlier analysis of natural monopolies tells us that profitability is not a good indicator of efficiency in this context. Indeed, we *expect* that a natural monopoly producing at the socially optimal position (in the interests of *allocative efficiency*) will make a financial loss. However, we also wish to monitor *production efficiency*—the question of whether the industry is operating on the lowest possible cost curve.

Do private firms tend to achieve higher productive efficiency than firms in the public sector? A study by George Yarrow suggested that they did—so long as they were operating in markets where there was sufficient competition to keep them on their toes. We must recognize that large private sector firms are run by managers, just as are public sector enterprises. The question then is whether the incentives for private sector managers are more effective than those for their counterparts in the public sector. In other words, the issue concerns the relative effectiveness of shareholders and government in the role of watchdog.

The monitoring and comparison problem is further clouded by the fact that the government may pursue political objectives that at times overrule questions of efficiency in the nationalized industries. For instance, there have been times when pay awards to workers in the public sector have been dictated by central government's anti-inflation policy. *Privatization* may itself constitute a pre-commitment by the government *not* to act in this way; indeed, this may be one of the major arguments in favour of privatization.

The recent wave of privatization has provided some interesting empirical observations and insights. The process began with the sale of council houses and flats, but since then a number of public sector companies have been privatized—and further sales are planned. In many cases, it has been observed that the performance of nationalized industries *prior to* privatization improved—substantially, in some instances. On the one hand, this suggests that some inefficiency may indeed have been present. On the other hand, it reveals that there is nothing intrinsic in public ownership that renders efficiency impossible. Perhaps it is a case of providing managers with appropriate targets and incentives. Privatization has been criticized for being a short-sighted policy on the part of the government, producing benefits only in the short run. The validity of this criticism depends to a great extent upon how the proceeds from the sales are used. If they serve to allow a tax-cut-financed consumer boom, or if the sale was underpriced, then the criticism may carry some weight, although as far as underpricing is concerned the government may claim that there are external benefits from expanding share ownership. However, if the proceeds are used for investment in physical capital or for the retirement of outstanding government debt, then the validity of the short-sightedness argument may be questioned.

Finally, it may be noted that government responsibility for these large, previously nationalized activities does not end with privatization: the question of regulation and monitoring remains.

IMPORTANT CONCEPTS AND TECHNICAL TERMS

Match each lettered concept with the appropriate numbered phrase:

(a) Regulation   (h) Marginal cost
(b) Peak load pricing   pricing
(c) Privatization   (i) Nationalization
(d) Employee buyout   (j) Test discount rate
(e) Allocative efficiency (k) Cash limits
(f) Efficiency audits   (l) Offer price
(g) Production
     efficiency

1 The acquisition of private companies by the public sector.

2 The sale of public sector companies to the private sector.

3 A price system where users pay a price equal to marginal production costs: a system that is not viable for a private natural monopoly as the firm would incur losses.

4 The price at which shares in an enterprise to be privatized are initially sold to investors: this often turned out to be below the free market price established on the first day of trading on the stock market.

5 A system of price discrimination whereby peak-time users pay higher prices to reflect the higher marginal cost of supplying them.

6 A target profit or loss for a nationalized industry, set by the government in the light of the industry's circumstances.

7 Measures adopted to ensure that privatized companies do not misuse their market situation.

8 The social rate of interest used after 1967 for evaluating investment decisions in nationalized industries.

9 A state in which firms are on the lowest possible cost curve so there is no slack or waste.

10 A state in which the balance of activities in the economy is Pareto-efficient such that no reallocation of resources could increase social welfare.

11 Investigations carried out by the Monopolies and Mergers Commission to check up on management performance of nationalized industries.

12 A privatization in which all shares are sold to employees of the enterprise, such as that of the National Freight Corporation.

EXERCISES

1 Which of the following have been advanced as reasons for the nationalization of an industry?
    (a) A natural monopoly situation exists, with large economies of scale meaning that average cost lies above marginal cost.
    (b) Externalities exist, such that the social gains from the provision of a commodity exceed the private benefits for which direct users are prepared to pay.
    (c) There is a need to protect the interests of some members of society who might lose out if profit maximization were the sole criterion for the provision of a service.
    (d) Certain basic industries should be under state control.
    Which of these reasons do *you* consider to be valid?

2 Which of the following effects is/are *not* claimed as being associated with privatization?
    (a) An increase in competition—and hence a lowering of costs and prices.
    (b) A reduction in political interference.
    (c) An increase in the efficiency of management.
    (d) A reduction in the money that the government needs to borrow to finance its expenditure programme.
    (e) A reduction of deadweight burden.
    (f) A widening of consumer choice, as private firms must be more sensitive to market demand.

3 Table 18.1 shows information about experience with share prices for a number of companies priva-

TABLE 18.1 Share prices and privatization

Company	Date of first trading	Offer price (pence)	Price at end of first day's trading (pence)
Amersham International	25/02/82	142	188
Enterprise Oil	2/07/84	185	185
TSB	10/10/86	100	136
British Gas	8/12/86	135	148
British Airways	11/02/87	125	169
Rolls Royce	20/05/87	170	232

Source: Economic Review Data Supplement, September 1988

tized during the 1980s. (Some similar information may be found in Table 18–2 of the main text.)

(a) Calculate the percentage change in the share price on the opening day's trading for each of the companies.

(b) Do your calculations necessarily imply that there was deliberate underpricing of the shares in setting the offer prices?

(c) Use the financial pages of the newspaper to check out the current share prices of these companies. By how much have the prices changed since the first day's trading? Do you observe much variation among the companies? What factors might help to explain any differences you observe?

(d) In the case of all but one of the companies in Table 18.1, the offer price was announced. In the other case, the initial price was based on tenders placed by individuals and institutions. Can you guess which company is the odd one out?

4 Suppose that you are in authority, and are contemplating the privatization of an industry currently within your responsibility. The following thoughts run through your mind. Identify each as being in favour of or against privatization, and assess their validity.

(a) The industry has consistently incurred losses over a period of many years and thus is a drain on the government's coffers.

(b) The industry enjoys substantial economies of scale and is a natural monopoly, so losses are to be expected. Society as a whole benefits from the scale economies, which would be sacrificed if the industry were to be broken up into a number of smaller firms.

(c) In the absence of competition, the industry has been operating less efficiently than it could have done.

(d) If the industry were to be privatized, the shareholders would be such a diverse group of people that they would be no spur to efficiency.

(e) Privatization would enable the industry to be freed from interference by the government in their pursuit of various political objectives.

(f) Keeping the industry under public control would be a safeguard, ensuring that needy groups in society are protected from a withdrawal of service.

(g) The proceeds from the sale of the industry can be used to finance necessary capital investment in other parts of the public sector.

What other arguments might influence your thinking on this matter? On balance, would you decide to privatize or to maintain the status quo?

5 In 1985, factor incomes in public corporations totalled £23.5 billion compared with a figure of £305.7 billion for the UK economy as a whole. Employment in these industries amounted to 1.3 million of a total employed labour force of 24.4 million. Net capital stock (at current replacement cost) was estimated to be £138.0 billion of a total of £649.9 billion (this excludes dwellings). (These figures all come from CSO, *United Kingdom National Accounts*, 1986 edn, HMSO.)

Calculate the percentage share of the nationalized industries (public corporations) in income, employment, and investment. Comment upon the relative labour or capital intensity of this sector and explain why this pattern should have occurred.

6 Suppose that you are the manager of a firm in the private sector considering a capital investment project. Three plans have been submitted for your consideration (all figures are in £ million).

Project	Private benefits	Private costs	Externalities Favourable	Unfavourable
A	400	380	20	80
B	320	350	120	20
C	350	300	70	80

(a) If your aim is to maximize financial profits for your firm, which project do you choose?

(b) Suppose you know that your shareholders are keen to see successful sales figures rather than large profits (so long as there is no financial loss). Which project do you now choose?

(c) Suppose now that the same projects are submitted to the manager of a nationalized industry. Which project would maximize economic welfare for society as a whole?

7 One area in which we have seen government intervention in the past is that of housing. This exercise considers the relative merits of two alternative schemes for public housing policy, namely, the provision of council housing and the issue of rent vouchers.

Figure 18.1 summarizes demand and supply conditions for each of the schemes. The initial equilibrium in the housing market is represented by the demand curve *DD* and supply curve *SS*.

(a) In this 'without-policy' state, identify equilibrium rent and quantity of housing.

(b) Suppose that the local authority now issues rent vouchers to needy families. Using the figure, describe the response in the housing market, and identify the new equilibrium rent and quantity of housing.

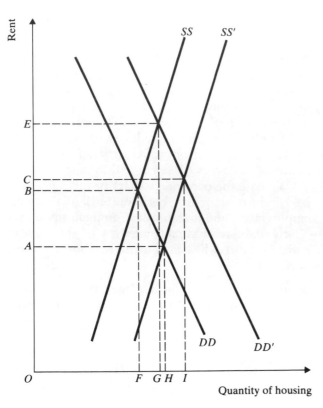

FIGURE 18.1   Council housing or rent vouchers?

(c)   Suppose that, instead of issuing rent vouchers, the local authority provides council housing. How will the market now respond, and what are the new equilibrium levels of rent and quantity of housing?

(d)   Which of the two schemes has the greatest effect on the quantity of housing? Why should this be?

(e)   Assess the relative merits of the two schemes.

TRUE/FALSE

1   _____ By the 1960s most countries in Europe had a significant sector of industrial production under public ownership and control.

2   _____ If a nationalized industry employs workers who would otherwise have been unemployed, their social opportunity cost is close to zero.

3   _____ To ensure efficiency, investment decisions made by nationalized industries should be made with reference to market rates of interest.

4   _____ Peak load pricing is a system of price discrimination.

5   _____ The Monopolies and Mergers Commission has no power to investigate nationalized industries—only private sector firms can be referred.

6   _____ Incentives for private managers to be efficient are strong because actual and potential shareholders monitor their performance carefully.

7   _____ Private industries are immune from government interference in the pursuit of political aims.

8   _____ Selling off state assets mortgages the country's future.

9   _____ In the period up to 1986, all privatization share offers were underpriced.

10   _____ The most successful of the early privatizations were those involving companies which faced significant competition after privatization.

QUESTIONS FOR THOUGHT

1   Discuss the incentives facing managers in public and private sector enterprises. Think about their relative effectiveness and the potential for improvement.

2   'Privatisation may have short-term benefits but in the long run it will reduce economic welfare.' Discuss.

(University of London GCE A level Economics Paper 1, June 1988)

ANSWERS AND COMMENTS FOR CHAPTER 18

Please note Where questions are reproduced from GCE examinations, the examination boards bear no responsibility for the answers provided in this volume, which are the sole responsibility of the authors.

Important Concepts and Technical Terms

1	*i*	4	*l*	7	*a*	10	*e*
2	*c*	5	*b*	8	*j*	11	*f*
3	*h*	6	*k*	9	*g*	12	*d*

Exercises

1 All have been advanced at one time or another: see Section 18–1 of the main text.

2 In recent privatization debates, many claims have been made, covering most of those mentioned, with the probable exception of (*e*). Some of the effects may be of limited significance in practice or of only short-run relevance. For instance, effect (*d*) is important only in the short run, when the proceeds from the sale of an industry can be used to help fund expenditure. Time alone will reveal the importance of these effects. Further discussion may be found in an article by George Yarrow in *Economic Review*, November 1988.

3 (*a*)

TABLE A18.1 Share prices and privatization

Company	% change in price on first day's trading
Amersham International	32.4
Enterprise Oil	0.0
TSB	36.0
British Gas	9.6
British Airways	35.2
Rolls Royce	36.5

(*b*) Not necessarily: it is no easy matter to fix an offer price several weeks ahead of the sale—after all, share prices in general may be volatile over such a period. None the less, it is noticeable that in all the cases cited there was a significant increase in the share price on the first day's trading—except in the case of Enterprise Oil. You should also notice that Table 18.1 does not list *all* the cases of privatization that have taken place.

(*c*) As we do not know when you will be tackling this question, we cannot provide an answer for you.

(*d*) Enterprise Oil.

4 Thoughts (*a*), (*c*), (*e*), and (*g*) might incline you towards privatization, but the remainder represent the opposite point of view. Unless you have strong prior views taking you in one direction or the other, I expect you found it quite difficult to weight up the arguments and come to a firm decision. As you learn more about economics, you will find that there are many topic areas like this where there are no clear-cut or definitive answers.

5 From the figures given, public corporations in 1985 accounted for 7.7 per cent of national income, 5.3 per cent of employment, and 21 per cent of net capital stock (excluding dwellings). The clear implication is that these industries are relatively capital-intensive. This should be no great surprise, as it is in such capital-intensive industries that we would expect fixed costs to be important, creating the conditions for a potential natural monopoly. With the privatization programme of the 1980s, these proportions have decreased: the corresponding figures for 1988 were respectively 5.4, 3.5, and 16.5 per cent.

6 Tabulating the net private and social gains from each of the projects, we find the following (notice that figures in brackets represent negative numbers):

Project	Financial profit (loss)	Net overall gain (loss)
A	20	(40)
B	(30)	70
C	50	40

The net overall gain (loss) column takes account of both private and social costs and benefits.

(*a*) Profits are maximized by choosing project C—but notice that the net overall gain, while positive, is smaller than the private gain accruing to the firm.

(*b*) Revenue is maximized by project A, but this is clearly bad news for the community at large, as this project shows a net overall loss.

(*c*) The project that maximizes economic welfare generally is project B, although this entails a financial loss for the enterprise.

True/False

1 True: see Introduction to Chapter 18 in the main text.

2 True: see Section 18–1 of the main text.

3 False: nationalized industries should use a lower discount rate, and undertake some projects that the private sector would consider unprofitable.

4 True: peak-time users pay higher prices to reflect the higher marginal cost of supplying them.

5 False: nationalized industries became subject to referral in the 1980 Competition Act (see Section 18–2 of the main text).

6 False: in practice, individual shareholders have little influence and face a free-rider problem (see Section 18–3 of the main text).

7 Not always true: for instance, private oil companies operating in the North Sea have been faced with petroleum revenue tax, often at very high rates.

8 There is no simple true/false response to this one: in part, it depends upon how the proceeds are disposed.

9 False: *most* were underpriced, in the sense that the opening free market price was higher than the offer price. However, Enterprise Oil opened at the offer price and Britoil opened below it. (See Section 18–4 of the main text.)

10 True.

Questions for Thought

1   This issue is discussed at some length in Section 18–3 of the main text.

2   We know this is a big question, covering much of the material of this chapter. However, it will do you no harm to try to marshal your thoughts and to focus on the salient points. This is part of the economist's skill.

19

General Equilibrium and Welfare Economics

This chapter brings together much of the subject matter of the book so far. In it we think of a complete economy as a series of interlocking and interrelated markets, and discuss whether (and how) it is possible to achieve a general equilibrium of all markets simultaneously. We also examine whether such a situation is a desirable state of affairs for society as a whole.

For simplicity, we consider an economy in which there are just two goods being produced and only one consumer. Labour input is variable, but capital is fixed. While it is quite possible to relax these assumptions, the essence of the results would be unaffected by so doing—and the analysis is more clearly seen in this simple world.

We begin by discussing *production efficiency*—that is, by seeing what combinations of the two goods can be produced in the economy if production is so organized as to avoid waste. These maximum attainable combinations can be depicted on a diagram as the *production possibility frontier* (PPF), which we first encountered back in Chapter 1.

The PPF can be derived using the production functions for the two goods, for instance by progressively switching labour from one industry to the other and calculating output of the two goods. During this process we see that there is a trade-off between producing more of one good and less of the other: this trade-off is measured as the *marginal rate of transformation* between the goods—that is, the slope of the PPF. This provides a representation of the opportunity cost of one good in terms of the other. The shape of the PPF is determined by the nature of the two production functions. Given diminishing marginal productivity in both industries, the PPF will be downward-sloping and concave to the origin.

Production efficiency is not sufficient of itself: we also need to consider consumption. In our single consumer model, we can overlay the indifference curves on to the PPF and thus determine the maximum attainable utility level—which will occur where an indifference curve just touches the frontier. This signals the optimum combination of the two goods, which in turn shows how the available labour force should be divided between the two industries.

How do we get to this optimum position? In a command economy, the planners could allocate labour to the appropriate industries in order to produce the 'correct' amounts of the two goods—or they could if they had enough information to know what the optimum quantities were! In a complex real-world economy, it is unlikely that this information would be available. How else can the best allocation be achieved? The *Invisible Hand* may take us there, and we have already seen that in the absence of distortions a free competitive market system would be Pareto-efficient. If this is so, then government intervention would be needed only to correct for market failure.

With a free competitive market system, flexibility of wages would ensure full employment, thus taking the economy to the PPF. The precise point on the frontier where the economy settles depends on the relative prices of the goods. With equilibrium in both goods and labour markets, the economy will move to a position on the PPF where the marginal rate of transformation is equal to the negative of the price ratio.

From the consumption side, our individual consumer chooses a point at which the budget line just touches an indifference curve—which must also be just touching the PPF, given that we have assumed production efficiency. Thus there are forces in the freely competitive market which might result in a *general equilibrium* position in which each agent is a price-taker and in which there is simultaneous equilibrium in all markets.

Given our assumptions about the shape of the indifference curves and the PPF, this optimum point is unique: there is only one ratio of prices which allows general equilibrium. Recall from Chapter 15 that a tax on one good which alters the price ratio destroys Pareto efficiency even if the economy remains on the PPF. When there is more than one consumer, society will also have to consider the distribution of resources between individuals. In this situation, there is no unique solution to the question of efficient resource allocation, but a number of alternative allocations represent different distributions between individuals.

This discussion seems to suggest that the free market system will produce an ideal outcome for society. However, it is important to bear in mind the qualifications which must accompany this analysis: in particular, the result depends upon the absence of distortions. Thus, the presence of imperfect competition, externalities, and public goods or other missing markets may impede general equilibrium. Government reaction to unavoidable distortions may need to be guided by the theory of the second best.

By setting up the problem of choice as deciding present against future consumption, we can use the analysis to examine the question of *savings* and *investment*. In choosing how much of the available resources are to be consumed *now*, society implicitly also chooses how much of current resources are invested in the form of new capital goods which will produce goods for consumption in the *future*. In this context, the shape and slope of the PPF depend upon the productivity of new capital goods, and the shape and slope of the indifference curves are strongly influenced by the consumer's attitude towards thrift. Bringing the two together, the *rate of interest* is seen as the 'price' which brings savings and investment into equality.

IMPORTANT CONCEPTS AND TECHNICAL TERMS

Match each lettered concept with the appropriate numbered phrase:

(a) Opportunity cost
(b) Production efficiency
(c) Invisible Hand
(d) Savings
(e) General equilibrium
(f) Investment
(g) Production possibility frontier
(h) Marginal rate of substitution
(i) Equilibrium rate of interest
(j) An allocation of resources
(k) Rate of return on investment
(l) Marginal rate of transformation

1 A doctrine by which a socially efficient general equilibrium is achieved in a free market even though individual agents are motivated by self-interest.
2 The amount lost by not using a resource in its best alternative use.
3 A complete description of the factors being used, the goods being produced, and the way these goods are distributed to consumers.
4 A curve showing the maximum quantity of one good that can be produced given the output of the other good, defining output combinations that are production-efficient.
5 The increase in future consumption relative to current consumption forgone.
6 The rate at which output of one good must be sacrificed to allow increased production of the other good: the slope of the PPF.
7 The use of current resources to increase the capital stock.
8 A situation in which there is equilibrium in factor markets, production, and consumption.
9 The rate at which a consumer sacrifices one good to increase consumption of another good without changing total utility: the slope of an indifference curve.
10 The rate of interest which brings savings and investment into equilibrium.

11 A situation in which, for a given output of all other goods, the economy is producing the maximum possible quantity of the last good, given the resources and technology available to the economy as a whole.
12 The difference between income and current consumption.

EXERCISES

1 An economy has six workers producing two goods, bread and beer. Capital is fixed and cannot be moved between the industries, although labour can so move. The short-run production functions for the two goods are given in Table 19.1

TABLE 19.1   Production functions for bread and beer

Number of workers	Production of bread (units/week)	Production of beer (units/week)
0	0	0
1	120	180
2	220	330
3	300	450
4	360	540
5	400	600
6	420	630

(a) Plot the production possibility frontier for the economy.
(b) What does the shape of the frontier suggest concerning the nature of returns to labour in these industries?
(c) What does the shape of the frontier suggest for the marginal rate of transformation as workers are moved from bread to beer production?
(d) Confirm your answer to (c) by filling in the columns of Table 19.2, beginning with all workers involved in bread production.

TABLE 19.2   The marginal rate of transformation between bread and beer

Extra workers in beer	Extra output of beer	Lost output of bread	Marginal rate of transformation
1			
2			
3			
4			
5			
6			

2 Figure 19.1 shows the PPF for an economy producing milk and cheese. The single consumer in this economy has preferences represented by the indifference curves U_0U_0, U_1U_1, and U_2U_2.

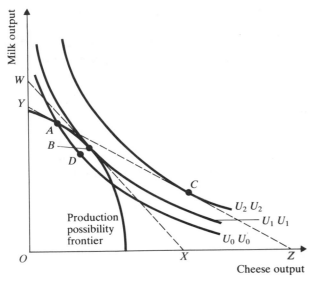

FIGURE 19.1 The consumer and general equilibrium

(a) Which of the points A, B, and C would be preferred by the consumer?
(b) What is the highest level of utility attainable?
(c) Which of the lines WX, YZ represents the relative prices of milk and cheese that would prevail if the consumer were able to choose this consumption point?
(d) Suppose the economy is at point D. What free market forces would move the economy towards the PPF?
(e) Suppose the price line is given by YZ. At what points will producers and consumers wish to be? How can they be reconciled?
(f) Which point is Pareto-efficient?

3 Figure 19.2 shows an economy in equilibrium,

with the single consumer choosing between current and future consumption.
(a) Identify the equilibrium point.
(b) How much is saved at this point?
(c) If all current resources were invested in new capital goods, what would be the maximum attainable future consumption level?
(d) How would you measure the rate of return on investment?
(e) What determines the slope of the price line?

4 Back in Chapter 6, we saw that a consumer's reaction to a price change can be analysed in terms of real income and substitution effects. Explain how the same sort of decomposition can be used to analyse the effect on savings of a change in the interest rate. What would you expect to be the net effect on savings of an increase in the interest rate?

5 Which of the following is/are *not* a feature of a general equilibrium in a two-good (x and y), one-consumer economy?
(a) $P_x MPL_x = P_y MPL_y$.
(b) $\dfrac{MPL_x}{MPL_y} = \dfrac{P_y}{P_x}$.
(c) $MRS = -\dfrac{P_y}{P_x}$.
(d) $-MRT = -MRS$.
(e) $P_x = P_y$.
(f) $P_x = \dfrac{wage}{MPL_x}$.

6 Figure 19.3 shows the maximum numbers of lorries and cars which can be produced with given factor inputs. From the diagram we can deduce that, as lorry output increases, the opportunity cost of one lorry in terms of cars

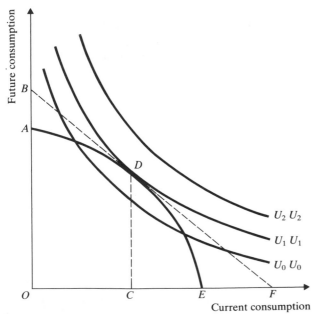

FIGURE 19.2 Current and future consumption

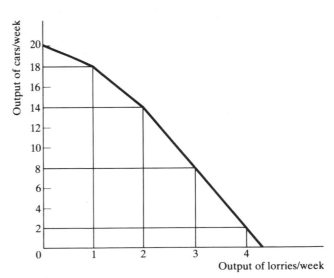

FIGURE 19.3 Production possibilities for a motor manufacturer

(a) is constant at first, then rises.
(b) is constant at first, then falls.
(c) rises at first, then is constant.
(d) falls at first, then is constant.

7 Consider a movement of a production possibility
   frontier between current and future consumption.
   Which of the following factors would cause the
   new frontier to have a steeper slope at each output
   of current consumption? (*Note:* more than one
   answer may be valid.)
   (a) An increase in thriftiness of members of so-
        ciety.
   (b) An increase in the productivity of new capital
        equipment.
   (c) A fall in the rate of interest.
   (d) A rise in the rate of interest.
   (e) An increase in investment.
   (f) A technological break-through improving
        efficiency in production.

8 Figure 19.4 shows a PPF between current and
   future consumption. Households must pay income
   tax on interest earnings that they receive. R_1 and
   R_2 represent 'price lines'.

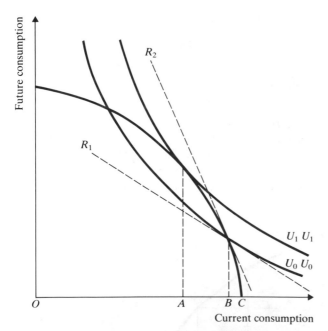

FIGURE 19.4 The distortionary effect of taxation

(a) What would be the level of savings in the
     absence of the tax?
(b) Which of the price lines represents that faced
     by households—i.e., the price line rep-
     resenting the households' after-tax trade-off
     between current and future consumption?
(c) How much will households save given the
     presence of the tax?

(d) Which of the price lines represents that faced
     by firms?
(e) What is the loss of welfare implied by this
     position for the society as compared with the
     socially efficient point?

TRUE/FALSE

1 _____ Any point within the production
   possibility frontier represents a position where an
   economy is failing to make full or efficient use of
   available resources.
2 _____ The slope of the production
   possibility frontier is known as the marginal rate
   of transformation between the two goods.
3 _____ The marginal rate of transformation is *usually* negative.
4 _____ Any point on the production
   possibility frontier is socially efficient.
5 _____ Many economists believe that
   the market mechanism is an important device
   because it economizes on the amount of information concerning tastes and production technology that the government needs to collect to
   ensure Pareto efficiency.
6 _____ Flexibility of wages and prices
   leads to a general equilibrium in which goods and
   labour markets clear.
7 _____ If perfect competition reigns in
   all markets, production efficiency is assured because all prices are set equal to marginal production costs.
8 _____ The marginal rate of substitution
   between two goods is the slope of the price line.
9 _____ The Pareto criterion may fail to
   provide a unique social optimum where we need
   to consider alternative distributions of resources
   between a number of individuals.
10 _____ It is not necessary to eliminate *all*
   distortions in order to prove that free markets
   work best.
11 _____ A resource allocation can still be
   Pareto-efficient even if the marginal rate of substitution is different from the marginal rate of
   transformation.
12 _____ The analysis of the choice between current and future consumption suggests
   that investment will depend upon the rate of
   interest.

QUESTIONS FOR THOUGHT

1 Suppose you want to analyse a general competitive
   equilibrium for an economy with two consumers
   as well as two goods. How would the problem

differ from the analysis of a one-consumer world? Can you think how this might be tackled?

2 Think back over the last month. In that time, you will have no doubt spent money on consumer goods—perhaps also you 'saved' some money. What were the most important factors which influenced your choice of how much to spend—and save? Can you relate these factors to the analysis of the choice between current and future consumption?

3 Discuss how market failure interferes with the achievement of Pareto efficiency.

ANSWERS AND COMMENTS FOR CHAPTER 19

Please note Where questions are reproduced from GCE examinations, the examination boards bear no responsibility for the answers provided in this volume, which are the sole responsibility of the authors.

Important Concepts and Technical Terms

1 *c*	4 *g*	7 *f*	10 *i*
2 *a*	5 *k*	8 *e*	11 *b*
3 *j*	6 *l*	9 *h*	12 *d*

Exercises

1 (a) Using the figures in Table 19.1, we see that, if all workers are employed in the bread industry, the economy produces 420 units of bread but no beer. If half the workers are in each industry, production is 300 units of bread and 450 units of beer. Plotting all such combinations gives us the *PPF*.

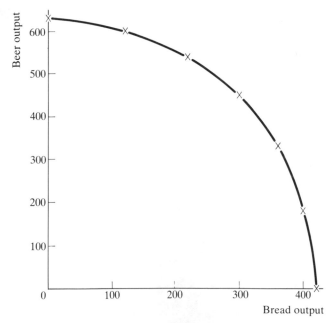

FIGURE A19.1 The production possibility frontier

(b) The shape suggests diminishing returns to labour in these industries (see Section 19–2 of the main text).

(c) We would expect the marginal rate of transformation to become numerically smaller: as more workers are employed in producing beer, their *MPL* falls, but increasing amounts of bread are sacrificed.

(d)

TABLE A19.1 The marginal rate of transformation between bread and beer

(1) Extra workers in beer	(2) Extra output of beer	(3) Lost output of bread	(4) Marginal rate of transformation −(Col (2)/ Col (3))
1	180	20	−9.0
2	150	40	−3.75
3	120	60	−2.0
4	90	80	−1.125
5	60	100	−0.6
6	30	120	−0.25

2 (a) Point C is on the highest indifference curve—but, of course, it cannot be reached, being beyond the PPF.

(b) U_1U_1 at point B.

(c) WX is tangent to PPF and the indifference curve U_1U_1 at point B, and thus represents relative prices.

(d) At D, the economy is below full employment. Flexibility of wages would enable a move towards the frontier.

(e) Producers will wish to be at A and consumers at C. There is excess demand for cheese, and excess supply of milk. The price of cheese will tend to rise and the price of milk to fall in response to these market conditions. Thus the economy moves back to a general equilibrium at B.

(f) B.

3 (a) D is the equilibrium, where the price line, PPF, and indifference curve all touch.

(b) OE represents maximum current consumption, OC is actual consumption, so the difference CE is savings.

(c) OA: but starvation may set in before the 'future' is reached if no resources are currently consumed.

(d) By the slope of the PPF.

(e) The rate of interest.

4 Suppose the interest rate increases. The consumer's trade-off between current and future consumption changes, as more future consumption can be obtained for a given sacrifice in the present. Thus, the substitution effect suggests that savings will increase with the interest rate. The real income effect is likely to operate in the reverse direction: at higher interest rates less saving is required to generate a given future income level. We cannot be certain of the net effect, but it is probable that the substitution effect will win—that is, higher interest rates will tend to encourage savings.

5 General equilibrium does not require all prices to be equal (as in (e)): it is price *ratios* that are important. All other relationships are features of general equilibrium (see Box 19–1 of the main text).

6 (c): this shows another use for the PPF: to analyse a firm's production possibilities rather than those for a complete economy.

7   (b) and (f) would cause the PPF to steepen.
    (a) affects the shape of the society's indifference curves.
    (c) and (d) affect the slope of the price line.
    (e) refers to a movement *along* the PPF.
8   (a)   AC.
    (b) R_1.
    (c)   BC.
    (d) R_2.
    (e)   The welfare loss is represented by the difference between U_0U_0 and U_1U_1.

True/False

1   True: the PPF shows all points of efficient production (see Section 19–1 of the main text).
2   True: see Section 19–2 of the main text.
3   False: the marginal rate of transformation is *always* negative.
4   False: points on the frontier represent production efficiency—but we must also consider consumer preferences (see Section 19–3 of the main text).
5   True.
6   True: see Section 19–4 of the main text.
7   True.
8   False: the *MRS* is the slope of an individual's indifference curve.
9   True: there is a different Pareto-efficient allocation for each possible welfare distribution (see Section 19–5 of the main text).
10 False: any market failure causes social inefficiency (see Section 19–6 of the main text).
11 False: see Section 19–7 of the main text.
12 True: see Section 19–8 of the main text. The relationship between investment and the rate of interest will be re-examined from a macroeconomic perspective in Chapter 25.

Questions for Thought

1   For hints, see Section 19–5 of the main text.
2   The important factors were probably your income, your preferences, and the return on savings. Each of these elements can be traced in the analysis.
3   For hints, see Section 19–6 and Chapter 15 of the main text, where we discussed various forms of market failure such as imperfect competition, externalities, and so on.

20

Introduction to Macroeconomics and National Income Accounting

If we look through a microscope at a grasshopper's leg, eye, or innards, we may learn a great deal about its make-up—but we would not get a clear view of the whole creature. So with an economy: we may learn a lot from the study of individual markets and of how individual agents behave, but at some stage we may wish to step back and form a broader view of how the economy fits together as a whole. This is the province of *macroeconomics*.

One way of introducing macroeconomics is to mention some of the questions to be examined. For instance, what determines the level of *output* of an economy, that is, the total amount of goods and services produced? What determines the rate at which output grows through time? What is unemployment and why should it occur? What determines the rate at which prices change—and why does it matter? Should the authorities attempt to intervene to try to affect these key variables?

The recent history of the UK highlights the importance of these issues: prices have risen rapidly, output growth has slowed, unemployment has risen substantially. Many other countries have also suffered, although not all as severely as the UK. These events have taken place against a backdrop in which governments have been trying to reduce the amount of intervention in the economy.

Before we can begin to *explain* how the economy operates, we must first be able to *describe* it. This is best done through the construction of a set of *national income accounts* which provides a framework for measuring national output and for describing its component parts and the interrelationships between them.

The *circular flow* of output, income, and expenditure provides the initial clues for our understanding of the national accounts, revealing three ways by which we can set about the measurement of national output. We can see these three methods in a simple model of a *closed economy* (that is, with no international trade) without government. Put at its most simple, factors are combined to produce *output* and are paid *income* which then becomes *expenditure*. These provide our three equivalent measures of national output.

Gross domestic product (GDP) in a closed no-government economy can be calculated by summing the *value added* by each industry in the economy. Equivalently, we can sum total expenditures on *final goods* or add up the income payments made to factors. *Inventories* may be regarded as working capital, and changes in inventory levels are thus to be included as part of *investment*. Income not spent by households is regarded as *saving*. Expenditure in this simple world is either on consumption goods or on investment; income is allocated either to consumption or to saving. We will always thus observe an equality between *actual* savings and *actual* investment. Firms borrow to finance their investment just that amount of funds which households do not spend and thus lend. It is important to notice that this equality describes what actually happens, and need not imply that *desired* savings and investment are always equal. For instance, a firm which sells less than planned will experience unplanned investment in the form of an addition to stocks.

The introduction of government into the economy requires some changes, as the government indulges in economic activity, raising revenue through *direct and indirect taxation*, undertaking *expenditure on goods and services*, and making *transfer payments*. Government spending on goods and services is incorporated into the calculations of total expenditure. Transfers and direct taxation lead us to the concept of *personal disposable income*, which represents the amount of income available to households for allocating between consumption and saving. The existence of indirect taxes results in two alternative valuations of GDP: we can measure *at market prices*, or we can deduct net indirect taxes and produce a valuation *at factor cost*.

If we consider an *open economy* and allow international trade to take place, we must take account of transactions between domestic residents and other countries. These may take the form of *exports* and *imports* of goods and services (affecting the expenditure identity) or may involve transfers of 'property income' between countries. Adding *net property income from abroad* to GDP gives us a measure of *gross national product* (GNP)—that is, total income earned by domestic citizens regardless of the country in which their factor services were supplied.

As a final refinement, we need to recognize the fact that capital goods wear out over time, so we need to deduct this *depreciation* (known in the UK accounts as *capital consumption*) from GNP. This provides an estimate of *national income* (or *net national product*)—the amount of money an economy has available for expenditure on goods and services after setting aside sufficient funds to maintain the capital stock.

Why do we wish to measure GNP? A major

motivation is to have some measure of the real total production of goods and services in an economy: we wish to know this because it affects the quality of life of the economy's citizens, and perhaps because we want to make international comparisons.

Depreciation is measured in different ways in different countries, so GNP rather than national income is the natural comparative measure. In order to ensure that we measure *real* output, we need to abstract from changing prices, which cause *nominal* GNP to change even when real output remains constant. We thus distinguish between GNP at *current prices* and GNP at *constant prices*, in which all items are valued at the prices prevailing in a specified base year. In economies where population changes rapidly, it is reasonable to consider GNP *per capita*.

In assessing real output, we naturally want our measure to be as comprehensive as possible. A complete measure might deduct the 'output' of bads such as pollution and add some 'production' which is not easily measured—for instance, the output of housewives or DIY experts. Differing national attitudes to tax evasion may influence the size of the unreported sector. Nordhaus and Tobin's *net economic welfare* measure is an example of a more comprehensive calculation of national output, but the cost and unreliability of such procedures means that GNP is likely to remain the best regularly available measure of economic activity.

IMPORTANT CONCEPTS AND TECHNICAL TERMS

Match each lettered concept with the appropriate numbered phrase:

(a)	Inventories	(o)	Personal disposable
(b)	Exports		income
(c)	Final goods	(p)	Net economic
(d)	Per capita GNP		welfare
(e)	Macroeconomics	(q)	Value added
(f)	Saving	(r)	GNP deflator
(g)	Depreciation	(s)	Investment
(h)	Factor cost	(t)	Imports
(i)	Current prices	(u)	Gross domestic
(j)	Intermediate goods		product
(k)	Constant prices	(v)	National income
(l)	Open economy	(w)	Market prices
(m)	Closed economy	(x)	Net property
(n)	Gross national		income from abroad
	product		

1 The study of the economy as a whole.
2 Goods that are produced abroad but purchased for use in the domestic economy.
3 The total income earned by domestic citizens regardless of the country in which their factor services were supplied.
4 The economy's net national product valued at factor cost.
5 The output produced by factors of production located in the domestic economy, regardless of who owns these factors.
6 A way of valuing domestic output inclusive of indirect taxes on goods and services.
7 The excess of inflows of property income from factor services supplied abroad over the outflows of property income arising from the supply of factor services by foreigners in the domestic economy.
8 The purchase of new capital goods by firms.
9 A valuation of expenditures or output using the prices prevailing at some base year.
10 A valuation of expenditures or output using the prices prevailing at the time of measurement.
11 A measurement of national output which adjusts GNP for the net value of non-market activities and leisure, devised by Professors William Nordhaus and James Tobin.
12 Partly finished goods which form inputs to another firm's production process and are used up in that process.
13 Goods that are domestically produced but sold abroad.
14 That part of income which is not spent buying goods and services.
15 The increase in the value of goods as a result of the production process.
16 GNP divided by the total population.
17 A measurement of the rate at which the value of the existing capital stock declines per period as a result of wear and tear or of obsolescence.
18 A way of valuing domestic output exclusive of indirect taxes on goods and services.
19 Household income after direct taxes and transfer payments: the amount that households have available for spending and saving.
20 An economy which does not transact with the rest of the world.
21 Goods purchased by the ultimate user: either consumer goods purchased by households, or capital goods such as machinery purchased by firms.
22 Goods currently held by a firm for future production or sale.
23 An economy which has transactions with other countries.
24 The ratio of nominal GNP to real GNP expressed as an index.

EXERCISES

Some of the relevant techniques and issues which you will need in the exercises in this chapter were first introduced in Chapter 2.

1 Table 20.1 presents consumer price indices (CPIs) for the UK, Japan, and Italy. (The consumer price index is the deflator of consumers' expenditure, calculated in similar fashion to the GNP deflator discussed in Section 20–5 of the main text.)

TABLE 20.1 Consumer price indices 1979–89

	UK		Japan		Italy	
	CPI	Inflation rate (%)	CPI	Inflation rate (%)	CPI	Inflation rate (%)
1979	59.9		80.9		43.4	
1980	70.7		87.4		52.5	
1981	79.1		91.7		61.9	
1982	85.9		94.1		72.1	
1983	89.8		95.9		82.7	
1984	94.3		98.0		91.6	
1985	100.0		100.0		100.0	
1986	103.4		100.6		105.8	
1987	107.7		100.7		110.9	
1988	113.0		101.4		116.5	
1989	121.8		103.7		123.8	

Source: based on data from Department of Employment, *Employment Gazette*

(a) Calculate the annual inflation rate for each of the countries.

(b) Plot your three inflation series on a diagram against time.

(c) By what percentage did prices increase in each country over the whole period—i.e. between 1979 and 1989?

(d) Which economy has experienced most stability of the inflation rate?

(e) Which economy has seen the greatest decline in the rate of inflation since 1980?

Table 20.2 presents some data relating to national output of the same three economies over a similar period, expressed as index numbers.

(f) Calculate the annual growth rate for each of the countries.

TABLE 20.2 National production (1985 = 100)

	UK		Japan		Italy	
	GDP	Growth rate (%)	GNP	Growth rate (%)	GDP	Growth rate (%)
1979	92.7		78.8		89.0	
1980	90.6		82.2		92.5	
1981	89.5		85.2		93.5	
1982	91.1		87.9		93.7	
1983	94.5		90.7		94.7	
1984	96.6		95.3		97.5	
1985	100.0		100.0		100.0	
1986	103.4		102.5		102.5	
1987	108.4		107.0		105.6	
1988	112.8		113.2		109.7	

Source: based on data from *OECD Main Economic Indicators*

(g) Plot your three growth series on a diagram against time.

(h) By what percentage did output increase in each country over the whole period?

2 In a hypothetical closed economy with no government, planned consumption is 150, planned investment is 50, and total production is 210.

(a) How much is total planned expenditure?

(b) Calculate unplanned stock changes.

(c) How much is savings in this situation?

(d) What is actual investment?

(e) How would you expect producers to react to this situation in the next period?

3 Table 20.3 lists a number of components of UK gross national product from both income and expenditure sides of the account for 1988. All quantities are measured in £million at current prices and are taken from CSO, *United Kingdom National Accounts*, 1989 edn, HMSO. Using the *expenditure* side of the accounts, calculate the following:

(a) Gross domestic product at market prices.

(b) Gross national product at market prices.

(c) Gross domestic product at factor cost.

(d) National income.

(e) Calculate gross domestic product at factor cost from the *income* side of the accounts.

(f) Can you explain why your answers to (c) and (e) are not identical?

TABLE 20.3

Consumers' expenditure	293 569	Capital consumption	45 918
Subsidies	5 883	Stock changes	4 371
Rent	27 464	Fixed investment	88 751
Net property income from abroad	5 619	Exports	108 533
General government final consumption	91 847	Wages	292 392
Taxes on expenditure	75 029	Other factor incomes, etc.	−2 708
Profits	77 458	Imports	125 194

4 Consider five firms in a closed economy: a steel producer, rubber producer, machine tool maker, tyre producer, and bicycle manufacturer. The bicycle manufacturer sells the bicycles produced to final consumers for £8000. In producing the bicycles, the firm buys tyres (£1000), steel (£2500), and machine tools (£1800). The tyre manufacturer buys rubber (£600) from the rubber producer, and the machine tool maker buys steel (£1000) from the steel producer.

(a) What is the contribution of the bicycle industry to GDP?

(b) Calculate total final expenditure.

5 Below are listed a number of components of UK personal income and taxation for 1988 together with some irrelevant items to try to put you off! The quantities are measured in £million at current prices and are taken from CSO, *United Kingdom National Accounts*, 1989 edn, HMSO.

Income from employment and self-employment	292 392
Income from rent, dividends, etc.	40 878
UK taxes on income, social security contributions, etc.	82 657
Taxes on consumers' expenditure	51 696
Saving	13 601
Transfers	56 557

(a) Calculate total personal income.

(b) Calculate personal disposable income.

6 According to the CSO *United Kingdom National Accounts* (1989 edn), GDP at 1985 market prices was £384 996m in 1987 and £400 999m in the following year. GDP at current market prices was £355 329m in 1985, £380 623m in 1986, and £463 933m in 1988. The implicit GDP deflator was 103.5 in 1986 and 108.5 in 1988.

For the period 1985–88, calculate the annual growth rates of real GDP, nominal GDP, and the price index.

7 All of the following form part of the UK National Income *except*:

(a) remuneration of the police

(b) payments to prisoners for tasks completed

(c) income from sickness benefit payments

(d) salaries of charity organisers

(e) dividends to equity holders

(University of London GCE A level Economics 3, January 1989))

8 The following table illustrates the domestic expenditure and national income of a certain country during three consecutive years.

	Year 1 £m	Year 2 £m	Year 3 £m
National income	500	600	700
Government expenditure	200	250	200
Private expenditure	300	300	250
Investment	50	200	200

In which year(s) did the country have a balance of payments deficit?

(a) Years 1, 2 and 3

(b) Years 1 and 2

(c) Years 2 and 3

(d) Year 1 only

(Associated Examining Board GCE A level Economics Paper 1, June 1988)

9 The following table refers to one country over two years:

	Index of gross national product	Retail price index	Index of population	Average working week (hours)
Year 1	105	102	103	44
Year 2	110	106	103	44

The figures indicate that, between year 1 and year 2,

I real income of the country increased

II standard of living of all people within the country increased

III working population increased in size

Choose one of the following permutations of the above statements

(a) I, II, III all correct

(b) I, II only correct

(c) II, III only correct

(d) I only correct

(Associated Examining Board GCE A level Economics Paper 1, June 1987)

10 Which of the following items are included in the calculation of GNP in the UK and which are excluded?

(a) Salaries paid to schoolteachers.

(b) Tips given to taxi drivers.

(c) Expenditure on social security benefits.

(d) The income of a second-hand car salesman.

(e) Work carried out in the home by a house-wife.

(f) Work carried out in the home by a paid domestic.

(g) The value of pleasure from leisure.

(h) Free-range eggs sold in the market.

(i) Blackberries picked in the hedgerows.

11 Below are quoted some UK data relating to national output in 1988 (in £b), taken from CSO, *United Kingdom National Accounts*, 1989 edn, HMSO.

	£billion
Gross national product at market prices	469.6
Taxes on expenditure	75.0
Capital consumption	54.8
Net property income from abroad	5.6
Subsidies	5.9

Calculate the following:
(a) Gross domestic product at market prices.
(b) Net national product at market prices.
(c) Net national product at factor cost.
(d) Gross domestic product at factor cost.
(e) National income.

TRUE/FALSE

1 _____ The increase in the quantity of goods and services which the economy as a whole can afford to purchase is known as economic growth.

2 _____ In the period 1973–84, Brazil, Korea and Japan grew significantly faster than European countries such as the UK, Switzerland, or West Germany.

3 _____ During the 1970s and early 1980s, the UK suffered more from price inflation than any other country.

4 _____ Unemployment in the UK increased tenfold between 1975 and 1985.

5 _____ Given full and accurate measurement, we should get the same estimate of total economic activity whether we measure the value of production output, the level of factor incomes, or spending on goods and services.

6 _____ A closed economy is one with excessive levels of unemployment.

7 _____ The calculation of value added is a way of measuring output without double-counting.

8 _____ In a closed economy with no government, savings are always equal to investment.

9 _____ Gross domestic product at factor cost is equal to gross domestic product at market prices plus net indirect taxes.

10 _____ Depreciation is an economic cost because it measures resources being used up in the production process.

11 _____ Gross national product at current prices is a measure of real economic activity.

12 _____ Gross national product at constant prices is a useless measure of economic welfare because it fails to measure so many important ingredients of welfare.

QUESTIONS FOR THOUGHT

1 Reconsider the items listed in exercise 10 of this chapter. Which of these items do you think *should* be included in a measure of national economic welfare? What additional items (positive or negative) should be incorporated?

2 In many less developed countries, much of economic activity is concentrated in small-scale subsistence agriculture. How would you expect this to affect comparisons of living standards based on GNP measurements? What other difficulties would you expect to encounter in making international comparisons of living standards?

3 Why is it so important to distinguish between real and nominal national income measures?

ANSWERS AND COMMENTS FOR CHAPTER 20

Please note Where questions are reproduced from GCE examinations, the examination boards bear no responsibility for the answers provided in this volume, which are the sole responsibility of the authors.

Important Concepts and Technical Terms

1 *e*	7 *x*	13 *b*	19 *o*
2 *t*	8 *s*	14 *f*	20 *m*
3 *n*	9 *k*	15 *q*	21 *c*
4 *v*	10 *i*	16 *d*	22 *a*
5 *u*	11 *p*	17 *g*	23 *l*
6 *w*	12 *j*	18 *h*	24 *r*

Exercises

1 **TABLE A20.1** Inflation, 1980–89

	UK		Japan		Italy	
	CPI	Inflation rate (%)	CPI	Inflation rate (%)	CPI	Inflation rate (%)
1979	59.9		80.9		43.4	
1980	70.7	18.0	87.4	8.0	52.5	21.0
1981	79.1	11.9	91.7	4.9	61.9	17.9
1982	85.9	8.6	94.1	2.6	72.1	16.5
1983	89.8	4.5	95.9	1.9	82.7	14.7
1984	94.3	5.0	98.0	2.2	91.6	10.8
1985	100.0	6.0	100.0	2.0	100.0	9.2
1986	103.4	3.4	100.6	0.6	105.8	5.8
1987	107.7	4.2	100.7	0.1	110.9	4.8
1988	113.0	4.9	101.4	0.7	116.5	5.0
1989	121.8	7.8	103.7	2.3	123.8	6.3

(a) The annual inflation rate is calculated from the consumer price index using the method described in Section 20–2 of the main text. Thus for the UK, the inflation rate for 1979–80 is calculated as:
$$100 \times (70.7 - 59.9)/59.9 = 18.0\%$$

(b) Figure A20.1

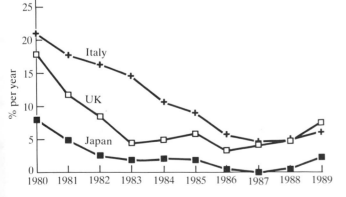

FIGURE A20.1 Inflation in the UK, Italy, and Japan

(c) UK 103.3 per cent. Japan 28.2 per cent. Italy 185.3 per cent.

(d) Japan.

(e) The UK—but the rate is still well above that of Japan. Italy is improving also.

(f) The growth rates are calculated in the same way as the inflation rates: see Table A20.2.

TABLE A20.2 National production and economic growth

	UK		Japan		Italy	
	GDP	Growth rate (%)	GNP	Growth rate (%)	GDP	Growth rate (%)
1979	92.7		78.8		89.0	
1980	90.6	−2.3	82.2	4.3	92.5	3.9
1981	89.5	−1.2	85.2	3.6	93.5	1.1
1982	91.1	1.8	87.9	3.2	93.7	0.2
1983	94.5	3.7	90.7	3.2	94.7	1.1
1984	96.6	2.2	95.3	5.1	97.5	3.0
1985	100.0	3.5	100.0	4.9	100.0	2.6
1986	103.4	3.4	102.5	2.5	102.5	2.5
1987	108.4	4.8	107.0	4.4	105.6	3.0
1988	112.8	4.1	113.2	5.8	109.7	3.9

(g)

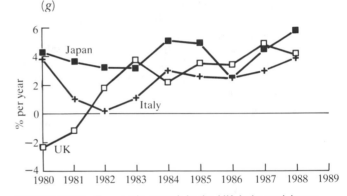

FIGURE A20.2 Economic growth in the UK, Italy, and Japan

(h) UK 21.7 per cent; Japan 43.7 per cent; Italy 23.3 per cent.

2 (a) Planned consumption plus planned investment is 150 + 50 = 200.

(b) Production less expenditure is 210 − 200 = 10. This quantity represents an unplanned addition to inventories.

(c) Income less consumption is 210 − 150 = 60.

(d) Planned investment plus stock changes is 50 + 10 = 60.
Thus actual investment = actual savings.

(e) Producers have not sold as much output as they expected and witness an increase in stock levels. Two responses are possible: to reduce output or reduce price. As we begin to build our model of an economy in the next chapter, we will initially assume that prices are fixed—so the response to an unplanned increase in stocks will be to reduce output.

3 It may be helpful to begin by translating these terms into the notation of the main text:

Item	Notation in main text
Consumers' expenditure	C
Fixed investment *plus* stock changes	I
General government final consumption	G
Exports	X
Imports	Z
Taxes on expenditure *less* subsidies	T_e

The remaining terms should be familiar.

(a) GDP at market prices is $C + I + G + X - Z = 461\,877$.

(b) GNP at market prices is GDP_{mp} + net property income from abroad $= 467\,496$.

(c) GDP at factor cost is $GDP_{mp} - T_e = 392\,731$.

(d) National income is $NNP = GNP_{fc}$ − capital consumption $= 352\,432$.

(e) From the income side, GDP_{fc} = wages + profits + rent + other factor incomes, etc. $= 394\,606$.

(f) In an ideal world, the two methods should give the same results. However, in practice the problems of accurate measurement are too great. If you look in the CSO Blue Book you will see that the recommended estimate of GDP is formed as an average of the income-, expenditure-, and output-based measures.

4 The simplest way to clarify this question is to tabulate the transactions as in Table A20.3, and then calculate the value added entailed in each transaction. This was done in Section 20–4 of the main text.

Check that you understand how column (5) is obtained. For instance, value added by the bicycle manufacturer is the transaction value (£8000) *less* the value of goods used up in the production process—namely, tyres (£1000) and steel (£2500)—but *not* the machine, which is not 'used up' but kept for future use also.

(a) The contribution is the sum of the value added in column (5) = £9800.

(b) Total final expenditure is composed of two elements—consumers' expenditure on bicycles (£8000) and the bicycle manufacturer's purchase of machine tools (£1800), totalling £9800.

5 (a) Total personal income is the sum of income from employment, self-employment, rent, dividends, and transfers, totalling £389\,827m.

(b) Personal disposable income (the amount available to households to spend or save) is total personal income less UK taxes on income, national insurance contributions, etc., $= 389\,827 - 82\,657 = 307\,170$. Personal disposable income is discussed in Section 20–4 of the main text.

6 The key relationship to remember is that the GDP deflator is the ratio of nominal GDP to real GDP expressed as an index; i.e.,

$$\text{price index} = \frac{\text{nominal } GDP}{\text{real } GDP} \times 100.$$

For any year, if we have two of these pieces of information, we can calculate the third. For instance, for 1988 the question furnishes the two GDP measures and we calculate the price index. Once we have our complete series, we can calculate the growth rates. Notice that 1985 is the base year, so nominal GDP equals real GDP, and the price index is 100. Results are summarized in Table A20.4.

7 (c).

8 (b).

9 (d).

10 The general rule to adopt is that, if an item can be valued and is reported, then, so long as it is notionally part of GNP, it will be included. This includes (a), (b), (d), (f), and (h), although we cannot always guarantee

TABLE A20.3 Calculating value added

(1) Good	(2) Seller	(3) Buyer	(4) Transaction value (£)	(5) Value added (£)
Steel	Steel producer	Machine tool maker	1000	1000
Steel	Steel producer	Bicycle manufacturer	2500	2500
Rubber	Rubber producer	Tyre producer	600	600
Machine	Machine tool maker	Bicycle manufacturer	1800	800
Tyres	Tyre producer	Bicycle manufacturer	1000	400
Bicycles	Bicycle manufacturer	Final consumers	8000	4500

TABLE A20.4 Real and nominal GDP calculations

	(1) GDP at 1985 market prices £m)	(2) Rate of growth of (1) (% p.a.)	(3) GDP at current market prices (£m)	(4) Rate of growth of (3) (% p.a.)	(5) Implicit GDP deflator	(6) Rate of change of (5) (% p.a.)
1985	355\,239		355\,329		100.0	
1986	367\,752	3.5	380\,623	7.1	103.5	3.5
1987	384\,996	4.7	417\,721	9.7	108.5	4.8
1988	400\,999	4.2	463\,933	11.1	115.7	6.6

the full reporting of all these items. Item (c) relates to a transfer payment and is not notionally part of GNP. (e) is immeasurable. (g) cannot easily be valued, although GNP will include wages paid to those responsible for providing leisure services. Hedgefruit are neither valued nor reported, unless you choose to visit a pick-your-own fruit farm!

11 (a) GDP_{mp} is GNP_{mp} less net property income from abroad: $469.6 - 5.6 = 464.0$.

    (b) NNP_{mp} is GNP_{mp} less capital consumption (depreciation): $469.6 - 54.8 = 414.8$.

    (c) NNP_{fc} is NNP_{mp} less *net* taxes on expenditure: $414.8 - (75.0 - 5.9) = 345.7$.

    (d) GDP_{fc} is GDP_{mp} less net taxes on expenditure: $464.0 - (75.0 - 5.9) = 394.9$.

    (e) National income is (by definition) the same as NNP_{fc}.

True/False

1 True: see Section 20–1 of the main text.

2 True: see Section 20–2 of the main text.

3 False: many other countries, especially in Latin America, have experienced much more rapid inflation than the UK—for instance, the average annual rate of inflation in Chile during the 1970s was 242.6 per cent!

4 False: although unemployment did increase substantially at this time, it was by no means as high as tenfold—it just felt that way!

5 True: see Section 20–3 of the main text.

6 False, and silly: whether an economy is 'closed' or 'open' depends upon whether it is open to international trade—not upon the rate of closure of firms (see Section 20–4 of the main text).

7 True.

8 It is true that actual savings will always equal actual investment in such an economy: this results from the way we choose to define these variables. There is no necessity, however, for *planned* savings and investment to be always equal.

9 False: indirect taxes must be deducted from GDP_{mp} to give GDP_{fc}.

10 True.

11 False: if measured at *current* prices, GNP incorporates price changes—this is *nominal* GNP, not *real* GNP.

12 False: real GNP may not be an ideal measure of welfare, but it is the best measure we have which is available on a regular basis.

Questions for Thought

1 Some discussion of more comprehensive measures is included in Section 20–5 of the main text.

2 The existence of unrecorded economic activity will bias downwards the measurements of GNP in whatever country. In making international comparisons, we may also have to face problems with income distribution and currency conversions.

3 You might like to illustrate your discussion by using your answers to exercise 6.

21

The Determination of National Income

In Chapter 20 we have seen how to go about measuring national income. As economists, this ability to describe the world is but the first step: we want to be able to go on to explain why an economy may settle at a particular level of income at a particular time. To do this, we begin to build a model which will help us to explore the interactions between the markets of the economy at an aggregate level.

The maximum level of output that an economy could produce in a particular period is known as the *potential output*. Notice that, even at this potential output level, there is likely to be some unemployment. The size of potential output of an economy grows through time as the labour force grows, capital accumulates, and technical progress takes place. We set aside these considerations until later, and enquire whether an economy at a point in time might settle at an actual output level which is below the potential level—that is, in a position where there is less than full employment.

Our initial simple model assumes that prices and wages are fixed and that there are spare resources in the economy. This enables us to neglect the supply side of the economy for the time being and to concentrate on a *short-run demand-determined Keynesian model*.

We also assume no government and no international trade. Thus, there are just two groups of agents in the economy: households, which supply labour and demand goods, and firms, which produce output, pay incomes to households, and demand investment goods. The importance of demand in the system is readily seen within the circular flow. If households were to decide to spend less of their income, the result is that aggregate demand would fall, . . . and so on.

In aggregate, we may think of aggregate consumption being determined mainly by national income, together with an autonomous component. (Later we will see that other factors will also be important.) The description of how consumption varies with national income is known as the *consumption function*. As income rises, consumption will also rise, but by less than the increase in income—i.e., some of the additional income will be saved. The *marginal propensity to consume* measures the fraction of additional income which is used for consumption. In this simple world, if we specify our consumption function, we also determine the *savings function*—for income which is not spent is saved.

The other component of aggregate demand is *investment*, which we assume to be independent of current income. In practice, it is more likely to depend upon firms' expectations about future changes in demand or upon the rate of interest, which we have yet to consider. For now, we therefore assume investment to be autonomous.

The *aggregate demand schedule* is formed by combining our consumption function with autonomous investment demand. It shows aggregate demand at different levels of national income.

Short-run equilibrium is achieved when planned aggregate demand is equal to actual supply. The 45° line on the income–expenditure diagram allows us to pinpoint this equilibrium output level given the aggregate demand schedule. If planned aggregate demand falls short of actual output, firms will observe unplanned accumulation of inventories. It is reasonable to assume that they will respond to this by reducing output in the next period, thus moving the economy towards equilibrium. Similar forces come into effect if output falls short of planned aggregate demand. In this way, the economy can be seen to move towards equilibrium, with unplanned stock changes acting as the signal to producers to change their output levels. Although this process brings the economy to equilibrium, we have said nothing to prove that this need necessarily be at the full potential output level.

An alternative view of the process sees short-run equilibrium as a position in which planned savings equal planned investment. In equilibrium, firms wish to borrow money to invest at just the rate at which households wish to lend (save) it. This equality of *planned*, or *desired*, savings and investment is very different from the equality of *actual* savings and investment which we saw in Chapter 20, which was caused by the way we defined these variables (especially investment).

The position of the aggregate demand schedule is dependent on the size of autonomous expenditures—investment and autonomous consumption. *Keynes* suggested that autonomous investment would be especially volatile, depending as it does on the *animal spirits* of investors, reflecting their optimism or pessimism about future demand conditions. A change in autonomous spending which shifts the aggregate demand schedule moves the economy to a new equilibrium position. Following such a change, it may be observed that the change in equilibrium output is larger than the original change in autonomous spending which initiated the change. This is because the change in income itself induces further changes in spending through what is known as the *multiplier process*. It should be noted that the size of these multiplier effects is much exaggerated in this greatly simplified model.

This process gives rise to the so-called *paradox of thrift*. If households decide to save less, does this mean falling investment and output? No. If households save less at each income, they spend more, output increases, household incomes rise—and so too do savings, the process continuing until we get back to equilibrium with planned savings again equal to planned investment. (Remember that investment is assumed to be autonomous.)

We close with a word of warning: no economic model is better than the assumptions on which it is based. So far, our model is very simple indeed, resting heavily on the short-run analysis of a closed economy without government, with wages and prices fixed, and with spare resources. We should not assume that all our results will continue to hold in the more complex models to be seen later. None the less, we now have our starting point.

IMPORTANT CONCEPTS AND TECHNICAL TERMS

Match each lettered concept with the appropriate numbered phrase:

(a) Investment demand
(b) Animal spirits
(c) Autonomous consumption
(d) Potential output
(e) Short-run equilibrium output
(f) Marginal propensity to save
(g) 45° line
(h) Consumption function
(i) Savings function
(j) Aggregate demand schedule
(k) Actual output
(l) Marginal propensity to consume
(m) Paradox of thrift
(n) Unplanned inventory change
(o) Personal disposable income
(p) Multiplier

1 The part of consumption expenditure which is unrelated to the level of income.
2 Firms' desired or planned additions both to their physical capital (factories and machines) and to their inventories.
3 An unanticipated increase or decrease in the level of stocks held by firms.
4 A relationship showing the level of planned savings at each level of personal disposable income.
5 The income that households have available for spending or saving.
6 A curve which shows the amount that firms and households plan to spend on goods and services at each level of income.
7 The level of output the economy would produce if all factors of production were fully employed.
8 The ratio of the change in equilibrium output to the change in autonomous spending that causes the change in output.
9 The situation whereby a change in the amount households wish to save at each income level leads to a change in the equilibrium level of income but no change in the equilibrium level of savings, which must still equal planned investment.
10 A line on the income–expenditure diagram which joins all the points at which income equals expenditure.
11 The fraction of each extra pound of disposable income that households wish to use for saving.
12 The amount of output produced in an economy in a particular period.
13 The fraction of each extra pound of disposable income that households wish to use to increase consumption.
14 The level of output in an economy when aggregate demand or planned aggregate spending just equals the output that is actually produced.
15 The current pessimism or optimism felt by firms concerning the future.
16 A relationship showing the level of aggregate consumption desired at each level of personal disposable income.

EXERCISES

1 Table 21.1 presents data on real consumers' expenditure and personal disposable income for the UK.

TABLE 21.1 Consumption and income

Year	Real consumers' expenditure (£m)	Real personal disposable income (£m)
1977	124 868	140 930
1978	131 742	150 624
1979	137 612	158 743
1980	137 234	161 581
1981	137 211	158 507
1982	138 277	158 736
1983	143 603	162 507
1984	146 657	166 951
1985	151 986	171 540
1986	159 715	178 849

Source: CSO, *Monthly Digest of Statistics*

(a) Calculate real savings in each year during the period and the percentage of income saved.
(b) Using graph paper, plot a scatter diagram with real consumption on the vertical axis and real personal disposable income on the horizontal axis.

(c) Draw a straight line passing as close as possible to these points on the diagram, and measure the approximate slope of the line.

(d) Under what conditions would you regard this slope as a reasonable estimate of the marginal propensity to consume?

(e) Using more graph paper, plot another scatter diagram of real savings against income.

(f) If you were to draw a straight line through *these* points, how would you expect it to relate to the one you drew in part (c)? Do it, and measure its approximate slope.

(g) Assuming this to be a sensible estimate of the marginal propensity to save, what is implied for the value of the multiplier?

2   Table 21.2 shows some data on consumption and income (output) for the economy of Hypothetica. Planned investment is autonomous, and occurs at the rate of $60 billion per period.

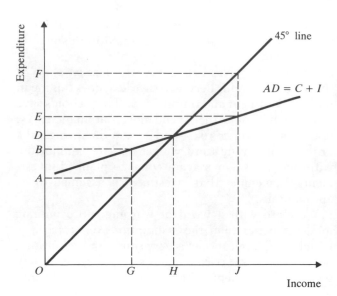

FIGURE 21.1   The income–expenditure diagram

TABLE 21.2   Income and consumption in Hypothetica (all in Hypothetical $billion)

Income (output)	Planned consumption	Planned investment	Savings	Aggregate demand	Unplanned inventory change	Actual investment
50	35					
100	70					
150	105					
200	140					
250	175					
300	210					
350	245					
400	280					

(a) Calculate savings and aggregate demand at each level of income.

(b) For each level of output, work out the unplanned change in inventory holdings and the rate of actual investment.

(c) If, in a particular period, income turned out to be $100 billion, how would you expect producers to react?

(d) If, in a particular period, income turned out to be $350 billion, how would you expect producers to react?

(e) What is the equilibrium level of income?

(f) What is the marginal propensity to consume?

(g) If investment increased by $15 billion, what would be the change in equilibrium income?

3   (a) Using the data of exercise 2, use graph paper to plot the consumption function and aggregate demand schedule.

(b) Add on the 45° line and confirm that equilibrium occurs at the same point suggested by your answer to 2(e) above.

(c) Show the effect on equilibrium of an increase in investment of $15 billion.

4   (a) Again using the data on Hypothetica from exercise 2, use graph paper to plot how savings vary with income.

(b) Add on the investment line and confirm that equilibrium again occurs at the same income level.

(c) Show that an increase in investment of $15 billion leads to a new level of equilibrium income.

(d) Explain the process by which this new equilibrium is attained.

5   Figure 21.1 shows the aggregate demand schedule for an economy, together with the 45° line.

(a) Suppose output is OG: identify the level of aggregate demand and specify whether there is excess demand or excess supply.

(b) What is the size of the unplanned inventory change with output OG?

(c) How will firms respond to this situation?

(d) Identify equilibrium income and expenditure.

(e) Suppose output is OJ; identify the level of aggregate planned expenditure and specify whether there is excess demand or excess supply.

(f) What is the size of the unplanned inventory change with output *OJ*—and how will firms react to it?

6 Figure 21.2 shows autonomous investment for an economy, together with the savings function showing how savings vary with income. I_B is the initial level of investment.

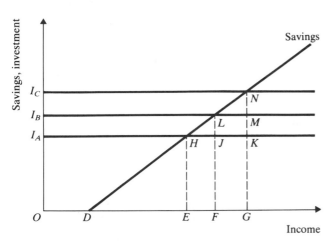

FIGURE 21.2 Savings and investment

(a) Identify the initial equilibrium levels of income and savings.
(b) Which level of investment represents the effect of an increase in business confidence—a surge in optimistic animal spirits?
(c) What is the new equilibrium level of income?
(d) What is the multiplier?
(e) Which level of investment shows an increase in pessimism on the part of firms?
(f) What would be the new equilibrium level of income?

7 In a closed economy with no government sector, consumption (C) and income (Y) are related by the function:

$C = £400 \text{ million} + \frac{3}{4}Y.$

Saving will be zero when national income is
(a) zero
(b) £100 million
(c) £300 million
(d) £700 million
(e) £1600 million
(University of London GCE A level Economics 3, June 1989)

8 The marginal propensity to save is
(a) the change in saving divided by the change in income
(b) the reciprocal of the marginal propensity to consume
(c) income which is not spent

(d) the sum that is saved if the individual receives greater income
(e) the reduction in purchasing power
(University of London GCE A level Economics 3, June 1988)

9

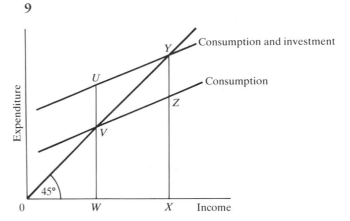

FIGURE 21.3

Figure 21.3 represents a closed economy with no government sector. At the equilibrium level of income, the average propensity to consume is calculated by
(a) UV/OW
(b) YZ/ZX
(c) YZ/OX
(d) ZX/OX
(Associated Examining Board GCE A level Economics Paper 1, June 1987)

10 Figure 21.4 shows an economy which initially has an aggregate demand schedule given by *AK*.

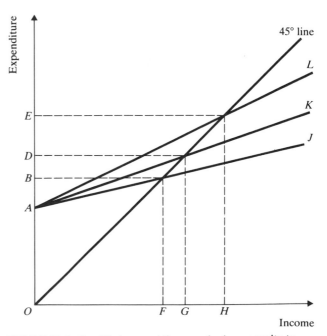

FIGURE 21.4 Equilibrium and the marginal propensity to consume

(a) What is the initial equilibrium level of income?

(b) Suppose there is an increase in the marginal propensity to save: which is the new aggregate demand schedule?

(c) What is the new equilibrium level of income?

(d) Suppose that, instead, the marginal propensity to consume had increased: which would be the new aggregate demand schedule?

(e) What is the new equilibrium level of income?

11 For the last exercise of this chapter we return to the economy of Hypothetica. Initially, consumption is determined (as before) as 70 per cent of income. Investment is again autonomous and occurs at the rate of $90 billion per period.

(a) What is the equilibrium level of income? (If it helps, you might create a table similar to that in exercise 2, for values of output between, say, 250 and 600.)

(b) What would be the equilibrium level of income if investment increased by $15 billion?

(c) Calculate the value of the multiplier.

Suppose that our Hypothetical consumers become more spendthrift, spending 80 cents in the dollar rather than 70. With investment again at $90 billion per period,

(d) Calculate the equilibrium level of income.

(e) Calculate the equilibrium level of income if investment increased by $10 billion.

(f) Calculate the value of the multiplier.

TRUE/FALSE

1 _____ Potential output includes an allowance for 'normal unemployment'.

2 _____ The Keynesian model suggests that output is mainly demand-determined.

3 _____ Consumption is linearly related to income.

4 _____ The marginal propensities to consume and save sum to unity.

5 _____ Investment is autonomous.

6 _____ The purpose of the aggregate demand schedule is to separate out the change in demand directly induced by changes in income.

7 _____ Short-run equilibrium occurs when spending plans are not frustrated by a shortage of goods and when firms do not produce more output than they can sell.

8 _____ Unplanned inventory changes are the signal to firms that there is disequilibrium.

9 _____ Planned savings always equals planned investment.

10 _____ The slope of the aggregate demand schedule depends only on the level of autonomous consumption.

11 _____ The multiplier in our simple model tells us how much output changes when there is a shift in aggregate demand.

12 _____ If only people were prepared to save more, investment would increase and we could get the economy moving again.

QUESTIONS FOR THOUGHT

1 We know that, in a closed economy with no governmental economic activity, savings and investment are always equal. How, then, does it make sense for economists to talk about situations in which they take different values?

2 Think about the consumption expenditures undertaken by your household. Is income the only factor influencing the aggregate amount? What other factors may help to determine aggregate consumption?

3 Suppose that equilibrium output for an economy entails high levels of unemployment. Does the analysis of this chapter suggest any action which the authorities might take to mitigate the effects of unemployment?

ANSWERS AND COMMENTS FOR CHAPTER 21

Please note Where questions are reproduced from GCE A level examinations, the examination boards bear no responsibility for the answers provided in this volume, which are the sole responsibility of the authors.

Important Concepts and Technical Terms

1	*c*	5	*o*	9	*m*	13	*l*
2	*a*	6	*j*	10	*g*	14	*e*
3	*n*	7	*d*	11	*f*	15	*b*
4	*i*	8	*p*	12	*k*	16	*h*

Exercises

1 (a)

TABLE A21.1 Consumption, income, and saving, 1977–86

	Real consumers' expenditure (£m)	Real personal disposable income (£m)	Real savings (£m)	Savings ratio (%)
1977	124 868	140 930	16 062	11.4
1978	131 742	150 624	18 882	12.5
1979	137 612	158 743	21 131	13.3
1980	137 234	161 581	24 347	15.1
1981	137 211	158 507	21 296	13.4
1982	138 277	158 736	20 459	12.9
1983	143 603	162 507	18 904	11.6
1984	146 657	166 951	20 294	12.2
1985	151 986	171 540	19 554	11.4
1986	159 715	178 849	19 134	10.7

(b)

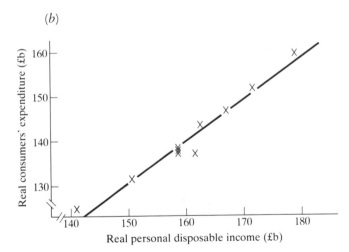

FIGURE A21.1 Consumption and income

(c) We drew our line using a statistical procedure called 'regression': its slope is 0.933.

(d) In focusing upon this simple relationship between consumption and income, we have made a number of assumptions, especially concerning autonomous consumption. We have also assumed that the relationship can be viewed as a straight line. Only if all these assumptions are valid can we regard our estimate of the marginal propensity as 'reasonable'. This must be interpreted in the light of economics (what we are trying to measure) as well as of statistics (how we try to measure it). The estimate seems high, but had we extended the data beyond 1986 we would have moved into the period of the so-called 'consumer boom'. Savings fell dramatically (to only 4.4 per cent in 1988) and our estimate would have been higher still. This underlines the fact that these results must be treated with extreme caution.

(e)

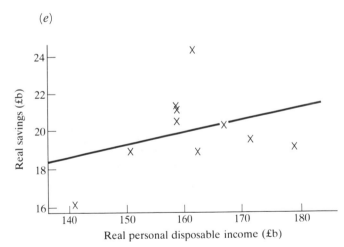

FIGURE A21.2 Savings and income

(f) Given $Y = C + S$, there must be a close correspondence between the two lines. If we write $C = a + bY$, then it is easily seen that $S = -a + (1 - b)Y$. It should thus be no surprise that the slope of the savings line is $1 - 0.933 = 0.067$.

(g) $1/0.067 = 14.9$.

Again, we should interpret this figure with caution.

2 **TABLE A21.2** Income, etc., Hypothetica ($billion)

(1)	(2)	(3)	(4)	(5)	(6)	(7)
Income (output)	Planned consumption	Planned investment	Savings	Aggregate demand	Unplanned inventory change	Actual investment
50	35	60	15	95	−45	15
100	70	60	30	130	−30	30
150	105	60	45	165	−15	45
200	140	60	60	200	0	60
250	175	60	75	235	15	75
300	210	60	90	270	30	90
350	245	60	105	305	45	105
400	280	60	120	340	60	120

(a) and (b): answers are contained in Table A21.2.

(c) With income at 100, aggregate demand is 130, so that stocks will be rapidly run down. Producers are likely to react by producing more output in the next period.

(d) With income at 350, aggregate demand is only 305 and producers will find that they cannot sell their output, so stocks begin to build up. They are thus likely to reduce output in the next period.

(e) Only at income of 200 do we find that aggregate demand equals aggregate supply—or, equivalently, that *planned* investment equals *planned* savings. This then is the equilibrium level of income.

(f) As income increases by 50, consumption increases by 35, so the marginal propensity to consume is 35/50 = 0.7.

(g) An increase of investment of $15 billion to $75 billion would carry equilibrium income to 250—an increase of 15/0.3 = 50.

3 (a)

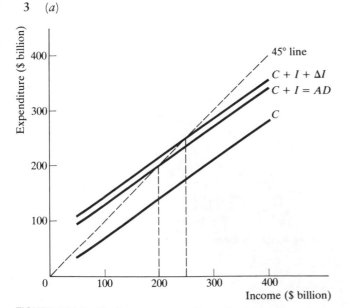

FIGURE A21.3 The income–expenditure diagram

(b) The diagram confirms that equilibrium occurs at income of 200—where the aggregate demand schedule meets the 45° line.

(c) The increase in investment shifts the aggregate demand schedule, giving a new equilibrium at income of 250.

4 (a)

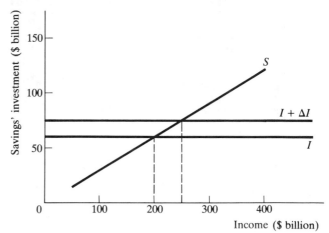

FIGURE A21.4 Savings and investment

(b) Equilibrium is again seen to be at income of 200.

(c) Equilibrium at the new level of investment is at income of 250.

(d) The increase in investment initially affects income, inducing higher savings; the process continues until planned savings equal planned investment.

5 (a) Aggregate demand is OB: there is excess demand at this point.

(b) Inventories will be run down to the extent of the excess demand, measured by AB.

(c) We expect firms to increase output in the next period.

(d) Income OH = planned expenditure OD.

(e) Aggregate planned expenditure is OE: there is excess supply at this point.

(f) Inventories will increase to the extent of the excess supply—namely, EF. Firms are likely to respond by reducing output.

6 (a) Income OF, savings OI_B.

(b) OI_C.

(c) OG.

(d) LM/NM.

(e) OI_A.
(f) OE.
7 (e).
8 (a).
9 (d).
10 (a) OG.
    (b) AJ.
    (c) OF.
    (d) AL.
    (e) OH.
11 (a) The column in Table A21.3 headed 'Aggregate demand 1' shows that equilibrium income is =300 (because consumption is then $0.7 \times 300 = 210$. So $C + I$ is $210 + 90 = 300$). Given the multiplier relationship, we could also calculate equilibrium as
$$Y = \frac{I}{(1 - MPC)} = 90/0.3 = 300.$$
    (b) Using 'Aggregate demand 2' or $Y = 105/0.3$, we see that equilibrium output is now 350.
    (c) The multiplier can be calculated as the ratio of the change in equilibrium income to the initiating change in investment (i.e., $50/15 = 3.33'$), or we simply calculate
$$\frac{1}{(1 - MPC)} = \frac{1}{0.3} = 3.33'.$$
    (d) With the higher propensity to consume, we get column 'Aggregate demand 3' and an equilibrium of 450:
$$\frac{I}{1 - MPC} = \frac{90}{0.2} = 450.$$
    (e) Using 'Aggregate demand 4', equilibrium income is now 500.
    (f) $50/10 = 5$.

True/False

1 True: see introduction to Chapter 21 in the main text.
2 True.
3 False: we make this simplifying assumption very often—but it is no more than assumption and may not always be accurate (see Section 21–2 of the main text).
4 True: we have set up the model such that income is either spent or saved.
5 False: we have assumed investment to be autonomous to keep the model simple for the time being; later we will treat it more realistically and consider its determinants.
6 True: see Box 21–1 of the main text.
7 True: see Section 21–4 of the main text.
8 True again.
9 False: this statement is true only in equilibrium. We note that savings and investment plans are formulated independently by different agents and need not always be equal (see Section 21–5 of the main text).
10 False: the *slope* depends upon the marginal propensity to consume; the *position* depends partly on the level of autonomous consumption (see Section 21–6 of the main text).
11 True: see Section 21–7 of the main text.
12 False: this is an expression of the paradox of thrift (see Section 21–8 of the main text).

Questions for Thought

1 Remember the distinction between planned and actual (see Section 21–5 of the main text).
2 We will reconsider consumption theory in Chapter 25.
3 This question looks ahead to Chapter 22.

TABLE A21.3 Hypothetica revisited

Income (output)	Planned consumption (MPC = 0.7)	Aggregate demand 1	Aggregate demand 2	Planned consumption (MPC = 0.8)	Aggregate demand 3	Aggregate demand 4
250	175	265	280	200	290	300
300	210	300	315	240	330	340
350	245	335	350	280	370	380
400	280	370	385	320	410	420
450	315	405	420	360	450	460
500	350	440	455	400	490	500
550	385	475	490	440	530	540
600	420	510	525	480	570	580

22

Aggregate Demand, Fiscal Policy, and Foreign Trade

The simple model of income determination developed in Chapter 21 is now to be extended to incorporate the economic actions of government and foreign trade, both of which are very important for an open economy like the UK. The government has significant effects upon how the level of aggregate demand varies with income. On the expenditure side, the government spends money on goods and services, thus adding a new component to aggregate demand. At the same time, the amount of spending power available to households is directly affected by the imposition of taxes and the payment of benefits. Foreign trade also has effects on aggregate demand, although for the moment we consider only the effects arising from expenditure on imports and exports.

In the UK, the government constitutes a major force in the economy, spending on the National Health Service, education, defence, and other items, and providing pensions and other social security benefits. Direct spending corresponded to nearly one-quarter of GNP in 1989, as did transfer payments. Revenue is raised by both direct and indirect taxation. The overall level of government activity is important in determining the level of aggregate demand, and hence can influence the level of equilibrium output. Decisions about the overall levels of government spending and taxes are known as *fiscal policy*. Attempts to keep output close to the full-employment level are known as *stabilization policy*.

In analysing the effects of government upon aggregate demand, we initially assume a closed economy and also set aside the question of indirect taxes. Government spending is assumed to be autonomous in the sense of being independent of the level of national income. However, *net taxes* (direct taxes net of transfers) are assumed to vary with income. As income increases, households pay more tax and the authorities need pay less in unemployment benefits. Taxation introduces a divergence between income and personal disposable income, the amount available for disposal by households. In the UK, net taxes comprise about 20 per cent of household income.

Government spending affects equilibrium output by influencing the *position* of the aggregate demand schedule. Tax rates have their influence by affecting its *slope*. The *balanced budget multiplier* reveals that an increase in government expenditure financed entirely and exactly by net taxation has the effect of increasing equilibrium income. The effect of introducing taxation is to reduce the size of the multiplier.

The government *budget deficit* is the excess of government spending over revenues. The size of the deficit (or surplus) can be seen to depend upon the net tax rate, the level of spending, and the level of national income. In equilibrium, planned savings plus planned net taxes must equal planned investment plus planned government expenditure. An increase in government spending, given the tax rate, increases equilibrium income and the government budget deficit. An increase in the tax rate decreases equilibrium income and the budget deficit.

At times in the past, the authorities have used fiscal policy for discretionary purposes, to try to influence the overall level of economic activity, one example being the actions of the Heath administration in the early 1970s. However, we cannot judge the fiscal stance of the government merely from the size of the budget deficit, as the size of the deficit may be influenced by whether the economy is in recession. A better indicator of government intentions is the *full-employment budget*—a measurement of what the deficit/surplus would have been if the economy had been at full employment with the same tax rate and level of government expenditure. The published deficit may also be misleading to the extent that government expenditure includes *nominal* interest payments on outstanding debt, rather than payments based on the *real* interest rate. Inflation-adjusting the deficit reveals a very different story about the UK in the 1970s and 1980s.

The size of the budget deficit responds to the overall level of activity through the operation of *automatic stabilizers*—by which the deficit tends to grow during a recession and to diminish in a boom.

The use of discretionary fiscal policy for stabilization may be inhibited by a number of factors. In particular, it takes time to monitor the progress of the economy and to decide what policy action is required. Once having decided to act, there are further uncertainties which make it difficult to predict the timing of policy effects. There may also be induced effects upon other components of aggregate demand which dilute the effects of policy (see Chapter 25).

If the government does run budget deficits, then it becomes necessary to borrow from the public to finance the deficit. In the UK, any deficit of the nationalized industries must also be covered—the total making the *public sector borrowing requirement*. The size of the accumulated stock of outstanding government debt is known as the *national debt*. Of itself, the size and importance of the national debt is easily exaggerated if we fail to adjust for inflation and the effects of economic growth. If debt were to become high relative to GNP, then the printing of money could be avoided only by higher taxation or by raising interest rates to encourage the public to lend. There is no indication that UK debt is getting out of hand in this way. Indeed, the late 1980s saw the emergence of a public sector surplus, with the public sector borrowing requirement becoming the *public sector debt repayment*. Between 1981 and 1990, UK net public sector debt fell as a proportion of GDP.

Analysis of the effects of exchange rate movements and of international capital transactions is left to a later chapter, but our model cannot be considered complete until we recognize the existence of international transactions involving goods and services— i.e. *exports* and *imports*—which have an effect on aggregate demand. Although *net* exports tend to be small, exports and imports have each accounted for an increasing share of UK GDP. Exports can be regarded as autonomous, depending more on world conditions than on domestic factors. Imports, however, may be thought of as being related to the size of national income. An effect of introducing net exports into the model is to reduce the size of the multiplier. As income rises, both households and firms are likely to demand more in the way of imported goods and services. With autonomous exports, this implies that the *trade deficit* tends to be larger at high income levels and may act as a constraint on economic growth. Individual economies may be tempted to try to avoid this by the use of *import controls*, but this raises the possibility of international retaliation.

IMPORTANT CONCEPTS AND TECHNICAL TERMS

Match each lettered concept with the appropriate numbered phrase:

(a)	Automatic stabilizers	(i)	Balanced budget
(b)	Trade surplus		multiplier
(c)	National debt	(j)	Net exports
(d)	Marginal propensity	(k)	Budget deficit
	to import	(l)	Fine-tuning
(e)	Stabilization policy	(m)	The full-
(f)	Import restrictions		employment budget
(g)	Discretionary fiscal	(n)	Trade balance
	policy	(o)	Fiscal policy
(h)	Public sector	(p)	Inflation-adjusted
	borrowing		government deficit
	requirement		

1 The government's decisions about spending and taxes.
2 Direct controls on the volume of imports.
3 Mechanisms in the economy that reduce the response of GNP to shocks.
4 The value of net exports.
5 The difference between exports and imports.
6 A situation in which exports exceed imports.
7 Government actions to control the level of output in order to keep GNP close to its full-employment level.
8 The government deficit adjusted for the difference between real and nominal interest rates.
9 The excess of government outlays over government receipts.
10 The process by which an increase in government spending, accompanied by an equal increase in taxes, results in an increase in output.
11 The government deficit plus the net losses of the nationalized industries.
12 The fraction of each additional pound of national income that domestic residents wish to spend on extra imports.
13 The government's total stock of outstanding debts.
14 Frequent discretionary adjustments to policy instruments.
15 A calculation of the government budget deficit under the assumption of full employment: an indicator of fiscal stance.
16 The use of active fiscal policy in response to economic conditions.

EXERCISES

1 Table 22.1 carries us back to the kingdom of Hypothetica, which we visited in Chapter 21. As then, planned consumption is 70 per cent of disposable income, but now the government imposes net taxes amounting to 20 per cent of gross income. Planned investment is still $60 billion and the government plans to spend $50 billion.
   (a) For each level of income in Table 22.1, calculate disposable income, planned consumption, savings, and net taxes.
   (b) Calculate the aggregate demand, showing it at each level of aggregate supply.
   (c) If, in a particular period, income turned out to be $350 billion, how would you expect producers to react?
   (d) What is the equilibrium level of income?
   (e) Calculate the government budget deficit at equilibrium income.
   Suppose government expenditure is increased by $22 billion:
   (f) What is the new equilibrium income?
   (g) Calculate the government budget deficit at this new equilibrium position.
   (h) What is the value of the multiplier?

TABLE 22.1 Government comes to Hypothetica. (All quantities in Hypothetical $billion.)

Income/ output	Disposable income	Planned consumption	Planned investment	Government spending	Savings	Net taxes	Aggregate demand
50							
100							
150							
200							
250							
300							
350							
400							

2 (a) Using the data of exercise 1, use graph paper to plot the consumption function and aggregate demand schedule.

(b) Add on the 45° line and confirm that equilibrium occurs at the same point suggested by your answer to 1(d) above.

(c) Show the effect on equilibrium income of an increase in government spending of $22 billion.

3 This exercise concerns the multiplier under different circumstances in a closed economy with and without government. Consumption is determined as 80 per cent of the income available to households. Investment is autonomous at a level of 450, as shown in Table 22.2.

(a) Calculate consumption 1 and aggregate demand 1, assuming there is no government.

(b) What is the equilibrium level of income?

(c) What would be equilibrium income if investment increased by 50?

(d) Calculate the value of the multiplier.

Suppose now that the government levies direct taxes of 10 per cent of income and undertakes expenditure of 250, with investment back at 450:

(e) Calculate disposable income, consumption 2, and aggregate demand 2.

(f) What is the equilibrium level of income?

(g) What is the size of the government budget deficit?

(h) Use your answers to parts (b), (e), and (f) to explain the balanced budget multiplier.

(i) What would equilibrium income be if investment increased by 70?

(j) Calculate the value of the multiplier.

4 The government in an economy undertakes expenditure on goods and services of £100 million and makes transfer payments amounting to 10 per cent of national income. The rate of direct taxation is 30 per cent.

(a) Draw a diagram showing autonomous government expenditure and the way in which net taxes vary with national income.

(b) At what level of income does the government have a balanced budget?

(c) Within what range of income does the government run a budget deficit?

(d) Within what range of income does the government run a budget surplus?

(e) What would be the government deficit/surplus if equilibrium income were £400 million?

(f) If full-employment income is £750 million, what is the full-employment budget?

5 A government has £100 billion of outstanding debt, on which it must make interest payments at the current nominal rate of 8 per cent. Inflation is running at 6 per cent per annum.

(a) Nominal interest payments are included in government expenditure and thus contribute to the government deficit. What is the nominal interest burden?

(b) What is the real interest rate? (*Note:* this was discussed in Chapter 13.)

(c) What is the real interest burden?

(d) If you have followed this line of reasoning through, you may feel suspicious that we have just been manipulating the figures. After all, holders of government bonds must be paid their (nominal) 8 per cent

TABLE 22.2 The multiplier with and without government

Income/ output	Consumption 1	Investment	Aggregate demand 1	Disposable income	Consumption 2	Government spending	Aggregate demand 2
2000		450					
2250		450					
2500		450					
2750		450					
3000		450					

return. How in practice will the government be able to meet the payments?

6   An economy exports £50 million worth of goods each period, this quantity being autonomous. Imports, however, vary with national income such that imports always comprise 20 per cent of income.
   (a)   Draw a diagram which shows imports and exports against national income.
   (b)   What is the trade balance when income is £1000 million?
   (c)   What is the trade balance when income is £500 million?
   (d)   At what level of income are imports equal to exports?
   (e)   If full-employment income is £1000 million, explain how the balance of trade may act as a constraint on government policy.

7   Figure 22.1 shows aggregate demand schedules with and without foreign trade, together with the 45° line.

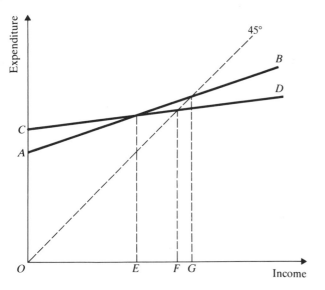

FIGURE 22.1   Equilibrium in an open economy

   (a)   AB and CD represent aggregate demand schedules with and without foreign trade. (Assume that imports are proportional to income, but exports are autonomous.) Which is which?
   (b)   Identify equilibrium income in the absence of foreign trade.
   (c)   Identify equilibrium income when there is foreign trade.
   (d)   At what level of income is there a zero trade balance?
   (e)   Explain whether the presence of foreign

trade increases or reduces the size of the multiplier.

8   Which of the following is the most accurate description of the National Debt?
   (a)   The annual gap between government expenditure and tax revenue
   (b)   The amount of money owed by the United Kingdom to the IMF
   (c)   The net accumulation of UK balance of payments deficits
   (d)   The net accumulation of UK budget deficits
   (e)   The total amount of outstanding UK foreign debt
         (University of London GCE A level Economics 3, June 1989)

9   In an open economy with government intervention, which of the following will ensure full employment?
   (a)   Savings = investment
   (b)   Taxation = government expenditure
   (c)   Savings + taxation + imports = investment + government expenditure + exports
   (d)   None of the above
         (Associated Examining Board GCE A level Economics 1, November 1988)

10   This exercise explores the balanced budget multiplier in a closed economy. Investment expenditure is fixed at 450, consumption is 80 per cent of disposable income. Initially, government expenditure is 250 and direct taxes are 10 per cent of income.
   (a)   Identify the initial equilibrium income for the economy.
   (b)   Calculate the amount of consumption expenditure, tax revenue, and the government budget deficit/surplus.
   Suppose now that government expenditure is increased by 500 and the tax rate raised from 10 to 25 per cent.
   (c)   Before output has had time to adjust, by how much is disposable income reduced?
   (d)   Calculate the resulting change in consumption expenditure and the net effect on aggregate demand, remembering the increase in government expenditure.
   (e)   What is the new equilibrium income level for the economy?
   (f)   What is the government budget deficit/surplus?
   (g)   Calculate the balanced budget multiplier.

11   Explain why each of the following items may constitute an obstacle to the use of active fiscal policy.
   (a)   Monitoring the economy's performance.

(b) Implementing changes in the spending programme.
(c) Timing the multiplier process.
(d) Uncertainty concerning the operation of the
multiplier.
(e) Uncertainty concerning future aggregate
demand.
(f) The possibility of indirect policy effects.
(g) Endangerment of other policy objectives.
(h) Uncertainty concerning the level of full
employment.

TRUE/FALSE

1 _____ In 1989, direct government
spending in the UK was nearly one-half the value
of GNP.

2 _____ The effect of net taxes is to
steepen the relationship between consumption
and national income.

3 _____ An increase in government
spending accompanied by an equal increase in
taxes results in an increase in output.

4 _____ The effect of net taxes is to reduce the multiplier.

5 _____ A negative public sector borrowing requirement is known as a public sector debt
repayment.

6 _____ For a given level of government
spending, an increase in the tax rate reduces both
the equilibrium level of national income and the
size of the budget deficit.

7 _____ The size of the budget deficit is a
good measure of the government's fiscal stance.

8 _____ The full-employment budget
shows the state of the government deficit/surplus
if the other components of aggregate demand
were such as to ensure the economy was at full-
employment output.

9 _____ In a world with significant inflation, it is sensible to count only the *real* interest
rate times the outstanding government debt as an
item of expenditure contributing to the overall
government deficit.

10 _____ Income tax, VAT, and unemployment benefit are important automatic stabilizers.

11 _____ Since the mid-1970s, governments in the UK have been reluctant to adopt
expansionary fiscal policy to offset rises in unemployment.

12 _____ The debt:GDP ratio fell in the
UK in the 1980s—as it did in most industrial
countries.

13 _____ Net exports in the UK in the early
1980s amounted to nearly 30 per cent of GDP.

14 _____ Direct import restrictions are
always good for domestic output and employment as they allow the economy to reach full
employment without hitting the constraint of the
trade balance.

QUESTIONS FOR THOUGHT

1 Examine the effect on the multiplier of the existence of government activity and international
trade. Discuss the problem of timing the multiplier
process and explore reasons why this model may
not provide an adequate explanation of how an
economy 'really' works.

2 Discuss the importance of automatic stabilizers.
To what extent may imports be regarded as one
such automatic stabilizer?

3 What do you regard as the principal shortcomings
of the model as developed so far?

ANSWERS AND COMMENTS FOR CHAPTER 22

Please note Where questions are reproduced from GCE examinations, the examination boards bear no responsibility for the answers provided in this volume, which are the sole responsibility of the authors.

Important Concepts and Technical Terms

1	o	5	j	9	k	13	c
2	f	6	b	10	i	14	l
3	a	7	e	11	h	15	m
4	n	8	p	12	d	16	g

Exercises

1 (*a*), (*b*).

TABLE A22.1 Government comes to Hypothetica. (All quantities in Hypothetical $billion.)

Income/ output	Disposable income	Planned consumption	Planned investment	Government spending	Savings	Net taxes	Aggregate demand
50	40	28	60	50	12	10	138
100	80	56	60	50	24	20	166
150	120	84	60	50	36	30	194
200	160	112	60	50	48	40	222
250	200	140	60	50	60	50	250
300	240	168	60	50	72	60	278
350	280	196	60	50	84	70	306
400	320	224	60	50	96	80	334

(*c*) At income $350b, aggregate demand amounts only to $306b; producers will see stocks building up and reduce output in the next period.

(*d*) Equilibrium is where aggregate demand equals aggregate supply, at income $250b. Equivalently, equilibrium occurs where $I + G = S + NT$— again, of course, at income $250b.

(*e*) Government spending is $50b; net taxes are $0.2 \times \$250b = \$50b$. The budget is in balance.

(*f*) With government spending at $72b, equilibrium income increases to $300b.

(*g*) Government spending is now $72b and net taxes are $0.2 \times \$300b = \$60b$: the government is running a deficit of $12b.

(*h*) The multiplier is $50/22 = 2.27$. Equivalently, it is $1/\{1 - c(1 - t)\} = 1/(1 - 0.56) = 2.27$.

2 (*a*) Notice in Figure A22.1 that the aggregate demand schedule is now less steep than previously (namely, Figure A21.3)—this is the result of the taxation.

(*b*) The diagram confirms that equilibrium occurs at income $250b—where the aggregate demand schedule cuts the 45° line.

(*c*) The increase in government spending moves the aggregate demand schedule to AD', giving a new equilibrium income of $300 billion.

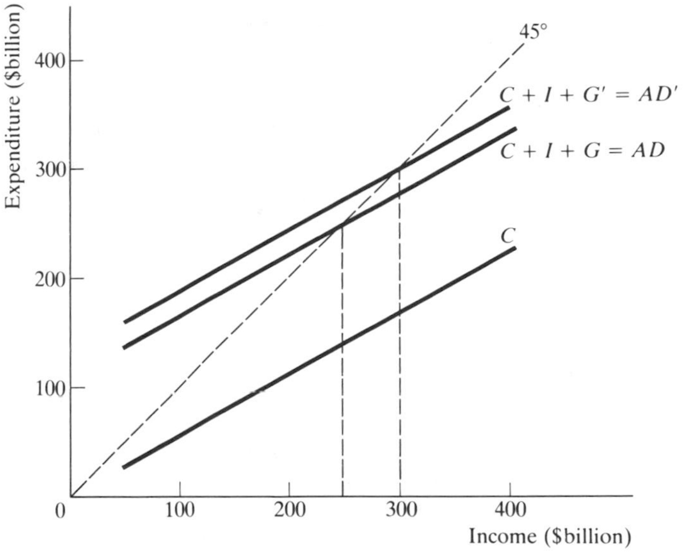

3 (*a*) See Table A22.2.

FIGURE A22.1 The income–expenditure diagram with government

TABLE A22.2 The multiplier with and without government

Income/ output	Consumption 1	Investment	Aggregate demand 1	Disposable income	Consumption 2	Government spending	Aggregate demand 2
2000	1600	450	2050	1800	1440	250	2140
2250	1800	450	2250	2025	1620	250	2320
2500	2000	450	2450	2250	1800	250	2500
2750	2200	450	2650	2475	1980	250	2680
3000	2400	450	2850	2700	2160	250	2860

(b)   2250.
(c)   2500.
(d)   250/50 = 5.
(e)   See Table A22.2.
(f)   2500.
(g)   Zero.
(h)   With the introduction of government, equilibrium income has increased from 2250 to 2500, even though the government is spending no more than is collected through taxation (see Section 22–2 of the main text).
(i)   2750.
(j)   250/70 = 3.57.

4   (a)

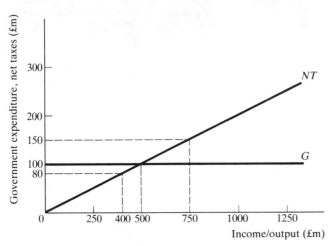

FIGURE A22.2   The government budget

(b)   £500m.
(c)   Up to £500m.
(d)   At income above £500m.
(e)   Net taxes at this point would be £80m, so with government expenditure at £100m, the government budget deficit is £20m.
(f)   A surplus of £50m.

5   (a)   £100b × 0.08 = £8b.
(b)   We can approximate the real interest rate as the difference between the nominal rate and the rate of inflation (see Section 13–2 of the main text). In this context, the real interest rate is 8 − 6 = 2 per cent.
(c)   £100b × 0.02 = £2b.
(d)   It's not really cheating: although the government must pay out the £8b in nominal interest payments, tax revenues will increase with inflation, clawing back part of this amount. If national income is also increasing in real terms, this will add further to tax revenues. It is valid to take these effects into account.

6   (a)   Figure A22.3.
(b)   At this income level, imports are £200m, exports are £150m—so there is a trade deficit of £50m.
(c)   Imports £100m, exports £150m; trade surplus is £50m.

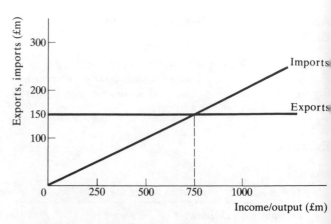

FIGURE A22.3   Imports and exports

(d)   At income £750m.
(e)   In part (b), we saw that this level of income entails a trade deficit of £50m. Such a deficit cannot be sustained in the long run, so fiscal policy to take the economy to full employment cannot be successful in the long run. Some commentators have regarded this constraint as the reason for Britain's slow rate of economic growth during the early postwar period.

7   (a)   AB is the aggregate demand schedule without foreign trade. Adding autonomous exports together with imports proportional to income moves the schedule to CD.
(b)   OG.
(c)   OF.
(d)   OE: this corresponds to the point at which exports = imports. At this point, aggregate demand is the same on both AB and CD, as net exports are equal to zero.
(e)   The multiplier is reduced by foreign trade through the effect of the marginal propensity to import (see Section 22–7 of the main text).

8   (d).

9   Option (c) states the condition for equilibrium output, but this does *not* guarantee full employment, so the appropriate response is (d).

10   (a) $Y = \dfrac{I + G}{\{1 - c(1 - t)\}} = \dfrac{700}{0.28} = 2500.$
(b) $C = 0.8 \times 2500 \times 0.9 = 1800;$
tax revenue = $0.1 \times 2500 = 250;$
government budget surplus = $tY - G = 0.$
(c)   Disposable income was $2500 \times 0.9\ = 2250$
but is now $2500 \times 0.75 = 1830$
                                ————
and has been reduced by   420
                                ————
(d)   Consumption falls by $0.8 \times 420 = 336$, but aggregate demand increases by $500 - 336 = 164.$
(e) $Y = 1200/0.4 = 3000.$
(f)   Government budget surplus = $tY - G = 750 - 750 = 0.$

(g) Multiplier $= \dfrac{\text{change in } Y}{\text{change in } G} = \dfrac{500}{500}$.

In this case the multiplier is unity.

1 (a) It takes time to collect information about the economy and to realize that policy action is required.

(b) Having decided to take action, further time is needed to put changes in spending into practice: capital expenditure is inflexible, individual government departments will resist cuts in their own budgets.

(c) The multiplier is not an instantaneous process, but takes some time to work through the system—remember, the policy relies upon influencing the behaviour of agents such as households.

(d) There is likely to be uncertainty about how strong, reliable, and rapid the effects of the policy will be.

(e) By the time the policy has taken effect, the other elements of aggregate demand may be at different levels, affecting the equilibrium level of income.

(f) Our model is still rudimentary: there are many routes by which fiscal policy may have indirect effects upon other components of demand—especially investment.

(g) There may be other policy objectives, such as the control of monetary growth or inflation, which could be endangered by the effects of fiscal policy.

(h) Before we are induced to take action to combat unemployment, we need to be sure that there really is a problem—that the economy is not already at full employment.

These issues are discussed in Box 22–1 of the main text.

True/False

1 False: more like a quarter (see Section 22–1 of the main text).

2 False: the reverse is true (see Section 22–2 of the main text).

3 True: although the proximity to full employment may be a relevant consideration.

4 True.

5 True.

6 True.

7 False: it may be misleading (see Section 22–4 of the main text).

8 True.

9 True.

10 True: see Section 22–5 of the main text.

11 True: see Box 22–1 of the main text.

12 False: the ratio fell for the UK and for Japan, but rose for many other countries: see Table 22–5 in the main text.

13 False: exports were nearly 30 per cent of GDP, but *net* exports (the difference between exports and imports) were much smaller (see Section 22–7 of the main text).

14 False: there is the possibility of retaliation from competitors to consider.

Questions for Thought

1 The introduction of government and foreign trade has the effect of reducing the multiplier. By comparing two alternative equilibrium positions, we neglect the process by which the new equilibrium is attained. This process may be spread over many time periods (see Section 21–6 of the main text). For hints on the inadequacy of the model so far, see the hints on question 3.

3 At this stage, the model is clearly much abstracted from reality. In particular, we have not considered the financial side of the economy; nor have we thought about what happens if prices are free to vary, or how the interest rate is determined. Neither have we explored how investment expenditure is decided. In addition, even a cursory look at the 'real' world suggests that the economy *changes* through time. All these issues are tackled in the following chapters.

23 Money and Modern Banking

Our study of macroeconomics so far has dealt with *real* variables, like output or expenditure on goods and services. We now turn our attention to the *financial* markets by examining the importance of money and banking in a modern economy. In this chapter and the next, we explore the uses of money and the means which the authorities may adopt in order to control its quantity.

The prime role for money in an economy is as a *medium of exchange*—it must be a generally accepted means of payment for the delivery of goods and services and for the settlement of debt. Imagine for a moment the problems of conducting trade in a *barter economy*, where you must find another person who not only can provide what you require but also needs whatever goods you happen to have on offer—the *double coincidence of wants*, as it is sometimes called. The existence of money makes the carrying out of transactions both more simple and more efficient.

A second role for money is as a *unit of account*: a standard measurement in which prices of goods and services can be quoted. Thirdly, money must be a *store of value*: it must have a value in future transactions if it is to operate effectively as a medium of exchange. Of course, there may be other commodities which store value—commodities which offer protection against inflation, or promise a rate of return. None the less, money must have this quality to some degree if it is to fulfil its role. Finally, money acts as a standard of deferred payment by establishing a value for the later repayment of loans.

At various times in various places, different commodities have performed the function of money—dogs' teeth, sea shells, gold, slaves, and cigarettes are all examples of *commodity money*. However, in the modern world such examples are rare, and *token money* is commonly accepted. Notes and coins (*legal tender*) are examples of token money and are supplemented by *customary* or *IOU money*, such as bank deposits.

The origins of modern banking can be traced back to the operations of the goldsmiths, who began by acting as 'safe-keepers', storing gold in their vaults on behalf of their clients. When these clients began to transfer ownership of their gold by means of paper transactions rather than physical exchange, the *cheque* was born. When the goldsmiths realized that their clients did not all demand their gold at once, then overdrafts and bank loans were on the way. Of course, the goldsmiths had to hold *reserves* of gold to avoid the danger of *financial panics*, but reserves needed to constitute only a proportion of total deposits.

The modern banking system works through the operation of *financial intermediaries* such as *commercial banks*. A key feature of the commercial banks is that part of their liabilities are used as a means of payment and are therefore to be regarded as part of the money supply of the economy. The commercial banks operate through the *clearing system*, which calculates on a daily basis the net flows of funds between its members resulting from the balance of transactions. In the UK the *central bank* (the Bank of England) acts as a banker for the commercial banks, who hold a proportion of their reserves as idle cash balances at the Bank of England to enable this banking activity.

Like any other private firm, we regard the commercial banks as profit-maximizers. They accept deposits in the form of *sight* and *time deposits*—which, together with *certificates of deposit*, comprise the liabilities side of their balance sheets. On the assets side, the banks hold various assets of differing *liquidity*—in general, the less liquid, the higher the return received on the asset. The skill of the bank trying to maximize profits is to judge the liquidity structure of its portfolio of assets so as to gain a safe high return while holding sufficient liquid assets to service the bank's customers. By granting loans and overdraft facilities, the commercial banks effectively add to the amount of customary money in the economy and can thus affect the size of the existing money stock.

The amount of notes and coins in circulation plus the cash reserves of the commercial banks is known as the *monetary base*. Inevitably, some cash is always required by the public for transaction purposes—and remember that in 1986 only 61 per cent of British households had chequing accounts. It can be shown that money supply is equal to the monetary base times the *money multiplier*. This reflects the ability of the banks to create credit. The size of the money multiplier depends upon the preferences of the commercial bank and of the public for holding cash. The lower is the banks' desired cash reserve ratio, the larger is the money multiplier and the larger will be the money stock. Similarly, the lower is the amount of cash held by the public, the larger will be the money stock.

The amount of cash held in reserve by banks will depend upon its opportunity cost—the return which could be obtained by lending the funds—and upon the predictability of withdrawals. Public preferences for holding cash will depend upon institutional factors determining how income payments are made, upon tax arrangements, upon the availability of credit cards, and perhaps upon the time of year. (More cash is needed at Christmas time, for instance.)

Until 1989, *M1* was a commonly used measure of *narrow money*. It comprised notes and coin in circulation, plus sterling sight deposits. However, in July 1989 Abbey National became a public limited company and was reclassified as a bank rather than a building society. The size of the company is such that the statistics for the monetary aggregates were seriously distorted. Consequently, data for *M1*, *M3*, and *M3c* are no longer published. Even narrower in coverage than M1 is *M0* (known as the *wide monetary base*), which comprises just cash in circulation plus the till money of commercial banks and their cash deposits at the Bank of England. There are also broader definitions of money which encompass other financial assets and *near money*. These include *M2*, *M4*, *M4c*, and *M5*. For example, *M4* is made up of private sector holdings of notes and coin, banks' retail deposits, building society shares and deposits, and other interest-bearing bank and building society deposits (including Certificates of Deposit). *M5* also includes money market instruments and certain national savings items. This is the broadest of the published definitions.

This multiplicity of assets and definitions of money turns out to be important when we come in Chapter 24 to consider how the authorities may attempt to control the growth of the money stock.

IMPORTANT CONCEPTS AND TECHNICAL TERMS

Match each lettered concept with the appropriate numbered phrase:

(a)	Medium of exchange	(j)	Deposit
(b)	Financial intermediary	(k)	Money supply
		(l)	Store of value
(c)	Token money	(m)	Liquidity
(d)	Money	(n)	Commercial banks
(e)	Near money	(o)	Reserve ratio
(f)	Financial panic	(p)	Money multiplier
(g)	M0	(q)	Unit of account
(h)	IOU money	(r)	Monetary base
(i)	Clearing system	(s)	Reserves
		(t)	Barter economy

1 Any generally accepted means of payment for the delivery of goods or the settlement of debt.

2 The function of money whereby it enables the exchange of goods and services.

3 The function of money by which it provides a unit in which prices are quoted and accounts are kept.

4 The function of money by which it can be used to make purchases in the future.

5 The quantity of notes and coin in private circulation plus the quantity held by the banking system, sometimes known as the stock of high-powered money.

6 In the time of the goldsmiths, the amount of gold immediately available to meet depositors' demands.

7 An economy with no medium of exchange, in which goods are traded directly or swapped for other goods.

8 The change in the money stock for a £1 change in the quantity of the monetary base.

9 A medium of exchange based on the debt of a private firm or individual.

10 Financial intermediaries with a government licence to make loans and issue deposits, including deposits against which cheques can be written.

11 An institution that specializes in bringing lenders and borrowers together.

12 Assets that are 'almost' as good as money: stores of value that can readily be converted into money but are not themselves a means of payment.

13 A means of payment whose value or purchasing power as money greatly exceeds its cost of production or value in uses other than as money.

14 A self-fulfilling prophecy whereby people believe that a bank will be unable to pay and, in the stampede to get their money, thereby ensure that the bank cannot pay.

15 Notes and coin in circulation plus bankers' operational deposits with the Bank of England.

16 The value of the total stock of money, the medium of exchange, in circulation.

17 A set of arrangements in which debts between banks are settled by adding up all the transactions in a given period and paying only the net amounts needed to balance inter-bank accounts.

18 The speed and certainty with which an asset can be converted into money.

19 In the time of the goldsmiths, the amount entrusted to the goldsmith for safekeeping.

20 The ratio of reserves to deposits.

EXERCISES

1 Eight individuals in a barter economy have and want the following goods:
Alice has some haddock but would like some apples;
Barry has some gin but fancies blackcurrant jam;
Carol is in possession of doughnuts but wants coconuts;
Daniel has obtained some jellied eels but really wants doughnuts;
Eva has some figs but would prefer jellied eels;

Frank fancies figs but has only blackcurrant jam;
Gloria has coconuts but yearns for gin;
Henry has apples but would like haddock.
  (a) Can you work out a series of transactions which would satisfy all concerned?
  (b) Can you now understand how money is so helpful in making the world go round?

2 Identify each of the following items as legal, token, commodity, or IOU money—or, indeed, as not-money:
  (a) Gold.
  (b) £1 coin.
  (c) Cigarettes.
  (d) Cheque for £100.
  (e) Petrol.
  (f) Camera accepted in part-exchange.
  (g) A building society deposit.
  (h) Pigs, turkeys, and cocoa nuts.

3 This exercise shows how the banks can create money through their loans policy. For simplicity, assume that there is a single commercial bank, which aims to hold 10 per cent of its deposits as cash. The public is assumed to have a fixed demand for cash of £10 million. We begin in equilibrium with the following situation:

Commercial bank balance sheet (£m)

Liabilities		Assets		Cash ratio	Public cash holdings	Money stock
Deposits	100	Cash	10			
		Loans	90			
	100		100	10%	10	110

Consider the sequence of events that follows if the central bank autonomously supplies an extra £10 million cash which finds its way into the pockets of Joe Public:
  (a) How will Joe Public react? (Remember the fixed demand for cash.)
  (b) How does this affect the cash ratio of the commercial bank?
  (c) How will the commercial bank react to this 'disequilibrium'?
  (d) How much cash does Joe Public now hold?
  (e) What will Joe Public do with the excess cash?
  (f) How does this affect the commercial bank's behaviour?
  (g) At what point will the system settle down again, with both bank and public back in equilibrium?
  (h) How does money stock alter as this process unfolds?

Note: if this sequence of questions does not make any sense to you, you are recommended to tackle them again in conjunction with the commentary provided in the 'Answers and Comments' section.

4 Which of the following would always be regarded as a requirement of money?
  1 Backed by a precious metal
  2 Authorised as legal tender by the government
  3 Generally acceptable as a medium of exchange
  (a) 1, 2 and 3 are correct
  (b) 1 and 2 only are correct
  (c) 2 and 3 only are correct
  (d) 1 only is correct
  (e) 3 only is correct
    (University of London GCE A level Economics 3, January 1987)

5 The commercial banks in an economy choose to hold 5 per cent of deposits in the form of cash reserves. The general public chooses to hold an amount of notes and coin in circulation equal to one-quarter of its bank deposits. The stock of high-powered money in the economy is £12 million.
  (a) Calculate the value of the money multiplier.
  (b) What is the size of the money stock if both public and banks are holding their desired amounts of cash?
  (c) Suppose the banks now decide that they need to hold only 4 per cent of deposits as cash. Calculate the value of the money multiplier.
  (d) What is now the size of 'equilibrium' money stock?
  (e) Suppose that the banks again choose to hold 5 per cent of deposits as cash, but the public increases its cash holdings to 30 per cent of its bank deposits. Now what is the value of the money multiplier?
  (f) What is now the size of 'equilibrium' money stock?
  (g) Does this analysis provide any clues to how the monetary authorities might try to influence the size of the money stock?

6 On p. 159 are listed items comprising the assets and liabilities of UK retail banks in March 1990, taken from the *Bank of England Quarterly Bulletin*, May 1990. Use these figures to compile the balance sheet of the retail banks.

	£b
Sterling sight deposits	131.5
Sterling cash holdings	3.7
Certificates of deposit	19.4
Market loans	51.4
Securities	11.5
Deposits in other currencies	67.1
Advances	222.1
Miscellaneous assets	38.5
Bills	12.2
Sterling time deposits	127.3
Miscellaneous liabilities	64.5
Lending in other currencies	70.4

7   Assume that the clearing banks maintain a minimum cash ratio of $12\frac{1}{2}\%$ and that an individual bank receives a cash deposit of £1000. On the basis of this additional cash, this particular bank will feel able to create additional deposits equal to
   (a)   £750
   (b)   £1250
   (c)   £7000
   (d)   £12 500
   (Associated Examining Board GCE A level Economics Paper 1, June 1987)

8   Which of the following would be regarded as an asset to a customer of a commercial bank?
   (a)   A current account bank deposit.
   (b)   A special deposit.
   (c)   Trade bills held by the bank as reserve assets.
   (d)   The bank's deposits at the Bank of England.
   (e)   An overdraft.
   (f)   Loans advanced by the commercial bank in US$.

9   Which of the following would appear as a liability in a commercial bank's balance sheet?
   (a)   Advances to customers
   (b)   Money at call and short notice
   (c)   Deposits of customers
   (d)   Bills discounted
   (University of London GCE A level Economics 3, June 1989)

10   Assess the liquidity and likely return of each of the following financial assets:
   (a)   Cash.
   (b)   Equities.
   (c)   Bonds.
   (d)   Bills.
   (e)   Industrial shares.
   (f)   Perpetuities.

TRUE/FALSE

1   _____ Dogs' teeth have been used as money in the Admiralty Islands.

2   _____ Trading is expensive in a barter economy.

3   _____ Money in current accounts in banks is legal tender.

4   _____ Financial panics are rare in present-day Britain because of the actions of the Bank of England.

5   _____ If the goldsmiths insisted that all transactions were backed by equal amounts of gold in the vaults, then their actions could not cause growth in the money supply.

6   _____ Banks are the only financial intermediaries.

7   _____ The clearing system represents one way in which society reduces the costs of making transactions.

8   _____ The more liquid an asset, the higher the return received.

9   _____ The modern fractional reserve banking system is an intrinsic part of the process of money creation.

10   _____ The monetary base is the quantity of notes and coin in circulation with the non-bank private sector.

11   _____ The more cash that the public wishes to hold, the higher is money supply.

12   _____ Building society deposits are so liquid that they ought to be included in the definition of money.

QUESTIONS FOR THOUGHT

1   Discuss why you think that people want to hold money rather than using the funds to earn a return.

2   How do you expect the increased use of credit cards to affect the money supply?

ANSWERS AND COMMENTS FOR CHAPTER 23

Please note Where questions are reproduced from GCE examinations, the examination boards bear no responsibility for the answers provided in this volume, which are the sole responsibility of the authors.

Important Concepts and Technical Terms

1 *d*	6 *s*	11 *b*	16 *k*
2 *a*	7 *t*	12 *e*	17 *i*
3 *q*	8 *p*	13 *c*	18 *m*
4 *l*	9 *h*	14 *f*	19 *j*
5 *r*	10 *n*	15 *g*	20 *o*

Exercises

1 (a) This exercise is intended to illustrate the inefficiency of the barter economy. It is possible in this case to arrange a sequence of transactions. For instance, Alice swaps with Henry; Daniel exchanges with Eva and then with Carol; Barry swaps with Gloria; Carol exchanges with Frank and then with Barry. The success of the sequence depends upon the ability of these people to agree fair quantities for exchange as well as being able to sort out with whom to exchange—notice that poor Carol in our sequence holds in turn doughnuts, figs, and blackcurrant jam before she finally gets coconuts in the last round!

   (b) Even in this simple world of only eight people with simple desires, the gains from there being a medium of exchange should be apparent—and notice that, by virtue of prices, the 'quantity' problem is also solved.

2 (a) Gold is an example of commodity money—it is a substance with industrial uses which has at times been acceptable as a medium of exchange.

   (b) A £1 coin is legal tender and token money—the value of the metal and cost of production is less than £1.

   (c) Cigarettes have been used as a commodity money—for example, in prisoner-of-war camps during the Second World War (see Section 23–1 of the main text), but normally would be considered not-money.

   (d) A cheque is an example of IOU money—and also token money.

   (e) Petrol is normally not-money—but *The Times* on 11 December 1981 reported that parking fines in some towns in Argentina could be paid only in petrol, as inflation was eroding the value of money at such a rapid rate.

   (f) The camera in part-exchange is not-money. It does not meet the requirement of being 'generally acceptable' and has value only in that particular transaction.

   (g) A building society deposit is near money: it is readily converted into cash but cannot be used directly in payment.

   (h) In general, these are considered not-money—but see the story of the singer Mademoiselle Zelie in Box 23–1 of the main text.

3 (a) Joe Public is now holding £20m instead of the desired £10m and will presumably deposit the extra £10m with the commercial bank.

   (b) The bank is now holding £20m cash with £90m loans—and the cash ratio has increased to 20/110 = 18.2 per cent.

   (c) The commercial bank will seek to make further loans to restore the desired 10 per cent cash ratio.

   (d) Joe Public has now borrowed an extra £9m, so cash holdings have increased to £19m.

   (e) The extra £9m eventually finds its way back into the bank.

   (f) And the bank's cash ratio is back up to 20/119 = 16.8 per cent, so the bank again will try to make further loans.

   (g) Equilibrium is restored in the following condition:

Commercial bank balance sheet (£m)

Liabilities		Assets				
Deposits	200	Cash	20	Cash	Public cash	Money
		Loans	180	ratio	holdings	stock
	200		200	10%	10	210

   (h) Each time the bank makes further loans to Joe Public, money stock increases by the amount of the loans. The original increase of £10m leads to a £100m increase of money stock by the time the system settles down.

4 (e)

5 (a) The money multiplier is $(c_p + 1)/(c_p + c_b)$
   where c_p = the proportion of deposits held by the public as cash
   c_b = the proportion of deposits held by the banks as cash.
   Here we have $\frac{(0.25 + 1)}{(0.25 + 0.05)} = \frac{1.25}{0.3} = 4.17$

   (b) $M1 = \frac{(c_p + 1)}{(c_p + c_b)} H = 4.17 \times 12 = 50.04.$

   (c) 1.25/0.29 = 4.31.

   (d) 4.31 × 12 = 51.72.

   (e) 1.30/0.35 = 3.71.

   (f) 3.71 × 12 = 44.52.

   (g) It is clear that both c_p and c_b influence the size of the money stock. The question is whether either of these ratios can be influenced by policy action. The alternative is to operate on the stock of high-powered money itself. The question of money stock policy is raised in Chapter 24.

6   Balance Sheet of Retail Banks, March 1990

Assets	£b	Liabilities	£b
Sterling: Cash	3.7	Sterling: Sight deposits	131.5
Bills	12.2	Time deposits	127.3
Market loans	51.4	Certificates of	
Advances	222.1	deposit	19.4
Securities	11.5		
Lending in other currencies	70.4	Deposits in other currencies	67.1
Miscellaneous assets	38.5	Miscellaneous liabilities	64.5
TOTAL ASSETS	409.8	TOTAL LIABILITIES	409.8

7   (c).

8   (a).

9   (c).

10   (a)   Cash is the ultimately most liquid asset, but offers no return.

(b)   Equities offer a return in the form of dividends but are not very liquid and highly risky—if the firm goes bankrupt, equities of that firm become worthless.

(c)   Bonds are long-term financial assets offering a return (the coupon value) and the possibility of capital gains (or losses) if bond prices change. They are potentially liquid, but are affected by the uncertainty of future bond prices. Bonds are to be redeemed at a specific future date.

(d)   Bills are short-term financial assets with less than one year to redemption. They are highly liquid and offer a reasonable return.

(e)   See equities (b).

(f)   Perpetuities are bonds which are never repurchased by the original issuer. They are not very liquid.

For further discussion of these financial assets, see Box 23–2 of the main text.

True/False

1   True: see the introduction to Chapter 23 in the main text.

2   True: see Section 23–1 of the main text.

3   False: only notes and coins are legal tender—bank deposits are customary or IOU money. Shopkeepers are not legally obliged to accept a cheque.

4   True: see Section 23–2 of the main text.

5   True: the goldsmiths could create money only by holding reserves of less than 100 per cent.

6   False: insurance companies, pension funds, and building societies are other examples of institutions which take in money in order to relend it (see Section 23–3 of the main text).

7   True.

8   False: in general, a higher return must be offered to compensate for loss of liquidity.

9   True: see Section 23–4 of the main text.

10   False: the monetary base also includes cash held by the banks (see Section 23–5 of the main text).

11   False: examination of the money multiplier relationship suggests that the reverse is true.

12   'Trueish': it depends partly on why you want your money definition. If it is narrow money that you are trying to measure, you might not want to include building society deposits which are no more liquid than time deposits. Notice that building society deposits are included in the M2, M4, and M5 definitions of money (see Section 23–6 of the main text).

Questions for Thought

1   So far we have talked mainly about the *supply* of money. This question is asking you to think about the *demand* for money. This is an important issue which will be considered in the next chapter.

2   How does the existence of credit cards affect the public's need to use cash? Suppose a significant number of motorists always buy petrol by credit card: what effect does this have on their need to hold cash? How does this affect the money multiplier—and hence money supply? There is some brief discussion of this topic in Section 23–5 of the main text.

24

Central Banking and the Monetary System

This important chapter discusses one of the burning issues of the 1990s: how can the monetary authorities attempt to control the growth of money stock? We examine the role of the central bank (in the UK, the *Bank of England*), the demand for money, and the way in which money market equilibrium is attained. Finally, we explore recent UK monetary policy and set out some of the problems encountered.

The Bank of England carries out two main functions, reflected in the titles of its two departments—the Issue Department and the Banking Department. As its name suggests, the former issues coins and banknotes, which are introduced into circulation by the purchase of financial securities—a process known as *open market operations*. The Banking Department acts as banker to the commercial banks and to the government. A unique feature of the central bank is that it can create liabilities in unlimited quantity without fear of bankruptcy—if required to do so. This was not the case in the days of the *gold standard*, when all liabilities issued by the Bank had to be backed by equal amounts of gold.

The Bank is also responsible for the conduct of monetary policy on a day-to-day basis. We may distinguish three ways in which the Bank may influence the money supply. Firstly, it can do so by the imposition of *reserve requirements*, by which the commercial banks (and perhaps other financial institutions) are required to hold a given proportion of reserves as cash or liquid assets. If this forces the banks to hold more cash than they otherwise would, this limits money creation by the banks, reduces the money multiplier and thus money supply, given the stock of high-powered money. In the past, *Special Deposits* were a good way of putting pressure on the banks by effectively reducing their reserve holdings. This method of control is much diluted if the banks respond by trying to attract extra deposits rather than by restricting their lending.

The amount of lending the banks undertake can also be influenced through the *discount rate*—the interest rate that the Bank of England charges when the commercial banks want to borrow money. (In the UK this used to be known as the *minimum lending rate*.)

The amount of reserves held by the banks is typically above the minimum required by regulation. The amount of *excess* reserves held depends upon the differential between the market rate available on loans and the discount rate. By raising the discount rate to a penalty level, the Bank can induce the banks to hold more excess reserves and thus reduce the rate of money creation.

Both of the effects discussed operate by affecting the money multiplier. An alternative is for the Bank to influence the stock of high-powered money through open market operations.

In its role as banker to the banking system, the Bank acts as *lender of last resort*. As we saw in the previous chapter, confidence in the banking system is essential for the avoidance of financial panics. The lender-of-last-resort facility guarantees that banks can get cash if they really need it, and this encourages confidence. Speculative lending has been discouraged by the Bank since the secondary banking crisis of 1973–74, when substantial Bank of England intervention proved necessary.

As banker to the government, the Bank must ensure that the government can meet its payments when running a budget deficit. The *public sector borrowing requirement* may be financed either through open market operations—borrowing from the public by selling bills and bonds—or by 'printing money'—selling securities to the Bank of England for cash. This affects the stock of high-powered money, and hence money supply, through the money multiplier. In addition, the Bank is responsible for *debt management*: the issue of new securities to finance the redemption of old ones. This entails decisions concerning the length and return to be offered on new issues.

So far, all our discussion has concerned money supply, but money *demand* is equally important. The main reasons for agents to hold money can be related to its two prime functions—as a medium of exchange, and as a store of value. Suppose for simplicity that there are just two assets (money and bonds) and that the decision of the individual is to divide his or her wealth between these two assets. Given that bonds offer a return but money does not, one relevant consideration will be the *opportunity cost* of holding money.

The *transactions motive* for holding money arises from the imperfect synchronization of receipts and payments. Individuals receive income at regular intervals but typically undertake transactions more sporadically. The amount of *nominal money holding* depends upon the price level, but the demand for money is bound up with its purchasing power in terms of goods and services, so it is more helpful to think about the demand for *real money balances*. We assume that the real value of desired transactions will be related to the level of real national income.

The *precautionary motive* reflects the existence of uncertainty. People wish to hold money in case they encounter bargains or emergencies during the coming period. The main influence on the size of money demand from this motive is again likely to be real income. Both transactions and precautionary motives relate to money's function as a medium of exchange.

The *asset motive* reflects the desire to hold a balanced portfolio of risky and safe assets—money being a non-risky asset. This motive is more relevant when we try to explain a broad definition of money. In explaining the asset motive, we return to the notion of the opportunity cost of holding money. Individuals will hold money up to the point where the marginal benefit is balanced with the marginal cost. The marginal cost depends upon the *nominal interest rate* (the differential rate between money and bonds). The marginal benefit will be relatively high when money holding is low, but will decline as money holdings increase.

Price changes will not affect the demand for real money balances. An increase in the interest rate raises the opportunity cost of holding money and reduces money demand. An increase in real income tends to increase the demand for real money balances because more transactions will be undertaken.

Money market equilibrium is seen by bringing money supply and money demand together. In principle, the central bank can control money supply by open market operations and cash requirements—but notice that this control relates only to *nominal* money supply and not to *real* money supply, which depends also upon prices. By assuming prices to be fixed, we have side-stepped this problem for the moment. Money market equilibrium is achieved when the quantity of real balances demanded is equal to the quantity supplied. For a given level of real income, the interest rate adjusts to bring about equilibrium. The mechanism by which this works involves the bond market: for instance, excess demand for money implies excess supply of bonds; the consequent fall in the price of bonds raises the rate of interest, equalizing money demand and supply. An increase in real income has the effect of shifting the money demand curve, which, given fixed money supply, results in a rise in the interest rate.

Before 1971 in the UK, monetary policy was less prominent than today. It rested on the use of the discount rate, on the imposition of reserve requirements on the commercial banks with occasional resource to Special Deposits, ceilings on interest rates and bank lending, and on open market operations to affect the monetary base. A major concern was the stability of interest rates. Problems arose because the merchant banks and other financial institutions were unregulated so that monetary control operating only through the commercial banks became increasingly ineffective. There was also unease about the distortionary effects of direct controls.

The *Competition and Credit Control* reforms of 1971 coincided with the floating of the exchange rate (which we will see later is crucial for the use of monetary policy). The reforms extended monetary control to a wider range of financial institutions, but freed the commercial banks to compete for deposits and advances. Interest rate ceilings were scrapped for clearing bank time deposits and advances; reserve requirements were modified to incorporate a $12\frac{1}{2}$ per cent liquid assets ratio and a $1\frac{1}{2}$ per cent cash ratio— these to be applied more widely than just the commercial banks. The first years of the reforms (1971–73) saw dramatic rises in money supply. (£M3 increased by more than 60 per cent in two years). The banks offered high rates of interest on time deposits, thus attracting more funds to enable the expansion of lending. Special Deposits were found no longer to have the intended effects, causing the introduction of the *Supplementary Special Deposit* scheme (the 'Corset'). However, the banks found ways of evading the controls, channelling loans through institutions not covered by the regulations—a process known as *disintermediation*.

Further reforms in August 1981 abolished reserve requirements, and discontinued the announcement of minimum lending rate. A $\frac{1}{2}$ per cent cash ratio was imposed—but this was to allow the Bank of England to conduct its banking business, and has not been used for control. Monetary policy was to act through open market operation and the publication of monetary targets. In the late 1980s the focus of policy again switched with the adoption of a high interest rate strategy, intended to combat inflation, as we shall see in Chapter 28.

What are the practical problems of monetary control? Monetary base control is rendered difficult because of disintermediation and the potentially destabilizing effect on interest rates. An alternative is to allow the banks freedom to choose their cash ratio and to affect high-powered money through open market operations. This has been the approach since 1981, but a key problem remains the Bank's role as lender of last resort. Another possibility would be to impose a liquid assets rather than a cash ratio, as happened during the 1970s. The liquid assets base would be manipulated by the buying and selling of long-term assets. However, problems would remain, as the banks could acquire liquid assets from the public by offering high interest rates on time deposits—and charging correspondingly high rates on advances. The cessation of the announcement of minimum lending rate had the effect of increasing uncertainty concerning the rate to be charged for lender of last resort facilities. Another alternative which was used in the late 1970s was control through the interest rate, whereby interest rates are set at a level which allows money demand to adjust to the desired target. This can be successful only if the money demand function is both known and stable and if equilibrium is rapidly achieved.

The late 1980s saw major changes in financial markets throughout the world, enabled by advances in technology, bringing both deregulation and new forms of regulation. *Big Bang* in 1986 allowed UK banks to expand their range of activities, and other financial institutions (like building societies) began to compete more directly with banks. The Basle Accord of 1988 recognized the effective globalization of world financial markets, and made international banking the first industry to be truly regulated at international level. In the face of these developments and the moves towards greater European integration, the role and conduct of central banks are changing.

IMPORTANT CONCEPTS AND TECHNICAL TERMS

Match each lettered concept with the appropriate numbered phrase:

(a)	Special Deposits	(k)	Lender of last resort
(b)	Central bank	(l)	Precautionary
(c)	Debt management		motive
(d)	Nominal money	(m)	The Corset
	balances	(n)	Required reserve
(e)	Discount rate		ratio
(f)	Liquid assets ratio	(o)	Money market
(g)	Asset motive		equilibrium
(h)	Open market	(p)	Transactions motive
	operations	(q)	Goodhart's law
(i)	Real money balances	(r)	Opportunity cost of
(j)	Big Bang		holding money

1   The most important bank in a country, usually having official standing in the government, having responsibility for issuing banknotes, and acting as banker to the banking system and to the government.
2   Holdings of money deflated by the price level.
3   The Supplementary Special Deposit scheme introduced in the UK in December 1973 to stem the growth of bank lending.
4   A situation in which the quantity of real money balances demanded equals the quantity supplied.

5   A motive for holding money arising from uncertainty by which people hold money to meet contingencies the exact nature of which cannot be foreseen.
6   Action by the central bank to alter the monetary base by buying or selling financial securities in the open market.
7   The role of the central bank whereby it stands ready to lend to banks and other financial institutions when financial panic threatens the financial system.
8   The interest rate that the central bank charges when the commercial banks want to borrow money.
9   A minimum ratio of cash reserves to deposits which the central bank requires commercial banks to hold.
10   A motive for holding money arising because people dislike risk and are prepared to sacrifice a high average rate of return to obtain a portfolio with a lower but more predictable rate of return.
11   The value of money holdings uncorrected for the price level.
12   A motive for holding money reflecting the fact that payments and receipts are not perfectly synchronized.
13   A set of measures that introduced deregulation in a number of aspects of financial trading.
14   The set of judgements by which the Bank decides the details of new securities in relation to redemption dates and rates of interest.
15   A control measure whereby the commercial banks must deposit at the Bank of England some of their cash reserves, which could *not* be counted as part of the banks' cash reserves in meeting their reserve requirements.
16   The interest given up by holding money rather than bonds.
17   A requirement for the commercial banks to hold a proportion of their deposits as cash plus short-term bills.
18   The proposition that attempts by the Bank to regulate or tax one channel of banking business quickly leads to the same business being conducted through a different channel which is untaxed or unregulated.

EXERCISES

1   The following items comprise the assets and liabilities of the Bank of England in March 1990:

	£b
Government securities (Issue Department)	10.8
Public deposits	0.1
Advances	0.5
Special deposits	0.0
Government securities (Banking Department)	1.4
Notes in circulation	15.2
Bankers' deposits	1.5
Reserves and other accounts	2.1
Other securities (Issue Department)	4.4
Other assets (Banking Department)	0.4

Source: *Bank of England Quarterly Bulletin*, May 1990

Identify each item as an asset or a liability and complete the balance sheets for the two departments of the Bank.

2 In a given economy, the public chooses to hold an amount of cash equal to 40 per cent of its bank deposits. The commercial banks choose to hold 5 per cent of deposits in the form of cash in order to service their customers. The stock of high-powered money is £12 million.

(a) What is the size of the money supply?

Each of the following four situations represents an attempt by the monetary authorities to reduce the size of money supply. In each case, assume that the banking system is initially as described above.

(b) What would be the size of money supply if the central bank imposed a 10 per cent cash ratio on the commercial banks?

(c) What would be the size of money supply if the central bank raised its discount rate to such a penalty rate that the banks choose to hold an extra 5 per cent of deposits as cash?

(d) What would be the size of money supply if the central bank called for Special Deposits of an amount corresponding to 5 per cent of bank deposits?

(e) What would be the reduction in money supply if the central bank undertook open market operations to reduce the stock of high-powered money by £1 million?

3 In what way would you expect each of the following items to affect the demand for real money balances?

(a) An increase in real income.
(b) An increase in confidence about the future.
(c) An increase in the opportunity cost of holding money.
(d) A fall in nominal interest rates.
(e) An increase in the price level.
(f) An increase in the interest differential between risky assets and time deposits.

(g) An increase in uncertainty concerning future transactions.
(h) A fall in the frequency of income payments—for example, a switch from weekly to monthly payment.
(i) An increase in the stock of high-powered money brought about by open market operations by the Bank of England.

4 Table 24.1 provides information concerning *nominal* national output, M1, £M3, and interest rates, comparing the years 1979 and 1983 in the UK, a period in which money supply was a well publicized policy target.

TABLE 24.1 Analysing money holdings 1979–83

	1979	1983
Nominal money holdings M1 (end 1979 = 100)	100	151.5
Nominal money holdings £M3 (end 1979 = 100)	100	178.0
Nominal GDP (1979 = 100)	100	137.5
GDP deflator (1979 = 100)	100	139.7
Nominal interest rate on 3-month Treasury bills	16.65	9.28

Source: CSO, *Economic Trends Annual Supplement*, 1984 edn, HMSO, and *Bank of England Quarterly Bulletin*, June 1984

(a) Calculate an index of real GDP for 1983 based on 1979 = 100.
(b) Explain how you would expect *real* money holdings to have changed between 1979 and 1983 on the basis of the evidence on GDP, prices, and the interest rate.
(c) Calculate an index of real M1 and real £M3 for 1983 based on 1979 = 100 and discuss whether your answer is consistent with your reasoning in part (b) of the exercise.
(d) Why is it more difficult for the Bank to control real money stock than it is to control nominal money stock—and why does it matter?

5 Figure 24.1 shows conditions in the money market. LL_0 and LL_1 are money demand schedules; MS_0 and MS_1 represent alternative real money supply schedules. In the initial state, the money market is in equilibrium with the demand for money LL_0 and money supply MS_0.

(a) Identify equilibrium money balances and rate of interest.
(b) Suggest why it might be that the money demand schedule shifted from LL_0 to LL_1.
(c) Given the move from LL_0 to LL_1, suppose that no adjustment has yet taken place:

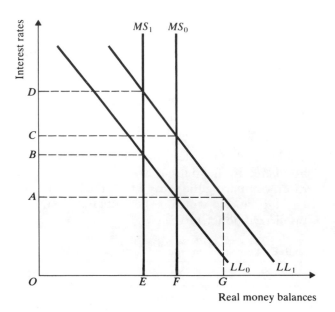

FIGURE 24.1   Money market equilibrium

what is the state of excess demand/supply in the bond market?

(d) How does this disequilibrium in the bond market bring about adjustments in the money market?

(e) Identify the new market equilibrium.

(f) Suppose that money demand remains at LL_1: what measures could the authorities adopt to move money supply from MS_0 to MS_1?

(g) Identify the new market equilibrium.

6   Complete Table 24.2 to show the various forms of monetary control used in the three main post-war periods in the UK.

7   All of the following are likely to lead to an increase in the transactions demand for money *except*
   (a) a general rise in the price of consumer goods
   (b) an expected rise in the price of consumer goods
   (c) an increase in the level of income
   (d) an increase in the standard rate of income tax
   (e) an increase in the rate of value-added tax
      (University of London GCE A level Economics 3, June 1989)

8   If the Bank of England increases the rate of interest at which it lends to the discount houses, this is likely to have the effect of
   1   raising the price of existing government stocks
   2   increasing the value of sterling
   3   reducing the tender prices of Treasury bills

   (a) 1, 2, 3 are all correct
   (b) 1 and 2 only are correct
   (c) 2 and 3 only are correct
   (d) 1 only is correct
      (Associated Examining Board GCE A level Economics Paper 1, November 1988)

9   Which of the following is (are) likely to bring about a rise in interest rates?
   1   A rise in liquidity preference
   2   A fall in the supply of money
   3   A fall in borrowing

   (a) 1, 2 and 3 are correct
   (b) 1 and 2 only are correct
   (c) 2 and 3 only are correct
   (d) 1 only is correct
   (e) 3 only is correct
      (University of London GCE A level Economics 3, June 1988)

TABLE 24.2   Monetary control in the UK

Control mechanism	Before 1971	Competition and Credit Control	After 20 August 1981
Cash ratio			
Liquid or secondary assets ratio			
Controls on advances			
Special Deposits			
Supplementary Special Deposits			
Discount rate			

10 Use a diagram to explain how the authorities may attempt to control money stock through interest rates. Comment on the problems of this procedure.

TRUE/FALSE

1 _____ There is no possibility that the Bank of England can go bankrupt because it can always meet withdrawals by its depositors by printing new banknotes a little more quickly.

2 _____ The central bank can reduce the money supply by reducing the amount of cash that the commercial banks must hold as reserves.

3 _____ The central bank can induce the commercial banks voluntarily to hold additional cash reserves by setting the discount rate at a penalty level.

4 _____ Open market operations are a means by which the Bank alters the monetary base, banks' cash reserves, deposit lending, and the money supply.

5 _____ When you've tried everywhere else to get money for your holidays, you go to the lender of last resort.

6 _____ Public sector borrowing requirement (PSBR) must be met by printing money; therefore there is a direct link between the size of PSBR and money supply.

7 _____ The strict regulation of British financial institutions, and the traditional demarcation between jobbers and brokers in stock exchange dealings, prevent UK companies from full participation in the world financial market.

8 _____ Money is a nominal variable, not a real variable.

9 _____ The existence of uncertainty increases the demand for bonds.

10 _____ The best measure of the opportunity cost of holding money is the real interest rate.

11 _____ The central bank can control the real money supply with precision more easily than the nominal money supply.

12 _____ An excess demand for money must be exactly matched by an excess supply of bonds: otherwise people would be planning to hold more wealth than they actually possess.

13 _____ Prior to 1971, Bank rate was announced by the Bank of England every Thursday.

14 _____ Since 1981 the Corset has been tightened.

15 _____ One of the main problems with monetary base control is Goodhart's law.

16 _____ The central bank can fix the money supply and accept the equilibrium interest rate implied by the money demand equation, or it can fix the interest rate and accept the equilibrium money supply implied by the money demand equation; but it cannot choose both money supply and interest rate independently.

QUESTIONS FOR THOUGHT

1 Imagine that you have a stock of wealth to be allocated between money and bonds, your main concern being to avoid the capital losses which might ensue if the price of bonds falls when you are holding bonds. Suppose that you expect the rate of interest to be at a particular level r_c.
   (a) How would you allocate your wealth between money and bonds if the current rate of interest were *below* r_c?
   (b) How would you allocate your wealth between money and bonds if the current rate of interest were *higher* than r_c?
   (c) What would be implied for the aggregate relationship between money holdings and the rate of interest if different individuals have different expectations about future interest rates?

2 Discuss why the Corset was introduced and why it was not wholly successful.

3 Suppose a given economy is working with a required liquid assets ratio, and that the central bank is adopting a restrictive monetary stance. Explain the conflict of interests that might arise if PSBR is large and is to be funded by the issue of Treasury bills.

4 The deregulation of the London stock exchange arose originally from legislation which extended the scope of the Restrictive Trade Practices Act to encompass service activities. What effects would you expect to observe from the changes?

ANSWERS AND COMMENTS FOR CHAPTER 24

Please note Where questions are reproduced from GCE examinations, the examination boards bear no responsibility for the answers provided in this volume, which are the sole responsibility of the authors.

Important Concepts and Technical Terms

1	b	4	o	7	k	10	g	13	j	16	r
2	i	5	l	8	e	11	d	14	c	17	f
3	m	6	h	9	n	12	p	15	a	18	q

Exercises

1   **TABLE A24.1**   Balance Sheets of the Bank of England, March 1990

Department	Assets	£b	Liabilities	£b
Issue	Government securities	10.8	Notes in circulation	15.2
	Other securities	4.4		
	Issue Department assets	15.2	Issue Department liabilities	15.2
Banking	Government securities	1.4	Public deposits	0.1
	Advances	0.5	Bankers' deposits	1.5
	Other assets	1.8	Reserves and other accounts	2.1
			Special Deposits	0.0
	Banking Department assets	3.7	Banking Department liabilities	3.7

2   (a)   Recall that
$$M = \frac{(c_p + 1)}{(c_p + c_b)} \times H = 3.11 \times 12 = £37.32\text{m}.$$

(b)   This has the effect of reducing the money multiplier from 3.11 to 2.8, so money supply falls to £33.6m.

(c)   This has the same effect as (b)—money supply falls to £33.6m.

(d)   This also has the same effect as (b)—money supply falls to £33.6m.

(e)   Reducing H by £1m reduces M by the size of the money multiplier—i.e. by £3.11m, to £34.21m.

3   (a)   An increase in real income leads to an increase in the demand for real money balances through both transactions and precautionary motives.

(b)   If this is interpreted as a decrease in uncertainty, then money demand will fall through the operation of the precautionary motive.

(c)   Reduces real money demand, mainly through the asset motive.

(d)   This is the reverse of (c): nominal interest rates represent the opportunity cost of holding money.

(e)   This will affect *nominal* money demand, but the demand for *real* money balances will be unaffected.

(f)   If we consider broad money, this differential again represents the opportunity cost of holding money—so we expect a fall in real money demand.

(g)   Increases real money demand through the precautionary motive.

(h)   The effect depends upon how people react: if they do not change their spending patterns, then they may increase real money demand. However, they may choose to switch funds between money and bonds to earn a return on cash otherwise idle for part of the period, or they may choose to alter spending patterns by visiting the freezer food centre once a month.

(i)   This item affects the *supply* of money: there may be an induced movement *along* the demand curve as interest rates change, but not a movement *of* the demand function. (This distinction between movements *of* and *along* the curve was first seen back in Chapter 3.)

4   (a) $137.5 \times 100/139.7 = 98.4$.

(b)   We see that real income fell during this period (but not by very much): this would tend to reduce the demand for real money balances (especially M1). However, nominal interest rates also fell, lowering the opportunity cost of holding money: this effect will tend to increase the demand for real money balances (especially £M3). Price changes should not affect *real* money demand, but no doubt would contribute to the substantial increases in demand for *nominal* money holdings.

(c)   For real M1: $151.5 \times 100/139.7 = 108.4$.
For real £M3: $178.0 \times 100/139.7 = 127.4$.
These results are consistent with our observations, especially reflecting the changes in nominal interest rates—notice that, as predicted, holdings of real £M3 increased by more than those of real M1.

(d)   The simple answer is that the authorities do not have precise control over prices: the available monetary instruments all affect nominal money supply—but it is *real* money supply that is relevant for influencing people's behaviour.

5   (a)   With money demand at LL_0 and money supply MS_0, equilibrium is achieved with real money balances OF and interest rate OA.

(b) The position of the *LL* schedule depends primarily upon real income, an increase in which could explain a move from LL_0 to LL_1.

(c) With money demand at LL_1, but money supply at MS_0 and interest rate still at *OA*, there is clearly an excess demand for money of an amount *FG*.

(d) This is mirrored by an equal excess supply of bonds, in response to which the price of bonds will fall, in turn causing the rate of interest to rise. This process continues until equilibrium is reached.

(e) The new equilibrium is at interest rate *OC*, at which point real money demand is equal to money supply *OF*.

(f) The authorities can operate either upon the stock of high-powered money or upon the money multiplier, as we have seen. The former could be achieved by open market operations to sell bills or bonds to the public. The money multiplier may be operated on by influencing the proportion of deposits held by the banks as cash.

(g) Equilibrium at interest rate *OD*, real money balances *OE*.

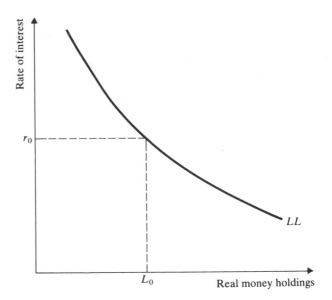

FIGURE A24.1 Monetary control through the interest rate

6

TABLE A24.2 Monetary control in the UK

Control mechanism	Before 1971	Competition and Credit Control	After 20 August 1981
Cash ratio	8%	$1\frac{1}{2}$%	$\frac{1}{2}$%
Liquid or secondary assets ratio	28% Liquid assets: deposits	$12\frac{1}{2}$% Reserve assets: deposits	No
Controls on advances	Quantitative ceilings	Quantitative controls	No
Special Deposits	Yes	Yes	Provided for but not so far used
Supplementary Special Deposits	No	Yes, after 1973	No
Discount rate	Bank rate	Minimum lending rate	No pre-announced rate; short term rates to be kept within chosen band by open market operations

This table is based on a similar one in an article by M. J. Artis, 'Monetary Control in the U.K.', *Economic Review*, Vol. 2(2), 1984

7 (d).

8 (c).

9 (b).

10 Suppose that the money demand schedule is known to be given by *LL* in Figure A24.1 and that the authorities set L_0 as the target level for money stock. By fixing the rate of interest at r_0, money supply can be allowed to self-adjust to the target level.

This technique relies on the stability of the *LL* curve—and upon the authorities having knowledge of it. If *LL* is neither known nor stable, the possibility of achieving targets by this route is remote. The method also requires that equilibrium is readily and quickly achieved.

True/False

1 True: see Section 24–1 of the main text.

2 False: in order to *reduce* money supply, the Bank must induce the banks to hold *larger* cash reserves (see Section 24–2 of the main text).

3 True.

4 True.

5 False: for discussion of the Bank's role as lender of last resort, see Section 24–3 of the main text.

6 False: printing money is not the *only* way of funding PSBR; an increase in PSBR does not necessarily mean an increase in money supply.

7 No longer true: the Big Bang deregulation measures were designed to remove many of the problems (see Box 24–1 of the main text).

8 True: see Section 24–4 of the main text.
9 False: uncertainty provides the motivation for the precautionary demand for money.
10 False: the *nominal* interest rate is a better reflection of the interest differential between holding money and bonds.
11 False: prices may vary in ways beyond the control of the Bank, so nominal money supply is more amenable to control (see Section 24–5 of the main text).
12 True.
13 True: see Section 24–6 of the main text.
14 False: the Corset was abandoned in 1980.
15 True: see Section 24–7 of the main text.
16 True.

Questions for Thought

1 (a) If you expect the rate of interest to rise, then you expect the price of bonds to fall—so you will hold all your wealth as money to avoid capital losses.
   (b) If the rate of interest is high, and bond prices correspondingly low, then you would probably choose to all your wealth into bonds to reap capital gains when bond prices rise. When the interest rate reaches r_c (the 'critical rate'), you no longer expect bond prices to change and will be indifferent between money and bonds.
   (c) This analysis appeared in Keynes's *General Theory*, which referred to it as the *speculative demand for money*. The aggregate relationship is

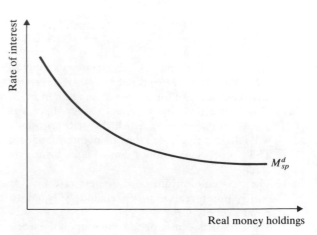

FIGURE A24.2 The speculative demand for money

shown in Figure A24.2. The downward slope results from the assumption that different individuals have different expectations about r_c, but at some point the rate of interest becomes so low that everyone agrees that it can fall no further.

2 For hints, see Box 24–2 of the main text.
3 Under Competition and Credit Control, Treasury bills were regarded as reserve assets.
4 *Hint* Perhaps the key words to consider are 'efficiency', 'competition', and 'monitoring'. Further details are contained in Box 24–1 of the main text or in an article by W. A. Thomas, 'Big Bang and the City', in the *Economic Review*, May 1987.

25

Monetary and Fiscal Policy in a Closed Economy

When manufacturing output in the UK fell by 16 per cent in response to the rapid fall in aggregate demand between June 1979 and December 1980, the CBI called for reductions in interest rates to aid recovery. Nothing we have said so far suggests why interest rates should be so important. We now begin to draw our model together, combining an extended version of the income–expenditure model of Chapters 21 and 22 with the analysis of the money market of Chapters 23 and 24. We will then be able to look more closely at the available policy options. For simplicity, we assume a closed economy and continue to hold prices fixed.

In 'Questions for Thought' in Chapter 21, you were asked to consider what factors other than income may affect aggregate consumption. One influence is the size of household *wealth*. What is more, an increase in real money supply may have direct and indirect influence upon wealth holdings. Direct effects arise from the fact that money is an asset in households' portfolios. The indirect effect works through the interest rate: an increase in money supply leads to a fall in the equilibrium interest rate. The associated increase in bond prices increases the value of financial assets held by households.

The *permanent income hypothesis* devised by Professor Milton Friedman suggests that consumption decisions are based upon average long-run or 'permanent' income. Changes in income which are viewed as temporary may not affect consumption patterns. The *life-cycle hypothesis*, developed by Professors Albert Ando and Franco Modigliani, also suggests that it is average income that governs consumption decisions. People form notions about their likely lifetime income and form a feasible consumption pattern in response, with the intention of achieving a steady consumption level even though income varies at different parts of the life-cycle. This requires borrowing, saving, and dissaving in turn as life goes on, and changes in interest rates may be an important factor.

These 'modern' theories of consumption re-emphasize the importance of the interest rate and stress that the way in which households react to changing circumstances depends upon whether a change is perceived as being permanent or temporary.

To date, the other major component of aggregate demand, *investment*, has been treated as autonomous: this is no longer adequate. Part of investment is expenditure on *fixed capital* (plant and machinery, factories, houses, and vehicles); part is *working capital* (inventories), this latter being relatively small but highly volatile. We continue to regard public sector investment as part of government expenditure, but consider private sector investment more carefully. Firms undertake investment after weighing the benefits and costs. Typically, the costs of investment are to be incurred in the present period, but the benefits accrue in the future. The future profit stream must be sufficient to cover both present costs and interest charges. In evaluating an investment project, it is the opportunity cost of the funds which is important. At higher market interest rates, a higher return on investment is required.

Suppose a firm ranks the alternative projects according to their returns. At high interest rates, relatively few projects will meet the necessary criterion—but as market interest rates fall, more projects become potentially profitable: this gives a downward-sloping *investment demand schedule*, whose position depends on the cost of capital, on the expected future profit stream, and on 'business confidence'. The importance of expectations in this decision-making process is central, and may cause the investment function to be volatile. The function will be steeper for long-lived assets.

Inventories may be held for speculative reasons or simply because the production process takes time. The cost of holding inventories is again the opportunity cost—the interest rate that could have been earned on the funds. Again, we expect a downward-sloping demand function.

We have now seen two routes by which interest rates may affect aggregate demand—through consumption, and through investment. Given the connection between money supply and interest rates, this provides a *transmission mechanism* by which changes in money supply may affect aggregate demand—we have established a link between the money and goods markets. Another way of viewing this is to see the position of the aggregate demand schedule in our income–expenditure model depending upon the interest rate, so there is a route by which changes in money supply lead to changes in equilibrium output. The initial effects of an increase in money supply may be later diluted because, as income rises, so too does transactions money demand, hence partially offsetting the fall in the rate of interest. This same damping effect reduces the impact of government spending—there is a *crowding-out* effect on both investment and consumption.

171

Our former model proves to be rather cumbersome for looking at simultaneous equilibrium in both goods and money markets. An alternative is the *IS–LM model*. The *IS curve* is the locus of combinations of real output and the interest rate which allow equilibrium in the goods market. The curve is downward-sloping as a lower interest rate allows higher equilibrium income because of the effect on investment and consumption. The slope of *IS* depends on the sensitivity of aggregate demand to the interest rate; its position depends upon the level of government expenditure and upon business confidence and other factors affecting autonomous investment and consumption.

The *LM* curve is the locus of combinations of real output and the interest rate which enable money market equilibrium—that is, where the demand for real money balances (which Keynes designated the liquidity preference schedule) equals the supply. The *LM* curve slopes upwards; its steepness depends on the sensitivity of money demand to the rate of interest and to income; for instance, the more responsive is money demand to the interest rate and the less to income, the flatter is *LM*. The position of *LM* depends upon real money supply and upon 'liquidity preference'. It should be remembered that real money supply depends on both nominal money supply and the price level, although we assume prices fixed for now.

Simultaneous equilibrium in both goods and money markets can be analysed by bringing *IS* and *LM* curves together, revealing the unique equilibrium combination of real output and interest rate. The economy tends to move towards this equilibrium position.

An increase in government expenditure financed by selling bonds shifts the *IS* curve and brings about an increase in equilibrium output and interest rate. Crowding out would be complete only if *LM* were vertical. An increase in government expenditure financed by an increase in money supply shifts both *IS* and *LM* and could be arranged such that the interest rate remains stable and only output increases—that is, such that no crowding out occurs. This illustrates the interaction of fiscal and monetary policy. As far as monetary policy is concerned, given the price level, an increase in money supply shifts *LM* and results in a fall in equilibrium interest rate and an increase in output, the fall in the rate of interest being necessary to induce an increase in aggregate demand.

Demand management is the use of monetary and fiscal policy to stabilize at a high average output level. Monetary and fiscal policy do not have the same effects and have different implications for the *composition* of aggregate demand. An *easy* fiscal policy represented by high levels of government spending, when combined with *tight* money, will tend to result in high interest rates and to discourage private expenditure. With tight fiscal policy and easy money, the relatively low interest rates encourage private expen-

diture. The effects of monetary policy may be unpredictable because of the indirect nature of the transmission mechanism.

In later chapters we will examine a number of further issues. There may be conditions in which we wish to encourage investment because of possible beneficial effects upon economic growth, or where easy money may have implications for inflation. These issues cannot be examined in our present static model.

Our model so far has a 'Keynesian' flavour in its emphasis on aggregate demand. In the years preceding the Second World War the inadvertent activism of rearmament was effective in raising output and employment: the Heath easy fiscal and easy monetary policy of 1972–73 was less successful because of the effect it had on inflation. Clearly, we can go no further without considering how the price level is determined. We must also abandon the assumption of spare capacity and explore the meaning of full employment. The complacency that the demand-side emphasis can bring must be avoided, and we need to be aware that an increasing government sector with its high taxation may affect private sector incentives. Keynesian demand analysis may still be pertinent for short-run analysis, but the supply side of the economy cannot be neglected: indeed, the supply side is considered in the next chapter.

IMPORTANT CONCEPTS AND TECHNICAL TERMS

Match each lettered concept with the appropriate numbered phrase:

(a)	Wealth effect	(i)	Permanent income
(b)	Monetary–fiscal		hypothesis
	policy mix	(j)	Tight fiscal policy
(c)	Investment demand	(k)	LM schedule
	schedule	(l)	Tight money
(d)	Easy money	(m)	Life-cycle
(e)	IS schedule		hypothesis
(f)	Crowding out	(n)	Demand
(g)	Easy fiscal policy		management
(h)	Transmission		
	mechanism		

1 A function showing how much investment firms wish to make at each interest rate.
2 The upward (downward) shift in the consumption function when household wealth increases (decreases) and people spend more (less) at each level of personal disposable income.
3 A policy stance in which the government restricts money supply and forces interest rates up.
4 The route by which a change in money supply affects aggregate demand.
5 A theory about consumption developed by Ando

and Modigliani which argues that people form their consumption plans by reference to their expected lifetime income.

6 A theory about consumption developed by Friedman which argues that consumption depends not on current disposable income but on average income in the long run.

7 The use of monetary and fiscal policy to stabilize the level of income around a high average level.

8 A curve which shows the different combinations of interest rates and income compatible with equilibrium in the money market.

9 The reduction in private demand for consumption and investment caused by an increase in government spending, which increases aggregate demand and hence interest rates.

10 A policy stance in which the government allows money supply to expand and interest rates to fall.

11 A policy stance in which the government reduces its expenditure and raises taxes.

12 A policy stance making use of a combination of fiscal and monetary measures.

13 A curve which shows the different combinations of income and interest rates at which the goods market is in equilibrium.

14 A policy stance in which the government lowers taxes and increases its expenditure.

EXERCISES

1 Table 25.1 presents UK data on the savings ratio and interest rates for the period 1978–89.
   (a) Examine the data and try to detect any trends.
   (b) Economists often find that visual display of data is more revealing. On graph paper, plot the savings ratio and the Treasury bill rate on the same diagram against time.
   (c) Comment on the apparent relationship between the two series.

TABLE 25.1 Interest rates and the savings ratio

	Treasury bill rate (%)	Savings ratio (%)
1978	11.91	11.1
1979	16.49	12.2
1980	13.58	13.5
1981	15.39	12.8
1982	9.96	11.6
1983	9.04	9.8
1984	9.33	10.2
1985	11.49	9.5
1986	10.94	8.2
1987	8.38	5.7
1988	12.91	4.1
1989	14.66	5.0

Source: CSO *United Kingdom National Accounts* and *Monthly Digest of Statistics*

2

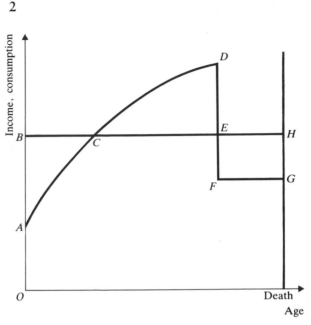

FIGURE 25.1 Consumption and the life-cycle

Figure 25.1 depicts income and consumption during the life-cycle. The path *ACDFG* represents the pattern of disposable income, increasing through the individual's working life and then reducing to pension level on retirement. *OB* represents long-run average, or 'permanent', income. The individual aims at a steady level of consumption through life so as just to exhaust total lifetime income.
   (a) What level of consumption will be chosen?
   (b) What does the area *ABC* represent?
   (c) How is the area *ABC* to be financed?
   (d) The area *CDE* represents an excess of current income over consumption. Why does the individual 'save' during this period?
   (e) What does the area *EFGH* (during pension years) represent?
   (f) How is *EFGH* financed?
   (g) How would consumption behaviour be affected if the individual begins life with a stock of inherited wealth?
   (h) Discuss the effect of an increase in interest rates upon the present value of future income and upon consumption.

3 Table 25.2 presents data for the UK relating to various components of investment in 1978 and 1988.

   (a) Calculate total fixed investment in each of the two years.
   (b) Calculate the percentage share of the public sector in each of the two years.

TABLE 25.2 Investment in the UK
(£billion at 1985 prices)

	1978	1988
Private sector		
Vehicles, ships, and aircraft	6.3	6.9
Plant and machinery	13.2	26.7
Dwellings	8.9	12.2
Other buildings, works, etc.	9.7	18.6
Public sector		
Vehicles, ships, and aircraft	0.8	0.6
Plant and machinery	5.1	3.5
Dwellings	3.9	2.6
Other buildings, works, etc.	6.9	3.8
Stockbuilding (private and public)	1.8	4.4

(c) Calculate total investment in each of the two years.

(d) Comment on the main trends revealed by these data.

4 A firm is appraising its investment opportunities. Table 25.3 shows the projects that are available.

TABLE 25.3 Investment opportunities

Project	Cost (£)	Expected rate of return (% p.a.)
A	4 000	6
B	6 000	12
C	4 000	2
D	5 000	20
E	3 000	10
F	10 000	16

Assume that the firm has sufficient internal funds to undertake as many of these projects as it desires without borrowing.

(a) Which projects will the firm undertake if the market rate of interest is currently 11 per cent per annum?

(b) Which (if any) projects would be abandoned if the market rate of interest rose from this level by 2 percentage points? Why would this decision be taken?

(c) Construct a schedule showing how much investment the firm will undertake at different values of the market rate of interest.

(d) How would you expect this schedule to be affected by an increase in the 'business confidence' of the firm? Relate your answer to Table 25.3.

5 This exercise concerns the transmission mechanism of monetary policy in a closed economy with fixed prices. Suppose that there is an increase in the real money supply.

(a) What effect does this policy have on the bond market?

(b) Outline the effect that this will have on consumption and investment.

(c) What does this imply for aggregate demand?

(d) How does this change in aggregate demand affect equilibrium output?

(e) How does this then affect money demand?

(f) What is implied for the rate of interest, and what further effects may follow?

(g) What do you expect to be the net effect on equilibrium output?

Please note: if you find that any links in this chain are obscure, you are advised to work through the question in conjunction with the commentary provided in the 'Answers and Comments' section.

6 This exercise concerns the crowding-out effects of fiscal policy in a closed economy with fixed prices. We begin this time with a cut in the rate of direct taxation. As with the previous question, if the chain does not make sense to you, follow the question in conjunction with the commentary.

(a) How will the policy change initially affect disposable income and aggregate demand?

(b) What is the subsequent effect on equilibrium output?

(c) What implications does this have for the demand for real money balances?

(d) Given fixed money supply, how will this affect bond prices and interest rates?

(e) How will this feed through to affect aggregate demand?

(f) What is the effect on equilibrium output?

(g) Under what circumstances will this crowding-out effect be complete?

7 Which of the following is *least* likely to stimulate an increase in investment?

(a) A fall in the rate of interest

(b) A rise in consumer spending

(c) A depletion of stocks

(d) An increase in imports

(e) Technological progress

(University of London GCE A level Economics 3, January 1989)

8 According to Keynesian theory, which of the following policies would be most suitable for a government seeking to reduce the level of unemployment?

(a) Reduce taxes and increase government expenditure

(b) Devalue, increase taxes, and reduce government expenditure

(c) Increase income tax only and increase government expenditure

(d) Devalue, reduce taxes and reduce government expenditure

(Associated Examining Board GCE A level Economics Paper 1, June 1987)

9   Figure 25.2 shows the *IS* and *LM* schedules for a closed economy with fixed prices.

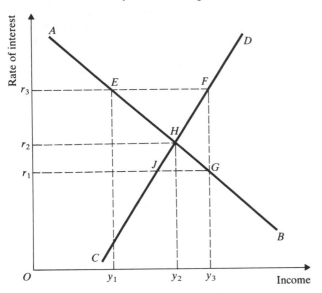

FIGURE 25.2   Equilibrium in the goods and money markets

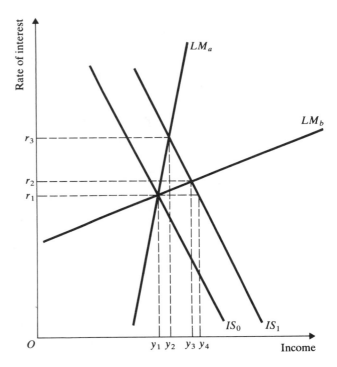

FIGURE 25.3   Fiscal policy

(a)   *AB* and *CD* are the *IS* and *LM* schedules—but which is which?

(b)   Comment on the equilibrium/disequilibrium states of the goods and money markets at each of the points *E*, *F*, *G*, *H*, and *J*.

(c)   How would you expect the economy to react if it is at point *J*?

(d)   For each of the following items, identify whether the *IS* or *LM* schedule is likely to shift—and in which direction (assume *ceteris paribus* in each case):

   (i)   An increase in business confidence.

   (ii)   An increase in nominal money supply.

   (iii)   A reduction in government spending.

   (iv)   A once-for-all increase in the price level.

   (v)   A redistribution of income from rich to poor.

   (vi)   An increase in the wealth holdings of households.

10   Figure 25.3 illustrates the effects of fiscal policy on equilibrium income and interest rate under alternative assumptions about the slope of the *LM* function. In each case, fiscal policy is represented by a movement of the *IS* curve from IS_0 to IS_1.

(a)   What is the initial equilibrium income and interest rate?

(b)   What could have caused the move from IS_0 to IS_1?

(c)   What would be the 'full multiplier' effect of the fiscal policy—that is, if the interest rate remains unchanged?

(d)   If the fiscal policy is bond-financed and the *LM* schedule is relatively *elastic*, what is the effect of the fiscal policy on the equilibrium position?

(e)   If the fiscal policy is bond-financed and the *LM* schedule is relatively *inelastic*, what is the effect of the fiscal policy on the equilibrium position?

(f)   Identify the extent of crowding out in each of these situations.

(g)   What determines the elasticity of the *LM* schedule?

(h)   How could the authorities arrange policy in order to achieve the 'full multiplier' effect?

11   Figure 25.4 illustrates the effects of a restrictive monetary policy on equilibrium income and interest rate under alternative assumptions about the slope of the *IS* schedule. Monetary policy is here represented by a movement of the *LM* schedule from LM_0 to LM_1.

(a)   What is the initial equilibrium income and interest rate?

(b)   What could have caused the move from LM_0 to LM_1?

(c)   What is the effect of monetary policy on the equilibrium when the *IS* schedule is relatively steep?

(d)   What is the effect when *IS* is relatively flat?

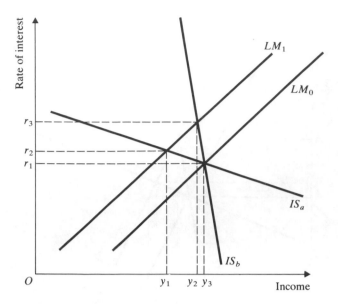

FIGURE 25.4 Monetary policy

(e) What factors determine the steepness of the *IS* curve and hence the effectiveness of monetary policy?

TRUE/FALSE

1 _____ An increase in transitory income may not have any effect on current consumption.

2 _____ Tax cuts lead to an increase in current consumption.

3 _____ The interest rate is the only determinant of investment.

4 _____ A higher interest rate increases the present value of the expected profit stream from an investment project and hence leads to an increase in investment.

5 _____ International banking was the first industry to be truly regulated at an international level.

6 _____ Changes in the rate of interest affect the position of the aggregate demand schedule in the income–expenditure model.

7 _____ When we take into account the money market and interest rate effects, the multiplier on government spending is enhanced.

8 _____ Movements *along* the *IS* schedule tell us about shifts in equilibrium income caused by shifts in the aggregate demand schedule as a result *only* of changes in interest rates.

9 _____ The position of the *LM* schedule depends on the price level.

10 _____ Monetary and fiscal policy affect aggregate demand through different routes but have very similar effects.

11 _____ The Heath government in the early 1970s adopted a mix of easy money and easy fiscal policy in an attempt to increase the rate of economic growth, whereas both monetary and fiscal policy were tight during the early years of the first Thatcher administration.

12 _____ The Keynesian model developed so far is deficient because it overemphasizes the demand side of the economy, holds prices fixed, and relies on the existence of spare capacity.

QUESTIONS FOR THOUGHT

1 Discuss the extent to which current consumption is a function of current income.
(Southern Universities' Joint Board GCE A level Economics 2, June 1987)

2 (a) How may a firm compare alternative investment projects with different capital costs, different expected income streams, and different expected economic lives?
(b) How would a rise in the rate of interest affect firms' decisions to invest?

3 This exercise requires some facility with simple algebra. Suppose that the following equations represent behaviour in the goods and money markets of a fixed price closed economy:

Goods market
Consumption:	$C = A + c(Y - T) - dR$
Investment:	$I = B - iR$
Taxes:	$T = tY$
Equilibrium:	$Y = C + I + G$

Money market
Money supply:	$M^s = \overline{M}$
Money demand:	$M^d = kPY + N - mR$
Equilibrium:	$M^s = M^d$

where A = autonomous consumption, B = autonomous investment, C = consumption, G = government expenditure, I = investment, M = real money, N = autonomous money demand, P = price level, R = rate of interest (%), T = net taxes, Y = income, output. Lower-case letters denote parameters of the model.

(a) Derive an expression for the *IS* curve—i.e., use the equations for the goods market to find a relationship between Y and r.
(b) Derive an expression for the *LM* curve.
(c) Suppose the variables and parameters in the model take the following values:

$A = 700$	$G = 649.6$	$m = 10$
$B = 400$	$i = 15$	$N = 200$
$c = 0.8$	$k = 0.25$	$P = 1$
$d = 5$	$\overline{M} = 1200$	$t = 0.2$

Plot *IS* and *LM* curves and read off the

approximate equilibrium values of income and the rate of interest.

(d) For these equilibrium values, calculate consumption and investment, and confirm that the goods market is in equilibrium.

(e) Check that the money market is also in equilibrium.

(f) Calculate the government budget deficit or surplus.

ANSWERS AND COMMENTS FOR CHAPTER 25

Please note   Where questions are reproduced from GCE examinations, the examination boards bear no responsibility for the answers provided in this volume, which are the sole responsibility of the authors.

Important Concepts and Technical Terms

1	*c*	5	*m*	9	*f*	13	*e*
2	*a*	6	*i*	10	*d*	14	*g*
3	*l*	7	*n*	11	*j*		
4	*h*	8	*k*	12	*b*		

Exercises

1 (a) Although it seems that there is some association between the series, it is not easy to evaluate them by simple eye-balling. However, some features do stand out, especially the divergence of the two series after 1987. This is associated with a boom in consumer spending which occurred at this time: for instance, see an article by Jon Shields in *Economic Review*, September 1988.

(b)

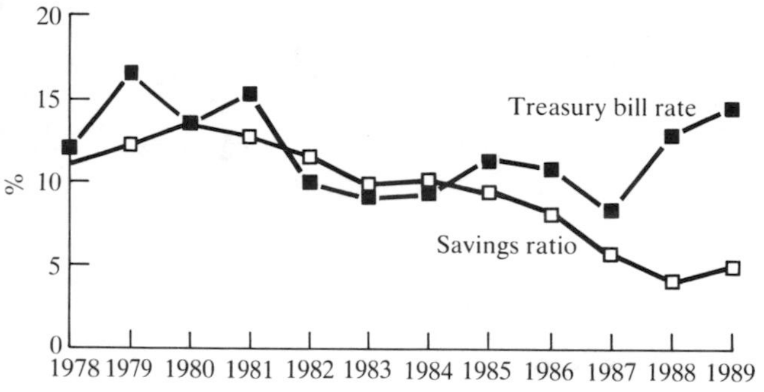

FIGURE A25.1   Interest rates and the personal savings ratio, UK

(c) In general, these series appear to be 'positively correlated'—that is, they tend to move together. For instance, both series 'dip' in 1971 and rise in the following years. This observation is not sufficient to *prove* that one variable *causes* the other. Nevertheless, it provides evidence in support of the theories outlined in Section 24–1 of the main text, where it is suggested that high interest rates will tend to be associated with high savings and correspondingly lower consumption expenditure.

2 (a) OB.

(b) The area ABC reflects the fact that our individual must borrow in early life to maintain consumption above current income.

(c) By borrowing at the market rate of interest.

(d) This 'saving' is for two reasons—firstly, the individual must pay back the money borrowed in early life, together with the interest payments. Secondly, money must be set aside in order to maintain consumption after retirement.

(e) EFGH represents dissaving.

(f) By saving in middle age (see *d*).

(g) An increase in initial wealth shifts up the permanent income line and increases consumption.

(h) An increase in the interest rate reduces the present value of future income. The cost of borrowing in early life is increased. The permanent income level falls—and so will consumption. For more detailed discussion, see Section 24–1 of the main text.

3 (a) 1978: £54.8b.
        1988: £74.9b.

(b) 1978: 30.5 per cent.
        1988: 14.0 per cent.

(c) 1978: £56.6b.
        1988: £79.3b.

(d) It is always potentially dangerous to single out two particular years for comparison. This is especially so with a highly volatile variable such as stockbuilding. We will thus comment only on the trends in fixed investment. Probably the most striking feature is the fall in public sector investment, especially in dwellings and other buildings and works. A result of this decline is that, although private sector fixed investment grew by nearly 70 per cent over this decade, total fixed investment rose by only about 37 per cent in real terms. Of course, the picture is complicated by the privatization programme of the 1980s, which involved the transfer of some public sector enterprises into the private sector.

4 (a) Projects D (return 20 per cent), F (16 per cent), and B (12 per cent) all offer returns superior to the market rate of interest and will be undertaken.

(b) With the market interest rate at 13 per cent, project B would not be selected. The firm could obtain a better return on the funds by lending at the market rate. The market rate of interest represents the opportunity cost of investment.

(c) We can construct the schedule by ranking the projects in order of their return and accumulating the amounts:

Project	Return (% p.a.)	Cumulative investment demand (£)
D	20	5 000
F	16	15 000
B	12	21 000
E	10	24 000
A	6	28 000
C	2	32 000

We can then produce the investment demand schedule (Figure A25.2).

(d) An increase in business confidence will move the investment demand schedule outwards. The firm will uprate all its estimates of rates of return.

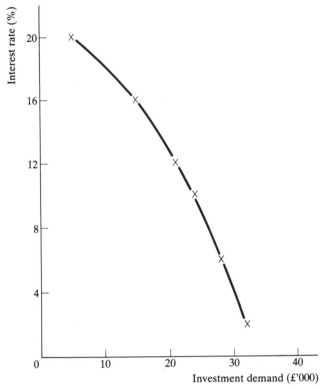

FIGURE A25.2 Investment demand

5 (a) An increase in real money supply creates excess supply of money—and hence excess demand for bonds: the price of bonds rises and the rate of interest falls.
   (b) As the rate of interest falls, private consumption and investment tend to rise;
   (c) so aggregate demand rises, and
   (d) this brings about an increase in equilibrium output. This shows the initial phase of the transmission mechanism of monetary policy.
   (e) As equilibrium output rises, there is an increase in the transactions and precautionary demands for money.
   (f) The increase in the demand for money leads to an increase in equilibrium interest rates (through the influence of the bond market); this will moderate the original increase in aggregate demand through the effects of the rate of interest on consumption and investment.
   (g) The net effect is likely to be an increase in equilibrium output, unless neither consumption nor investment is sensitive to the rate of interest.

6 (a) Reducing direct tax rates has an immediate effect in increasing disposable income, which leads to an increase in consumption expenditure and hence aggregate demand . . .
   (b) which leads to an increase in equilibrium output.
   (c) As income rises, there is an increase in transactions and precautionary demand for money, which,
   (d) given fixed money supply, leads to a fall in bond prices and an increase in interest rates.

(e) In turn, this leads to a fall in both investment and consumption;
(f) and there is a reduction in equilibrium output, owing to this 'crowding out' of private expenditure.
(g) Complete crowding out occurs when the demand for money is perfectly inelastic with respect to the interest rate: in this case the interest rate continues to rise until consumption and investment fall sufficiently to return aggregate demand to its initial level.

7 (d).
8 (a).
9 (a) AB is the (downward-sloping) IS curve.
        CD is the (upward-sloping) LM curve.
   (b)

Point	Money market	Goods market
E	Excess supply	Equilibrium
F	Equilibrium	Excess supply
G	Excess demand	Equilibrium
H	Equilibrium	Equilibrium
J	Equilibrium	Excess demand

Only at point H is there equilibrium in both markets.
(c) At J the money market is in equilibrium but there is excess demand for goods, tending to lead to an increase in output (and interest rates). A similar story could be told for each disequilibrium point—and under reasonable assumptions the economy can be seen to move towards equilibrium.
(d) (i)   Shifts IS to the right.
     (ii) Shifts LM to the right.
     (iii) Shifts IS to the left.
     (iv) This reduces real money supply—and so shifts LM to the left.
     (v)   This may be expected to increase autonomous consumption, as the poor tend to have a higher average propensity to consume: IS shifts to the right.
     (iv) A messy one—an increase in wealth may lead to higher consumption (IS shifts to the right) but also to an increase in the asset demand for money (LM shifts to the left).

10 (a) Income y_1, interest rate r_1.
    (b) An increase in government expenditure (or cuts in taxation).
    (c) Income increases from y_1 to y_4.
    (d) Income y_3, interest rate r_2 using LM_b.
    (e) Income y_2, interest rate r_3 using LM_a.
    (f) With LM_b (relatively elastic), crowding out is $y_4 - y_3$.
         With LM_a (relatively inelastic), crowding out is $y_4 - y_2$.
    (g) The sensitivity of money demand to the interest rate and to income.
    (h) By financing spending through an expansion of

money supply, shifting LM to intersect IS_1 at income y_4, interest rate r_1; this works all right in this fixed price world, but may have side-effects if prices are free to vary—as we shall see.

11 (a) Income y_3; interest rate r_1.

    (b) A reduction in real money supply. The methods by which this may be achieved were discussed in Chapter 24.

    (c) Income y_2; interest rate r_3 using IS_b.

    (d) Income y_1; interest rate r_2 using IS_a.

    (e) The degree to which private expenditure (investment and consumption) is sensitive to the rate of interest. The flatter is IS, the greater effect does monetary policy have on the level of income.

True/False

1 True: as specified in Friedman's permanent income hypothesis (see Section 25–1 of the main text).

2 False: if tax cuts are perceived to be temporary, consumption habits may not alter.

3 False: business confidence, the cost of capital, and other factors affect the position of the investment demand schedule (see Section 25–2 of the main text). Further analysis of investment takes place in Chapter 30.

4 False: a higher interest rate *reduces* the present value and leads to a *fall* in investment.

5 True: see Box 25–1 in the main text.

6 True: see Section 25–3 of the main text.

7 False: the multiplier is reduced, perhaps substantially (see Section 25–2 of the main text).

8 True: see Section 25–5 of the main text.

9 True: the price level affects real money supply.

10 False: monetary and fiscal policy have very different effects, especially in their influence on the *composition* of aggregate demand (see Section 25–6 of the main text).

11 True.

12 True: consideration of flexible prices, aggregate supply, and full employment are the next topics to be considered.

Questions for Thought

1 No hints provided.

2 You may wish to look back at Chapter 13 of the main text as well as Section 25–2.

3 (a) The IS curve is derived by substituting for T in the consumption equation and then for C and I in the equilibrium condition—i.e., we *impose* equilibrium.

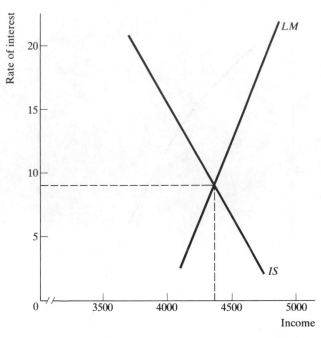

FIGURE A25.3   *IS–LM* equilibrium

$Y = A + c(Y - tY) - dR + B - iR + G.$

We can then collect terms in Y and R and rearrange the equation:

$$Y = \frac{A + B + G}{\{1 - c(1 - t)\}} - \frac{(d + i)}{\{1 - c(1 - t)\}}R.$$

The first term represents the autonomous element.

  (b) Similar steps are taken for the money market equation:

$$R = \frac{N - \overline{M}}{m} + \frac{kP}{m}Y.$$

  (c) Plugging in the values of the parameters yields:

IS: $Y = 4860 - 55.556R.$

LM: $R = -100 + 0.025Y.$

These are plotted in Figure A25.3.

Equilibrium occurs with the rate of interest at 9 per cent, income at 4360.

  (d) $C = 700 + 0.8 \times (1 - 0.2) \times 4360 - 5 \times 9$
      $= 3445.4.$

     $I = 400 - 15 \times 9 = 265$

     $C + I + G = 3445.4 + 265 + 649.6 = 4360.$

  (e) $M^d = 0.25 \times 1 \times 4360 + 200 - 10 \times 9$
      $= 1200.$

  (f) $T = 0.2 \times 4360 = 872$

     $G - T = 649.6 - 872 = -222.4$

     A surplus of 222.4.

26

Aggregate Supply, the Price Level, and the Speed of Adjustment

The Keynesian model we have developed so far has assumed that prices are fixed and that the economy has spare capacity: output has been demand-determined in the sense that an increase in aggregate demand finds producers ready to increase production. The *classical model* now to be explored allows both wages and prices to be flexible, so we always end up at full employment. We analyse how the economy responds both to demand and to supply shocks, persisting with a static model in which capital stock and technology remain fixed—as does potential output. The labour market is to be added to the model, and *aggregate supply* is seen as the result of interaction between goods and labour markets.

The price level we define as the average price of all goods produced in an economy. We continue to use the *IS–LM* model to ensure goods and money market equilibrium, but now recognize that the position of the *LM* curve depends on real money supply, which in turn depends upon the potentially variable price level. This provides us with a link between price and aggregate demand through the real money supply. For any given price level, equilibrium in goods and money markets implies the level of aggregate demand. As price changes, *LM* moves and hence leads to a new equilibrium level of aggregate demand. The locus of such combinations of price and aggregate demand is known as the *macroeconomic demand schedule* (*MDS*). At each point along it, planned spending equals actual output with the rate of interest ensuring money market equilibrium. The position of *MDS* depends on the level of autonomous spending. The *MDS* is not a demand curve in the usual sense, but is so named because it reflects the demand side of the economy—it shows levels of aggregate demand presupposing that producers are prepared to produce the necessary output.

Clearly, analysis of the supply side is also vital, as supply decisions are taken independently of demand decisions. (But notice that the supply decision influences the level of aggregate demand by fixing household incomes.) The *MDS* slopes downwards, reflecting that, as price changes, we slide along the *IS* schedule. This is reinforced by the *real balance effect*—an additional wealth effect on households, recognizing that a fall in prices leads to an increase in the real value of household asset holdings, which shifts *IS* through its effect on consumption.

The analysis of aggregate supply begins naturally with the *labour market*, as we have assumed other inputs to be fixed. In Chapter 11, we saw that firms maximize profits by employing labour up to the point where the *marginal product of labour* equals the *real wage*: this provides the *labour demand* schedule. As for *labour supply*, we first note a distinction between those in the *labour force* and those *accepting jobs*. As the real wage increases, more people join the labour force, but not all may accept jobs. At any time, there may be people between jobs, or people who find that the real level of unemployment benefit allows them to be choosy about the jobs they accept (more of this in Chapter 27). Labour market equilibrium is achieved when labour demand matches the number of people willing to accept jobs at the going real wage. At this point there will be some *voluntary* unemployment—*the natural rate of unemployment*. If real wages rise above this equilibrium level, there will be some *involuntary* unemployment.

The *real* wage is relevant because it represents real purchasing power to households, and to firms it represents the cost of labour relative to the output produced. We assume that households and firms do not confuse real and nominal values—that there is no *money illusion*.

The classical model assumes fully flexible wages and prices, implying that the labour market is always in equilibrium. With no money illusion, labour demand and supply depend only on real factors, and employment will be stable at the full-employment level. Output is thus always at the 'potential' level, and the *aggregate supply schedule* is vertical.

The intersection of aggregate supply and macroeconomic demand schedules shows the equilibrium price level. In the classical model, adjustment to equilibrium is rapid, and occurs through changes in price.

Monetary and fiscal policy can now be re-examined. Monetary policy is now found to leave all real variables unaffected. For instance, an increase in nominal money supply leads to increases in wages and prices but leaves employment and output unchanged. (This provides one of the basic tenets of *monetarism*.) Expansionary fiscal policy also leaves output unchanged—there is complete crowding out through the interest rate. An increase in government expenditure leads to increases in prices, wages, and the rate of interest, and alters the composition of aggregate demand. In the classical model these adjustments are instantaneous.

We can highlight the difference between the classical and Keynesian models by analysing the effects of an adverse demand shock. In the classical model, prices and wages adjust immediately and output is stable. In the Keynesian world, wages and prices are fixed, and output, being demand-determined, falls, together with employment. Eventually, firms may adjust prices and carry the economy back to full employment—but it is a moot point as to how long the process takes. We may suggest that Keynesian analysis is appropriate for the short run and the classical for the long run. In the Keynesian model the government can boost demand when there is spare capacity and hence secure an increase in output and employment; in the classical model, it is *supply* conditions that must change.

Experience of recession in modern industrial nations suggests that adjustment can take time and that prices and wages are not fully flexible. Clues to help explain this may be found by looking more closely at the labour market. It is in the interests of both firms and workers to come to long-term arrangements over terms of work. Hiring and firing impose costs on firms and job search on workers. Wage levels are just one component of the *explicit* or *implicit contracts* between firms and workers. Sluggishness in wage adjustment may come from a number of reasons. In the short run, firms may cushion their response to changes in demand by varying hours worked rather than wages or employment. The costs of the bargaining process encourage only occasional wage adjustment. Firms may smooth out fluctuations in wages in order to maintain good labour relations. In Chapter 11 we saw a number of possible explanations for non-instantaneous adjustment in a labour market.

How *do* wages adjust? Suppose an economy in full employment faces a permanent fall in aggregate demand. Initially, firms are likely to adjust hours worked and to 'hoard' labour. In time they begin to reduce the labour force and wage rates. Prices follow, raising real money supply, reducing the interest rate, and nudging up aggregate demand. Wages continue to fall until equilibrium is restored. If we make the simplifying assumption that prices follow wages, we can derive the *short-run aggregate supply schedule* (*SAS*), which mirrors this labour adjustment in terms of output.

An economy's reaction to demand and supply shocks can be seen by combining aggregate supply and macroeconomic demand schedules. We assume that even in the short run the goods market clears, but supply adjusts in time with wages, and the labour market carries any short-run disequilibrium. Consider a once-for-all reduction in nominal money supply in an economy initially at full employment. The first response is a movement along *SAS*; output falls, wages are rigid, but price falls a bit, raising the real wage and leading to some involuntary unemployment. In the medium term, there is downward pressure on wages, and *SAS* begins to shift. Price falls further, real money supply begins to rise, interest rates fall, aggregate demand rises a bit—and adjustment has begun. Eventually we return to full employment.

An increase in supply (e.g., in labour force participation) has no immediate effect (except on unemployment), but in time wage settlements will be affected, wages and prices fall, real money supply and aggregate demand increase, and the economy moves to a new potential output level. An external adverse supply shock, like an increase in the price of oil, pushes up price and reduces output in the short run. In the long run either there is wage and price adjustment to carry the economy back to the original equilibrium, or else, in this case, substitution against oil inputs may reduce the marginal product of labour and lead to a shift in labour demand, reducing potential output.

In the real world, shocks are always coming along, requiring the economy to adjust. Recent economic history shows evidence of severe supply shocks (1973–74 and 1979–80) and demand shocks (1971–73). Another fact worth remarking is that prices and wages do not seem to *fall* these days—instead, we experience inflation at differing rates. We return to analyse this *dynamic* phenomenon in Chapter 28.

IMPORTANT CONCEPTS AND TECHNICAL TERMS

Match each lettered concept with the appropriate numbered phrase:

(a) Real wage
(b) Aggregate supply schedule
(c) Labour input
(d) Business cycle
(e) Classical model
(f) Overtime and short-time
(g) Supply-side economics
(h) Job acceptance schedule
(i) Voluntary unemployment
(j) Money illusion
(k) Involuntary unemployment
(l) Marginal product of labour
(m) Real balance effect
(n) Short-run aggregate supply schedule
(o) Registered unemployment
(p) Labour force schedule
(q) Lay-off
(r) Price level
(s) Adverse supply shock
(t) The natural rate of unemployment

1 The average price of all the goods produced in the economy.

2   A schedule showing how many people choose to
be in the labour force at each real wage.
3   A temporary separation of workers from a firm.
4   The increase in autonomous consumption
demand when the value of consumers' real
money balances increases.
5   A schedule which shows the prices charged by
firms at each output level, given the wages they
have to pay.
6   A schedule which shows the quantity of output
that firms wish to supply at each price level.
7   A situation in which people confuse nominal and
real variables.
8   The percentage of the labour force that is unemployed when the labour market is in equilibrium.
9   A schedule showing how many workers choose
to accept jobs at each real wage.
10 The number of people without jobs who are
registered as seeking a job.
11 The nominal or money wage divided by the price
level.
12 Devices used by firms to vary labour input without affecting numbers employed.
13 The pursuit of policies aimed not at increasing
aggregate demand but at increasing aggregate
supply.
14 The tendency for output and employment to
fluctuate around their long-term trends.
15 An event such as an oil price rise which leads to a
contraction in supply, increasing prices and reducing output in the short run.
16 A school of macroeconomic thought in which
wages and prices are assumed to be fully flexible.
17 A situation in which some people have chosen not
to work at the going wage rate.
18 The increase in output produced from a given
capital stock when an additional worker is
employed.
19 A situation in which some people would like to
work at the going real wage but cannot find a job.
20 For a firm, the total number of labour hours it
employs in a given period.

EXERCISES

1   This exercise explores the relationship between
price and aggregate demand. Figure 26.1 shows
an economy's IS and LM schedules. The economy begins in equilibrium with IS_0 and LM_0
being the relevant schedules.
   (a) Identify equilibrium income, interest rate,
        and aggregate demand.
   Suppose the price level rises to a new level:
   (b) Which of the LM schedules is appropriate?
   (c) In the absence of the real balance effect,

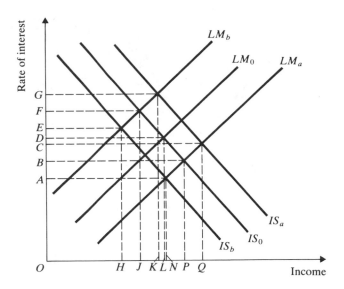

FIGURE 26.1   Price and aggregate demand

        identify the new equilibrium levels of
        income, interest rate, and aggregate
        demand.
   (d) Explain and identify the influence of the
        real-balance effect.
   (e) Repeat questions (b), (c), and (d) for a *fall* in
        price level from its original level.
   (f) Explain why the price level affects the posi-
        tion of the LM curve.
   (g) Draw a diagram to illustrate the macro-
        economic demand schedule with and with-
        out the real balance effect.

2   Which of the following characteristics are valid
for all points along the macroeconomic demand
schedule? *Note*: more than one response may be
valid.
   (a) Planned spending equals actual output.
   (b) Planned demand for real money balances is
        equal to nominal money supply divided by
        the price level.
   (c) Demanders of goods receive the quantities
        they want to buy.
   (d) The money market is in equilibrium.
   (e) There is no disequilibrium in the goods
        market.

3   Figure 26.2 shows the labour market of an economy. LD is labour demand, AJ is the job acceptances schedule, and LF the labour force schedule.
   (a) What is the equilibrium real wage?
   (b) Identify the level of employment and regis-
        tered unemployment.
   (c) In this situation, what is the natural rate of
        unemployment, and the quantity of invol-
        untary unemployment?

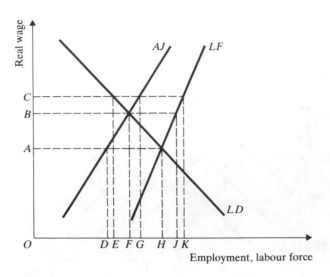

FIGURE 26.2   The labour market

Suppose the real wage is at OA:

(d)   Identify the level of employment, registered unemployment, and quantity of involuntary unemployment.

(e)   How will the market react?

Suppose now the real wage is at OC:

(f)   Identify the level of employment, registered unemployment, and quantity of involuntary unemployment.

(g)   How will the market react?

(h)   Explain why there should be a connection between employment and aggregate supply.

(i)   What are the implications for aggregate supply if the labour market is always in equilibrium?

4   This exercise examines monetary and fiscal policy, using the MDS and the aggregate supply schedule. Figure 26.3 shows two macroeconomic

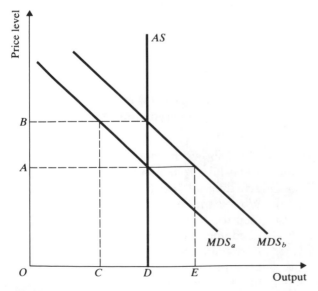

FIGURE 26.3   Monetary and fiscal policy

demand schedules (MDS_a and MDS_b) and the aggregate supply schedule (AS). First, we consider the effects of monetary policy in the *classical* model—specifically, an increase in nominal money supply.

(a)   Identify the 'before' and 'after' MDS.

(b)   What was the original equilibrium price and output?

(c)   What is equilibrium price and output after the policy is implemented?

Next, consider fiscal policy—again in the classical model. Suppose there is a reduction in government expenditure:

(d)   Identify the 'before' and 'after' MDS.

(e)   What was the original equilibrium price and output?

(f)   What is the equilibrium price and output after the policy is implemented?

The Keynesian model is characterized by sluggish adjustment. Consider the period *after* the policy but *before* adjustment begins:

(g)   Identify price and output.

(h)   The MDS represents points at which goods and money markets are in equilibrium. In the position you have identified in (g), adjustment has still to take place—so in what sense is the goods market in 'equilibrium'?

5   Consider the following factors. Explore which of them encourage and which discourage rapid adjustment in the labour market. For each of the factors, state whether you expect firms or workers primarily to be affected.

(a)   The costs of job search.

(b)   Lack of redundancy agreement.

(c)   Predominantly unskilled workforce.

(d)   Production process well suited to short-time or overtime working.

(e)   Concern of firm for its reputation as an employer.

(f)   Unemployment at low level.

(g)   Acquisition of firm-specific skills.

6   The following symptoms describe the response of an economy to a leftward movement of *either* the demand *or* the supply schedule, in a situation where adjustment is not instantaneous. In each case, deduce whether the shock was to the demand side or the supply side:

(a)   A short-run fall in the price level.

(b)   Lower long-run output.

(c)   No short-run change in price.

(d)   Price lower in the long run.

(e)   A short-run fall in output.

(f)   No long-run change in output.

(g)   Price higher in the long run.

(h)   Output unchanged in the short run.

7 Which of the following factors would you expect to affect the demand side of the economy and which the supply side? State whether each leads to an increase or a decrease in demand (or supply):
  (a) An increase in the number of married women going out to work.
  (b) An increase in the price of a vital imported raw material.
  (c) An increase in business confidence.
  (d) An autonomous increase in money wages.
  (e) A fall in nominal money supply.
  (f) A shift in the distribution of income from rich to poor.
  (g) An increase in the demand for leisure.

8 If the aggregate supply curve is perfectly inelastic, an increase in aggregate demand will lead to an increase in
  1 production
  2 money income
  3 prices

  (a) 1, 2 and 3 are correct
  (b) 1 and 2 only are correct
  (c) 2 and 3 only are correct
  (d) 1 only is correct
  (e) 3 only is correct
      (University of London GCE A level Economics 3, January 1989)

9 In an economy with all resources fully employed, which of the following would tend to result in a rise in the general level of prices?
  1 An increase in the demand for exports from that economy
  2 An increase in personal consumption
  3 A fall in the productivity of labour

  (a) 1, 2, 3 are all correct
  (b) 1 and 2 only are correct
  (c) 2 and 3 only are correct
  (d) 1 only is correct
      (Associated Examining Board GCE A level Economics Paper 1, June 1987)

10 This exercise explores the effects on price and output of a once-for-all increase in nominal money supply in the short, medium, and long runs. These effects are to be examined using Figure 26.4, in which AS is aggregate supply, $SAS_{a,b,c}$ are short-run aggregate supply schedules, and $MDS_{a,b}$ are macroeconomic demand schedules.
  (a) If Figure 26.4 is to be used to analyse the policy described, and if the economy begins in equilibrium, what are the initial levels of price and output?
  (b) How would the economy react to the in-

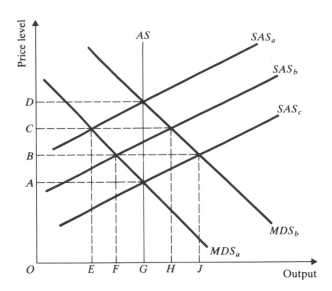

FIGURE 26.4 An increase in nominal money supply

crease in nominal money supply if it functions according to the classical model?
If adjustment is sluggish,
  (c) Identify the initial reaction of price and output and explain how it comes about.
  (d) Using Figure 26.4, describe how adjustment begins and identify the position of the economy in the medium term.
  (e) What is the final position of the economy when all adjustment is complete?
  (f) Draw a diagram showing how the adjustment process is mirrored in the labour market.
  (g) Do you expect adjustment to this change to be slower or more rapid than adjustment to a *decrease* in nominal money supply?
  (h) If the increase in nominal money supply were 10 per cent, what would be the *eventual* percentage increase in the price level?

TRUE/FALSE

1 _____ The position of the MDS depends upon the nominal money supply, government spending, and all other variables relevant to the level of aggregate demand.

2 _____ The real balance effect is the decrease in autonomous consumption demand when the value of consumers' real money balances decreases.

3 _____ Full employment is achieved when there is no unemployment.

4 _____ Money illusion is when people are tricked by forged banknotes.

5 _____ The labour market is in equilibrium anywhere on the classical aggregate supply schedule.

6 _____ In the classical model a change in nominal money supply leads to an equivalent percentage change in nominal wages and the price level.

7 _____ Fiscal policy in the classical model leads mainly to an increase in price and only to a modest increase in output.

8 _____ Sluggish wage adjustment is the most likely cause of a slow adjustment of price to changes in aggregate demand.

9 _____ In the short run firms adjust to an increase in labour demand by hiring additional workers.

10 _____ In the model developed in this chapter, the labour market bears the brunt of any short-run disequilibrium.

11 _____ An increase in full-capacity output resulting from a favourable supply shift leads to a higher price and output.

12 _____ In the UK, the supply shocks of 1973 and 1979 were quickly followed by sharp rises in the unemployment rate.

QUESTIONS FOR THOUGHT

1 (a) Explain how cuts in money wages lead to higher output if real wages are initially set at too high a level.

Suppose an economy is in *IS–LM* equilibrium, as shown in Figure 26.5. LM_a shows the initial *LM* schedule, LM_b shows how the *LM* schedule moves when the price level falls. *IS* is the *IS* schedule, y_0 is equilibrium income, r_0 the equilibrium interest rate, and y_{FE} represents full employment.

(b) Re-examine the story you told in part (a). Why might the cut in money wages fail to restore full employment?

(c) How might the story be affected if account is taken of the real balance effect?

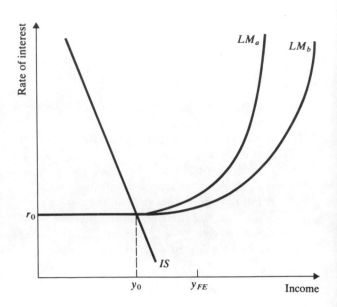

FIGURE 26.5 The liquidity trap

2 The Keynesian concept of the 'liquidity trap' refers to

(a) the inability of businesses with poor profit performances to obtain funds on loan for investment.

(b) the international problems of insufficient funds to finance any growth in world trade and payments.

(c) the downward inflexibility of interest rates as the money supply expands above a certain level.

(d) the disincentive of high income tax rates on savers depositing money with commercial banks or building societies.

(Associated Examining Board GCE A level Economics Paper 1, June 1986)

3 In Chapter 25 we saw that 'both fiscal and monetary policy were tight during the early years of the first Thatcher government' (Section 25–6 of the main text). Using the model developed in this chapter, investigate why this policy stance may impose costs on society in the short run. In what respects is the model still deficient in its application to the real world?

ANSWERS AND COMMENTS FOR CHAPTER 26

Please note   Where questions are reproduced from GCE examinations, the examination boards bear no responsibility for the answers provided in this volume, which are the sole responsibility of the authors.

Important Concepts and Technical Terms

1	r	6	b	11	a	16	e
2	p	7	j	12	f	17	i
3	q	8	t	13	g	18	l
4	m	9	h	14	d	19	k
5	n	10	o	15	s	20	c

Exercises

1   (a)   Income OL; interest rate OD; aggregate demand OL.

    (b) LM_b.

    (c)   Income OJ; interest rate OF; aggregate demand OJ.

    (d)   As price rises, the real value of money balances and other assets held by households is reduced. This has an effect on consumption and reduces aggregate demand, shifting IS to IS_b and equilibrium income, interest rate, and aggregate demand respectively to OH, OE, and OH.

    (e)   A fall in price moves LM from LM_0 to LM_a. In the absence of the real balance effect, equilibrium income and aggregate demand move to OP and the rate of interest to OB. The real balance effect moves IS from IS_0 to IS_a, so equilibrium income and aggregate demand are OQ with interest rate OC.

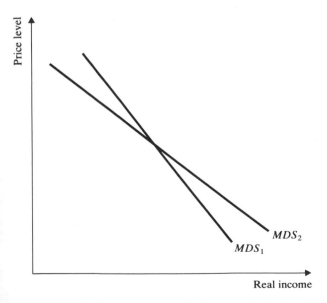

FIGURE A26.1   The macroeconomic demand schedule and the real balance effect

(f)   The position of the LM schedule is partly determined by the size of real money supply. A change in price given fixed nominal money supply affects real money supply and thus moves the LM schedule.

(g) MDS_1 shows the macroeconomic demand schedule without taking account of the real balance effect, which affects the slope, resulting in MDS_2. The intersection of the two represents our original equilibrium point.

2   *All* the characteristics listed are features of the macroeconomic demand schedule—that's how we constructed it!

3   (a) OB: where labour demand = job acceptances.

    (b)   Employment OF: registered unemployment FJ.

    (c)   The natural rate of unemployment is FJ—there is no involuntary unemployment.

    (d)   Employment OD: this represents the number of people prepared to accept jobs at this real wage. Registered unemployment is DH. All those wishing to work at this real wage can obtain work—there is excess demand for labour—so there is no involuntary unemployment.

    (e)   With excess demand for labour, firms will be prepared to offer high wages to attract labour, so the market moves towards equilibrium.

    (f)   Employment OE: this represents labour demand at this real wage. Registered unemployment is EK, of which EG is involuntary, representing people who are willing to work but cannot find employment.

    (g)   Eventually—or instantly, in the classical model—wages will drift downwards, and the market moves towards equilibrium.

    (h)   In our static model, labour is the only variable input, so fixing employment implies the level of output/aggregate supply.

    (i)   If the labour market is always in equilibrium, the level of employment—and hence aggregate supply—will be stable.

4   (a)   An increase in nominal money supply increases aggregate demand at each price, so the move must be from MDS_a to MDS_b.

    (b)   Output OD; price OA.

    (c)   Output OD; price OB; prices adjust instantaneously leaving output unaffected; money feeds only prices.

    (d)   A reduction in government spending is represented by a move from MDS_b to MDS_a.

    (e)   Price OB; output OD.

    (f)   Price OA; output OD.

    (g)   Price still at OB, output reduced to OC.

    (h) MDS represents points at which planned spending equals *actual* output—to this extent the goods market is in equilibrium. However, this may not represent equilibrium from the *producers'* perspective: there is no implication that *planned* output is equal to actual output.

5   (a)   This factor affects the workers' willingness to become unemployed and discourages adjustment.

(b) In the absence of a redundancy agreement, firms may be more willing to make adjustments to the size of workforce.

(c) This may encourage adjustment, as firms have less need to 'hoard' unskilled labour.

(d) This may discourage firms from adjusting employment and wage rates, as there is flexibility in labour input without needing to negotiate a new wage deal or indulge in hiring and firing. However, in the long run such adjustments, may have to be made.

(e) This also discourages firms from making adjustments to employment and wages.

(f) If labour is scarce, firms may not be able to increase employment, and may be reluctant to lose workers. Workers may be more prepared to change jobs as they will perceive that it will not be difficult to find new jobs.

(g) Firms may wish to hold on to trained labour if demand falls temporarily. Workers may recognize that their skills are not readily transferred to other firms.

6 (a) Demand shock.
   (b) Supply shock.
   (c) Supply.
   (d) Demand.
   (e) Demand.
   (f) Demand.
   (g) Supply.
   (h) Supply.

7 (a) An increase in supply, increasing potential output.
   (b) A decrease in supply (see the discussion of an oil price increase in Section 26–8 of the main text).
   (c) This increases autonomous investment demand, so represents an increase in demand.
   (d) A (short-run) decrease in supply.
   (e) A decrease in demand.
   (f) Given the differing propensities to consume of the 'rich' and the 'poor', this leads to an increase in autonomous consumption and in aggregate demand.
   (g) This represents a fall in labour supply at any given real wage, so there is a reduction in supply and potential output.

8 (c).
9 (a).
10 (a) If the economy is in equilibrium, then it must be on the (long-run) aggregate supply curve AS; if we are to illustrate an increase in nominal money, MDS is to move to the right—so initially must be on MDS_a. The initial position is thus at output OG, price OA.
   (b) Given full wage and price flexibility the economy moves straight to output OG, price OD.
   (c) The increase in nominal money supply moves the macroeconomic demand schedule from MDS_a to MDS_b; with sluggish adjustment, the economy moves to a position on the short-run aggregate supply curve SAS_c with output OJ, price OB. In the short run, this increase in output will be

brought about through overtime working, etc., as firms cannot instantly adjust wages and employment.

(d) Firms find that there has been an increase in demand for their output and prices rise. In time, firms take on new workers, as adjusting employment is a more sensible long-run strategy than varying hours worked by the existing workforce. The SAS schedule begins to move—from SAS_c to SAS_b in the medium term, by which stage price has reached OC and output has fallen back to OH.

(e) Output OG, price OD.

(f)

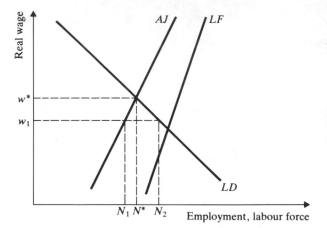

FIGURE A26.2 Labour market adjustment

The market starts in equilibrium with real wage w^* and employment N^*. As the price level rises, the real wage falls—say, to w_1—at which point we have to think rather carefully about what is happening. Labour demand has increased to N_2 but job acceptances have fallen to N_1. There is excess demand for labour, and if agents are always on the AJ function, employment *falls* at a time when output is *rising*. How do we explain this situation? It could be that in the short run workers prefer to hold on to their jobs rather than immediately incurring the costs of job search, perhaps because they realize that the real-wage reduction is temporary and are prepared to be 'off' the AJ schedule. In addition, firms may be prepared to offer lots of overtime, increasing output by this means rather than by increasing employment. As firms seek to adjust employment levels, wages will be bid up, carrying the economy back towards equilibrium—back at w^*N^*.

(g) When wages need to *fall* we may expect resistance from workers and unions. When the adjustment is upwards, we may expect firms to be keen to adjust wages (there is excess demand for labour) and workers are unlikely to protest. We may thus imagine that the adjustment in *this* case may be more rapid.

(h) 10 per cent (see Section 26–7 of the main text).

True/False

1 True: see Section 26–1 of the main text.
2 True.
3 False: there will always be some unemployment even at full employment (see Section 26–2 of the main text). Unemployment is more carefully examined in Chapter 27.
4 Silly: money illusion is the confusion of real and nominal variables.
5 True: see Section 26–3 of the main text.
6 True: see Section 26–4 of the main text.
7 False: output is unaffected and *only* prices change.
8 True: see Section 26–5 of the main text.
9 False: firms are more likely to vary hours worked in the short run (see Section 26–6 of the main text).
10 True: see Section 26–7 of the main text.
11 False: a favourable supply shock leads to higher output, but lower price level (see Section 26–8 of the main text).
12 True: see Section 26–9 of the main text.

Questions for Thought

1 (a) The story should be familiar by now: briefly, a reduction in money wages leads to a falling price level, an increase in real money supply, a fall in interest rates, and an expansion of consumption and investment—hence aggregate demand and output.

(b) The *LM* schedule of Figure 26.5 has a horizontal section. This results from the (Keynesian) speculative demand for money discussed in 'Questions for Thought' (1) of Chapter 24. r_0 represents an interest rate at which all agents expect a fall in bond prices and thus hold no bonds. It breaks the chain of part (a) because the interest rate cannot fall below r_0 and equilibrium income cannot increase beyond y_0. The economy is stuck in what is often known as the *liquidity trap*.

(c) If the real balance effect is strong enough, then falling prices have the effect of increasing autonomous consumption, thus shifting the *IS* schedule. Examination of Figure 26.5 shows that, if *IS* moves to the right, the economy is able to escape from the liquidity trap.

2 (c) If you do not recognize the jargon 'liquidity trap', refer back to the immediately preceding 'Questions for Thought', which talks you through the idea.

3 The analysis here parallels the discussion of a reduction in aggregate demand/nominal money supply (see Section 26–7 of the main text). Some transitional increase in unemployment may occur while the economy is adjusting towards equilibrium. There are still a number of themes to be further developed: in particular, we need to be able to analyse *inflation*—a situation of rising prices over time. We cannot easily do this with our static model. In order to analyse the UK economy fully, we also need to consider open economy effects. The following chapters explore these issues.

27 Unemployment

Unemployment was one of the dominating themes of the 1980s. The experience of persistent unemployment during the 1930s induced a reaction in the attitudes of policy-makers in the postwar period, with a steadfast commitment to maintain full employment. The classical model re-emerged in the 1970s with its emphasis on flexibility, on adjustment to full-employment equilibrium, and on voluntary unemployment. This re-emergence was at a time when inflation threatened to become uncontrollable, and policy attitudes were ripe for change. The adverse OPEC supply shock of 1979–80 triggered widespread unemployment, not only in the UK but in many parts of the world. In the UK the unemployment rate rose to 1930s levels for the first time in the postwar period.

What is unemployment? It is measured as the percentage of the labour force who are without a job but willing and available for work, where the *labour force* is defined as those of the population who choose to register as being available for work or who have jobs. The fact that people *choose* whether to register casts doubts on the reliability of the statistics, as there may be those willing and available to work who do not bother to register, especially if not eligible for benefit.

It is a mistake to think of unemployment as a static, stagnant pool of unfortunates languishing at street corners. Although the number of *long-term unemployed* increased considerably during the 1980s, there were still substantial flows into and out of unemployment. In 1988, 3.75 million joined the unemployment register, but 4.40 million also left it! In any period, people leave the ranks of the unemployed to become employed or re-employed, or to leave the labour force altogether as *discouraged workers*. Also, there are workers becoming unemployed through choice, having quit or having been temporarily laid off or fired—and there are those who rejoin the labour force to look for work. There are changes too among those in work: some leave the labour force through retirement or other reasons; some previously not part of the labour force accept jobs. Some groups within society are more prone to unemployment than others—notably the young (lacking human capital) and the old.

Frictional unemployment occurs because people are between jobs—perhaps because of the need to undertake job search. *Structural unemployment* occurs when there is a mismatch between the demand and supply of labour: for instance, some industries in an economy may be contracting and shedding labour while other sectors may be trying to expand by hiring new labour. If the skills of those leaving employment are not those required by the expanding sectors, unemployment results. As we saw in the previous chapter, sluggish adjustment within an economy may lead to *demand-deficient* ('*Keynesian*') *unemployment* if there is a decline in aggregate demand, or to *classical unemployment* if real wages are set above the equilibrium level.

Also in Chapter 26 we encountered the *natural rate of unemployment*, reflecting the idea that even in equilibrium there may be some unemployment, perhaps owing to frictional or structural factors. The distinction between *voluntary* and *involuntary unemployment* is an important one, as it colours the way we regard unemployment. Keynesian unemployment may be regarded as transitional or disequilibrium unemployment. Whereas monetary and fiscal policy may be able to reduce such unemployment, supply-side policies will be necessary if it is desired to affect the natural rate.

In asking why unemployment was relatively so high in the 1980s, we need to explore whether it is demand factors that are relevant or whether there has been an increase in the natural rate. Layard and Nickell considered a number of factors which might be argued to affect the male unemployment rate. Increases in trade union power turned out to have been an important source of higher UK unemployment, and labour taxes also made some contribution. However, increases in the *replacement ratio* (that is, the ratio of unemployment benefit to average after-tax earnings of those in work) were not observed in practice, and neither changes in real import prices, skill mismatch, nor incomes policy emerged as major causes. According to these estimates, two-thirds of UK unemployment in the 1980s reflected an increase in the natural rate; the rest was due to a Keynesian recession. Research in the late 1980s suggested that the long-run equilibrium level of employment may be affected by the short-run market experience, a process known as *hysteresis*. By this argument, a temporary fall in labour demand is said to lead to a permanent fall in labour supply. This could result from insider–outsider distinctions, or from discouraged worker, search-and-mismatch, or capital stock effects. These explanations were born of an attempt to explain high and persistent unemployment in a number of European countries.

In order to affect the long-run equilibrium rate, supply-side policies are essential. *Supply-side economics* involves the use of microeconomic incentives to affect the level of full employment output. In the context of this chapter, policies which affect labour supply or demand are especially important. Labour supply may be influenced by cuts in income tax rates to induce the substitution of work for leisure. (This may be diluted by the 'income effect'.) The likely effectiveness of such a move is in some doubt. Similar effects could be achieved by reducing unemployment benefits or national insurance contributions. Other possibilities might include measures to weaken trade union power, incomes policies (to be considered in Chapter 28), and policies to reduce frictional and structural unemployment, especially training and retraining schemes.

There may also be ways of increasing labour demand, for instance by encouraging adoption of modern capital equipment (which would increase the marginal product of labour). This could be done by investment subsidies or lower interest rates to increase the share of investment. The Thatcher administration cut public spending to allow 'crowding in' to take place. Another approach would be to improve expectations about the future and thus to encourage investment by improving business confidence. However, there is conflict here—some would argue that this is best accomplished by conquering inflation, others that expectations would be best improved by demand management.

The impact of *Okun's law* reduces the potential of demand policy to affect Keynesian unemployment. This concerns the way in which output and employment vary over the business cycle: output tends to grow by more than employment during boom periods and to fall more rapidly during a recession. This partly results from the effect of workers joining and leaving the labour force and partly because firms tend to hoard labour during recessions.

The way we view the *private and social costs of unemployment* depends crucially on whether unemployment is voluntary or involuntary. Presumably the private costs borne by the voluntarily unemployed can be neglected, as they have judged the benefits of not working to exceed the costs. However, we may not wish to ignore the social costs: allocative inefficiency results from the payment of unemployment benefit, which means that 'too many' workers choose to be unemployed. Notice, however, that some voluntary unemployment is desirable to allow changes in industrial employment structure to occur. Involuntary unemployment involves high social and private costs, both in terms of lost output and in private suffering which cannot be calculated.

It is sometimes easy to lose sight of the international perspective surrounding unemployment in the 1980s. The oil price supply shock of 1979–80, coupled with anti-inflation policy, led to unemployment being high in many countries throughout the world. Some economies may seem to have escaped: Japan with its individual social structure, Sweden with its compulsory high redundancy payments. However, we should remember that the UK is by no means alone.

IMPORTANT CONCEPTS AND TECHNICAL TERMS

Match each lettered concept with the appropriate numbered phrase:

(a) Unemployment rate
(b) Incomes policy
(c) Labour force
(d) Replacement ratio
(e) Okun's law
(f) Supply-side economics
(g) Private cost of unemployment
(h) Structural unemployment
(i) Discouraged worker effect
(j) Demand-deficient unemployment
(k) Hysteresis
(l) Social cost of unemployment
(m) Frictional unemployment
(n) Long-term unemployed
(o) Natural rate of unemployment
(p) Classical unemployment

1 In the UK, all those people holding a job or registered with the local office of the Department of Employment as being willing and available for work.

2 The percentage of the labour force who are without a job but are registered as being willing and available for work.

3 Those members of the labour force who have remained in unemployment for a time span measured in months rather than weeks—in the UK in April 1986, 41 per cent of the unemployed had been out of work for longer than a year.

4 People who have become depressed about the prospects of ever finding a job and decide to stop even trying.

5 The rate of unemployment when the labour market is in equilibrium.

6 Unemployment which occurs when aggregate demand falls and wages and prices have not yet adjusted to restore full employment—sometimes known as Keynesian unemployment.

7 The ratio of unemployment or supplementary benefit that an unemployed worker gets from the government (transfer payments) relative to the average after-tax earnings of people in work.

8 The unemployment created when the wage is deliberately maintained above the level at which the labour supply and labour demand schedules intersect.

9 The irreducible minimum level of unemployment in a dynamic society: comprising people who are almost unemployable or are spending short spells in unemployment while between jobs.

10 The cost to an individual worker of being out of work, the largest component being the wage forgone by not working.

11 The use of microeconomic incentives to alter the level of full employment, the level of potential output, and the natural rate of unemployment.

12 A situation experienced by an economy when its long-run equilibrium depends upon the path it has followed in the short run.

13 The cost to society of being below full employment, including lost output and human suffering.

14 A relationship between output and employment such that a 1 per cent increase in demand and output would lead to a smaller percentage increase in employment and an even smaller reduction in the percentage of the labour force unemployed.

15 A policy entailing the direct regulation of wages.

16 Unemployment arising from a mismatch of skills and job opportunities as the pattern of demand and production changes.

EXERCISES

1 Remember the economy of Hypothetica? They're now having unemployment problems. Below are presented some data on the flows in the labour market in a particular year. ('Real' data on some of these flows are hard to come by, so any resemblance between these numbers and those for any real economy you know about is purely fortuitous!) Data are in thousands. At the beginning of the year the labour force is 26 900, of whom 2900 are unemployed. We also have:

(i)	Discouraged workers	600
(ii)	Job-losers/lay-offs	1500
(iii)	Retiring, temporarily leaving	100
(iv)	Quits	700
(v)	New hires, recalls	2000
(vi)	Re-entrants, new entrants	500
(vii)	Taking a job (not previously unemployed)	100

(a) How many workers joined and left the unemployed during the year?

(b) How many people joined and left the labour force during the year?

(c) How did the size of the employed labour force change during the year?

(d) Calculate the size of total labour force and unemployment at the end of the year.

(e) In the UK in 1989, unemployment began the year at 2.05 million. During the year, 3.19 million joined the register, 3.62 million left it. What would this suggest for the level of unemployment at the end of the year?

2 State whether each of the following reasons for unemployment would be classified as frictional, structural, demand-deficient, or classical, and which represent voluntary or involuntary unemployment:

(a) Unemployment resulting from the decline of the textile industry and expansion of the microcomputer industry.

(b) Individuals between jobs.

(c) People whose physical or mental handicaps render them unemployable.

(d) Unemployment resulting from the real wage being too high for labour market equilibrium.

(e) Unemployment arising from slow adjustment following a reduction in aggregate demand.

3 Table 27.1 presents unemployment rates as a percentage of the national average for the standard regions in Great Britain for 1974 and 1989. *Health warning*: this question requires thought!

TABLE 27.1 Regional unemployment rate as a percentage of the national average

	1974 (%)	1989 (%)
South East	60	65
East Anglia	80	60
West Midlands	84	105
East Midlands	88	90
Yorkshire & Humberside	104	123
South West	108	87
North West	136	137
Wales	148	124
Scotland	156	152
North	180	160
Great Britain	100	100

Source: Department of Employment, *Employment Gazette*.

(a) The figures in the above table are ranked in ascending order of unemployment in 1974. Comment on the major differences and similarities revealed in the 1989 rankings.

(b) How does the analysis of types of unemployment help you to think about *why* these regional disparities have arisen and persist through time?

4 Table 27.2 shows how labour demand and supply vary with the real wage in a small economy.

TABLE 27.2 Labour demand and supply (in thousands)

Real wage ($/hour)	Labour demand	Job acceptances	Labour force
1	130	70	101
2	120	80	108
3	110	90	115
4	100	100	122
5	90	110	129
6	80	120	136

Suppose the real wage is fixed at $5 per hour:

(a) What is the level of employment?

(b) Calculate the level of unemployment.

(c) How much of the unemployment is involuntary and how much is voluntary?

Suppose now that workers base their decisions on take-home pay, that the real wage is flexible, and that workers are paying $2 in income tax:

(d) What is the equilibrium wage as paid by firms and the net take-home pay of those employed?

(e) What are the levels of employment and unemployment? Is there excess demand for labour?

(f) How much of the unemployment is involuntary and how much is voluntary?

Finally, suppose that income tax is removed:

(g) What is the equilibrium real wage?

(h) What are the levels of employment and unemployment? By how much has unemployment changed?

(i) How much of the remaining unemployment is involuntary and how much is voluntary?

5 Suppose that a labour market begins in equilibrium. We are to investigate the effects of a change in real oil prices such as happened in the 1970s, causing many energy-intensive firms to become economically obsolete. The effects of this on the labour market are shown in Figure 27.1.

(a) If Figure 27.1 is to illustrate the situation described, which of the labour demand schedules LD_a and LD_b represents the *initial* position? Explain your answer.

(b) Identify the equilibrium levels of employment and the real wage in this initial position.

(c) What is the natural rate of unemployment?

Now suppose that the oil price shock occurs.

(d) Assume that the real wage fails to adjust immediately—identify the levels of employment and unemployment.

(e) As real wages adjust, to what equilibrium values of employment and the real wage will the market tend?

(f) What will be the natural rate of unemployment?

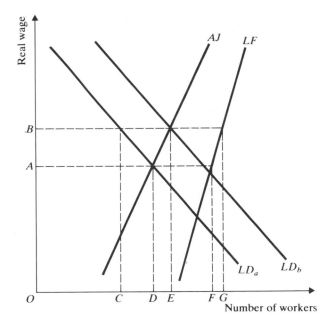

FIGURE 27.1 The effects of a supply shock

(g) Has the natural rate increased, decreased, or stayed the same? Why should that be?

6 Which of the following factors may have contributed to the rise in the natural rate of unemployment in the UK since the 1970s?

(a) An increase in the replacement ratio.

(b) A decline in international competitiveness.

(c) An increase in trade union power.

(d) A decline in world trade.

(e) The recession in British manufacturing industry.

(f) Technical progress.

(g) A decrease in the participation rate of married women.

(h) Changes in employers' labour taxes.

7 Below are listed a number of policies which could be used to reduce (or prevent a rise in) the long-run rate of unemployment. In each case, explain the disadvantages of the policy.

(a) Force firms to make high redundancy payments to discourage firms from sacking workers too readily.

(b) The reduction or elimination of unemployment benefit.

(c) Wages cut by an incomes policy.

(d) An expansionary fiscal policy.

(e) Subsidize manufacturing industry.

8 Other things being equal, the working population of a country would be likely to increase if

(a) the school-leaving age were raised.

(b) the retirement age were lowered.

(c) more full-time places were made available at universities.

(d) the amount of nursery provision were increased.

(Associated Examining Board GCE A level Economics Paper 1, November 1988)

9 Which of the following statements is *not* implied by Okun's law?

(a) In boom periods, employment increases by more than recorded unemployment decreases.

(b) An increase of 1 per cent in unemployment is associated with a fall of more than 1 per cent in real output.

(c) In slump periods, employment changes by less than recorded unemployment.

(d) Average labour productivity varies over the business cycle.

10 This exercise involves an application of indifference curves, which we first encountered early on in the book. You may wish to remind yourself of their application to labour supply (see Section 11–4 of the main text). Figure 27.2 is to be used to analyse the effects of a cut in the rate of income tax on the supply of labour by an individual (Jayne). I_1, I_2, and I_3 are indifference curves depicting Jayne's preferences for income and leisure. ACD and BCD are alternative budget lines, which assume that Jayne receives some non-labour income, some of which must be given up if she chooses to work. The horizontal axis is

labelled '*additional*' hours of leisure as Jayne never chooses to have less than 12 hours of leisure daily.

(a) How would you expect a cut in the income tax rate to affect the budget lines?

(b) This being so, which must be the initial budget line in our story?

(c) Identify Jayne's initial choice point.

(d) At this point, what is Jayne's total income? How many hours does she work?

(e) Identify Jayne's choice point *after* the income tax cut. How many hours does she now work?

11 Figure 27.3 shows the changing conditions in an economy's labour market. Suppose that this market has moved from an initial equilibrium in which employment was L_1 and the real wage was w_1, and has now settled at a new long-run equilibrium with employment L_2 and real wage w_2. LD represents labour demand, and AJ is the job acceptances schedule. Notice that employment is lower in this final situation. Which of the following arguments could explain the situation?

(a) A temporary recession increases unemployment and discourages potential workers from looking for jobs. This carries over even when the recession is over.

(b) Firms reduce capital stock during a recession, so that labour demand fails to readjust fully when the recession is over.

(c) A recession makes workers less enthusiastic about job search and reduces firms' need to advertise for workers. Previous levels of job search are not recaptured after the recession.

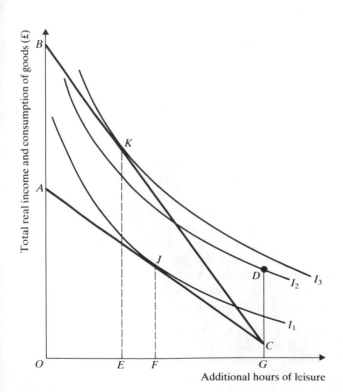

FIGURE 27.2 Income tax and the supply of labour

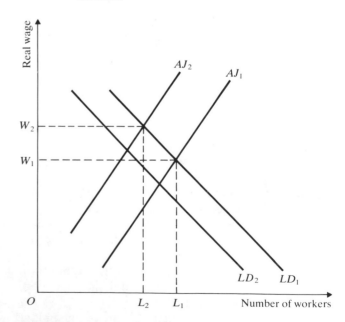

FIGURE 27.3 The effects of hysteresis

(d) Wage-bargaining is carried out by employed workers (insiders). A recession reduces employment and this situation is exploited by the still-employed workers in negotiating higher real wages for themselves at the recession's end.

TRUE/FALSE

1 _____ The Department of Employment publishes accurate monthly figures of the number of people who are unemployed in the UK.

2 _____ The unemployment rate is lower for women than for men.

3 _____ Minimum wage legislation may result in classical unemployment.

4 _____ The natural rate of unemployment is entirely composed of voluntary unemployment.

5 _____ Voluntary unemployment is known as the natural rate of unemployment.

6 _____ The actual rate of unemployment is always close to the natural rate.

7 _____ A major reason for the increase in unemployment in the UK in recent years has been the changing composition of the labour force, with increasing numbers of young workers and women seeking employment.

8 _____ In the long run the performance of the economy can be changed only by affecting the level of full employment and the corresponding level of potential output.

9 _____ Much empirical work in the UK suggests that the 1979 income tax cut should *not* have been expected to lead to a spontaneous eruption of work effort.

10 _____ Government expenditure on extra police officers will add less to employment than an equivalent increase in the value of spending on electricity.

11 _____ When unemployment is involuntary, the case for active policy is stronger, as the private costs are higher.

12 _____ Unemployment is always a bad thing.

13 _____ Freedom of choice is important; people choose to be unemployed; society need not be concerned about voluntary unemployment.

14 _____ Unemployment in Japan is relatively low partly because of implicit agreements between firms and workers that male workers have lifetime jobs.

QUESTIONS FOR THOUGHT

1 This exercise explores some of the differences between classical and demand-deficient unemployment within our labour market diagram.
   (a) Identify the equilibrium real wage, employment, and the natural rate of unemployment.
   Now we consider classical unemployment, which is readily shown in Figure 27.4. Suppose that the real wage is stuck at *OB*.

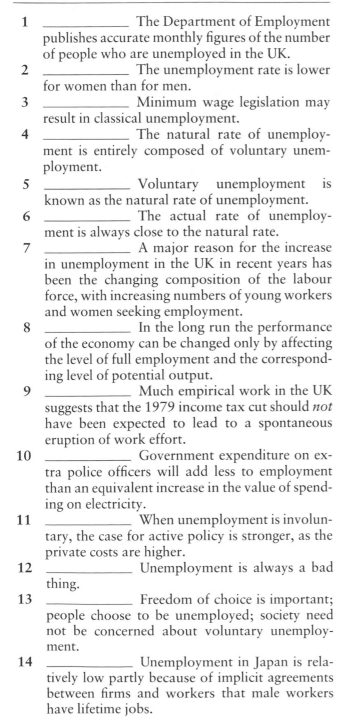

FIGURE 27.4 Classical and demand-deficient unemployment

   (b) Identify labour demand and the amounts of voluntary and involuntary unemployment.
   This much we have seen already—but how may we show demand-deficient unemployment? We have seen that this unemployment results from sluggish adjustment. Suppose that prices and wages are rigid in the short run, with the price level at too high a level to clear the goods market.
   (c) Firms see stocks building up but cannot adjust price immediately—how do they react?
   (d) Suppose that the real wage is at *OA*, but firms reduce output to prevent the build-up of stocks, so employ only *OC* workers. Identify the amounts of voluntary and involuntary unemployment.
   (e) How does this affect households' incomes?
   (f) Discuss how unemployment policy must be tailored to the underlying cause.

2 Why has unemployment in the UK been higher in the 1980s than in the 1970s?
   (University of London GCE A level Economics 1, June 1989)

ANSWERS AND COMMENTS FOR CHAPTER 27

Please note Where questions are reproduced from GCE examinations, the examination boards bear no responsibility for the answers provided in this volume, which are the sole responsibility of the authors.

Important Concepts and Technical Terms

1 *c*	5 *o*	9 *m*	13 *l*
2 *a*	6 *j*	10 *g*	14 *e*
3 *n*	7 *d*	11 *f*	15 *b*
4 *i*	8 *p*	12 *k*	16 *h*

Exercises

1 (a) Categories (ii), (iv), and (vi) joined the unemployed, a total of 2700.
Categories (i) and (v) left = 2600.

(b) Categories (vi) and (vii) joined = 600.
Categories (i) and (iii) left = 700.

(c) Categories (ii), (iii), and (iv) = 2300 left jobs; (v) and (vii) became employed = 2100; so the employed labour force fell by 200.

(d) Labour force 26 800, unemployed 3000. Although the *employed* labour force fell by 200, unemployment has risen by only 100.

(e) $2.05 + 3.19 - 3.62 = 1.62$m.
The way the figures are compiled leaves a discrepancy between this and the actual figure of 1.64m.

2 (a) This is structural unemployment. If textile workers are refusing jobs which do not match their acquired skills, then we regard them as voluntarily unemployed.

(b) Frictional unemployment. Voluntary. Of course, there is a sense in which all unemployed (except school-leavers) are 'between jobs', but here we refer to those in the process of changing jobs, perhaps having left one job in the knowledge that they have a new job starting in the near future.

(c) Usually regarded as part of frictional unemployment. This is a situation in which we may wish to remember that economists use words in a particular way. Some people in this group may *want* to work, but are incapable of work. As people, we may recognize these desires, but as economists we include them as part of voluntary unemployment—the wedge between *AJ* and *LF* in the diagrams.

(d) Classical unemployment. As individuals, those suffering unemployment for this reason may see themselves as being involuntarily unemployed. However, we remember that they may be unemployed through the choices of their ex-colleagues—for instance, if real wages are sustained at a high level through union market power. In this sense, this unemployment is voluntary.

(e) This is demand-deficient unemployment. Involuntary.

3 The regional variation in unemployment has not been discussed explicitly in this chapter, which is why this question carries a health warning. However, you should by now have had sufficient practice to be able to think through some of the main issues, using the techniques presented.

(a) Comparing the two columns, it is firstly apparent that some regions have maintained their relative positions. The South East, East Anglia, and East Midlands continue to enjoy lower unemployment rates than the national average, while the North, Yorkshire and Humberside, the North West, Wales, and Scotland continue to suffer more than most. The West Midlands fell dramatically down the rankings, starting below the national average and finishing well above. This in large measure may be attributed to the decline of manufacturing industry (especially motor vehicles) after 1974. The South West, on the other hand, improved its relative position.

(b) A fundamental issue is whether unemployment rates reflect the characteristics of the regions themselves or of the people who live there. If an area has a high proportion of young people, then we might expect high *frictional* unemployment, as such workers tend to switch between jobs more frequently. However, we are not presented with such information.
Structural unemployment may well contribute to our explanation, in the sense that different regions have differing employment structures. The immobility of labour between regions may create a mismatch between labour demand and supply. The decline of manufacturing in the West Midlands provides one instance of such unemployment.
Classical unemployment is less likely to vary between regions, but it is possible that national industry wage agreements may create wage scales which are locally inappropriate.
Demand-deficient unemployment may affect regions differently because of local product structure. In addition, regional disparities may be perpetuated by this route—if unemployment is high in a region, local demand will be low.
No doubt you have thought of many other factors.

4 (a) Employment is 90 (thousand).

(b) At a real wage of $5, 129 register as being part of the labour force, so total unemployment is $129 - 90 = 39$.

(c) From the table we see that 110 would be prepared to accept jobs at this real wage, so involuntary unemployment is $110 - 90 = 20$—the remainder is voluntary.

(d) Firms pay $5 per hour and workers receive $3.

(e) Employment is 90, given by labour demand at $5 per hour. As for unemployment, net real wages are $3, so the registered labour force is 115 and unemployment is $115 - 90 = 25$. The labour market is in equilibrium, so there is *no* excess demand for labour—remember that the real wage paid by firms exceeds that received by workers. The workers receive $3 per hour, at which rate job acceptances amount to 90.

(f) All unemployment here is voluntary.

(g) Without tax, the equilibrium real wage is $4.

(h) Employment is 100, unemployment is $122 - 100 = 22$. Unemployment has fallen by 3.

(i) With the labour market in equilibrium, all unemployment is voluntary.

If you found this difficult, you might find that it helps to draw a diagram using the figures of Table 27.2. There is a similar figure in Section 27–4 of the main text.

5 (a) LD_b must be the original labour demand schedule. The effect of the adverse supply shock will be to reduce the marginal product of labour and hence labour demand.

(b) Real wage OB, employment OE.

(c) EG.

(d) Employment falls to OC, unemployment rises to CG.

(e) Real wage OA, employment OD.

(f) DF.

(g) The natural rate has risen. As the real wage falls, the replacement ratio rises and affects the natural rate.

6 (a) cannot be a culprit as it has actually *fallen* since the 1970s.

(b) is a demand-side effect, which may have contributed to demand-deficient unemployment, but not to the natural rate.

(c) is cited in Section 27–3 of the main text as a major influence on the natural rate.

(d) is another demand-side effect.

(e) has no doubt contributed greatly to the rise in the natural rate, having generated structural unemployment.

(f) Changes in technology may have led to a fall in the demand for *some* types of labour—for instance, few clerks are required with computer-based filing systems. None the less, there is an increase in demand for computer operators ... but again, there may be some structural unemployment.

(g) The participation rate of married women has *increased* in recent years—this may have added to the natural rate.

(h) These have made some contribution to the natural rate.

7 (a) may cause immobility of labour and lead to distortions in resource allocation.

(b) may cause high levels of personal suffering but not have substantial effects. It would appear that in countries where no unemployment benefits are paid, high unemployment is associated with poverty and high rates of criminal activity.

(c) may be politically difficult to enforce, and the effectiveness of incomes policy is in some doubt. Incomes policy is discussed in Chapter 28.

(d) may affect demand-deficient unemployment but will affect the natural rate only if it has an effect

on expectations of firms and thus encourages investment, or if marginal tax cuts have an effect on labour supply by improving the incentive to work.

(e) is potentially distortionary. It may prevent structural unemployment in the short run, but eventually the adjustment of employment structure will be necessary.

8 (d).

9 (c).

10 (a) A cut in the income tax rate would *steepen* the budget line.

(b) ACD.

(c) D: I_2 is the highest indifference curve that Jayne can choose. If she works, the best she can do is at J on I_1.

(d) Income is GD; she does not work.

(e) K on I_3; she works EG hours.

11 This exercise is based on the discussion of hysteresis in Box 27–2 of the main text. All of the arguments may be found there.

(a) This is the discouraged-worker effect emphasized by Professor Richard Layard.

(b) This argument has been studied by Professor Charlie Bean, but notice that it does not correspond directly to Figure 27.3: in this story, it is labour *demand* which remains to the left of its original position after the recession, and labour supply is not affected.

(c) This explanation of hysteresis has been explored by Professor Chris Pissarides.

(d) This explanation has been emphasized by writers in both Europe and the United States.

Notice that if hysteresis does occur, it has important implications for policy strategy on the demand-side as well as on the supply-side. Read Box 27–2 of the main text for more details.

True/False

1 False: the published series relate to those *registered* as unemployed, but this is almost certainly an underestimate of those who are actually unemployed (see Section 27–1 of the main text).

2 True.

3 True: see Section 27–2 of the main text.

4 True.

5 False: voluntary unemployment may still occur when the labour market is out of equilibrium.

6 False, although some economists would judge it to be closer than would others (see Section 27–3 of the main text).

7 False.

8 True: see Section 27–4 of the main text.

9 True: see Box 27–1 of the main text.

10 False: the reverse is true (see Section 27–5 of the main text).

11 True: see Section 27–6 of the main text.

12 False: for instance, some frictional unemployment may be necessary to allow reallocation of resources.

13   False: society may wish to take the social costs of unemployment into account.

14   True: see Section 27–7 of the main text.

Questions for Thought

1   (a)   Real wage OA, employment OD, natural rate DF.
    (b)   Labour demand OC, voluntary unemployment EG, involuntary CE.
    (c)   With prices rigid, firms may well choose to reduce output—and hence employment—so that for a time they may be 'off' their LD schedule.
    (d)   Voluntary unemployment DF, involuntary CD. In this situation, we have involuntary unemployment even though the real wage is at its equilibrium level!
    (e)   The fall in employment reduces wage income and leads to a fall in demand for goods, confirming firms' beliefs that they cannot sell as much output as they would like!
    (f)   You can probably think this part through without hints.

2   Supply-side factors are vital in deciding whether there are grounds for believing that the natural rate has increased in the UK in recent years, and it is to these that your thoughts should turn.

28 Inflation

Sustained and persistent inflation is a relatively recent phenomenon in the UK, but was soon established in the minds of the Thatcher government as the greatest evil in the land, at least from the perspective of macroeconomic policy. In this chapter we look in turn at the causes, consequences, and costs of inflation.

In Chapter 24 we saw that the demand for real money balances depends on real income and the nominal interest rate. We now assume that interest rates adjust rapidly to keep the money market in equilibrium. An increase in nominal money supply initially implies an increase in real money supply and a fall in the interest rate, which stimulates aggregate demand and pushes up the price level, a process which continues until the economy returns to the same equilibrium output but at a higher price level. Thus in the long run, changes in money lead to changes in price. This sequence illustrates the *quantity theory of money*.

Two important issues are the extent to which the observed association between money and prices reflects the above chain of causality, and the extent to which it is valid to treat real money demand as constant. Could price changes 'cause' changes in money supply? An autonomous increase in money wages which puts upward pressure on prices could threaten a fall in real output, such that the authorities choose to follow an *accommodating monetary policy*. Only if this happens can prices continue to rise.

An exact relationship between money and prices would require that real money demand was stable. However, as real income grows over time, so too will real money demand. An added complication is that high nominal interest rates which raise the opportunity cost of holding money will tend to reduce real money demand. However, real money demand changes slowly, so when we switch from our static analysis into a dynamic environment, we can expect to see a relationship between *inflation* (the rate of change in prices) and the *growth* of money supply.

Back in Chapter 13, we encountered the *real rate of interest* as the difference between the nominal interest rate and the rate of inflation. According to the *Fisher hypothesis*, the real interest rate remains relatively stable—otherwise there would be large excess demand for or supply of loans. Thus, an increase in monetary growth leads not only to inflation but to high nominal interest rates. In periods of *hyperinflation* this brings problems and may lead to the *flight from money*, in which people do all they can to avoid holding money. At the height of the German hyperinflation in the early 1920s, prices rose by nearly 30 000 per cent in a single month, so people held as little money as possible.

A key factor in triggering the German hyperinflation was that the government was trying to finance a large deficit by printing money. This may hint at a link between *fiscal* and monetary policy, recently reflected in the UK in the *Medium-Term Financial Strategy*, which during the 1980s published targets for both monetary growth and PSBR.

Why should there be a direct link between the budget deficit and the inflation rate? International evidence does not suggest that such links are always present; and after all, the government need not finance its deficit only by printing money—it may instead use bond-financing. The UK data show no obvious short-run relationship between PSBR and changes in £M3. In the long run, the links may be stronger, as a persistently high PSBR will eventually push up interest rates, adding to the national debt and curtailing aggregate demand.

We next consider the effects of inflation on output and unemployment. Phillips in 1958 demonstrated a seemingly well-established relationship between the rate of change of money wages and unemployment (the *Phillips curve*), which seemed to offer policy-makers a range of options for combinations of inflation and unemployment, as low unemployment seemed to be associated with high inflation and vice versa. The 1970s thus came as a nasty shock with a combination of high wage inflation *and* high unemployment. What happened to the Phillips curve? We saw earlier that there exists a natural rate of unemployment towards which the economy will eventually adjust. This might suggest that the Phillips curve represents a short-run phenomenon, the trade-off occurring only during the adjustment period. This in turn would suggest that the Phillips curve cannot be exploited for long-run policy purposes.

What then is the long-run position? Milton Friedman has argued that people are concerned about *real* variables which are not affected by inflation in long-run equilibrium. The long-run Phillips curve is vertical by this argument, and long-run equilibrium may be typified by unemployment at the natural rate and by a steady rate of inflation. Indeed, the natural rate these days is sometimes referred to as the non-accelerating inflation rate of unemployment (NAIRU).

This being so, the combination of high unemployment and inflation of the 1970s is explained in terms of movement of the short-run Phillips curve (SRPC). An important determinant of the position of the SRPC is expectations about inflation. Suppose the authorities want to reduce inflation: they announce that the growth of nominal money stock is to be reduced to a level consistent with target inflation. In the short run, the economy slides along the SRPC; inflation is reduced a bit, unemployment rises above the natural rate. If the workers believe in the authorities' determination to reduce inflation, then the next round of wage negotiations can be at a lower level, and the SRPC moves down, until eventually we return to the natural rate with lower inflation. The key step is workers' expectations: the policy succeeds only if they believe in the policy and adjust expectations to move the SRPC. If expectations do not adjust, it is possible that unemployment will continue to rise above the natural rate until the government's nerve cracks. In this context, the *credibility* of policy is vital—hence the stress laid on the Medium-Term Financial Strategy being a long-term policy and the 'no U-turn' statements of the Thatcher government.

By the mid-1980s, the credibility of the government's commitment to controlling inflation was thought to be sufficiently well established to allow some relaxation of policy. The resultant boom had to be moderated somewhat by a high interest rate policy introduced in 1989.

In the UK, governments throughout the 1960s and early 1970s had a commitment to full employment, even to the extent of following an accommodating monetary policy. As will be seen in Chapter 29, the operation of fixed exchange rates in the 1960s forced monetary responsibility, but in the early 1970s an acceleration of monetary growth followed the transition to floating exchange rates and inflation resulted, aggravated by the oil price shock of 1973–74. By the early 1980s attitudes had changed, and anti-inflation measures and the restrictive monetary policy moved the economy along the SRPC, so that involuntary demand-deficient unemployment was superimposed on an increasing natural rate. Again, this was aggravated by oil price rises in 1979–80.

The differing reactions to the oil price aggregate supply shocks highlight the policy dilemma: in 1973–74 the authorities accommodated the price rise, and the result was high inflation. In 1979–80 they did not—and the result was high unemployment. '

Why do we worry about inflation? Although most would agree that inflation is 'bad', many of the common arguments are spurious, arising partly from *inflation illusion*. Also, inflation may wrongly get the blame for the effects of an adverse supply shock.

In considering the *costs of inflation*, it is important to distinguish between anticipated and unanticipated inflation and to ask whether an economy's institutions are able to adapt to its presence—for instance, whether nominal interest rates properly reflect inflation and whether monetary contracts incorporate adequate inflation allowance. Even if inflation is fully anticipated and there is full adaptation, there are *shoe-*

leather and *menu* costs of inflation, as people reduce their demand for real money balances and as firms must change price lists, slot machines, and so on. These costs may be significant only in times of hyperinflation.

Further costs are incurred when inflation is fully anticipated but there is not full adaptation. Nominal interest rates may be sluggish or may not be offered on all bank accounts: the taxation system may not adjust, so that low earners become liable to tax and others are carried into higher rates of tax. There may also be problems with income tax on interest payments and with profits tax. The latter problems may be avoided if firms use *inflation accounting*.

When inflation is not fully anticipated, there may be a redistribution of wealth and of income which may bear heavily on some groups within society. Perhaps most importantly, inflation may create uncertainty and damage business confidence and investment. Some evidence hints that the variability of inflation increases as inflation itself increases.

Three reactions to inflation are possible—we must control it, prevent it in the long run, or learn to live with it. Given that inflation is already present, control requires monetary responsibility and careful fiscal policy together with the will-power to endure the transition. It is possible that *incomes policy* may speed the transition, in spite of an unpromising past track record. This may be explained in that past policies of this sort were not single-tracked in their objectives, were accompanied by monetary irresponsibility, or were too rigid, causing distortions in a changing environment. Incomes policy might work if it is known to be temporary and to be used as support for other policies. Layard has suggested that past incomes policies failed partly because the incentives were wrong, and that a permanent tax-based scheme which provided suitably incentives for both unions and employers would be more successful.

The prevention of inflation in the long run requires reforms to remove the temptation for governments to increase money supply (especially near elections). Reforms to control money creation by the banks would also be needed, together with safeguards against disintermediation.

Some steps could be taken to help an economy to live with inflation—the regular raising of transfer payments in line with inflation, the speeding of adjustment of nominal interest rates, and the increased use of inflation accounting. *Indexation* of wages and loans could help further, but can never be perfect. The toleration of high inflation may be a precarious route because of the danger of hyperinflation. In practice, it is likely that some degree of inflation is here to stay.

IMPORTANT CONCEPTS AND TECHNICAL TERMS

Match each lettered concept with the appropriate numbered phrase:

(a) Real money supply   (l) Inflation illusion
(b) Fiscal drag   (m) Quantity Theory of
(c) Hyperinflation   Money
(d) Shoe-leather costs   (n) Indexation
(e) Pure inflation   (o) Stagflation
(f) Incomes policy   (p) Inflation accounting
(g) Phillips curve   (q) Inflation
(h) Real rate of interest   (r) Medium-Term
(i) Menu costs   Financial Strategy
(j) Accommodating   (s) Flight from money
     monetary policy   (t) Tax-based incomes
(k) Fisher hypothesis   policy

1 A rise in the average price of goods over time.
2 The inflation-adjusted interest rate, approximated by the difference between the nominal interest rate and the inflation rate.
3 An attempt to influence wages and other incomes directly.
4 The nominal money supply divided by the price level.
5 A policy stance in which a change in price induces the government to provide a matching change in the nominal money supply precisely to avoid any change in the real money supply in the short run.
6 The costs imposed by inflation because physical resources are required to reprint price tags, alter slot machines, and so on.
7 A theory which states that changes in the nominal money supply lead to equivalent changes in the price level but do not have effects on output and employment; this is sometimes summarized in the equation $MV = PY$.
8 The increase in real tax revenue when inflation raises nominal incomes and pushes people into higher tax brackets in a progressive income tax system.
9 A period of both high inflation and high unemployment, often caused by an adverse supply shock.
10 The costs imposed by inflation because high nominal interest rates induce people to economize on holding real money balances, so that society must use a greater quantity of resources in undertaking transactions.
11 The adoption of definitions of costs, revenue, profit, and loss that are fully inflation-adjusted.
12 A situation in which all prices of goods and factors of production are rising at the same percentage rate.
13 A situation in which people confuse nominal and real changes, although their welfare depends on real variables, not nominal variables.
14 The dramatic reduction in the demand for real money when high inflation and high nominal interest rates make it very expensive to hold money.
15 Periods when inflation rates are extremely high.
16 An annual policy statement which emphasizes the need to reduce the budget deficit in order to reduce monetary growth by publishing targets for both PSBR and monetary aggregates.
17 A theory by which a 1 per cent increase in inflation would be accompanied by a 1 per cent increase in nominal interest rates.
18 A process by which nominal contracts are automatically adjusted for the effects of inflation.
19 A policy for the control of wage settlements through tax incentives rather than direct legislation.
20 A relationship showing that a higher inflation rate is accompanied by a lower unemployment rate, and vice versa. It suggests we can trade off more inflation for less unemployment, or vice versa.

EXERCISES

1 The long-run position of an economy is described by the quantity theory of money
$$MV = PY$$
where M = nominal money stock
       V = the velocity of circulation
       P = price level
       Y = real income
This economy does not immediately adjust to equilibrium, so we can distinguish both short-run and long-run effects. (Notice, however, that when we *observe* the economy it is always the case that $MV = PY$, because we define velocity as the ratio of nominal income to nominal money.) The economy begins in equilibrium.
Suppose there is a demand shock—namely, a 10 per cent increase in nominal money supply used to finance an increase in government expenditure:
(a) By what percentage will nominal income change?
(b) Describe the effects upon real income and the price level in the short run.
(c) Describe the effects upon real income and the price level in the long run.
Suppose now that the economy, again from equilibrium, experiences a supply shock, say, an increase in the cost of a vital raw material:
(d) Describe the short-run effect of the supply shock.

(e) How would the government be likely to act if its primary concern was the level of unemployment?

(f) What effect would this policy have on the long-run equilibrium position?

(g) How would the government have been likely to have acted if its primary concern had been the rate of inflation?

(h) What effect would this policy have had on the long-run equilibrium position?

2 Another 'quantity theory' economy adjusts instantaneously to equilibrium, velocity of circulation being a constant 4. The following observations relate to consecutive years:

	Year 1	Year 2
Nominal interest rate	9	9
Nominal money supply	2000	2200
Real income	4000	4065

(a) Calculate the growth rate of nominal money supply.

(b) What was the rate of inflation between year 1 and year 2?

(c) Calculate the real interest rate in year 2.

(d) Calculate real money demand in each of the two years.

3 Table 28.1 presents data on inflation and unemployment in the UK for the period 1972–86.

TABLE 28.1 Inflation and unemployment, UK

Year	Rate of change of retail price index (% p.a.)	Unemployment rate (%)
1972	7.3	3.1
1973	9.1	2.2
1974	16.0	2.1
1975	24.2	3.2
1976	16.5	4.8
1977	15.9	5.2
1978	8.3	5.1
1979	13.4	4.6
1980	18.0	5.6
1981	11.9	9.0
1982	8.6	10.4
1983	4.6	11.2
1984	4.9	11.2
1985	6.1	11.5
1986	3.4	11.6

Source: Calculated from data in CSO, *Economic Trends Annual Supplement*, HMSO, and Department of Employment, *Employment Gazette*.

(a) Using graph paper, plot a scatter diagram with inflation on the vertical axis and unemployment on the horizontal axis. You will find it helpful to mark each point with the year.

(b) To what extent does your diagram support the idea of a trade-off between inflation and unemployment?

(c) In the main text it was pointed out that the government of the day reacted very differently to the oil price shocks of 1973–74 and 1979–80. Use your diagram to compare the differing reactions of the economy following these supply shocks.

4 Figure 28.1 shows two short-run Phillips curves ($SRPC_0$ and $SRPC_1$). $SRPC_0$ corresponds to a situation in which workers expect no inflation.

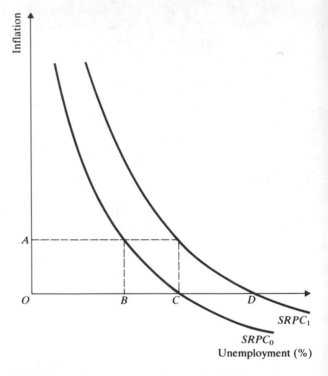

FIGURE 28.1 Government policy and the Phillips curve

(a) What is the natural rate of unemployment?

(b) What is the *expected* rate of inflation if the Phillips curve is $SRPC_1$?

Suppose that the economy begins in long-run equilibrium with zero inflation and that the authorities adopt a policy of constant monetary growth because they wish to reduce unemployment below its existing level:

(c) Identify the short-run effect on inflation and unemployment.

(d) Explain why this new position for the economy is untenable in the long run.

(e) Towards what long-run equilibrium position will the economy tend?

Suppose that the government now wishes to return to zero inflation and holds money supply constant:

(f) Identify the short-run impact on inflation and unemployment.

(g) Identify the long-run equilibrium position.

(h) Under what conditions will this long-run equilibrium be attained?

(i) Can you see a role for incomes policy in this process?

5 This exercise shows how taxing capital is complicated by the presence of inflation. Initially, suppose there is no inflation, a nominal interest rate of 3 per cent, and income tax levied at 30 per cent on earnings from interest. Being a money-lender, this fact is of interest to you!

Suppose you lend £5000 to a client for the purchase of a car:

(a) Calculate your gross earnings from this transaction in the year.

(b) For how much tax are you liable?

(c) Calculate net earnings and the after-tax real rate of return on the deal.

Suppose now that the same deal goes through when inflation is 10 per cent per annum, but that institutions have adapted, so the market nominal interest rate is 13 per cent (i.e., the real pre-tax interest rate is still 3 per cent):

(d) Calculate gross earnings and tax liability.

(e) Calculate net earnings and the after-tax real rate of interest on the deal.

6 Which of the following initial causes of inflation stem from the demand side of the economy and which from the supply side?

(a) An increase in government expenditure on goods and services financed by printing money.

(b) An increase in the price of oil.

(c) An increase in value added tax.

(d) An increase in income tax allowances for individuals.

(e) An increase in money wage rates.

(f) A decrease in the marginal propensity to save of households.

7 Positive real interest rates will always occur when

1 money rates of interest are greater than the inflation rate

2 the level of prices is falling

3 the level of interest rates is increasing

(a) 1, 2, 3 are all correct

(b) 1 and 2 only are correct

(c) 2 and 3 only are correct

(d) 1 only is correct

(Associated Examining Board GCE A level Economics Paper 1, June 1988)

8 According to the Quantity Theory of Money, a rise in the supply of money relative to its demand will

1 cause a reduction in the velocity of circulation

2 invariably raise the level of real output

3 increase the price level when an economy is at full employment

Choose one of the following:

(a) 1, 2, 3 are all correct

(b) 1, 2 only are correct

(c) 2, 3 only are correct

(d) 1 only is correct

(e) 3 only is correct

(University of London GCE A level Economics Paper 3, June 1987)

9 Which of the following items is most likely to have caused the move from PC_0 to PC_1 in Figure 28.2?

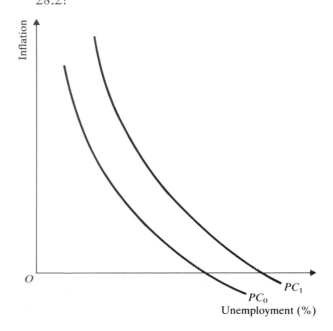

FIGURE 28.2 Inflation and unemployment

(a) A decrease in the natural rate of unemployment.

(b) An increase in wage inflation.

(c) The expectation of a future increase in the rate of unemployment.

(d) The expectation of a future increase in the rate of inflation.

(e) An increase in labour supply.

10 State whether each of the following costs of inflation are real or illusory and whether they apply to anticipated or only to unanticipated inflation:

(a) Fiscal drag.

(b) A redistribution of income affecting those on fixed incomes.
(c) All goods becoming more expensive.
(d) Shoe-leather and menu costs.
(e) An increase in uncertainty.
(f) A fall in the real wage arising from the inflation set off by the monetary expansion following a supply shock.

11 Incomes policy has, and has had, many critics. Explain why each of the following items has been a problem area in the past, and whether it nullifies the potential use of incomes policy in the future:
(a) The lack of support from other policy instruments.
(b) Multiplicity of objectives.
(c) The temporary nature of incomes policy.
(d) Inflexibility in a changing employment structure.
(e) Inappropriate incentive structures.

TRUE/FALSE

1 _____ The UK price level was no higher in 1950 than it was in 1920.

2 _____ Sustained inflation is always and everywhere a monetary phenomenon.

3 _____ The simple quantity theory says that the inflation rate always equals the rate of nominal money growth.

4 _____ According to the Fisher hypothesis, an increase in the rate of money growth will lead to an increase in the inflation rate and to an increase in nominal interest rates.

5 _____ The German hyperinflation of the 1920s was so severe that the government had to buy faster printing presses to print money quickly enough.

6 _____ A large budget deficit necessarily leads to inflation by forcing the government to print money.

7 _____ The velocity of circulation is the speed at which the outstanding stock of money is passed round the economy as people make transactions.

8 _____ The Medium-Term Financial Strategy is concerned only with monetary targets.

9 _____ UK inflation is determined by the rate of growth of £M3 with a two-year lag.

10 _____ The Phillips curve shows that a decrease in unemployment can be achieved at the expense of higher inflation.

11 _____ In the long run the Phillips curve is vertical at the natural rate of unemployment, whereas the short-run Phillips curve shows the temporary trade-off between inflation and unemployment while the economy is adjusting to an aggregate demand shock.

12 _____ The menu costs of inflation reflect the fact that the faster the inflation rate, the more frequently menus have to be reprinted if real prices are to remain constant.

13 _____ There are no costs to inflation so long as it can be fully anticipated.

14 _____ In order to incur the permanent benefits of lower inflation, the economy must first undergo a period of low output and employment.

15 _____ Indexation may make inflation tolerable in the long run.

QUESTIONS FOR THOUGHT

1 Given the relationship between inflation and unemployment outlined in this chapter, which do you think should be the prime target of economic policy?

2 The simple quantity theory assumes that the velocity of circulation is constant. What factors might lead velocity to vary in the short and long runs?

3 Discuss the costs of inflation. Which of these cost items is likely to have encouraged Western governments in their adoption of inflation as public enemy number one?

ANSWERS AND COMMENTS FOR CHAPTER 28

Please note Where questions are reproduced from GCE examinations, the examination boards bear no responsibility for the answers provided in this volume, which are the sole responsibility of the authors.

Important Concepts and Technical Terms

1	*p*	6	*i*	11	*q*	16	*r*
2	*h*	7	*m*	12	*e*	17	*k*
3	*f*	8	*b*	13	*l*	18	*n*
4	*a*	9	*o*	14	*s*	19	*t*
5	*j*	10	*d*	15	*c*	20	*g*

Exercises

1 (a) 10 per cent: the same percentage as nominal money stock. This follows from the assumption of the Quantity Theory that the velocity of circulation is constant.

   (b) In the short run, producers react to the increase in demand by increasing output. The price level may also begin to rise—but the main effect is on output. (Recall Section 26–7 of the main text.) The nominal interest rate falls to induce people to hold a larger quantity of real money balances.

   (c) As adjustment takes place, the level of real output falls back to its original equilibrium level and prices rise. In the eventual equilibrium, the price level will have risen by the full extent of the original increase in money stock, but real output will be unchanged and interest rates will have gradually climbed back to their original level.

   (d) Using the analysis of Chapter 26, we may argue that the cost increase is passed on as a price increase, reducing real money supply, raising interest rates, and reducing aggregate demand. Sluggish wages lead to unemployment.

   (e) A government worried about unemployment may be tempted to accommodate the price rise by allowing an increase in nominal money.

   (f) If the supply shock reduces long-run potential output, then the economy will eventually settle at this lower output level, which may entail higher unemployment. The more the authorities have tried to maintain output and employment by printing money, the higher the eventual price level—but output will still tend to its equilibrium level.

   (g) A government concerned about inflation may refuse to accommodate the price rise, preferring to see unemployment rise in the short run.

   (h) In the eventual equilibrium, real output will be at its potential level, but prices will be less high than in (f).

2 (a) 10 per cent.

   (b) Given $MV = PY$, we calculate that in year 1 $P = MV/Y = 8000/4000 = 2$. In year 2,

$P = 2.16$(ish). So the inflation rate was about 8 per cent.

   (c) The real interest rate is approximately the difference between the nominal interest rate and the inflation rate. Here, $9 - 8 = 1$ per cent.

   (d) Given that the money market is in equilibrium, then from $MV = PY$, $M/P = Y/V$.
   Year 1: $4000/4 = 1000$
   Year 2: $4065/4 = 1016.25$.

3 (a)

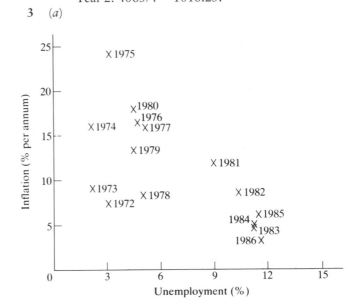

FIGURE A28.1   Inflation and unemployment in the UK

   (b) There is little evidence of a *stable* relationship between inflation and unemployment. The points from 1980 onwards are perhaps not far from the 'classic' picture in shape, but are nowhere near the original position as established by Phillips. The years 1974 and 1975 fit no particular pattern. Between 1976 and 1979, unemployment varied little but there were substantial changes in inflation. We might perhaps speculate that under some policy conditions a short-run trade-off will emerge but that some policy stances may shift the position of the trade-off relationship. For instance, it could be that the Social Contract incomes policy enabled inflation to be reduced in 1977 and 1978 without a significant rise in unemployment.

   (c) The authorities in 1974–75 followed an accommodating monetary policy. The result was that unemployment did not rise immediately, but the economy experienced high inflation. In 1980–84, no such accommodation ensued and inflation was reduced—but at the cost of rising unemployment. The remaining question is whether the adjustment of expectations will move the Phillips curve back to a lower inflation–unemployment combination or whether there has been an increase in the natural rate. For further discussion of the

Phillips curve in the UK, see an article by John Driffill in *Economic Review*, January 1990.

4 (a) $SRPC_0$ is the zero-inflation Phillips curve, so the natural rate of unemployment is OC where $SRPC_0$ cuts the horizontal axis.

(b) OC is the natural rate, and the rate of inflation which will be stable at OC with $SRPC_1$ is OA.

(c) Initially unemployment falls to OB, inflation rises to OA.

(d) This position is untenable because $SRPC_0$ is valid for zero expected inflation. Once workers realize that prices are rising at the rate OA, they will adjust expectations and $SRPC$ will move.

(e) Given answer (b), the economy ends up back at unemployment OC but with inflation OA.

(f) A determined government would carry the economy to D in the short run.

(g) As expectations adjust, the short-run Phillips curve moves back down and unemployment falls back to the natural rate OC with zero inflation.

(h) The attainment of equilibrium requires that expectations adjust before the government loses its nerve at the sight of all that unemployment.

(i) It is possible that incomes policy may speed up the adjustment process by affecting expectations, and that unemployment need not rise so high or for so long.

5 This exercise closely follows the example pursued in Section 28–5 of the main text.

(a) Gross earnings are 3 per cent of £5000 = £150.

(b) 30 per cent of £150 = £45.

(c) Net earnings are £105; the rate of return is (105/5000) × 100 = 2.1 per cent. In the absence of inflation nominal and real rates of return are the same.

(d) Gross earnings are 13 per cent of £5000 = £650. Tax is 30 per cent of £650 = £195.

(e) Net earnings are £455. Nominal rate of return is (455/5000) × 100 = 9.1 per cent. Real rate of return is 9.1 − 10 = −0.9 per cent.

6 Factors (a), (d), and (f) stem from the demand side, whereas factors (b), (c), and (e) affect the supply side. Item (d) may be debatable, in the sense that, whereas aggregate demand may be increased, future wage negotiations may be at lower levels if take-home pay has been improved. Some economists have argued that item (e) is an unlikely *initial* cause of inflation, as unions react to past events but do not initiate autonomous wage increases.

7 (d).

8 (e).

9 (d).

10 (a) is a real cost of inflation, but if inflation is anticipated it can be offset by the adjustment of tax thresholds.

(b) is also a real cost, which can be minimized by indexation or by building in anticipated inflation.

(c) is mere illusion, as it ignores changes in money income.

(d) are real costs which are present whether or not inflation is anticipated.

(e) is a real cost of inflation at an unpredictable rate; it is the effects of inflation on uncertainty and business confidence which have made inflation public enemy number one.

(f) is an illusion: the cost is not a cost of inflation but the inevitable response to the adverse supply shock.

11 (a) Incomes policy can stem inflation only temporarily if other policy instruments are not used consistently and responsibly. At times in the past, incomes policy has been used against a backdrop of monetary expansion and thus had no chance of success. However, there could be a role for it if used in harness with other policies.

(b) A problem in the past has been that governments have tried to achieve too much through a single policy.

(c) Layard has argued that a *permanent* policy is needed; others have suggested that a policy *known* to be both temporary and consistent with other policies has a better chance of success.

(d) If applied too rigorously, incomes policy could have the effect of preventing desirable relative price changes.

(e) Another Layard suggestion is that policies should be sure to offer proper incentives to both sides in the wage bargaining process.

True/False

1 True: see the introduction to Chapter 28 of the main text.

2 True: in the sense that sustained inflation must always be accompanied by monetary expansion in excess of output growth. The direction of causality is not always clear (see Section 28–1 of the main text).

3 False: this is correct only when real money demand is constant.

4 True: see Section 28–2 of the main text.

5 True. For further discussion of hyperinflation, see an article by Derek Aldcroft in *Economic Review*, January 1990.

6 False: printing money is not the only way of financing a budget deficit (see Section 28–3 of the main text).

7 True: see Box 28–1 of the main text.

8 False: the MTFS also incorporates fiscal targets, notably for PSBR.

9 False: for a while in the 1970s there seemed to be such a relationship, but with time it has become less clear.

10 False: recent experience suggests that the Phillips curve cannot be exploited for policy purposes (see Section 28–4 of the main text). This may be a manifestation of Goodhart's law, which we encountered in Chapter 24.

11 True.

12 True: see Section 28–5 of the main text.

13 False: the shoe-leather and menu costs remain; other costs result if institutions do not fully adapt.

14 True: see Section 28–6 of the main text.

15 False: in the long run, a tolerant attitude may lead to high rates of inflation with the consequent high menu and shoe-leather costs.

Questions for Thought

2   In the long run, velocity is likely to be determined by factors affecting the efficiency with which transactions may be carried out and will reflect real money demand. (What happens to velocity in a hyperinflation?) In the short run, velocity may at times reflect disequilibrium in the money market. For instance, in the mid-1970s velocity fell dramatically at a time when the authorities pursued an 'easy' money policy and there was perhaps excess supply of money. This was followed in the late 1970s by a period of higher-than-normal velocity. This was at a time when output was growing but Healey was beginning to restrict money growth. Since 1979, as inflation fell more rapidly than the rate of monetary growth, velocity fell again. Velocity may thus be a signal of conditions in the money market in the short run. Velocity is discussed in Box 28–1 of the main text.

3   See Section 28–5 of the main text.

29
Open Economy Macroeconomics

This chapter examines the effects of international transactions on the domestic economy. These are very important for economies such as Britain, Japan, and Germany, which rely heavily on exports and imports. The *exchange rate* and the way it is determined is also seen to have a far-reaching impact on the economy.

The exchange rate is the price at which two currencies exchange; its equilibrium level is determined in the *foreign exchange market* by the interaction of demand and supply. For convenience, we focus on a two-country situation and consider the US$/£ exchange rate. This is not to say that the dollar is the only other important currency—at times the *sterling effective rate* is more useful, this being an index of the international value of sterling based on its rate against the currencies of Britain's major trading partners. In our two-country world, the demand for pounds arises because US residents buy British goods, services, and assets; the supply arises because UK residents buy American goods and assets.

The exchange rate regime describes the conditions under which national governments permit the exchange rate to be determined. Under a *fixed exchange rate regime* the government agrees to maintain *convertibility* of the currency at a particular exchange rate. The central bank holds a stock of foreign exchange reserves to enable the agreed rate to be maintained. A disequilibrium rate cannot be maintained indefinitely. For instance, if the currency is overvalued, the loss of reserves eventually leads to the need for *devaluation*. Under a *floating exchange rate regime*, the exchange rate is free to find its equilibrium level without government intervention. 'Dirty floating', in which the government intervenes in a limited way, is discussed in Chapter 33.

The *balance of payments* is a systematic record of the international transactions of an economy. Transactions involving goods and services comprise the *current account*. This incorporates 'visible' and 'invisible' items (together yielding the *trade balance*) and also international transfer payments and property income. The accounts also incorporate an analysis of the capital transactions that take place. This includes transactions involving the sale and purchase of assets, together with changes to official reserves. The sum of current and capital transactions (together with the balancing item) is always zero.

A fall in the international value of sterling tends to make British goods cheaper in foreign currency and foreign goods more expensive in pounds, but it does not necessarily lead to an increase in competitiveness, which depends also on the relative inflation rate in Britain and abroad. As usual, we must distinguish between nominal and real variables. International competitiveness is measured by the *real exchange rate*. Over a period of years, the *purchasing power parity (PPP)* path is that path of the nominal exchange rate that would keep the real exchange rate constant.

The demand for exports depends upon world income and the real exchange rate; the demand for imports depends upon domestic real income and the real exchange rate. These together determine the current account of the balance of payments; both may be sluggish in adjusting to changing conditions.

The capital account has become more important in the postwar years with the dismantling of controls and the development of technology which facilitates the rapid movement of capital around the world. That 1973–74 oil crisis again rates a mention, as in its aftermath the OPEC countries ran large current account surpluses and had to be encouraged to balance them with capital account deficits by buying assets in the West. There are now enormous amounts of internationally footloose funds chasing the best rate of return on assets and switching between currencies in the process. These accounts are so large that they could totally swamp current account transactions.

For an open economy, long-run equilibrium requires not only full employment (*internal balance*) but also current account balance (*external balance*). In the absence of government intervention in the exchange market, current account balance also implies capital account balance. From this long-run equilibrium, shocks may carry an economy away from both internal and external balance, but there is no necessary relationship between booms or slumps and current account surpluses or deficits. Whether or not policy can speed the adjustment to equilibrium depends crucially on the exchange rate regime in operation.

Only one real exchange rate is compatible with both internal and external balance. Under a fixed exchange rate regime, it is the nominal exchange rate that is fixed, so maintenance of internal and external balance relies on keeping domestic inflation in line with world rates.

There are strong links between the balance of payments and money supply under fixed rates: a balance of payments deficit leads to a reduction in money supply, and the government cannot decide in isolation how much money should be printed. The authorities may choose to neutralize this effect through open market operations—a procedure known as *sterilization*.

Under a fixed exchange rate system, the ability of

the economy to achieve equilibrium following a shock depends on the source of the shock. Natural wage and price adjustment does not suffice to restore equilibrium following a *domestic* demand shock, as *perfect capital mobility* means that domestic interest rates cannot diverge from the world level. However, wage and price adjustment may enable an economy to cope with an *external* demand shock.

Monetary policy cannot work under fixed exchange rates with perfect capital mobility as the required interest rate changes cannot occur and sterilization will be frustrated. However, the same interest rate rigidity enhances the short-run power of fiscal policy by preventing crowding out. In the long run, higher aggregate demand will lead to higher wages and prices and thus reduce competitiveness, but fiscal policy may help in restoring the economy to its long-run equilibrium.

The UK operated under a fixed exchange rate system until the early 1970s, with devaluations in 1949 and 1967. What are the effects of devaluation? If an economy is initially in long-run equilibrium, devaluation improves competitiveness in the short run by increasing the price of imports and reducing the price of exports. Adjustment may be slow as it takes time to renegotiate contracts and to adapt production levels. The short-run effect on the current account depends upon the elasticities of demand for imports and exports: according to the Marshall–Lerner condition, devaluation improves the current account only if the sum of these price elasticities is more negative than −1. If the economy began at full employment, output cannot increase, so in the medium term, wages and prices will drift upwards until the real exchange rate has readjusted. If the economy began with a current account deficit, then devaluation may work in the medium term supported by fiscal contraction. In the long run the effect of higher import prices will work through and force the real exchange rate back to its equilibrium level. In some cases, devaluation may speed an economy's adjustment to an external demand shock.

How is the exchange rate determined with no government intervention? Recall that there is a unique real exchange rate compatible with internal and external balance. Under fixed rates, adjustment must take place wholly through domestic prices, but under floating rates the nominal exchange rate can also contribute to adjustment. In the long run (in the absence of shocks) the nominal exchange rate tends to follow the PPP path, but in the short run the real exchange rate may vary. The foreign exchange market clears day by day, and, given the footloose funds mentioned earlier, *speculation* cannot be ignored. Speculators will compare the interest rate on sterling lending with the total return on lending abroad, which depends on foreign interest rates and on expected changes in the exchange rate. If domestic interest rates deviate from foreign interest rates, nominal exchange rate movements will be required to prevent capital account flows.

Under freely floating exchange rates, we now see that monetary policy has a powerful short-run effect, in contrast to the position under fixed rates. A change in money supply induces changes in interest rates which in turn trigger a change in the nominal exchange rate to offset capital flows. In fact, the exchange rate can be seen to *overshoot* the change required. In the long run, wages and prices will adjust and the real exchange rate returns to equilibrium. The government is now seen to be free to determine domestic money supply so long as it is prepared to see the nominal exchange rate find its own level. It is not possible to control *both* exchange rate and money supply.

As for fiscal policy, with interest rates now free to diverge from world levels in the short run, an active fiscal policy now leads to changes in both domestic interest rates and the nominal exchange rate, and we find that crowding out affects not only consumption and investment, but also net exports.

The real exchange rate was reasonably steady in Britain in the early 1970s, but it rose dramatically in the period 1979–81. This was due partly to the tight money policy which pushed up interest rates, but it also reflected the advent of North Sea oil. The exploitation of North Sea oil altered the external balance position of the economy by reducing the demand for imports of oil. This required an increase in the real exchange rate which was exaggerated by the oil price shock of 1979–80 and (in the short run) by overshooting. The recession of the time may thus have been deepened by the short-run loss of competitiveness in the period before wages and prices had time to adjust. Since 1981 the real exchange rate has fallen gradually, but even in 1989 UK competitiveness was still noticeably worse than it had been in 1975. By the late 1980s North Sea oil was becoming much less important to the UK economy, making the sterling exchange rate less sensitive to oil price variations. This decline in importance is likely to affect the level of the real sterling exchange rate in the 1990s as compared with the previous decade.

IMPORTANT CONCEPTS AND TECHNICAL TERMS

Match each lettered concept with the appropriate numbered phrase:

(a)	Trade balance	(d)	Purchasing power
(b)	Convertibility		parity path
(c)	Balance of payments	(e)	Appreciation

(f) Real exchange rate
(g) Overshooting
(h) Exchange rate regime
(i) External balance
(j) Foreign exchange reserves
(k) Capital account
(l) Current account
(m) Foreign exchange market
(n) Revaluation
(o) Internal balance
(p) Open economy macroeconomics
(q) Sterling effective exchange rate
(r) Exchange rate
(s) Sterilization
(t) Devaluation
(u) Depreciation
(v) Perfect capital mobility

1   The study of economies in which international transactions play a significant role.
2   The price at which two currencies exchange.
3   The international market in which one national currency can be exchanged for another.
4   A fall in the international value of a currency.
5   A systematic record of all transactions between residents of one country and the rest of the world.
6   A record of international flows of goods and services and other net income from abroad.
7   A characteristic of a currency by which the government, acting through the central bank, agrees to buy or sell as much of the currency as people wish to trade at the fixed exchange rate.
8   The stock of foreign currency held by the domestic central bank.
9   A record of international transactions in financial assets.
10 An average of $/£, DM/£, FF/£, and yen/£ exchange rates, weighted by the relative importance of each country in Britain's international trading transactions, expressed as an index.
11 A situation in a country when aggregate demand is at the full-employment level.
12 A description of the conditions under which national governments allow exchange rates to be determined.
13 A rise in the international value of a currency.
14 A situation in which speculation causes the nominal exchange rate to move beyond its new equilibrium value.
15 Net exports of goods and services.
16 A situation in which an enormous quantity of funds will be transferred from one currency to another whenever the rate of return on assets in one country is higher than the rate of return in another.
17 A reduction in the exchange rate which the government commits itself to defend.
18 A situation in a country when the current account of the balance of payments just balances.
19 A measurement of the relative price of goods from different countries when measured in a common currency.

20 An increase in the exchange rate which the government commits itself to defend.
21 The path of the nominal exchange rate that would keep the real exchange rate constant over a given period.
22 An open market operation between domestic money and domestic bonds, the sole purpose of which is to neutralize the tendency of balance of payments surpluses and deficits to change the domestic money supply.

EXERCISES

1   This question is based on the following items in a country's balance of payments:

	£m
Imports	5000
Exports	6000
Financial and other services (net)	−400
Profits from investments abroad (net)	+500
Short term capital movements (net)	−750
Long term capital movements	+250
Repayment of I.M.F. loans	300
Fall in reserves	100
Balancing item	−400

Which of the following represents the balance on current account?
(a) +£1100 million
(b) +£1000 million
(c) +£400 million
(d) +£200 million
(e) −£200 million
(University of London GCE A level Economics Paper 3, January 1987)

2   Figure 29.1 shows the position in the foreign

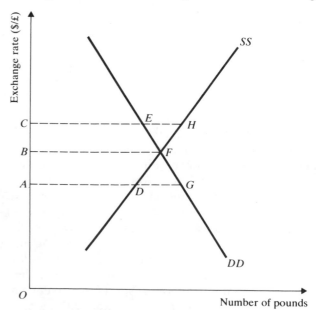

FIGURE 29.1   The foreign exchange market

exchange market: *DD* is the demand schedule for sterling and *SS* the supply schedule. Assume a two-country world (UK and USA):

(a) Explain briefly how the two schedules arise.

(b) Identify the exchange rate that would prevail under a clean float. What would be the state of the overall balance of payments at this exchange rate?

(c) Suppose the exchange rate were set at *OA* under a fixed exchange rate regime. What intervention would be required by the central bank? What would be the state of the balance of payments?

(d) Suppose the exchange rate were set at *OC*. Identify the situation of the balance of payments and the necessary central bank intervention.

(e) If the authorities wished to maintain the exchange rate at *OC* in the long run, what sort of measures would be required?

3 This exercise considers the effect of various shocks upon the internal and external balance of an economy. For each shock in Table 29.1, indicate the effects on the assumption that the economy is initially in both internal and external balance.

4 Table 29.2 presents data relating to price movements in the UK and West Germany and the nominal DM/£ exchange rate for the years 1978–89.

(a) Using these data, calculate the real exchange rate for the years 1978–89.

(b) Using graph paper, plot both real and nominal exchange rates against time.

(c) Comment on the path of the real exchange rate during this period.

(d) Calculate the purchasing power parity path for the exchange rate relative to 1978.

5 This exercise explores the effects of a devaluation for an economy operating under a fixed exchange rate regime. The economy to be considered adjusts sluggishly to shocks and is initially in a state of both internal and external balance. We consider the effects of devaluation in the short, medium, and long runs.

The short run

(a) What is the immediate effect of the devaluation on international competitiveness?

(b) Mention some of the factors that may impede adjustment in the short run.

(c) What determines the initial impact on the current account balance?

TABLE 29.1 Shocks and balances

	Internal		External Current account balance	
Nature of shock	Boom	Slump	Deficit	Surplus
Reduction in autonomous consumption				
Increase in real exchange rate				
Tighter monetary and fiscal policy				
Increase in world income				
Increase in consumption with easier monetary and fiscal policy				

TABLE 29.2 Prices and the exchange rate

	DM/£ exchange rate	UK price index (1985 = 100)	West German price index (1985 = 100)	Real exchange rate	'PPP' exchange rate
1978	3.85	52.8	75.3		
1979	3.89	60.0	78.4		
1980	4.23	70.7	82.7		
1981	4.56	79.1	87.9		
1982	4.24	85.9	92.5		
1983	3.87	89.8	95.6		
1984	3.79	94.3	97.9		
1985	3.78	100.0	100.0		
1986	3.18	103.4	99.8		
1987	2.94	107.8	100.1		
1988	3.12	113.0	101.2		
1989	3.08	121.8	103.7		

Source: *Economic Review Data Supplement*, September 1990

The medium term

(d) Recall that the economy began at full employment: what does this imply for output and prices in the medium term?

(e) Are there any policy measures that could evade this problem?

The long run

(f) Can the lower real exchange rate be sustained in the long run? Explain your answer.

(g) Under what circumstances might a devaluation be an appropriate policy reaction?

6 Comment briefly on the short-run effectiveness (or otherwise) of monetary and fiscal policy in each of the following economies:

(a) A closed economy.

(b) An open economy with fixed exchange rate and perfect capital mobility.

(c) An open economy with floating exchange rate and perfect capital mobility.

(d) An open economy with floating exchange rate and imperfect capital mobility.

7 Suppose that you have £100 idle which you wish to lend for a year. In Britain the current market rate of interest is 12 per cent, but if you choose you could lend your funds in the USA where the current interest rate is 9 per cent. The present nominal exchange rate is $1.70/£.

(a) What additional piece of information is required to enable you to take a decision on whether to lend in Britain or in the USA?

(b) Suppose that you expect the exchange rate at the end of the year to be $1.50/£: where will you invest?

(c) Where would you invest if you expected the exchange rate to fall only to $1.65/£.

(d) Given that you expect the exchange rate to fall to $1.65/£, where would you invest if the US interest rate were 8 per cent?

(e) Would you suppose expectations about future exchange rates to be stable or volatile? Why does it matter?

8 Within a two-country (UK and USA) model, identify the effect on the UK exchange rate of each of the following:

(a) Americans want to buy more British assets.

(b) A fall in the American demand for Scotch whisky.

(c) An increase in the British demand for bourbon.

(d) An increase in the number of US tourists visiting the UK.

(e) A drop in the UK demand for shares in American companies.

(f) An increase in US interest rates.

9 Which of the following would *not* move the United Kingdom's Balance of Payments towards a current account surplus?

(a) An increased number of holiday-makers visiting the United Kingdom from France and West Germany

(b) An increase in dividends from United Kingdom investments in the USA

(c) Increased export earnings from the sale of antiques to the USA

(d) The hiring of fewer American films for showing in the United Kingdom, the cost per film remaining unchanged

(e) The sale of United Kingdom investments in American industry
(University of London GCE A level Economics 3, January 1989)

10 Consider an open economy which adjusts sluggishly to shocks. A floating exchange rate regime is operating and the economy begins in long-run equilibrium. The authorities initiate a 20 per cent increase in nominal money supply.

(a) What will be the eventual increase in the domestic price level?

(b) What will be the eventual change in the real and nominal exchange rates?

(c) What will be the initial change in domestic interest rates?

(d) Sketch a diagram to show the adjustment path of the nominal exchange rate towards its long-run equilibrium, and comment briefly on the pattern.

TRUE/FALSE

1 _____ The $/£ exchange rate measures the international value of sterling.

2 _____ Under a fixed exchange rate regime the authorities undertake to maintain the exchange rate at its equilibrium level.

3 _____ Invisible trade is a component of the capital account.

4 _____ In the absence of government intervention in the foreign exchange market, the exchange rate adjusts to equate the supply of and demand for domestic currency.

5 _____ A fall in the international value of sterling makes British goods cheaper in foreign currency and foreign goods more expensive in pounds, and thus tends to increase the quantity of British exports and reduce the quantity of goods imported to Britain.

6 _____ Perfect capital mobility means that machines are easily moved across international borders.

7 _____ In the early 1980s, Kuwait experienced a domestic boom with a current account surplus, the UK a slump and surplus, Brazil a recession and deficit, and Mexico a boom and deficit.

8 _____ Sterilization of the domestic money supply under fixed exchange rates can be effective only in the short run.

9 _____ Under fixed exchange rates, the ability of an economy to deal automatically with a shock depends on its source.

10 _____ Devaluation need not improve the current account.

11 _____ There is only one real exchange rate compatible with both internal and external balance.

12 _____ The nominal exchange rate always follows the purchasing power parity path.

13 _____ The best policy for the government to adopt is to choose exchange rate and money supply to ensure internal and external balance.

14 _____ The exploitation of North Sea oil led to an increase in the real sterling exchange rate which deepened the recession in the UK in the early 1980s.

QUESTIONS FOR THOUGHT

1 During the mid-1980s, the government began to pay increasing attention to the exchange rate as a target for economic policy. Why should this be? What implications would it have for the general conduct of policy?

2 What are the disadvantages to a country of running a persistent Balance of Payments deficit on current account? Contrast the likely results of *two* policies which a government might use to rectify a current account deficit.

(University of London GCE A level Economics 1, June 1989)

ANSWERS AND COMMENTS FOR CHAPTER 29

Please note Where questions are reproduced from GCE examinations, the examination boards bear no responsibility for the answers provided in this volume, which are the sole responsibility of the authors.

Important Concepts and Technical Terms

1	p	7	b	13	e	19	f
2	r	8	j	14	g	20	n
3	m	9	k	15	a	21	d
4	u	10	q	16	v	22	s
5	c	11	o	17	t		
6	l	12	h	18	i		

Exercises

1 We hope you weren't too confused at the difference in the words used here compared with the main text. In fact, it's the first four items in the list which need to be combined to calculate the balance on current account. Imports and exports are straightforward: we can begin by deducting the former from the latter to give the trade balance. Financial and other services (net) and profits from investments abroad (net) were previously included as *invisibles*. If you re-read the relevant section in the main text, you will see this. Combining these with the trade balance, we arrive at a figure of +£1100 million (answer (a)) as the current balance.

Perhaps we can add a few words concerning the remaining items in the list. In recent years, the structure of the UK balance of payments accounts has altered, with the *Capital Account* no longer appearing as a separate entity. Instead, a table is published which offers a 'summary of transactions in UK external assets and liabilities'. These transactions include those undertaken by both private sector and government. 'Official financing' is no longer distinguished. The other items mentioned in the question (except of course the balancing item) represent items from this new summary table.

2 (a) The *DD* schedule represents the demand for pounds by US residents wishing to buy British goods and assets. The *SS* schedule shows the supply of pounds from UK residents wanting to buy American goods and assets.

(b) *OB* is the equilibrium exchange rate with no government intervention. The balance of payments is zero at this point.

(c) At *OA* there is an excess demand for pounds (the distance *DG*) which must be supplied by the Bank of England in exchange for additions to its foreign exchange reserves. The balance of payments is in surplus here.

(d) At *OC* there is a balance of payments deficit of an amount *EH*; the Bank of England must purchase the excess supply of pounds, depleting its foreign exchange reserves in the process.

(e) In the long run, the balance of payments deficit cannot be sustained, as foreign exchange reserves are finite. To maintain *OC* as the exchange rate, the authorities must influence *DD* and *SS* such that *OC* is in equilibrium. Promotion of British goods in the USA is unlikely to do much for *DD*, so it is more likely that the authorities will have to discourage imports, perhaps by a contractionary policy. Direct import controls may be tempting but may invoke retaliation from trading partners. We saw similar arguments back in Chapter 22 (see exercise 6(e) of that chapter).

3 **TABLE A29.1** Shocks and balances

	Internal		External Current account balance	
Nature of shock	Boom	Slump	Deficit	Surplus
Reduction in autonomous consumption		✓		✓
Increase in real exchange rate		✓	✓	
Tighter monetary and fiscal policy		✓		✓
Increase in world income	✓			✓
Increase in consumption with easier monetary and fiscal policy	✓		✓	

For more detail, see Section 29–4 of the main text.

4 (a)

TABLE A29.2   Prices and the exchange rate

	DM/£ exchange rate	UK price index (1985 = 100)	West German price index (1985 = 100)	Real exchange rate	'PPP' exchange rate
1978	3.85	52.8	75.3	2.70	3.85
1979	3.89	60.0	78.4	2.98	3.53
1980	4.23	70.7	82.7	3.62	3.16
1981	4.56	79.1	87.9	4.10	3.00
1982	4.24	85.9	92.5	3.94	2.91
1983	3.87	89.8	95.6	3.64	2.87
1984	3.79	94.3	97.9	3.65	2.80
1985	3.78	100.0	100.0	3.78	2.70
1986	3.18	103.4	99.8	3.30	2.61
1987	2.94	107.8	100.1	3.17	2.51
1988	3.12	113.0	101.2	3.48	2.42
1989	3.08	121.8	103.7	3.62	2.30

(b)

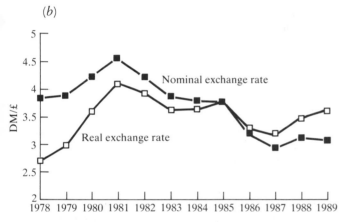

FIGURE A29.1   Nominal and real exchange rates

(c) Most noticeable is the steep rise in the real exchange rate up to 1981. This reflects both policy stance and the exploitation of North Sea oil. The divergence between real and nominal exchange rates results from the difference between the inflation rates of West Germany and the UK. Remember that a rise in the real exchange rate implies a loss of competitiveness of British goods.

(d) See Table A29.2.

5 (a) Competitiveness is improved: domestically produced goods become relatively cheap in both internal and external markets.

(b) Purchasers take time to adjust to new prices and may have existing contractual commitments; suppliers need time to adjust production levels.

(c) The elasticities of demand for imports and exports (the Marshall–Lerner condition), which determine the revenue response to the price changes.

(d) Eventually output will return to the full-employment level: competitiveness is eroded by increases in domestic prices and wages.

(e) A fiscal contraction could alleviate the pressure on aggregate demand.

(f) No: in the long run the supply side of the economy adjusts to the increase in import prices.

(g) The most obvious circumstance is if initially the exchange rate were being held above its equilibrium level, resulting in balance of payments deficits.

6 (a) In a closed economy, both monetary and fiscal policy may have short-run effects. In the long run, real output returns to its 'natural' level, but its *composition* may be affected by crowding out following fiscal action.

(b) Monetary policy is totally ineffective domestically in this situation, with the authorities committed to maintaining the exchange rate. Fiscal policy has a relatively powerful effect in the short run.

(c) The effectiveness of fiscal policy is much reduced here by the rapid adjustment of interest rates, but monetary policy is rendered more effective.

(d) If capital is not perfectly mobile, interest rates will be slower to adjust, so the crowding-out effect of fiscal policy is retarded: fiscal policy may have short-run effects. Monetary policy is somewhat diluted by the same argument.

7 In all the cases, if the funds are invested in Britain, £112 is the end year result. If funds are invested in the USA there are $170 to be loaned at the current exchange rate. Now read on.

(a) The key missing element is the end-of-year exchange rate, which we need to convert our dollars back into sterling.

(b) Return in $ is $170 \times 1.09 = 185.3$. Converting to £ at the expected exchange rate yields $185.3/1.5 = £123.5$. The depreciation more than compensates for the interest rate differential: you lend in the USA.

(c) $185.3/1.65$ is approximately £112. You will be indifferent as to where you lend.

(d) $170 \times 1.08 = 183.6$; $183.6/1.65 = £111$: you invest in Britain.

(e) The expected exchange rate depends upon how you view the current rate as compared with the long-run equilibrium rate. Such expectations could be very volatile, varying with your perception of factors affecting the economy. It matters because there are enormous quantities of internationally footloose funds in search of the best return.

8 If you have any difficulty with these, work out the effect on demand/supply of pounds and thus on the equilibrium exchange rate, perhaps with the help of a diagram.

(a) Sterling appreciates.

(b) Sterling depreciates.

(c) Sterling depreciates.

(d) Sterling appreciates.

(e) Sterling appreciates.

(f) An increase in US interest rates induces capital flows from UK to USA, so there is a depreciation of sterling.

9   (e).
10 (a) 20 per cent.
    (b) The real exchange rate will be unchanged in the long run, but the nominal rate will need to fall by 20 per cent to maintain the real rate, given the price change.
    (c) A fall.
    (d) In Figure A29.2, e_1 shows the original equilibrium nominal exchange rate. At time t the shock occurs, domestic interest rates fall, and the nominal exchange rate must fall to prevent capital outflows and to maintain equilibrium in the exchange market. The nominal exchange rate overshoots its new equilibrium value (e_2), falling initially to e_3 and then gradually adjusting as domestic prices adjust. The path thus involves a jump from A to B at the time of the shock and then adjustment to C.

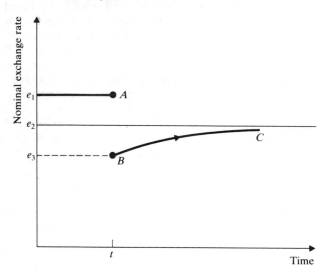

FIGURE A29.2   Nominal and real exchange rates

True/False

1   False: the dollar rate is important, but is not the *only* relevant rate (see Section 29–1 of the main text).

2   False: there is no guarantee that the chosen rate will turn out to be the equilibrium rate.

3   False: sale and purchase of services and other invisibles belong to the current account (see Section 29–2 of the main text).

4   True.

5   False: competitiveness also depends on relative inflation rates (see Section 29–3 of the main text).

6   False and silly: if you responded 'true' to this you are confusing financial capital with capital goods.

7   True: see Section 29–4 of the main text.

8   True: see Section 29–5 of the main text.

9   True: external shocks are more easily accommodated than domestic ones.

10 True: see Section 29–6 of the main text.

11 True: see Section 29–7 of the main text.

12 False: it may deviate in the short run.

13 False: this seems to imply that the government can independently choose *both* exchange rate and money supply, which is not the case (see Section 29–8 of the main text).

14 True: see Section 29–9 of the main text.

Questions for Thought

1   It must be remembered that any rapid depreciation of sterling tends to put upward pressure on prices in the short run. Import prices rise, increasing the demand for domestic substitutes for imported goods. We also expect the demand for exports to increase as competitiveness improves. This, of course, sounds like good news, but if domestic supply is relatively inelastic in the short run, there will inevitably be upward pressure on prices. In other words, if the government is intent on curbing inflation, it may be reluctant to allow the exchange rate to fall rapidly. Of course, once the exchange rate becomes the object of policy action, the government relinquishes independent control of the money supply.

2   This was of course, a topical issue in the late 1980s at a time when the current account deficit for the UK was substantial.

30

Long-term Growth and Short-term Fluctuations

Our macroeconomic analysis has so far been concerned with whether the economy can reach full employment. In a broader perspective, we see that potential output may change over time: clearly, the potential output of the UK today is very different from what it was 100 years ago. In this chapter we consider the nature and sources of *economic growth* and explore some policy possibilities.

Economic growth is an elusive concept. In Chapter 20 we saw that real GDP has flaws as a measurement of economic output—let alone as a measure of society's happiness! When we consider long-term issues, these problems are especially marked. The development of new products makes it hard to compare different periods; the fall in the average working week reduces measured output but conceals the increase in leisure; externalities are not easily incorporated; per capita real output measures may disguise inequity. None the less, real output per capita is probably the best measure we have; material goods may not be all there is to life, but they help!

In the long-run perspective of this chapter, it is worth remembering that even a modest growth rate accumulates over long periods. Throughout the discussion, we assume that the economy is at full employment and consider changes in potential output.

Through the *production function*, we have seen that the level of output depends upon inputs (capital, labour, land, raw materials) and upon the state of technology. Growth of potential output thus comes either from an increase in inputs or from an improvement in the efficiency with which they are used. Taking each in turn, one route for growth is an increase in capital per worker. Labour input may increase through population growth or through an increase in quality: an increase in human capital (skill and knowledge). Land is in virtually fixed supply for today's industrialized nations and does not contribute to growth. The characteristics of raw materials may constrain growth: we must be aware that a *depletable resource* has a finite lifespan and that a *renewable resource* requires careful management. Economies of scale offer another source of growth.

Technical knowledge is important in the growth process. *Invention* may result from *research and development* (R & D), but such activity is costly and risky. Protection of new ideas is required to avoid market failure. The granting of patents is one such measure; alternatively, the government may choose to subsidize research activity. Invention alone does not suffice: ideas must also be put into practice via *innovation*. This may require investment.

Are there limits to economic growth? Malthus at the end of the eighteenth century warned that, with fixed land supply and diminishing marginal product of labour, there were limits to the size of population that could be adequately fed. Increases in agricultural productivity and technical changes averted the Malthusian trap for industrialized nations, but his warnings have been echoed by present-day doomsters. The price system helps to ensure a proper use of finite resources. Scarcity brings price increases, which induce increased efficiency of use and render economic some reserves of the resource not formerly recognized.

Costs of growth such as pollution, congestion, and the quality of life have sometimes been invoked to support the *zero-growth proposal*, which argues that economies should aim at zero growth of measured real output. This ignores a number of issues—for instance, the argument of Chapter 15 that zero pollution is not necessarily socially optimal.

A slowdown of the growth of productivity was evident in the OECD nations in the late 1970s, but opinion is divided as to its cause. Some have pointed out that, if more resources are devoted to pollution control, measured output per head will appear to fall; others have blamed our old friend the price of oil for diverting resources to R & D in search of ways to economize on energy use; yet others say that the great inflation affected expectations and led to a decline in the rate of investment. In addition, it may be difficult to distinguish long-run changes in the growth rate from short-run deviations around the long-run trend.

As far as policy is concerned, we should not confuse supply-side policies which produce a once-for-all increase in output with policies intended to produce sustained long-run growth. Policies for investment may help but would not suffice—a doubling of the rate of UK investment might add only about 1 per cent to the annual growth rate of real output. Technical progress might be increased through the encouragement of R & D, but this is a risky route also requiring innovation and investment. Investment in human capital might have a promising pay-off. A comparison of British and German productivity levels in the *National Institute Economic Review* in 1985 showed that there were large differences in skill levels between British workers and their German counterparts.

Economies tend not to grow steadily, but are subject to the *business cycle*—successively passing through phases of *slump*, *recovery*, *boom*, and *recession* in a typical four- or five-year period. Output per worker also varies with the cycle, rising during booms and falling in slumps. One suggestion is that economies are subject to a political business cycle, whereby governments allow aggregate demand to expand near election time. However, we can find economic explanations of the cycle not requiring us to be so cynical about governments.

Variations in activity during the cycle must be associated with variations in some element of aggregate demand—but which? International trade may help to explain the transmission of the cycle between countries but does not initiate it. If we discount the political cycle and regard consumption as relatively rapid in adjustment, we are left with investment as a candidate. We have already argued that investment may be sluggish—and the cycle story is essentially a story about sluggish adjustment.

The *multiplier–accelerator* model offers one explanation. The multiplier is relevant because it communicates the effects of changing investment to aggregate demand, but why should investment vary? Given that the real interest rate is relatively stable, changes in investment may depend crucially upon expectations of future profits, which in turn depend upon expected future sales. The accelerator model assumes that firms gauge future demand by reference to past output *growth*. An increase in output growth (i.e. an acceleration) triggers an increase in investment. This simple model can be seen to produce cycles in response to an initial shock. These may be explosive, but will be constrained by a *ceiling* and *floor*. Aggregate supply provides the ceiling; the floor results because there are limits to how far investment can fall. The existence of stocks may help to explain sluggish output adjustment during the cycle.

Finally, it is worth mentioning those economists who believe that the economy adjusts rapidly to equilibrium, such as the New Classical school, for instance. For these, there is an *equilibrium business cycle*. The cycle cannot represent demand movements, but rather indicates that potential output itself does not grow according to a smooth trend but is subject to fluctuations.

IMPORTANT CONCEPTS AND TECHNICAL TERMS

Match each lettered concept with the appropriate numbered phrase:

(*a*) Innovation
(*b*) Economic growth
(*c*) Accelerator model
(*d*) Embodied technical progress
(*e*) Production function
(*f*) Human capital
(*g*) Renewable resource
(*h*) Political business cycle
(*i*) R & D
(*j*) Ceilings and floors
(*k*) Business cycle
(*l*) Equilibrium business cycle
(*m*) Depletable resource
(*n*) Trend path of output
(*o*) Invention
(*p*) Zero-growth proposal

1 A relationship which shows the maximum output that can be produced using specified quantities of inputs, given the existing technical knowledge.
2 Departments in firms devoted to research activity and the development of new ideas.
3 The annual percentage increase in the potential real output of an economy.
4 A resource which need never be exhausted if harvested with care.
5 An argument which suggests that, because increases in measured GNP are accompanied by additional costs of pollution, congestion, and so on, the best solution is to aim for zero growth of measured GNP.
6 The discovery of new knowledge.
7 The short-term fluctuation of total output around its trend path.
8 A theory that short-term fluctuations of total output represent fluctuations of potential output.
9 Constraints which prevent cycles from exploding indefinitely.
10 A suggestion that the business cycle is related to the election cycle.
11 The smooth path which output follows in the long run once the short-term fluctuations are averaged out.
12 Advances in knowledge incorporated in 'new' capital or labour inputs.
13 The stock of expertise accumulated by a worker.
14 A theory that firms guess future output and profits by extrapolating past output growth, so that an increase in the desired level of investment requires an increase in output growth.
15 A resource of which only finite stocks are available.
16 The incorporation of new knowledge into actual production techniques.

EXERCISES

1 Which of the following items reflect genuine economic growth?
   (*a*) A decrease in unemployment.
   (*b*) An increase in the utilization of capital.
   (*c*) An increase in the proportion of the population entering the labour force.

(d) An increase in the rate of change of potential output.

(e) A movement towards the production possibility frontier.

(f) Continuous movement of the production possibility frontier.

2 We have seen that output may be increased either by an increase in inputs or by technical progress. (We neglect economies of scale for the moment.) This exercise explores how this may happen in a practical situation. Below are listed a number of ways by which the output of a typist might be increased. State whether each involves an increase in input or technical progress.

(a) Modification introduced to improve the quality of the existing typewriter.

(b) Purchase of a new improved typewriter.

(c) Making the typist work her or his lunch hour without pay.

(d) Sending the typist to night school to improve her or his technique.

(e) Our typist gaining experience and producing better quality work.

(f) Introduction of a word processor.

If technical progress is to be measured as a residual, which of the above items will be included?

3 Identify each of the following as a depletable or renewable resource:

(a) Wheat.

(b) Oil.

(c) Whales.

(d) Copper.

(e) Trees.

(f) Rain.

4 Figure 30.1 shows the path of a hypothetical economy fluctuating around a smooth trend. For each of the labelled points, identify the phase of the cycle.

How would you interpret the horizontal distance from A to F?

5 This exercise should be approached with a dose of scepticism. Table 30.1 offers some data on

output and productivity in three European countries.

(a) Calculate average annual percentage growth rates for gross product and output per person-hour for 1974–79 and 1979–83 for each country.

(b) Explain why these calculations may give a distorted view of the world.

6 Which of the following items might be said to have contributed to the productivity slowdown of the 1970s?

(a) Inflation.

(b) Reductions in company profitability.

(c) The growth of the black economy.

(d) Oil price shock.

(e) The dawning of the post-industrial society.

(f) Completion of recovery from the Second World War.

7 Which of the following policy suggestions are appropriate for improving economic growth in an economy?

(a) The encouragement of R & D.

(b) A reduction in marginal tax rates to increase labour supply.

(c) Investment grants.

(d) The establishment of training and education schemes to improve human capital.

(e) An expansion of aggregate demand to increase the level of employment.

(f) The encouragement of dissemination of new knowledge and techniques.

TABLE 30.1 Output per head and gross product (1980 = 100)

	Germany GNP	Italy GDP	UK GDP	Output per person-hour in manufacturing Germany	Italy	UK
1974	85.4	85.9	93.2	87	78	95
1979	100.0	96.2	102.4	96	96	101
1983	99.8	98.6	104.7	110	102	115

Source: National Institute Economic Review, August 1984

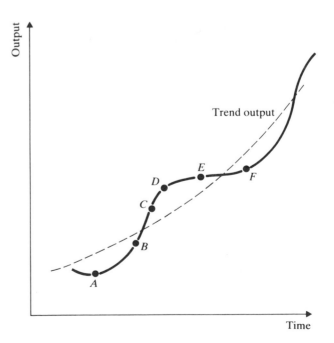

FIGURE 30.1 The business cycle

8   The accelerator principle states that
    (a) the rate of interest determines the rate of investment
    (b) the capital/output ratio is altered by changes in demand
    (c) the rate of change in demand for consumer goods has a more than proportionate effect on the rate of investment
    (d) the rate of change in investment affects the rate of change in output
    (e) an increase in induced investment will lead to a more than proportionate increase in autonomous investment
         (University of London GCE A level Economics 3, June 1989)

9   A country may *not* wish to maximise economic growth if this leads to
    1   a reduction in its non-renewable resources
    2   a greater inequality of incomes
    3   social costs greatly exceeding private costs
    Choose one of the following:
    (a) 1, 2, 3 all correct
    (b) 1, 2 only correct
    (c) 2, 3 only correct
    (d) 1 only correct
         (Associated Examining Board GCE A level Economics Paper 1, June 1987)

10 This exercise concerns the multiplier–accelerator model and entails some simple calculations. Suppose we have a fixed-price closed economy with no government, such that
    $Y_t = C_t + I_t$
    where Y_t = national income in time period t
          C_t = consumption in period t
          I_t = investment in period t.
    Further, suppose that consumption in the current period depends upon income in the *previous* period:
    $C_t = 0.5\,Y_{t-1}$
    (0.5 is the marginal propensity to consume).
    Investment comprises two parts, an autonomous element (A) and a part which depends upon past changes in output:
    $I_t = A + v(Y_{t-1} - Y_{t-2})$
    where v is the 'acceleration coefficient'.
    Initially, autonomous investment is 30 and the economy is in equilibrium with $Y = 60$ and $C = 30$, $I = 30$.
    We now consider what happens if there is an increase in autonomous investment from 30 to 40. The new equilibrium is $Y = 80$, $C = 40$, $I = 40$, but our model enables us to trace the adjustment path through time. This can be done as in Table 30.2, under alternative assumptions about v, the acceleration coefficient. For $v = 0.2$,

TABLE 30.2 A multiplier–accelerator model

Time period	C (v = 0.2)	I (v = 0.2)	Y (v = 0.2)	C (v = 0.8)	I (v = 0.8)	Y (v = 0.8)
0	30	30	60	30	30	60
1	30	40	70	30	40	70
2	35	42	77			
3						
4						
5						
6						

we have provided some initial calculations with explanation below.

For $v = 0.2$, period 0 shows the original equilibrium. In period 1, investment increases to 40 but consumption has not yet changed. In period 2, consumption is 0.5×70 and investment is $40 + 0.2 \times (70 - 60) = 42$ and $Y = 77$.
If you repeat the exercise for $v = 0.8$, you will find that the adjustment path is very different.
(If you have access to a microcomputer, you may like to write yourself a program to simulate adjustment paths for other values of c and v.)

TRUE/FALSE

1   _____ Per capita real GDP is a reasonable measure of the living standards of people in a country.

2   _____ An annual growth rate of just 2 per cent per annum leads to a sevenfold increase in real output in less than a century.

3   _____ The purpose of investment is to increase the capital stock.

4   _____ Invention is futile without innovation which in turn requires investment.

5   _____ Governments are heavily involved in financing R & D and often contribute up to half of its cost, equivalent to about 1 per cent of GDP in some cases.

6   _____ Sustained growth cannot occur if production relies on a factor whose supply is largely fixed.

7   _____ The assessment of the desirable growth rate will always remain a normative question, hinging on the value judgements of the assessor.

8   _____ In the long run, fluctuations of output around potential output are unimportant.

9   _____ The potential rate of return on investment in people in the UK is probably quite high.

10 _____ Short-run fluctuations in output can be explained by fluctuations in aggregate demand.

11 _____ In the multiplier–accelerator model, the less firms' decisions respond to changes in past output, the more pronounced will be the cycle.

12 _____ Changes in stocks help to explain why the economy is likely to spend several years during the phase of recovery or recession.

QUESTIONS FOR THOUGHT

1 Explain how the price system helps to deal with the problem of depletion of a scarce resource, but may not always cope with the preservation of a renewable resource.

2 This exercise considers the political business cycle and uses concepts developed earlier in the book, in particular, notions about indifference curves and short- and long-run Phillips curves.

In Figure 30.2, $LRPC$ is the long-run Phillips curve; SPC_0 and SPC_1 are short-run Phillips curves reflecting different inflation expectations. The curves I_1–I_4 are indifference curves which represent how the government perceives the preferences of the electorate for different combinations of inflation and unemployment. The shape of these curves reflects the fact that the two 'goods' are 'bads'! Utility increases from I_1 to I_2 to I_3 to I_4. The economy begins in long-run equilibrium with no inflation.

(a) What is the current unemployment level?

(b) What is the perceived utility level of the electorate?

(c) An election approaches; what measures can the government take to make the electorate feel better off? At what point would the economy be in the short run?

(d) What happens as the economy adjusts?

(e) What is the perceived utility level of the electorate?

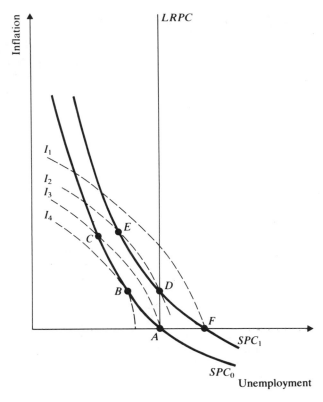

FIGURE 30.2 The political business cycle

(f) Supposing that the next election is five years away, where might the economy be taken next, and where might it eventually settle?

(g) Do you think that this model explains the actions of the Thatcher administration?

3 What are the major factors affecting the rate of economic growth? Comment on whether the government should introduce a policy to stimulate growth. At which factors should the policy be aimed?

ANSWERS AND COMMENTS FOR CHAPTER 30

Please note Where questions are reproduced from GCE examinations, the examination boards bear no responsibility for the answers provided in this volume, which are the sole responsibility of the authors.

Important Concepts and Technical Terms

1 *e*	5 *p*	9 *j*	13 *f*
2 *i*	6 *o*	10 *h*	14 *c*
3 *b*	7 *k*	11 *n*	15 *m*
4 *g*	8 *l*	12 *d*	16 *a*

Exercises

1 Items (*d*) and (*f*) describe an increase in potential output, and *this* is what we intend by talking about 'economic growth'. The other items all represent once-for-all changes in output, but not sustained growth.

2 (*a*) Technical progress: but possibly measured in practice as an increase in capital input, the cost of improvement being registered as investment.

  (*b*) Technical progress and/or an increase in capital.

  (*c*) An increase in the utilization of labour—but will not be measured as such.

  (*d*) This represents an increase in human capital—an improvement in the quality of the labour input.

  (*e*) Human capital again—but unmeasured.

  (*f*) As with (*b*), this is a combination of technical progress and an increase in capital input.

  Much of the genuine technical progress is embodied either in capital input ((*a*), (*b*), (*f*)) or in labour ((*d*), (*e*)). The extent to which technical progress is properly measured depends to a great extent on how carefully inputs are measured, and clearly the 'residual method' of calculation will be at best imprecise. Notice that item (*c*), which has nothing to do with technical progress, may well be measured as such.

3 (*a*) Renewable.

  (*b*) Depletable.

  (*c*) Renewable.

  (*d*) Depletable.

  (*e*) Renewable—but with long gestation lags.

  (*f*) We don't usually think of rain as a resource, but the terrible drought in Ethiopia in the mid-1980s and the associated famine remind us of the fragility of the ecological balance. It is said that overenthusiastic tree-felling had dire effects upon rainfall.

4 *A* is the slump phase, being the trough of the cycle;
B: recovery;
C: boom;
D: boom—the peak of the cycle;
E: recession;
F: slump—the trough again.
The horizontal distance from *A* to *F* represents the (trough to trough) length of the cycle.

5 (*a*)

TABLE A30.1 Average annual growth rates (%)

	Germany GNP	Italy GDP	UK GDP	Output per person-hour in manufacturing Germany	Italy	UK
1974–79	3.42	2.40	1.97	2.07	4.62	1.26
1979–83	−0.05	0.62	0.56	3.65	1.56	3.47

  (*b*) There are a number of criticisms that could be levelled. In particular, we would want to check whether the years chosen correspond to similar points of the business cycle. If not, there may be considerable distortion. If you were to look up our source for the data, you would find that we had simply taken the earliest and latest years in the table, together with one in the middle. Only by extreme coincidence would this be a sensible procedure! For the UK, at least, it seems unlikely that a comparison of 1979 and 1983 would be appropriate. Placing GDP side by side with manufacturing productivity is also unhelpful. The improvement in UK 'productivity' is more likely a result of falling employment than of rising output. For reasons mentioned elsewhere, GDP may be an inaccurate measure of economic growth and welfare.

6 *All* the items mentioned have been invoked as potential contributors to the slowdown. Inflation is said to have increased uncertainty and thus affected investment, and in addition to have wrought havoc with taxation systems and necessitated anti-inflation policies which have slowed growth. Increasing international competition has reduced profit margins and reduced investment. It has also been suggested that increased under-reporting of transactions has affected measured output. The oil price shock cannot be excluded, having (it is said) diverted resources to R & D and caused premature scrapping of capital equipment. Increased preferences *for* leisure and *against* pollution as society moves beyond the industrial age have also received mention. It has also been argued that the revival of economies following the Second World War allowed rapid expansion based on new technology—and that the 1970s represented the return to normal growth rates. We leave you to filter these ideas for yourself, to discover which *you* think are most reasonable.

7 A policy for growth is one which enables sustained long-run growth of potential output, not mere once-for-all increases. Items (*a*), (*c*), (*d*), and (*f*) would thus be appropriate, but not (*b*) or (*e*).

8 (*c*).

9 Any of these items may be valid reasons for wishing to avoid maximizing economic growth, and may thus influence policy decisions.

10 **TABLE A30.2** A multiplier–accelerator model

Time period	v = 0.2			v = 0.8		
	C	I	Y	C	I	Y
0	30	30	60	30	30	60
1	30	40	70	30	40	70
2	35	42	77	35	48	83
3	38.5	41.4	79.9	41.5	50.4	91.9
4	39.95	40.58	80.53	45.95	47.12	93.07
5	40.26	40.13	80.39	46.54	40.94	87.48
6	40.20	39.97	80.17	43.74	35.52	79.26

With $v = 0.2$, the economy converges quite rapidly on the new equilibrium, but with $v = 0.8$, the adjustment path is cyclical and takes a lot longer. Other values of v and c can induce explosive cycles which *never* allow the economy to reach the new equilibrium.

True/False

1 False: in some countries (e.g. Brazil) there may be great inequality of income distribution (see Section 30–1 of the main text).
2 True.
3 False: part of investment is for replacement of existing capital (see Section 30–2 of the main text).
4 True: see Section 30–3 of the main text.
5 True.
6 False: this rather Malthusian argument ignores the potential for productivity changes (see Section 30–4 of the main text).
7 True.
8 Trueish—so long as we can afford to take a long-run view. Very often, the short-run problems are more obvious (see Section 30–5 of the main text).

9 True: see Section 30–6 of the main text.
10 False: there may be an *association* between the two, but for an *explanation* we need to understand *why* demand may fluctuate (see Section 30–7 of the main text).
11 False: see Section 30–8 of the main text.
12 True.

Questions for Thought

1 *Some hints* What happens to price as a resource becomes more scarce? How does this affect incentives? On the matter of a renewable resource, think about short-run/long-run and private/social costs aspects.
2 (a) OA—the natural rate.
  (b) I_3.
  (c) An expansion of aggregate demand could exploit the short-run Phillips trade-off and take the economy to point B on I_4.
  (d) Back to the natural rate at D.
  (e) I_2: worse than originally because inflation is higher.
  (f) Sliding 'up' SPC_1 does not produce much gain and cannot be sustained anyway—better to contract aggregate demand and move to point F (making people worse off), recognizing that as expectations adjust, the economy returns to A—hopefully in time to slide back up to B as the next election comes round!
  (g) The Thatcher administration's unswerving commitment to the long run could not have countenanced such a procedure—indeed, the very existence of the short-run trade-off has been questioned.
3 No hints offered.

31

Macroeconomics: Where Do We Stand?

The last eleven chapters have covered a lot of ground as we have invoked ever more complicated ways of looking at the macroeconomy. This has involved much careful thinking and reasoning, but it is still apparent that there are many issues on which macroeconomists fail to agree. The purpose of these chapters has not been to convince you of the validity of a particular viewpoint, but to prepare a framework to enable you to assess for yourself the different points of view. This chapter offers a perspective on macroeconomic views and identifies some contentious issues.

In the media and elsewhere, the macroeconomic controversy is sometimes portrayed as a debate between the 'monetarists' on the one hand and the 'Keynesians' on the other, as if all economists were to be found in one camp or the other. An important aim of this chapter is to emphasize that this polarization is an over-simplification: it is more sensible to think of there being a spectrum of views with no very clear divide between them. We examine four snapshots taken at different points along that spectrum.

Why should there be disagreements between economists? Some can be understood by recalling the distinction between positive and normative statements, first introduced in the opening chapter. It is perfectly possible for two economists to agree about the nature of a problem facing an economy, to agree about the theoretical analysis of the problem, but yet to disagree about the appropriate policy response. This arises simply from differing value judgements about the proper objectives of policy. However, it is clear that some disagreements go beyond this, extending to views about how the economy operates. This is perhaps inevitable in a subject denied the luxury of conducting laboratory experiments. By its very nature, empirical evidence may often be open to alternative interpretations, especially when so many vital variables are unobservable. For example, we have many times seen the importance of expectations in affecting macroeconomic behaviour—and yet we cannot measure expectations.

This issue of how agents form expectations is one of three important areas of disagreement which colour the way that macroeconomists think. *Exogenous expectations* are formed independently of other economic influences explained within our model. *Extrapolative expectations* rest on the assumption that people frame their expectations on the basis of past experi-

ence. Agents who form *rational expectations* are smart enough to make the best possible use of all available information and to avoid making systematic errors.

A second issue concerns market clearing, of which we have already seen hints. Will wages and prices adjust so as to take the economy to equilibrium? How long will the adjustment process take? This is very clearly an area where there is plenty of scope for different views to coexist. The third issue is closely bound up with the second. It involves the relative priority to be given to the short run as opposed to the long run. With rapid market clearing, the short run can be neglected, but if adjustment is a lengthy business, then intervention may be needed in the short run.

A further issue concerns the importance of *hysteresis*, which we encountered in Chapter 27. If temporary shocks can affect the long-run equilibrium of an economy, then it is no longer the case that long-run equilibrium is a unique situation. If hysteresis can occur, then it is important that policy should avoid the onset of recession as far as possible, so the short run is significant.

Our first snapshot is of *New Classical macroeconomics*, which may be thought of as being one end of the spectrum. The twin characteristics of this school of thought are rational expectations and instant market clearing. Under these conditions, unemployment is always at the natural rate, and fluctuations reflect the equilibrium business cycle. Monetary and fiscal policy may affect the composition but not the level of aggregate demand, and only surprises can move the economy away from full employment, because the rational expectations assumption ensures that all anticipated events have been taken into account in the decision-making process. The short run can be ignored because it essentially does not exist, the economy remaining in long-run equilibrium at all times. Hysteresis is not a problem. Policy should be concentrated entirely on the supply side and should be designed to avoid distortions, minimize surprises, and ensure smooth adjustment to equilibrium. Above all, policy must be clear, credible, and predictable.

The *Gradualist monetarists* would accept that markets may not clear instantaneously, but would not expect adjustment to be too lengthy a process. However, they would recognize that the economy may be temporarily away from full employment, although we need not worry about hysteresis. The costs of the transition from high to low inflation are such that monetary control must be introduced gradually. Although the short run must be considered, it is still the long run that is most important, and concern about short-run unemployment must not trigger monetary and fiscal policy which would jeopardize the achievement of long-run objectives. Policy should thus focus mainly on the supply side. It is probably fair to characterize the Thatcher government as having been here or hereabouts on the spectrum.

Our third snapshot is of the *Eclectic Keynesians*— 'short-run Keynesians and long-run monetarists'. According to this view, the economy will eventually reach equilibrium, but it may take some considerable time, so there is a possibility of severe recession during the adjustment period. What is more, hysteresis is a potential problem. For the long run, there need to be supply-side policies with monetary responsibility, but some short-run stabilization may also be needed. It may be argued that demand management may be effective both in achieving short-run stabilization and in increasing long-run potential output through its effect on investment. Some members of this group may also subscribe to the idea that adjustments may be accelerated by use of an incomes policy.

Finally, we have the *Extreme Keynesians*, who argue that markets not only do not clear in the short run, but may not clear in the long run either. There is thus the possibility of sustained demand-deficient unemployment with inflexible real wages. Members of this group might also argue that the government is unable to control real money supply. A cut in nominal money supply which leads to a fall in aggregate demand results in a fall in money demand, leaving the interest rate unchanged, thus nullifying the usual adjustment process. It might also be argued that investment depends mainly on profits and not very much on the rate of interest. In such a world, demand management is all-important, perhaps coupled with direct control of imports. The possibility of hysteresis adds weight to the arguments in favour of demand-management policies to avoid the onset of recession, as there may be long-term consequences for the economy.

As we have moved across the spectrum, we have seen that the question of whether or not the free market works has been crucial. This points to the breaking of another great divide in economics, that between macroeconomics and microeconomics. Concern with the microeconomic basis of macroeconomics has increased greatly of late. An important aspect of the spectrum is that our position along it determines our attitude towards policy in regard to both the nature and the extent of government intervention.

IMPORTANT CONCEPTS AND TECHNICAL TERMS

Match each lettered concept with the appropriate numbered phrase (included are some key revision terms used in the chapter):

(a) Aggregate demand
(b) Exogenous expectations
(c) Eclectic Keynesians
(d) Demand management
(e) Market clearing
(f) Rational expectations
(g) New Classical macroeconomics
(h) Full employment
(i) Real wage hypothesis
(j) Extrapolative expectations
(k) Gradualist monetarists
(l) Potential output
(m) Extreme Keynesians
(n) Supply-side policies
(o) Hysteresis

1 Policies to stabilize aggregate demand close to its full-employment level.
2 The demand for domestic output.
3 The level of output that firms wish to supply when there is full employment.
4 The level of employment when the labour market is in equilibrium.
5 A group of economists who insist that markets not only fail to clear in the short run but also may not clear in the long run.
6 The assumption that real wages are rigidly inflexible.
7 Policies aimed at increasing potential output.
8 A school of economists who believe that the restoration of full employment is not immediate but that adjustment is not too lengthy.
9 A theory of expectations formation which says that people make good use of the information that is available today and do not make forecasts that are already knowably incorrect.
10 A school of economists, including Nobel prize winners John Hicks, James Mcade, and James Tobin, whose ideas may be summarized as 'short-run Keynesian and long-run monetarist'.
11 Expectations formed on the basis of past experience.
12 Expectations formed independently of the rest of the analysis being undertaken.
13 A situation in which the quantity that sellers wish to supply in a market equals the quantity that purchasers wish to demand.
14 The view that temporary shocks affect the long-run equilibrium.
15 A school of economists whose analysis is based on the twin principles of almost instantaneous market clearing and rational expectations.

EXERCISES

1 Which of the following could be called a 'normative' economic statement?
  (a) 'The level of inflation has increased by more

this year in the United Kingdom than in France.'

(b) 'A rise in the price of apples will lead, other things remaining constant, to a fall in the demand for them.'

(c) 'A fall in the value of sterling against the dollar means that British goods may be more competitive in the United States.'

(d) 'Direct taxes should be increased, to redistribute income more fairly.'
(Associated Examining Board GCE A level Economics Paper 1, November 1986)

2 Associate each of the following viewpoints with one of the 'schools' discussed in this chapter.

(a) Full employment will be reached in a reasonable period of time.

(b) Long-run demand-deficient unemployment is feasible.

(c) Short run and long run are indistinguishable because adjustment is rapid.

(d) Short-run stabilization could be important because adjustment may be sluggish.

(e) Policies should be concentrated on the short run.

(f) Expectations are formed rationally.

3 (a) What do you expect to be the rate of inflation in the coming year?

(b) What information did you use to form that expectation?

(c) If you had responsibility for setting prices or negotiating wage settlements, would you form your expectations more carefully? What additional information would you seek?

4 Figure 31.1 shows our usual labour market story: LD_0, LD_1 represent labour demand curves; LF shows the number of people prepared to register in the labour force at each real wage; AJ shows those prepared to accept jobs. The economy begins in equilibrium with labour demand LD_0. An exogenous shock affects labour productivity and reduces labour demand to LD_1.

(a) Identify the original real wage and unemployment level.

After the shock:

(b) How would an Extreme Keynesian view the long-run prospects for the labour market?

(c) How would a Gradualist monetarist and an Eclectic Keynesian view the labour market in the medium and long terms? How would you distinguish the two?

(d) Identify the new short-run position of the market according to the New Classical school.

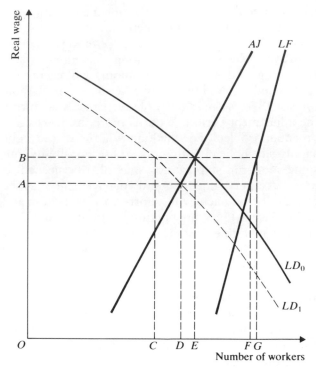

FIGURE 31.1 The labour market

(e) How would the groups differ in their approach to policy?

(f) How would the analysis be affected by hysteresis?

5 Which of the schools are most likely to adopt the following policy measures?

(a) Contractionary monetary policy to combat inflation, as the transitional cost of unemployment will be quite shortlived.

(b) Reduction of money supply to eliminate inflation; output and employment will not be affected.

(c) Import controls to protect domestic employment during an expansion of aggregate demand.

(d) Incomes policy to speed adjustment.

(e) Demand management to stimulate investment and thus raise potential output.

6 Rank the following markets in order of their likely speed of adjustment (most rapid first):

(a) The market for goods.

(b) The money market.

(c) The labour market.

(d) The foreign exchange market.

Explain your answer.

7 Macroeconomics: where do *you* stand?

TRUE/FALSE

1 _____ Economists agree about positive issues but disagree on normative matters.

2 _____ A rise in unemployment provides support for the Keynesian analysis of the economy in which a deficiency of aggregate demand may move the economy away from full employment.

3 _____ According to the New Classical macroeconomics, government policy can move the economy away from full employment only if agents are surprised by the policy.

4 _____ The New Classicals believe that the dramatic rise in UK unemployment in the early 1980s had almost nothing to do with a fall in aggregate demand.

5 _____ Gradualist monetarists subscribe to the view that an increase in money supply can increase output and employment in the long run, but that the adjustment process is gradual.

6 _____ According to the Gradualist monetarists, the government's chief responsibility is to increase potential output by supply-side policies and by bringing inflation under control.

7 _____ Eclectic Keynesians argue that supply-side policies are irrelevant and that attention should be focused on demand management.

8 _____ According to some Eclectic Keynesians, demand management may operate as a significant supply-side policy.

9 _____ Extreme Keynesians argue that supply-side policies are irrelevant and that attention should be focused on demand management.

10 _____ Macroeconomists never consider microeconomic issues.

QUESTIONS FOR THOUGHT

1 Discuss the proposition that the best stabilization policy is one of non-intervention.

2 Discuss whether government policy should be permitted to react to changing circumstances or whether it should be guided by predetermined rules.

3 Consider the economic policies of the current government and opposition. Can you trace these policies to particular areas of the macroeconomic spectrum?

ANSWERS AND COMMENTS FOR CHAPTER 31

Please note Where questions are reproduced from GCE examinations, the examination boards bear no responsibility for the answers provided in this volume, which are the sole responsibility of the authors.

Important Concepts and Technical Terms

1 *d*	5 *m*	9 *f*	13 *e*
2 *a*	6 *i*	10 *c*	14 *o*
3 *l*	7 *n*	11 *j*	15 *g*
4 *h*	8 *k*	12 *b*	

Exercises

1 (*d*).

2 (*a*) Gradualist Monetarist.
   (*b*) Extreme Keynesian.
   (*c*) New Classical.
   (*d*) Eclectic Keynesian.
   (*e*) Extreme Keynesian.
   (*f*) Rational expectations are not uniquely identified with a single school. It is an essential assumption of the New Classical macroeconomics, but there are also devotees in the Gradualist monetarist and Eclectic Keynesian groups.

3 (*a*) We cannot of course supply you with an answer to this: apart from anything else, we don't know when you are reading it!
   (*b*) Most people asked for a casual guess about inflation will think back to what inflation has been in the last year—perhaps with an adjustment for current conditions or recent TV reports. The dominance of past experience in this process suggests extrapolative expectations.
   (*c*) We always take more care when it matters! Whether people research sufficiently thoroughly to justify the rational expectations hypothesis is, however, more contentious.

4 (*a*) Real wage *OB*, unemployment *EG*—the natural rate.
   (*b*) Given real wage inflexibility, the real wage could well remain at *OB* and unemployment would rise to *CG*.
   (*c*) In the 'medium' term, the market could still be at real wage *OB*, unemployment *CG*; but in the long run, adjustment would take the real wage to *OA* and unemployment to *DF*. The two groups would differ in their definitions of 'medium' and 'long' term, with the Gradualist expecting the long run to be relatively close.
   (*d*) The New Classicals would expect rapid adjustment to the new equilibrium with real wage *OA*, unemployment at the new natural rate *DF*.
   (*e*) The Extreme Keynesians would want demand management to combat the unemployment, which

they view as being due to deficient demand. The Eclectic Keynesians would perhaps want to allow some demand management to alleviate the short-run problem, or incomes policy to speed the adjustment—together with some long-run supply-side policies also. The Gradualists would probably want to ride out the short-run crisis and concentrate on long-run supply-side policies. The New Classicals would not recognize the short-run problem, but might wish to take steps to reduce the natural rate of unemployment.
   (*f*) Under hysteresis, the temporary fall in *LD* could lead to a permanent shift in *AJ*, and a new long-run equilibrium with a lower employment level. See exercise 11 of Chapter 27.

5 (*a*) Gradualist.
   (*b*) New Classical.
   (*c*) Extreme Keynesian.
   (*d*) Eclectic Keynesian.
   (*e*) Eclectic Keynesian.

6 (*d*), (*b*), (*a*), (*c*).
   The foreign exchange market clears very rapidly indeed—at least, under floating exchange rates. The money market is hardly less quick. The goods market is more sluggish for a number of reasons—remember the oligopoly models of Chapter 10? There are also the menu costs of changing prices. The labour market is likely to be the slowest. For more detail, see Box 31–1 of the main text.

7 You may find that your views do not place you firmly in any one school. This is not surprising, as there are considerable grey areas between our snapshots—which is why we refer to it as a spectrum.

True/False

1 False: there are some positive issues which would command general agreement, but there are others where a variety of opinion exists (see Section 31–1 of the main text).
2 False: the statement presumes that demand deficiency is the *only* cause of unemployment. Some economists would attribute much of the rise to an increase in the natural rate.
3 True: see Section 31–2 of the main text.
4 True.
5 False: they would argue that output and employment may change in the short run but will gradually readjust to full employment. It is *prices* that are affected in the long run (see Section 31–3 of the main text).
6 True.
7 False: they would recognize the potential importance of supply-side policies in the long-run while wishing to carry out stabilization in the short run (see Section 31–4 of the main text).
8 True.
9 True: see Section 31–5 of the main text.
10 False: see Section 31–6 of the main text.

Questions for Thought

1 This proposition rests on the belief that the economy will stabilize itself within a reasonable time span if left alone. In addition, it may be argued that misguided or mistimed policy action may have a destabilizing effect.

2 The debate about 'rules versus discretion' has been a long-lasting one. The discussion of the problems of fine-tuning (Chapter 22) is worth reviewing, as it highlights some of the problems of discretionary policy. Friedman and other Gradualists are heavily committed to the idea of pre-set rules.

3 No comment.

32

International Trade and Commercial Policy

In Chapter 29 we saw something of the importance of international transactions for the macroeconomy. Other facets of international trade must also be examined. Some of the reasons for studying international trade are readily apparent—for instance, there are likely to be effects on the exchange rate, and there are a number of issues relating to commercial policy which are important. We also explore why it is that international trade takes place, and find that it has its basis in *exchange* and in *specialization*.

By 1988 the level of world exports was equivalent to about 18 per cent of world GNP. World trade had been inhibited by the Great Depression and the Second World War, but greatly increased in importance in the postwar period. Almost half of world trade is carried out among the industrialized nations, which in 1986 accounted for 67 per cent of world income and 69.7 per cent of world trade. The only significant trade not involving these countries was trade within the Soviet bloc. Recent years have seen an increase in the share of manufactures in world exports, especially engineering goods and road vehicles. Fuels also increased in importance (partly a result of changing oil prices), but other primary commodities became relatively less important.

The gains from international trade are readily demonstrated by the *law of comparative advantage*, formulated by David Ricardo in the early nineteenth century. This rests on international differences in the opportunity cost of goods. Suppose a two-country, two-good world for simplicity; it may be that one economy has an *absolute advantage* in the production of both goods—that is, can produce both goods more cheaply. International trade can be shown to be still worth while if one country has a *relative advantage* in the production of one of the goods. If each country specializes in the good which it can produce *relatively* cheaply, total joint output can be increased. The level of the equilibrium exchange rate will reflect the difference in absolute advantage. A common cause of comparative advantage arises when economies have different *factor endowments* and hence different relative factor prices. For instance, economies with high capital:labour ratios will tend to export capital-intensive goods, in which their comparative advantage lies.

In some commodities, we observe *intra-industry trade* between countries—the UK, for instance, both imports and exports cars. Why should this be? Analysis of the commodities involved suggests that they are characterized by a degree of product differentiation. It may be that by specializing even within a commodity group it is possible to benefit from economies of scale. The extent of international integration is also relevant: for instance, there is substantial intra-industry trade within the EC.

International trade may bring gains in the form of higher output, but, as ever, the question of the distribution of the gains remains. We must ask who benefits? And does anyone lose? The fact that potentially everyone could be made better off does not mean that everyone will actually benefit. For example, international trade has allowed UK car buyers to gain from an increase in the imports of cheap foreign cars (whose producers have also gained), but in addition there has been a sharp fall in employment in the British car industry, which has hit some regions like the West Midlands very severely. The question naturally arises as to whether the government should intervene to affect the distribution of the gains or to protect domestic industries. Such measures are known as *commercial policy*, and aim to influence international trade through taxes or subsidies, or through direct restrictions on imports or exports.

A *tariff* requires the importer to pay a given fraction of the world price to the government. This protects domestic producers by raising the domestic price above the world price—but this affects consumers as well, of course! A tariff works rather like a tax from the consumer's perspective: there are transfers from consumers both to government in the form of revenue and to producers in the form of higher profits. In addition, there is a *deadweight burden*. In the long run, it may be desirable to allow free trade and to permit resources to be transferred to industries in which the domestic economy has a comparative advantage.

Over the years, many 'justifications' for tariffs have been advanced—many of them invalid. The strongest (some would say the *only*) argument in favour of a tariff begins with the recognition that a domestic economy imports such a significant share of the world market for a commodity that an increase in imports will affect the world price. In such a case, the cost to society of the last unit imported may exceed the benefit, as all consumers must pay the higher world price. Society as a whole could then gain by the imposition of an *optimal tariff* which restricted imports to the point where the marginal benefit of importing was just equal to the marginal cost. This is a *first-best* argument in favour of a tariff.

The *principle of targeting* states that the most efficient way to attain a given objective is to use a policy that has a direct influence on that activity. Policies which operate indirectly through other activities are known as second-best because of the distortions they introduce. Most of the other arguments in favour of tariffs fall into this category. These usually constitute attempts to protect domestic producers or consumers, and in most cases production subsidies or consumption taxes that bear directly on the problem would be preferred. The *infant industry argument* is often advanced, by which a domestic industry is to be protected until strong enough to flourish alone. Such protection is presumably required only for ventures which cannot acquire bank backing. In some cases the banks' judgement about the likelihood of long-run viability may well be correct! All too often, the infant never grows up.

The earlier analysis of game theory in Chapter 10 might lead us to advance a strategic argument in favour of a tariff to protect domestic producers and to prevent entry by foreign producers. However, retaliation by other countries in this situation is likely to result in everyone being worse off. This may be seen as another instance of the Prisoners' Dilemma game.

Other arguments for tariffs are mainly groundless. Complaints about cheap foreign labour cannot be sustained in the light of the law of comparative advantage. There may be a case for protecting domestic industries against temporary 'dumping' of foreign produce, but, again, production subsidies would be preferable.

If the case is so strong, why do tariffs still exist? The answer may be partly political. The costs of tariffs are diffuse but the benefits concentrated. It may be politically more tactful to collect tariff revenues and have consumers suffer high prices than to impose taxation in order to subsidize production.

Major periods of unemployment such as the 1930s have tended to trigger increases in tariffs. In the postwar period the *General Agreement on Tariffs and Trade* (GATT) has been successful in bringing tariffs to tolerably low levels by the early 1980s. Some economists have been worried lest tariffs may be due for a comeback in the world recession.

Although tariffs are the most common form of commercial policy, there are others also. The World Bank has suggested that more than 14 per cent of the UK's imports in the early 1980s were covered by *non-tariff barriers*. These may take the form of administrative regulations which impede trade. Alternative policies include *export subsidies*, which may boost exports, but only at the expense of a deadweight loss borne by the domestic consumer. *Quotas* are quantity restrictions which in practice work in a similar way to tariffs, raising the domestic price of the restricted good, but allowing the foreign supplier to reap extra profits rather than bringing revenue to the home government.

IMPORTANT CONCEPTS AND TECHNICAL TERMS

Match each lettered concept with the appropriate numbered phrase:

(a) Intra-industry trade
(b) Dumping
(c) Opportunity cost
(d) Non-tariff barriers
(e) Import tariff
(f) Absolute advantage
(g) Import quotas
(h) Principle of targeting
(i) Export subsidy
(j) Commercial policy
(k) Optimal tariff
(l) Infant industry argument
(m) Law of comparative advantage
(n) GATT
(o) Factor endowments
(p) Deadweight loss of a tariff

1 The quantity of other goods that must be sacrificed to produce one more unit of a good.
2 Trade in goods made within the same industry.
3 An import duty requiring the importer of a good to pay a specified fraction of the world price to the government.
4 A commercial policy designed to increase exports by granting producers an additional sum above the domestic price per unit exported.
5 The amounts of capital and labour available in an economy.
6 Government policy that influences international trade through taxes or subsidies or through direct restrictions on imports and exports.
7 Administrative regulations that discriminate against foreign goods and favour home goods.
8 The waste arising from the domestic overproduction and domestic underconsumption of a good where imports are subject to a tariff.
9 A principle which states that countries specialize in producing and exporting goods that they produce at a lower *relative* cost than other countries.
10 Restrictions imposed on the maximum quantity of imports.
11 The ability to produce goods with lower unit labour requirements than in other countries.
12 Tariffs designed to restrict imports until the benefit of the last import equals its cost to society as a whole.
13 A justification of a tariff on the grounds that a developing industry needs protection until established.
14 A commitment by a large number of countries in the postwar period to reduce tariffs successively and to dismantle trade restrictions.
15 A situation when foreign producers sell at prices

below their marginal production costs, either by making losses or with the assistance of a government subsidy.

16 An argument that the most efficient way to attain a given objective is to use a policy that influences that activity directly.

EXERCISES

1 Table 32.1 shows how the exports of a number of countries were divided between five commodity groups in 1987.

TABLE 32.1 Structure of merchandise exports, 1987

Country	Percentage share of merchandise exports				
	Fuels, minerals, and metals	Other primary commodities	Textiles and clothing	Machinery and transport equipment	Other manufactures
Ethiopia	3	96	0	0	1
Pakistan	1	32	41	3	23
Ivory Coast	4	86	1	2	6
Trinidad & Tobago	72	5	0	1	22
Saudi Arabia	90	1	…	4	5
Singapore	17	11	6	43	23
Hong Kong	2	6	34	22	36
UK	14	9	4	37	36
West Germany	4	6	5	49	36
Japan	1	1	3	65	29

Source: World Bank, *World Development Report 1989*

(a) What do these figures suggest about the factor and resource endowments in these countries and the pattern of comparative advantage?

(b) Given recent changes in the composition of world exports (see Section 32–1 of the main text), how would you assess the future prospects for these countries?

(c) What additional information would you require to feel confidence in your answers?

2 This exercise examines the gains from trade in a two-country, two-good model. To simplify matters for the time being, we assume that the two countries share a common currency; this allows us to ignore the exchange rate. The two countries are called Anywaria and Someland; the two goods are bicycles and boots. The unit labour requirements of the two goods in each country are shown in Table 32.2; we assume constant returns to scale.

(a) Which of the countries has an absolute advantage in the production of the two commodities?

(b) Calculate the opportunity cost of bicycles in terms of boots and of boots in terms of bicycles for each of the countries.

TABLE 32.2 Production techniques

	Unit labour requirement (hours per unit output)	
	Anywaria	Someland
Bicycles	60	120
Boots	30	40

(c) Which country has a comparative advantage in the production of bicycles?

Suppose there is no trade. Each of the two economies has 300 workers who work 40 hours per week. Initially, each country devotes half of its resources to producing each of the two commodities.

(d) Calculate the following:

TABLE 32.3 Production of bicycles and boots, no-trade case

	Anywaria	Someland	'World' output
Bicycles			
Boots			

Trade now takes place under the following conditions: the country with a comparative advantage in boot production produces only boots. The other country produces sufficient bicycles to maintain the world 'no-trade' output, devoting the remaining resources to boot production.

(e) Calculate the following and comment on the gains from trade:

TABLE 32.4 Production of bicycles and boots

	Anywaria	Someland	'World' output
Bicycles			
Boots			

(f) On a single diagram, plot the production possibility frontier for each country. What aspect of your diagram is indicative of potential gains from trade?

3 This exercise extends the analysis of the previous one by recognizing that our two economies have different currencies and labour costs. Unit labour requirements are as set out before in Table 32.2. The hourly wage rate in Anywaria is A$5; in Someland it is S$4.50.

(a) Calculate unit labour costs for the two goods in each country.
(b) Calculate unit labour costs in terms of Somelandish dollars if the exchange rate is A$1 = S$1.8.
(c) Calculate unit labour costs in terms of Somelandish dollars if the exchange rate is A$1 = S$1.2.
(d) Comment on the range of values for the exchange rate within which trade may take place. Explain your answer.
(e) Within this simple world, what factors will determine the equilibrium exchange rate?

4 Which of the following factors favour(s) intra-industry trade and which act(s) against it?
(a) Product differentiation.
(b) International integration.
(c) Existence of tariff barriers.
(d) Availability of economies of scale in the production of individual brands.
(e) High transport costs.
(f) Homogeneous commodity.

5 Figure 32.1 shows the domestic demand (DD) and supply (SS) of a commodity with and without the imposition of a tariff, the world price being given by OB.
(a) Identify the domestic price and the quantity imported in a situation of free trade.
Suppose now that a tariff is imposed on imports of this commodity.

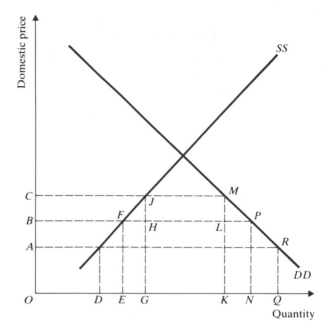

FIGURE 32.1 A tariff

(b) Identify the domestic price in the new situation, and the quantity imported.
(c) By how much does domestic production of this commodity change?
(d) Identify the area which represents the extra consumer payments for the quantity purchased.
(e) How much of this accrues to the government as tariff revenue, and how much to domestic producers as additional rents?
(f) Explain the remaining part of these extra consumer payments.
(g) Identify the surplus of consumer benefits over social marginal cost which is sacrificed by society in reducing its consumption of this good.
(h) What is the total welfare cost of this tariff?

6 Below are listed a selection of arguments which have been advanced to support the existence of tariffs. Identify each as a 'first-best', 'second-best', or 'non-'argument:
(a) The need to defend domestic producers against unfair competition based on cheap foreign labour.
(b) The need to maintain a national defence industry in case of war.
(c) A desire to restrict imports until the benefits of the last imported unit are equalized with its cost to society as a whole.
(d) The need to nurture a newly developing domestic industry.
(e) A wish to prevent dumping by foreign producers.

(f)   The government needs a cheap and easy way of obtaining revenue.

7   Figure 32.2 shows the domestic demand (DD) and supply (SS) of a commodity, the export of which the government wishes to encourage. OA represents the world price.

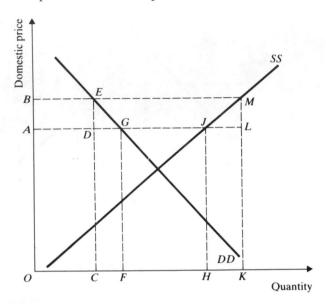

FIGURE 32.2   An export subsidy

(a)   Identify the domestic price and the quantity exported in a situation of free trade.

The government now imposes an export subsidy.

(b)   Identify the new domestic price and quantity exported.

(c)   By how much does domestic production increase?

(d)   By how much does domestic consumption fall?

(e)   Identify the decrease in 'consumer surplus' (i.e., the surplus of consumer benefits over social marginal cost which is sacrificed).

(f)   What is the social cost of the extra production (i.e., the social cost of producing goods whose marginal cost exceeds the world price)?

(g)   Why would the government wish to introduce this policy?

(h)   How else could the same objective be achieved?

8   Attempts to protect the level of employment by imposing tariffs can have adverse results as a result of

1   retaliation in export markets
2   reduced exploitation of comparative advantage
3   increased export penetration

(a)   1, 2 and 3 are correct

(b)   1 and 2 only are correct
(c)   2 and 3 only are correct
(d)   1 only is correct
(e)   3 only is correct
(University of London GCE A level Economics Paper 3, June 1989)

9   Assume that countries A and B only produce the following quantities of X and Y

	Units of X	or	Units of Y
Country A	12		16
Country B	8		8

If each country specialises in accordance with the law of comparative advantage the terms of trade will be

(a)   1 unit of X for $1\frac{1}{3}$ units of Y
(b)   1 unit of X for 2 units of Y
(c)   1 unit of X for 1 unit of Y
(d)   between 1 and $1\frac{1}{3}$ units of Y for 1 unit of X
(e)   between $\frac{1}{2}$ and $\frac{3}{4}$ units of X for 1 unit of Y
(University of London GCE A level Economics Paper 3, June 1987)

10   The view that protectionism may be used to increase total world economic welfare might be supported by the argument that

(a)   there are some products in which a country has a long-term comparative advantage which can only be developed, at first, behind a tariff barrier

(b)   governments can increase their expenditure through tariff revenue gained at the expense of foreigners

(c)   a tariff curtails the demand for imported goods, thus helping to protect the real wealth of the country

(d)   a tariff is necessary to equalise the costs of production between countries
(Associated Examining Board GCE A level Economics Paper 1, June 1986)

11   The Multi-Fibre Arrangement restricts the increase of imports of many textiles and clothes from the developing into the developed countries including the UK. This exercise explores the effect of such quota agreements on the domestic market using Figure 32.3, which shows the domestic demand curve (DD) and supply curves (SS) for a commodity. OA is the world price.

(a)   What would be the level of imports in the absence of restriction?

A quota restriction is now imposed which limits imports to the amount FJ.

(b)   What is the new domestic price?

(c)   Identify the change in domestic production and consumption.

(d)   Explain what is represented by the area FGKJ.

(e)   Identify the total welfare cost.

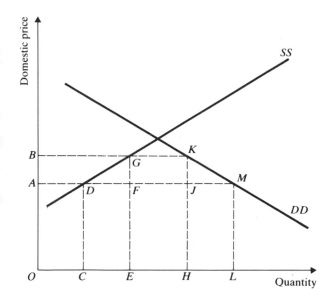

FIGURE 32.3 Quota restrictions

TRUE/FALSE

1 _____ Almost half of world trade is between the industrialized countries.

2 _____ Taken together, about one-third of the exports of the less developed countries are manufactured goods.

3 _____ International trade is worth while so long as one country has an absolute advantage in production.

4 _____ Comparative advantage reflects international differences in the opportunity costs of producing different goods.

5 _____ If a country has a relatively abundant endowment of a particular factor, it will tend to have a comparative advantage in the production of goods which use that factor intensively.

6 _____ The existence of comparative advantage tends to increase the amount of intra-industry trade.

7 _____ The law of comparative advantage ensures that there are gains from trade which make everyone better off.

8 _____ The imposition of a tariff stimulates domestic consumption.

9 _____ The case for free trade rests partly on the analysis of the deadweight burden arising from the existence of tariff barriers.

10 _____ The need to protect infant industries is a powerful argument in favour of tariff barriers.

11 _____ At the start of the 1980s, tariff

levels throughout the world economy were probably as low as they had ever been.

12 _____ Some countries attempt to restrict imports by imposing rigorous or complicated rules concerning the specification of imported goods.

QUESTIONS FOR THOUGHT

1 In April 1985 the Japanese prime minister went on nationwide Japanese television, exhorting his viewers to 'buy more foreign goods . . . [because] we depend on free trade to survive . . . Japan is the country most vulnerable to any erosion of the free trade system.' (*Guardian*, 10 April 1985.) Explain his concern and suggest what positive action could be taken.

2 What are the economic benefits of international trade? Given these benefits, explain why governments often place restrictions on imports.
(Northern Ireland Schools Examination Council GCE A level Economics Paper 2, June 1988)

3 This exercise extends some aspects of the analysis in this chapter of a two-country, two-good world. The two countries are A and B, the two goods X and Y. Figure 32.4 focuses on country A, illustrating the production possibility frontier (PPF) and some indifference curves (I_1, I_2) depicting the community's preference for the two goods.

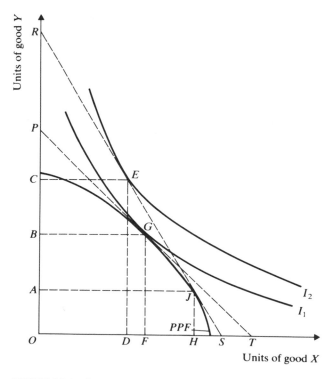

FIGURE 32.4 Country A: production and preferences

Suppose that initially there is no trade, and that the domestic price ratio is given by the line *PT*.

(*a*)   At what point will the economy choose to produce?

(*b*)   If the 'world' price ratio is also given by *PT*, what is implied for comparative advantage and the gains from trade?

Suppose now that the world price ratio is given by *RS*, but the domestic price ratio by *PT*.

(*c*)   What are the implications for the comparative advantage of country A?

With international trade in this situation, country A can move to any point along *RS* by exporting and importing goods.

(*d*)   At what points will country A choose to produce and consume?

(*e*)   Identify exports and imports.

In parts (*d*) and (*e*), we have seen that the quantities offered for exchange internationally depend upon the *terms of trade* (the world price ratio) and upon the preferences of people in country A. Of course, a similar story could be told for country B, showing the offers made for exchange. By examining the offers made by the two countries at different relative world prices, we can gain some insight into the equilibrium terms of trade.

Consider Figure 32.5. The curve *UV* is the *offer curve* for country A: it shows the quantities of

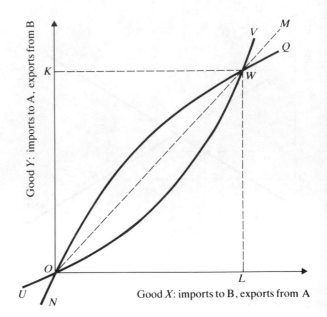

FIGURE 32.5   Offer curves

good X offered in exchange for good Y at different terms of trade. The curve *NQ* shows the offer curve for country B, constructed in similar fashion.

(*f*)   Interpret the line *OM*, and explain the sense in which the point W represents an equilibrium.

ANSWERS AND COMMENTS FOR CHAPTER 32

Please note Where questions are reproduced from GCE examinations, the examination boards bear no responsibility for the answers provided in this volume, which are the sole responsibility of the authors.

Important Concepts and Technical Terms

1	*c*	5	*o*	9	*m*	13	*l*
2	*a*	6	*j*	10	*g*	14	*n*
3	*e*	7	*d*	11	*f*	15	*b*
4	*i*	8	*p*	12	*k*	16	*h*

Exercises

1   (*a*)   In general, goods in the last two categories tend to require relatively capital-intensive production techniques—which explains why countries like Ethiopia and the Ivory Coast have a low concentration of exports in these commodities. 'Other primary commodities' comprises mainly agricultural produce. The importance of oil to Saudi Arabia stands out. Trinidad's exports are also dominated by oil and pitch. The North Sea oil effect is apparent for the UK. The relatively labour-intensive nature of the Hong Kong economy can also be seen—together with its relative lack of natural resources. It turns out that Hong Kong and Singapore are both rather special cases when it comes to exports. This is discussed further in Chapter 35.

   (*b*)   In recent years the categories 'other primary commodities' and 'textiles and clothing' have been declining in relative importance while the other categories have been on the increase. The change in 'fuels' has been due in part to the oil price changes, but engineering and road vehicles have become increasingly important without such help from prices. If these trends continue, we would expect prospects to be good for Japan, Germany, and the UK, but poor for Ethiopia and the Ivory Coast. However, . . .

   (*c*)   . . . it is dangerous to read too much into these figures. In particular, the commodity groups are broad in coverage. No doubt there are some goods within 'other manufacturing' or 'other primary commodities' whose prospects are markedly different from the norm. We would thus need more detailed information about the commodities exported by each country. In addition, we are given only percentage shares, which do not provide clues to the importance of exports to each country. For instance, merchandise exports for Ethiopia comprised only 8 per cent of GDP in 1987, compared with 23 per cent for the UK. (In Singapore the figure was about 144 per cent—but that is another story!)

2   (*a*)   Anywaria has the absolute advantage, having lower unit labour requirements for each good.

   (*b*)   The opportunity cost of a unit of bicycle output is 2 units of boots in Anywaria and 3 units in Someland. The opportunity cost of a unit of boots output is $\frac{1}{2}$ a unit of bicycles in Anywaria and $\frac{1}{3}$ of a unit in Someland.

   (*c*)   Anywaria has the comparative advantage in bicycles, having the lower opportunity cost.

   (*d*)   **TABLE A32.1**   Production of bicycles and boots, no-trade case

	Anywaria	Someland	'World' output
Bicycles	100	50	150
Boots	200	150	350

   (*e*)   **TABLE A32.2**   Production of bicycles and boots

	Anywaria	Someland	'World' output
Bicycles	150	–	150
Boots	100	300	400

World output of bicycles has been maintained at the no-trade level, but it has proved possible to increase the output of boots from 350 to 400 units. How these gains are distributed between the two economies is of course a separate issue. Indeed, the very feasibility of trade may depend on the exchange rate if the two countries do not share a common currency (see exercise 3).

   (*f*)   In Figure A32.1, PPF_A and PPF_S represent the production possibility frontiers for Anywaria and Someland, respectively. The key element which reveals the potential gains from trade is the difference in the slope of the two curves, reflecting the difference in opportunity costs.

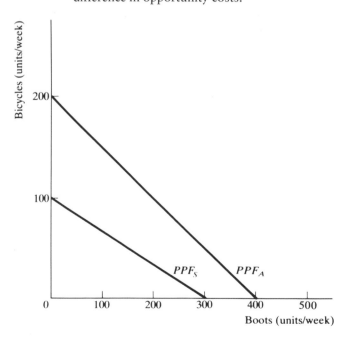

FIGURE A32.1   Production possibilities for Anywaria and Someland

3   (a)   Unit labour costs:

Bicycles: A\$300 in Anywaria, S\$540 in Someland.

Boots: A\$150 in Anywaria, S\$180 in Someland.

(b)

	Anywaria	Someland
Bicycles	540	540
Boots	270	180

(c)

	Anywaria	Someland
Bicycles	360	540
Boots	180	180

(d)   Trade will take place only at exchange rates between the values analysed in parts (b) and (c), as *one-way* trade is not viable. With an exchange rate above A\$1.8 = S\$1, there would be no demand for Anywaria produce; below A\$1.2, there is no demand for Somelandish output.

(e)   The equilibrium exchange rate will depend upon the size of demand for the goods in the two economies (see Section 32–2 of the main text).

4   (a), (b), and (d) encourage intra-industry trade, but (c), (e), and (f) work against it.

5   (a)   Price OB (= world price), imports FP (the excess of domestic demand over domestic supply at this price).

(b)   Price OC, imports JM.

(c)   EG.

(d)   BCML.

(e)   Tariff revenue HJML, rents BCJF.

(f)   FHJ remains: this is the extra that society spends by producing cars domestically rather than importing them at the world price.

(g)   LMP.

(h)   FHJ + LMP.

6   (c)   is a first-best argument; (b), (d), and (f) are second-best arguments—in each case there are preferable and more direct methods of achieving the desired object. (e) is at *best* a second-best argument and may join (a) as a non-argument.

7   (a)   Price OA, exports GJ.

(b)   Price OB, exports EM.

(c)   HK.

(d)   CF.

(e)   DEG.

(f)   JLM.

(g)   It is sometimes argued that economic growth can take place only if accompanied by an expansion of aggregate demand. If the authorities perceive the domestic market to be too limited, they may wish to encourage exports—but notice that part of the increase achieved is at the expense of domestic consumption.

(h)   A production subsidy would keep the domestic price at OA; the social cost would then be JLM rather than JLM + DEG (see Section 32–8 of the main text).

8   (b).

9   (d).

10   (a).

11   (a)   DM.

(b)   OB.

(c)   Domestic production increases from OC to OE, but consumption falls from OL to OH.

(d)   If this diagram had been describing a tariff, this area would have represented tariff revenue. With a quota, this revenue accrues either to foreign suppliers or to domestic importers.

(e)   DFG + JKM + the proportion of FGJK accruing to foreign suppliers. It has been estimated that, if the Multi-Fibre Arrangement were to be abandoned, British consumers would pay £550 million (at 1985 prices) less for textiles and clothes annually. Two-thirds of these savings would be losses to foreign producers and only one-third to British firms (see Aubrey Silberston, *The Multi-Fibre Arrangement and the UK Economy*, HMSO, 1984).

True/False

1   True: see Section 32–1 of the main text.

2   True.

3   False: it is *necessary* for one country to have an absolute advantage in the production of at least one commodity, but it is not *sufficient*—comparative advantage is also important (see Section 32–2 of the main text).

4   True.

5   True.

6   False: see Section 32–3 of the main text.

7   False: comparative advantage ensures that *potentially* everyone may be better off but cannot guarantee that they will actually be so (see Section 32–4 of the main text).

8   False: see Section 32–5 of the main text.

9   True.

10   False: it is a *common* argument but not a powerful one, and has often been misused (see Section 32–6 of the main text).

11   True: see Section 32–7 of the main text.

12   True: this is very common (see Section 32–8 of the main text).

Questions for Thought

1   At the time, Japan's trade surplus was a prime concern. Any increase in protectionism elsewhere in the world would affect the demand for Japan's exports. A preferable way of coping with the surplus would be to allow more imports into Japan. The measures announced included 'tariff cuts, abolition of import restrictions, simplification of standards and certification systems and expansion of government procurement'. Internal political pressure from some domestic industries prevented the measures from being as vigorous as some other countries would have liked.

2   This is an essay question which strikes to the heart of the discussion in this chapter as to whether governments should intervene in the arena of international trade.

3   (a)   The choice point is at G; production and consumption are OF units of good X and OB units of good Y. We saw how this point is reached in Chapter 19.

    (b)   If the world price ratio is equal to the domestic ratio, then country A holds no comparative advantage in the production of either good and there is no incentive for trade to take place.

    (c)   With the world price ratio at RS, a unit of good X exchanges for more units of good Y in the world market than at home, implying that country A has a comparative advantage in the production of good X.

    (d)   Country A can now *produce* at point J, making OH units of X and OA of Y. By trading at the world price ratio, country A can *consume* at point E, consuming OD of X and OC of Y. In the process, the economy moves to a higher indifference curve.

    (e)   Country A exports DH units of X and imports AC of Y.

    (f)   OM represents the terms of trade when the countries are at point W. This can be seen to be the equilibrium terms of trade—the point where the offer curves intersect represents the point at which the offers made by the two countries are consistent.

The International Monetary System and International Finance

In Chapter 29 we examined the exchange rate and its importance from the perspective of an individual economy. We now take a broader view by looking at the significance for the *world economy* of the exchange rate regime adopted by nations. We investigate the controversial issue of whether a fixed or floating exchange rate system is best for the world economy, basing the exploration partly on evidence of the working of various regimes in the past—the 'fixed' systems of the gold standard and the adjustable peg, the more recent experience with a managed float, and the potential for a clean float.

The *gold standard* held sway until the 1930s and had three distinguishing characteristics. Firstly, the government of each country fixed the price of gold in terms of domestic currency—known as the *par value*. Secondly, the government maintained the convertibility of domestic currency into gold. Finally, domestic money creation was directly tied to holdings of gold such that the money supply could be increased only through the purchase of gold from the public. The exchange rate between two economies thus reflected the ratio of gold prices in the two currencies—the gold *parity rate*. By this mechanism, the exchange rate is automatically fixed.

The gold standard provides an automatic mechanism by which internal and external balance can be achieved. This essentially works by forcing the central bank to intervene in the foreign exchange market. An economy with a balance of payments deficit finds that gold reserves and money supply fall, forcing the economy into a recession, which lasts until domestic wages and prices fall to restore international competitiveness. If the adjustment of wages and prices is sluggish, the recession is prolonged. The temptation exists for economies to push up domestic interest rates in order to achieve balance of payments equilibrium via the capital account. If successful, wage and price adjustment is further postponed. This vulnerability of economies to prolonged deep recessions was the great

disadvantage of the system, but it was not without its merits—for instance, there was no possibility of persistent high inflation.

Under the gold standard, a country's exchange rate is fixed indefinitely. In the postwar period the *Bretton Woods system* came into operation; it is sometimes known as the *dollar standard*, as other countries agreed to fix the value of the domestic currency in dollars. The system is best described as an *adjustable peg*, as rates were not fixed for ever but could be adjusted if an economy could demonstrate that conditions had so changed as to make the existing rate inappropriate. A key difference between this system and the gold standard was that *100 per cent backing* for the domestic currency was dropped, the result being that governments could attempt sterilization. This may prevent unemployment in the short run but it cannot be sustained in the long run. The main effect of such attempts is to inhibit the adjustment of domestic money and prices, removing the automatic equilibrating mechanism.

Two problems emerged. Firstly, it seemed that the system almost encouraged the development of crisis situations, the onus being on individual countries to convince others that a change in the exchange rate was required. The second problem arose because the dollar, unlike gold, was not in (virtually) fixed supply. As the supply of dollars increased, there was a gradual acceleration of inflation.

Under a *freely floating exchange rate system*, the balance of payments is brought automatically into equilibrium. In the long run, the exchange rate tends towards the PPP path, which maintains international competitiveness through time. Whereas under a fixed exchange rate system a single country cannot have domestic inflation markedly out of line with world levels, such divergence *is* possible under a floating system if the nominal exchange rate adjusts to maintain PPP. Experience suggests that exchange rate adjustment can cope with substantial discrepancies in inflation rates.

In the short run, the exchange rate may diverge from PPP under the influence of movements of the large quantities of internationally footloose funds. (Many of these are owned by OPEC countries and are known as *petrodollars*.) The existence of these funds renders exchange and interest rates highly sensitive and subject to short-run fluctuations. A restrictive monetary policy in an individual economy which pushes up interest rates leads to exchange rate appreciation, reducing international competitiveness and deepening the transitional increase in unemployment.

Under a *managed* or *dirty float* there is some intervention from governments, either to smooth short-run fluctuations or to influence the direction of the change in the exchange rate. However, the quantity of footloose funds is so great that no single government has sufficient funds to out-manoeuvre the speculators.

Does the evidence allow us conclusively to favour one regime over the others? In the modern world, the adopted system must be robust. A fixed rate system can cope only if individual countries pursue domestic policies which keep inflation close to world levels; otherwise there is a need for continual devaluation and revaluation, compounded by speculative action. This argument is not conclusive, for critics of floating rates would see the financial discipline imposed by a fixed rate system as one of its strengths; some, indeed, would argue for a return of the gold standard which would give individual economies no choice but to be responsible in their domestic policies. As ever, the validity of this argument depends on a balancing of costs and benefits. The adjustment to an adverse supply shock would be by domestic recession, not exchange rate changes. It is by no means clear that the adjustable peg system would have effectively handled the oil price shocks.

A common criticism of floating rate systems is the uncertainty caused by the potential for day-to-day fluctuations in exchange rates. How telling this criticism is depends upon whether the volatility would have happened anyway and found expression in interest rates or tax rates under fixed exchange rates. Some would argue that shocks are more likely under a floating exchange rate regime which does not force domestic policy responsibility.

Fixed rate systems have been criticized on the grounds that the need to defend a fixed exchange rate makes protectionism more likely. Again, the evidence is not clear-cut. The steady reductions in tariffs under GATT occurred under the Bretton Woods system, but the dismantling of controls on capital transactions was accomplished under the managed float of the 1970s. The pressures of the mid-1970s were negotiated without a rise in protectionism—but new pressures emerged in the early 1980s as industrial nations tried to protect domestic employment.

When governments decide on an economic policy, they must remain aware of possible repercussions on other countries. In this sense they operate rather like oligopolists. If a single government allows a rise in the domestic exchange rate to help combat inflation, an externality is imposed on other countries—who experience a corresponding fall in their exchange rates. *International policy co-ordination* may prevent some of the damage caused by such externalities. It may also provide a pre-commitment to 'tight' policies; co-ordinated financial discipline may thus add credibility to policy actions.

The *European Monetary System* (EMS) represents one attempt to achieve co-ordination among members of the EC. The UK joined the EMS, but delayed participation in one of its important provisions, the *Exchange Rate Mechanism* (ERM) until 1990. Under the ERM, members agree to fix exchange rates against each other (within bands), but jointly float against the rest of the world. A number of realignments have taken place, but their frequency has reduced since 1983. Inflation rates were gradually brought into line between the participating countries, but it is not clear whether this reflects the discipline of ERM, or the independent determination of individual countries to cure inflation. Foreign exchange controls were progressively reduced within the EC, partly in connection with the moves towards European integration, which are discussed fully in the following chapter.

IMPORTANT CONCEPTS AND TECHNICAL TERMS

Match each lettered concept with the appropriate numbered phrase:

(a) PPP path
(b) Adjustable peg regime
(c) International competitiveness
(d) Petrodollars
(e) Gold parity exchange rate
(f) Exchange rate speculation
(g) Policy harmonization
(h) Gold standard
(i) Managed float
(j) European Monetary System
(k) Financial discipline
(l) 100 per cent gold backing
(m) Par value of gold
(n) Dollar standard

1 Measured by comparing the relative prices of the goods from different countries when these are measured in a common currency.

2 The path for the nominal exchange rate that would maintain the level of international competitiveness constant over time.

3 A rule by which each pound in circulation must be backed by an equivalent value of gold in the vaults of the central bank.

4 An exchange rate system under which the government of each country fixes the price of gold in terms of its home currency, maintains convertibility of the domestic currency into gold, and preserves 100 per cent cover.

5 The price of gold in terms of domestic currency.

6 A regime in which the exchange rate floats but is influenced in the short run by government intervention.

7 An exchange rate system which operated after the Second World War in which countries agreed to fix their exchange rates against the dollar.

8 A feature of fixed exchange rate systems by which governments are forced to pursue policies which keep domestic inflation in line with world rates.

9   The movement of investment funds between currencies in pursuit of the highest return in the light of expected exchange rate changes.

10 Footloose investment funds in the control of OPEC countries.

11 A tentative step back towards fixed exchange rates involving members of the EC.

12 A regime in which exchange rates are normally fixed but countries are occasionally allowed to alter their exchange rate.

13 Under the gold standard, the equilibrium exchange rate between two currencies, reflecting the relative gold prices.

14 A concerted attempt by a group of countries to formulate monetary and fiscal policies which recognize that one country's policy affects other members of the group.

EXERCISES

1   Below are listed a number of policy actions and situations. In each case, identify the sort of exchange rate regime in operation.
    (a) The government carries out open market operations to prevent the exchange rate from falling so rapidly as to endanger the target inflation rate.
    (b) The money supply decreases following a balance of payments deficit and a fall in the economy's gold reserves.
    (c) A major crisis leads to a devaluation of the domestic currency.
    (d) A contractionary fiscal policy is introduced following successive years of balance of payments deficits and falls in the foreign exchange reserves.
    (e) The foreign exchange markets are in continuous equilibrium with no government intervention via foreign exchange reserves.
    (f) There is a fixed exchange rate regime with automatic government reaction to disequilibrium.
    (g) There is a flexible exchange rate system in which the government has some discretion in exchange rate policy.
    (h) A country experiencing high rates of inflation relative to other countries also experiences a depreciating nominal exchange rate which in the long run maintains a constant real exchange rate.

2   This exercise and the following one investigate the operation of the gold standard. Suppose the USA has fixed the par value of gold at $20.67 per ounce, and the UK par value is £4.25.
    (a) What is the $/£ exchange rate?

Suppose that you begin with £85 and the exchange rate is $6/£.
    (b) How much gold could you buy in the UK?
    (c) Suppose instead that you exchange your pounds for dollars: how much gold could you then buy in the USA?
    (d) If you then ship the gold back to Britain, what would it be worth in sterling?
    (e) For how long would you expect the exchange rate to remain at $6/£?
    (f) Describe the likely events should the exchange rate be $3/£.

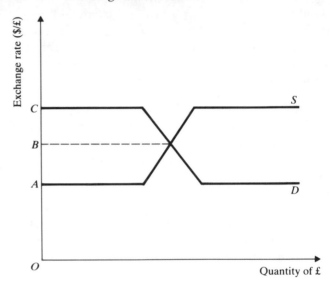

FIGURE 33.1   The exchange rate and the gold standard

Figure 33.1 shows the demand for (D) and supply of (S) pounds at different exchange rates under the gold standard.
    (g) Identify the gold parity exchange rate.
    (h) Describe what happens at exchange rate OC.
    (i) Describe what is happening between exchange rates OA and OC.

3   Two countries, called the UK and the USA, are operating under the gold standard, both countries beginning in both internal and external balance. There is then a fall in the American average propensity to import from the UK at each income level.
    (a) What is the short-run impact on UK exports and the balance of payments?
    (b) Describe the effect of this on aggregate demand, output, and employment if UK wages and prices do not immediately respond.
    (c) How does this affect the exchange rate and UK gold reserves?
    (d) What does this in turn imply for money supply?

(e) Describe how the UK now manages to return to internal and external balance.

(f) Briefly outline the effects upon the American economy.

4 Three countries, A, B, and C, are all experiencing relatively high rates of inflation. A floating exchange rate regime is in operation.
Country A wants to reduce the rate of inflation, so introduces a restrictive monetary policy.

(a) What effect does this have on A's exchange rate relative to the other two countries?

(b) How does this affect A's competitiveness?

(c) Meanwhile, back in B and C, what is happening to the inflation rate?

Country B now gets worried about inflation and initiates a tight money policy.

(d) What effect does this have on B's exchange rate relative to the other two countries?

(e) Outline the effects of B's policy on country A.

We could now, of course, consider what happens when country C decides to have a go at tight money—but instead,

(f) comment briefly on the potential advantages of policy harmonization.

5 Which of the following were features of the dollar standard?

(a) The provision of an automatic mechanism for resolving imbalances in international payments.

(b) The removal of speculation problems, given the fixed nature of the exchange rate.

(c) At the fixed exchange rate, central banks were committed to buy or sell dollars from their stock of foreign exchange reserves or dollar holdings.

(d) A series of gradual exchange rate adjustments at frequent intervals.

(e) 100 per cent backing of domestic currencies by dollar reserves.

(f) A relatively rapid increase in the world supply of dollars in the late 1960s, partly as a result of the Vietnam war.

6 Which of the following describe the response of an economy to a shock under a system of freely floating exchange rates? (*Note:* more than one response may be valid.)

(a) An autonomous increase in aggregate demand leads to an increase in imports, a balance of payments deficit (in the immediate run), and a depreciation of the domestic currency.

(b) A once-for-all reduction in domestic money supply leads to an appreciation of the exchange rate, which may overshoot in the short run.

(c) A decrease in aggregate demand leads to a balance of payments surplus and an increase in foreign exchange reserves.

(d) Domestic interest rates are increased by government action to slow down a depreciation of the exchange rate.

(e) A succession of balance of payments deficits enables the domestic government successfully to request a devaluation of the currency.

7 Which of the following is *not* a feature of a managed float?

(a) In the long run, the nominal exchange rate tends to follow the PPP path.

(b) Governments may sometimes intervene to smooth out short-run fluctuations in the exchange rate.

(c) The foreign exchange reserves remain constant.

(d) The net monetary inflow from abroad need not always be zero.

(e) Governments may operate in the foreign exchange market to influence the direction of movement of the exchange rate.

8 Below are listed four criteria by which an exchange rate regime may be evaluated. Outline the merits and demerits of fixed and floating systems under each criterion:

(a) Robustness.

(b) Financial discipline.

(c) Volatility.

(d) Freedom from restrictions on trade and payment.

TRUE/FALSE

1 _____ Under the gold standard, 100 per cent backing for the money supply was always strictly adhered to.

2 _____ Victorians were wrong to believe that Britain's trade deficits in the late nineteenth century were the result of laziness or decadence.

3 _____ The crucial difference between the gold standard and the dollar standard was that under the latter there was no longer 100 per cent backing for the domestic currency.

4 _____ The adjustable peg system effectively eliminated speculation by creating a state of certainty regarding future exchange rates.

5 _____ The floating exchange rate regime is flexible but not sufficiently so to cope with substantial differences in inflation rates between countries.

6 _____ In practice, exchange rates have rarely been allowed to float absolutely freely during the period since 1973.

7 _____ The volatility of the exchange rate under a floating system leads to great uncertainty and is likely to reduce the level of international trade and the amount of investment undertaken by firms competing in world markets.

8 _____ Protectionism is more likely to occur under a fixed exchange rate system.

9 _____ Policy harmonization might have allowed the world economy to reduce inflation in the late 1970s/early 1980s at a lower short-run cost in unemployment.

10 _____ The EMS committed the central banks of member countries to intervene in foreign exchange markets whenever any of the currencies threatened to deviate from its par value against other member countries by more than an agreed amount.

QUESTIONS FOR THOUGHT

1 Discuss the proposition that governments will not behave responsibly unless forced to.

2 Consider the advantages and disadvantages of a fixed exchange rate system.
(Welsh Joint Education Committee GCE A level Economics A2, June 1987)

3 Why might greater stability in exchange rates stimulate the volume of international trade?
(Oxford and Cambridge Schools Examination Board GCE A level Economics Paper 2, June 1988)

ANSWERS AND COMMENTS FOR CHAPTER 33

Please note Where questions are reproduced from GCE examinations, the examination boards bear no responsibility for the answers provided in this volume, which are the sole responsibility of the authors.

Important Concepts and Technical Terms

1	*c*	5	*m*	9	*f*	13	*e*
2	*a*	6	*i*	10	*d*	14	*g*
3	*l*	7	*n*	11	*j*		
4	*h*	8	*k*	12	*b*		

Exercises

1. (a) Managed float.
   (b) Gold standard.
   (c) Adjustable peg.
   (d) Adjustable peg (or conceivably a managed float in which the authorities have been holding up the exchange rate for an extended period).
   (e) Clean float.
   (f) Gold standard.
   (g) Managed float.
   (h) Clean or managed float: in either case, the nominal exchange rate tends to follow the PPP path in the long run.

2. (a) 20.67/4.25 = 4.86.
   (b) 20 ounces.
   (c) £85 converts to $510, which buys 24.67 ounces of gold.
   (d) 24.67 ounces of gold is worth £104.85 at the UK price—it would then pay to repeat the exercise, selling gold in Britain, converting to dollars, and buying gold in the US.
   (e) Such a rate could hold only in the very short run because of the potential return from the sort of transactions already examined.
   (f) With the exchange rate below the gold parity rate, the reverse set of transactions becomes profitable, selling gold in the USA and buying gold in the UK.
   (g) *OB*: the equilibrium rate.
   (h) *OC* is the rate at which everyone wants to convert into dollars, so demand for pounds falls to zero.
   (i) Between *OA* and *OC* it is possible for the exchange rate to be out of equilibrium without all agents indulging in gold and currency transactions. This band arises because there are transaction costs—either brokerage or transport. It costs to ship gold about the world.

3. (a) Exports fall and the balance of payments moves into deficit.
   (b) Aggregate demand falls and so too will output and employment if wages and prices are slow to adjust.
   (c) As we have seen, the exchange rate can never move far away from the gold parity rate. The balance of payments deficit must be matched by a fall in the UK gold reserves.
   (d) Domestic money supply must fall also to preserve 100 per cent gold backing. This tends to push up interest rates, further depressing aggregate demand.
   (e) Eventually wages and prices must adjust, and this will lead to an improvement in British competitiveness. This continues until internal and external balance are restored.
   (f) Adjustment in the US mirrors that in the UK—the balance of payments moves into surplus, aggregate demand increases, gold reserves and money supply rise, wages and prices are pushed up, competitiveness falls as internal and external balance are restored.

4. (a) The restrictive monetary policy leads to high interest rates and to an appreciation of A's exchange rate.
   (b) Competitiveness declines, deepening the transitional fall in output and employment.
   (c) As competitiveness in A declines, so it rises in B and C, as their exchange rates have depreciated. There is thus some upward pressure on prices.
   (d) B's exchange rate now appreciates.
   (e) A's exchange rate now falls relative to B and C, threatening upward pressure on prices.
   (f) If all three countries were to co-ordinate their policies, the see-saw effect on exchange rates would be avoided and there would be much more stability. There would be less speculative movement in financial capital. In this more stable environment, it may well be that the transitional cost of anti-inflation policy would be less strong and less long-lasting.

5. (c) and (f) were features of the dollar standard, but none of the other items mentioned.

6. Only (a) and (b) are valid under a clean float.

7. (c) is a feature only of a clean float.

8. These headings are used in the examination of fixed versus floating exchange rates in Section 33–5 of the main text. Some salient points are mentioned below.
   (a) Flexible rates are probably better at coping with real shocks. Flexible rates also cope with nominal shocks, but a fixed rate system may discourage the occurrence of such shocks (see (b)).
   (b) Fixed rate systems force financial discipline upon countries, which must adopt domestic policies that keep their inflation rates in line with world rates. The discipline is lacking with a floating exchange rate, which is able to cope with variations in inflation rates between countries.
   (c) Fixed rate systems by definition offer stability of exchange rates (except, of course, at the time of a devaluation), whereas under a flexible regime there may be day-to-day variability. Defenders of flexible rates point out that the volatility may find alternative expression in interest rates or tax rates.
   (d) It is by no means clear whether protectionism is more likely under fixed or under floating exchange rates.

True/False

1 False: governments bent the rules at times (see Section 33–2 of the main text).
2 True: see Box 33–1 of the main text.
3 True: see Section 33–3 of the main text.
4 False: speculators were well aware that a country experiencing balance of payments deficits was liable to devalue—and could take appropriate action in anticipation.
5 False: experience suggests that exchange rates can be sufficiently flexible to maintain PPP even in extreme conditions (see Section 33–4 of the main text).
6 True.
7 Not proved: see Section 33–5 of the main text.

8 Also not proved: tariffs were substantially dismantled through GATT under the adjustable peg. In the recession of the early 1980s there were moves towards protectionism under the managed float.
9 True: see Section 33–6 of the main text.
10 True: but only for those members of the EMS who were also participating in the ERM.

Questions for Thought

1 This issue lies at the heart of the 'fixed v. floating' debate—can policy harmonization be achieved without the discipline of a fixed exchange rate regime?
2 and 3   No hints provided.

34 European Integration in the 1990s

The rapidity of change in Europe at the threshold of the 1990s was startling. The moves towards a single European market and European monetary union, and the breaking down of barriers with Eastern Europe, offered a new challenge for economics in attempting to understand the new shape of Europe.

The European Community (EC) was established in 1957. During the following three decades the EC expanded in membership to the 12, but this enlargement occurred without fundamental structural change, with the member-states anxious to retain their identity and sovereignty. As we have seen in earlier chapters, the 1980s brought renewed belief in the importance of market forces in guiding the evolution of economies, together with a desire for less intrusive government. These developments paved the way for a change in attitudes towards European integration. It now became more acceptable to think in terms of a general level of agreement on the broad outline of economic policy with individual states free to meet those general outlines in their own way, together with mutual recognition of regulations.

One manifestation of this change in attitudes was the agreement to establish a single market in Europe by *1992*. This harmonizing process involved the abolition of all remaining foreign exchange controls, the removal of *non-tariff barriers*, the elimination of bias in public sector purchasing policies, the removal of frontier controls, and progress towards the harmonization of tax rates. The single market created by these reforms would be an economic area greater in size than either the United States or Japan.

What would be the benefits of this enlarged market? The removal of non-tariff barriers and the increased mobility of factors within the EC would be expected to allow more efficient allocation of resources and exploitation of comparative advantage. The larger market would also enable firms in some countries to exploit economies of scale previously denied them. The greater freedom of trade within the EC would intensify competition between firms, although there is a possibility that some of the resulting benefits would be diluted by cross-border mergers and takeovers.

The Cecchini Report estimated that the once-for-all gains from 1992 could amount to between 2.5 and 6.5 per cent of EC GDP, but according to Baldwin, the gains could be even more substantial if we take into account the potential gains from externalities.

Which countries are likely to gain the most from 1992? Economic analysis of the problem suggests that the countries who stand to make the largest gains will be those who were previously constrained in their exploitation of comparative advantage or scale economies, probably those countries specializing in labour-intensive production. This would include countries in southern Europe such as Greece, Portugal, and Spain. However, it is also possible that countries in the North may gain through externality arguments, making them more able to compete with the United States and Japan.

For countries outside the EC, such as the members of *EFTA*, it is probable that 1992 will make them no worse off, but that they could gain in the long run by joining the EC. Countries outside Europe have been watching developments with some trepidation, fearing that the stimulus to intra-European trade will diminish the amount of trade with the rest of the world.

Monetary union for an economic area involves internally fixed exchange rates, freedom of capital movement, and co-ordinated control of money supply by a single monetary authority. It is possible for a monetary union to operate without a common currency, but it is clearly more convenient if there is one. *European monetary union* (EMU) has been viewed by some commentators as the logical consequence of the *European Monetary System* and the 1992 reforms. Others see it as just one more step on the road to a fully united Europe.

Monetary union has significant implications for member countries. With freedom of capital movements, it becomes essential to harmonize interest rates across countries, so individual countries must be prepared to surrender sovereignty over domestic monetary policy.

The entry of sterling into the *Exchange Rate Mechanism* (ERM) was delayed, but by 1990 most of the arguments against entry were weakened. The Thatcher government had been proud of its independent conquest of inflation, but this argument was weakened by the re-acceleration of inflation in 1989–90 and sterling entered the ERM in October 1990.

The *Delors Report* set out a three-stage transition process towards European monetary union. In stage 1 all EC members would join the ERM, which would become tighter. Stage 2 would see a rehearsal of EC-wide decision-making, setting ceilings for budget deficits and beginning to formulate a common monetary policy. Realignments of exchange rates would become rare during this stage. In the final stage 3, the *European System of Central Banks* (ESCB) would take on full responsibility for EC monetary policy. The 1989

Madrid summit at which the Delors Report was discussed ratified only the stage 1 proposals.

The main benefits of EMU would be to reinforce the 1992 reforms, to eliminate exchange rate uncertainty (a benefit already enjoyed to some extent by members of the ERM), and to reduce transaction costs through the move to a single currency. A potentially important cost would be to restrict the freedom of individual governments in coping with a loss of competitiveness, in the sense that the Delors ceilings on budget deficits would prevent independent fiscal action by individual countries. The United States (another example of a monetary union) handles this problem through the working of federal (cross-state) fiscal policy, but at present the EC has no adequate equivalent mechanism. The Delors system is intended to provide a credible pre-commitment to the containment of inflation; but, arguably, this could have been better achieved by ensuring the political independence of the ESCB.

In Eastern Europe, the rapid moves towards liberalization and the adoption of market-oriented policies came as a surprise. Past borrowing on the part of many East European countries left a legacy of outstanding debt, which will have to be carefully handled. Supply-side reforms will not be a painless process after years in which production and prices had been determined by bureaucrats rather than market forces. Substantial relative price changes will undoubtedly be needed to ensure a more efficient resource allocation, and will require a willingness on the part of members of society to accept short-run costs, especially where wage adjustments are required.

In recognition of the importance of international trade, it seems likely that some Eastern European countries will be given associate EC member status. In addition, it is likely that there will be direct investment of EC firms in East Europe and the establishment of joint ventures between firms from West and East. Macroeconomic policy needs to be firm (perhaps austere) and credible, in order to avoid the potential problem of hyperinflation as prices adjust. In the special case of East Germany, the most affluent and best educated of East European countries, reunification in 1990 included *German Monetary Union*, a process given credibility by the involvement of the Bundesbank in controlling monetary policy.

IMPORTANT CONCEPTS, TECHNICAL TERMS, AND INITIALS

Match each lettered concept with the appropriate numbered phrase:

(a) A monetary union   (d) CAP
(b) 1992   (e) GMU
(c) EMU   (f) EFTA

(g) Structural Funds   (m) Cross-border
(h) Delors Report   takeovers
(i) Non-tariff barriers (n) European Bank for
(j) ERM   Reconstruction and
(k) Federal fiscal system   Development
(l) ESCB

1 Differences in national regulations or practices which prevent free movement of goods, services, and factors across countries.
2 The largest programme administered by the EC, involving a system of administered high prices for agricultural commodities.
3 A system by which each member country fixes a nominal exchange rate against each other participant, while jointly floating against the rest of the world.
4 A system in which a group of states agrees to have permanently fixed exchange rates within the union, free capital movements, and a single monetary authority responsible for setting the union's money supply.
5 A free trade area outside the EC comprising Austria, Finland, Iceland, Norway, and Sweden.
6 A programme to establish a single European market in goods, services, assets, and people.
7 The joining together of members of the EC in a monetary union.
8 A new authority to be set up to take full responsibility for EC monetary policy when European monetary union is complete.
9 A system under which fiscal transfers between states helps to cushion individual states from the effects of temporary local recession.
10 A modest EC programme designed to provide subsidies for social infrastructure, especially in poorer areas of the Community.
11 Discussed at the 1989 Madrid Summit of heads of EC government, it proposed three stages of transition towards European monetary union.
12 An institution set up to finance market-oriented reforms in Eastern Europe.
13 A situation in which domestic firms buy into or sell out to firms based in other countries.
14 Part of the move to German reunification, by which the Germanies agreed to adopt a common currency and to confirm the Bundesbank in charge of common monetary policy.

EXERCISES

1 The creation of a single European market by 1992 entails a number of changes for EC members. For each of the following, state whether or not they are part of the 1992 reforms:

(a) The abolition of all remaining foreign exchange controls between EC members.

(b) The removal of frontier controls (delays), subject to retention of necessary safeguards for security, social and health reasons.

(c) The harmonization of all tax rates in EC member countries.

(d) The removal of all non-tariff barriers to trade within the EC.

(e) The creation of an economic area without frontiers in which the free movement of goods, persons, services, and capital is ensured.

(f) Mutual recognition of regulations such that, for instance, a doctor who qualified in England could practise medicine in any other EC country.

(g) The adoption of a common currency within the EC.

2 Which of the following constitute non-tariff barriers to trade?

(a) Differences in patent laws between countries.

(b) Safety standards which act to segment national markets.

(c) Voluntary export restraints—bilateral agreements whereby an exporting country agrees to limit exports to a quota.

(d) Taxes imposed on imported goods.

(e) Sanitary requirements for imported meats and dairy products which are more stringent than for domestic goods.

(f) Quota limits on the import of particular commodities.

(g) Packaging and labelling requirements.

3 The entry of sterling into the Exchange Rate Mechanism of the European Monetary System was delayed until 1990. A number of reasons were put forward for this delay, some of which are listed below. In each case, consider the strength of the case made against entry.

(a) Sterling is a petrocurrency because of North Sea oil, and is thus subject to volatility because of possible fluctuations in the price of oil.

(b) With London and Frankfurt being the only decontrolled financial centres in Europe, it would be inconvenient for the UK to join the ERM, as this would require the co-ordination of monetary policy.

(c) A significant proportion of UK trade is conducted with countries outside the EC.

(d) UK inflation was being controlled independently by the policies of the government in power, so the additional stability of the ERM was unnecessary.

(e) Independence of domestic monetary policy is important for the UK.

(f) The EMS was a result of muddled thinking, so it is better to bide time until things settle down.

4 Which of the following is/are characteristic of a monetary union?

(a) Fixed exchange rates within the union.

(b) A single currency.

(c) Freedom of capital movement.

(d) A single monetary authority for setting the union's money supply.

(e) A common interest rate policy.

(f) A federal government.

(g) A federal fiscal system.

5 Consider a country that is part of a monetary union that has no federal system of fiscal transfers. Suppose that for some reason—perhaps trade union pressure—firms in the economy face an increase in costs which is passed on by producers in the form of higher prices. This exercise traces the path taken by the economy as it adjusts towards equilibrium.

(a) If the cost increase is restricted to firms in the domestic economy, what is the effect on competitiveness?

(b) Given that the exchange rate cannot adjust because of the rules of the monetary union, what is the effect on exports?

(c) What will be the consequences for output and employment?

(d) By what process will the economy now return to equilibrium?

(e) The Delors Report favoured the placing of ceilings on government budget deficits so that the return to equilibrium could not be encouraged by domestic fiscal policy. Would such expansionary fiscal action be effective, and why should it be outlawed?

(f) Explain how a system of federal fiscal transfers would alter the sequence of events.

6 Identify each of the following as a cost *or* a benefit of 1992 *or* European Monetary Union:

(a) Greater efficiency in resource allocation.

(b) The removal of frontier controls.

(c) Loss of protection of domestic activity.

(d) Loss of sovereignty over interest rates.

(e) Intensified competition.

(f) Enhancement of labour mobility.

(g) Reduction of trade between Britain and the Commonwealth.

(h) Exchange rate certainty.

(i) Fuller exploitation of economies of scale.

(j) Establishment of a credible pre-commitment to controlling inflation.

(k) Inflexibility in adjusting to a loss of competitiveness.

(l) A reduction in transaction costs.

(m) A politically acceptable way for moving towards European integration.

7 Imagine that you are a planner working in one of the centrally planned economies of Eastern Europe in the early 1980s. (You may wish to tackle parts of this question in conjunction with the commentary in the 'Answers and Comments' section.)

(a) The rules of the economy do not permit the industry for which you are responsible to make profits, so profit maximization cannot be your objective: on what basis do you take decisions about the number of workers to hire and the amount of output to be produced?

(b) How do you think prices will come to be fixed?

(c) If the output of your industry (e.g. steel) is used for defence goods, industrial goods, and consumer goods, how will priorities be determined?

(d) What is likely to be the state of equilibrium or disequilibrium in the market for consumer goods?

(e) Discuss the incentives for workers and management.

(f) Reforms are introduced to move the economy towards a more market-oriented system. What is the likely effect upon prices, especially in the market for consumer goods?

(g) Must inflation occur?

(h) Under what conditions will the market reforms be successful?

(i) By the time you get to tackle this question, market reforms in Eastern Europe will have progressed. Discuss the degree of success that has been achieved.

TRUE/FALSE

1 _____ The swing in thinking against big government and extensive regulation of the economy accelerated the moves towards European integration.

2 _____ Big Bang gave London a flying start towards becoming the only surviving European financial centre, but the contest is not yet over.

3 _____ A bank registered in Germany will, after 1992, be permitted to operate in France or the UK.

4 _____ The 1992 reforms will create a European economic area almost as large as the United States or Japan.

5 _____ 1992 will outlaw tariffs on trade between EC members.

6 _____ Cross-border takeovers and mergers of European firms will effectively preserve market power and prevent gains from the intensified competition that was intended to follow the 1992 reforms.

7 _____ The gains from the 1992 reforms could be between 2.5 and 6.5 per cent of EC GDP.

8 _____ According to Neven, Spain, Greece, and Portugal stand to gain most from exploiting new gains from scale economies after 1992.

9 _____ English and Scottish banknotes both circulate in Scotland, proving that a monetary union need not have a single currency.

10 _____ The Delors Report was discussed and ratified at the Madrid Summit of EC heads of government in 1989.

11 _____ European Monetary Union would bring exchange rate certainty, but this is not much of a change for existing ERM members.

12 _____ The EC Structural Funds provide a system of federal fiscal transfers which can help countries suffering from a temporary loss of competitiveness.

13 _____ The high standards of education and health provision in the countries of Eastern Europe put them in a better position to be able to attain large productivity gains than many of today's less developed countries.

14 _____ The substantial debts incurred by Eastern European countries to Western creditors are a substantial obstacle to further development.

QUESTIONS FOR THOUGHT

1 How would you establish whether the UK economy gained or lost from membership of the European Community since 1973?
(University of London GCE Economics Special Paper, June 1989)

2 'The pressure for reform in Eastern Europe came more from discontent with past performance than from belief in the superiority of capitalist economies.' Do you think this overstates the situation?

3 Explore the extent to which East Germany is a special case among the reforming countries of Eastern Europe. How successful has German reunification been since 1990?

ANSWERS AND COMMENTS FOR CHAPTER 34

Please note   Where questions are reproduced from GCE examinations, the examination boards bear no responsibility for the answers provided in this volume, which are the sole responsibility of the authors.

Important Concepts, Technical Terms, and Initials

1	*i*	5	*f*	9	*k*	13	*m*
2	*d*	6	*b*	10	*g*	14	*e*
3	*j*	7	*c*	11	*h*		
4	*a*	8	*l*	12	*n*		

Exercises

1 (a) This was certainly a key part of the 1992 reforms—indeed, many EC members had dismantled all controls much earlier.

(b) This was also part of the reforms.

(c) The harmonization of tax rates was seen as a desirable aspect of a single European market, but politically tricky to achieve. The 1992 reforms thus made provision for *progress towards* harmonization of tax rates.

(d) This was part of the reforms, but some non-tariff barriers are subtle in nature, so enforcement could be a problem in some cases.

(e) This is the wording used in the EC 'Directives' on trade and competition policies setting out the objectives for 1992. (See George McKenzie and Tony Venables, 'The Economics of 1992', in *Economic Review*, May 1989.)

(f) This also is part of the reforms.

(g) This is not envisaged as part of the 1992 reforms.

2 Option (d) describes a tariff; all the other items are non-tariff barriers which have been used.

3 (a) The gradual depletion of the reserves of North Sea oil dilutes this argument.

(b) This argument disappears as other EC members dismantle controls on capital movements.

(c) The proportion of UK trade with other EC members has increased substantially since Britain's entry into the Community, so this argument becomes less powerful with time.

(d) Look at what happened to the inflation rate in 1989/90.

(e) It is argued that monetary policy is required as a short-term weapon against inflation to avoid the use of fiscal policy for this purpose. There is no definitive answer to whether this is a valid argument—it depends upon your evaluation of the consequences of fiscal management.

(f) Time inevitably must dilute this argument.

4 Items (a), (c), (d), and (e) are necessary characteristics of a monetary union; the others may be.

5 (a) Competitiveness will fall.

(b) The loss in competitiveness will presumably lead to a reduction in the demand for exported goods;

(c) so both output and employment are likely to be reduced.

(d) Adjustment will rely on the gradual restoration of competitiveness through changes in relative wage and price levels. Of course, this may take some time, and during the interim period the economy is likely to suffer from unemployment.

(e) The danger of adopting fiscal management is that it could lead to an increase in the inflation rate; this is what the Delors proposals were intended to avoid. A key question to consider is whether there are alternative ways of achieving the same objective.

(f) In the United States, an example of a monetary union, if one state suffers a temporary recession, the federal fiscal system will provide some automatic stabilization. See Section 34–5 of the main text for the full story.

6 (a) One of the benefits expected from the 1992 reforms.

(b) This is also part of the 1992 reforms; the hope is that transaction costs will be reduced by this move.

(c) The abolition of non-tariff barriers to trade (part of 1992) opens domestic industry up to intensified competition. Although this might be seen as a cost in the short run if it causes unemployment, the long-run effect should be beneficial.

(d) Monetary union will bring this loss of sovereignty, but hopefully the benefits of the union will be adequate compensation.

(e) A benefit of 1992.

(f) A benefit of 1992, although the extent to which labour mobility will be enhanced remains to be seen.

(g) This has been happening over the years in any case.

(h) Exchange rate certainty would come with monetary union—at least internally, rates would be fixed—but 1992 is also a step in this direction.

(i) An expected benefit of 1992.

(j) Monetary union is one way of establishing this, but not necessarily the only way.

(k) This is one possible result of a monetary union—see exercise 5.

(l) The establishment of a common currency is one way in which a monetary union could have the effect of reducing transaction costs, but notice that in principle it is possible to have a monetary union operating without a common currency.

(m) Both 1992 and European Monetary Union may be regarded as moves towards European integration—whether this is politically acceptable is to some extent a separate issue.

7 (a) In the absence of the profit motive, a planner responsible for an industry will probably be concerned to demonstrate his or her skills by producing as much output as possible by whatever means necessary. This is a recipe for waste, and there is no guarantee that the output will actually be useful or appropriate. Output may at times be overstated for effect.

(b) Prices will be centrally fixed, but not necessarily with relative scarcity in mind. In many cases, prices will tend to be held at artificially low levels to create the impression that inflation is not a problem in the economy.

(c) This is straightforward: defence and industry will take highest priority, as consumers can wait—and queue.

(d) With prices held at artificially low levels, and consumers queuing for goods, there is of course a state of excess demand in the market.

(e) Incentives for managers are poor in the absence of proper signals to which they can react in their output decisions. Workers have little incentive to work hard, as they cannot obtain consumer goods in any case. This may perhaps exaggerate a little . . . but perhaps not.

(f) If prices are to begin to reflect relative scarcity, they will naturally have to rise towards the equilibrium market levels . . .

(g) . . . but this need not mean inflation. A once-for-all upwards adjustment in the price level is not the same as a persistent rise in the general level of prices, which is how we define inflation.

(h) The key is to have a firm and credible macroeconomic strategy that can avoid the spectre of hyperinflation, even at the cost of some short-term unemployment. See Section 34–6 of the main text for a fuller discussion.

(i) No comment.

True/False

1 True: see Section 34–1 of the main text.
2 True: see Box 34–1 of the main text.
3 True.
4 Not quite accurate: the EC of 1993 will have a population *larger* than either the United States or Japan.
5 False: tariffs were already outlawed *before* 1992.
6 Hopefully false: it is possible that such merger and takeover activity represents companies' attempts to restructure so as to be in a better position to exploit economies of scale and comparative advantage in the enlarged single market. Much will depend upon the strength and wisdom of European merger policy in the transition period and beyond.

7 Possible: these were the estimates presented by the Cecchini Report. However, taking externalities into account, the gains could in fact be much greater. See Section 34–3 of the main text.

8 True.

9 True: see Section 34–4 of the main text.

10 False: the report was discussed at the Summit, but agreement was reached only on stage 1.

11 True: see Section 34–5 of the main text.

12 False: the EC Structural Funds programme is not sufficient to fulfil that role.

13 True: see Section 34–6 of the main text. The plight of less-developed countries is discussed in Chapter 35.

14 True, but Western governments have taken steps to reduce the burdens, for example by the establishment of the European Bank for Reconstruction and Development to finance market-oriented reforms.

Questions for Thought

1 The question here is whether the UK would have managed better had it stayed outside the EC. This, of course, is by no means an easy thing to establish. The discussion must include some mention of the moves towards closer European integration and monetary union, which are open to the UK as a result of the earlier decision to join the EC.

2 Both discontent and envy probably had some part to play in the pressure for reform: see an article by Paul Hare in *Economic Review*, May 1990.

3 It seems sure that the option to reunify with West Germany put East Germany in a very different position as compared with other countries in Eastern Europe, especially in terms of the credibility of policy. See Section 34–6 of the main text for further discussion.

35

Problems of Developing Countries in the World Economy

A visitor to our world from another galaxy would probably be struck less by the unemployment in the industrialized nations than by the global maldistribution of income, by which a vast number of people in the *less developed countries* (LDCs) live in conditions of poverty which are unimaginable to most of us. The LDCs have long felt that they have been exploited by the rich nations, and in 1974 they used the forum of the UN to call for a *New International Economic Order* (NIEO). In this chapter we examine the position of the LDCs and look at ways in which it could be improved.

International comparisons are always difficult, but it is undeniable that most of the world's people live in extreme poverty. Whatever measure we look at, the story is the same: income per capita, literacy, education, life expectancy, and medical care are all at appallingly low levels for the majority of the world's population. Conditions have improved since 1960, but the *relative* position of the LDCs worsened in that period. The division is often portrayed as between the rich North and the poor South.

The reasons for low per capita growth rates in LDCs are myriad. Partly they result from relatively high population growth, which, combined with diminishing returns to labour, keeps productivity low. This is often compounded by a scarcity of natural resources and capital. The poverty of the LDCs means that they have few resources to spare to devote to physical investment or the development of infrastructure. The low productivity of the agricultural sector means that disproportionate amounts of resources must be taken up in trying to feed the increasing population. Multinational companies that have invested in LDCs have tended to take their own workers (which inhibits the growth of local human capital) and to repatriate profits, preventing the accumulation of local financial capital. In some LDCs the cultural background of the people may not favour the development of high productivity methods of production.

How may economic development be achieved? One possible route is through *trade in primary commodities*. Remember that comparative advantage tends to reflect relative factor endowments. The fact that many LDCs have abundant land suggests that they should specialize in the production and trade of land-intensive primary commodities. For a number of reasons, the LDCs have not found this an attractive route. One problem is that the long-term trend in the price of many primary commodities has been emphatically downwards. Ironically, this in part reflects the success of LDCs in increasing the supply of such goods, but it also reflects technical developments in the industrial countries creating cheap artificial substitutes and reducing demand for some primary commodities such as rubber.

A second problem is that real commodity prices tend to be highly volatile. Both demand and supply tend to be relatively inelastic, so a small shift in one of the curves leads to a large change in equilibrium price. What is more, many primary commodities tend to be ones where either demand or supply may be subject to variations. Demand may vary with the business cycle; the supply of an agricultural product depends on the weather and the success of the harvest.

These problems combined make life hard for the LDCs, many of whom have high *export concentration*. In many countries a single commodity constitutes a very large proportion of total exports. There are thus potential gains from diversification.

Commodity stabilization schemes offer one possible escape route. For some commodities, attempts have been made to establish *buffer stocks*. If a number of producers can get together, it may be possible to stockpile a commodity during times of high supply and sell from those stocks when supply is low. By this means, it is possible to set the price at an appropriate level—if set too high, stocks build up too quickly and the scheme becomes expensive to operate. Such organizations have not always been successful, as they require resources in order to become established. Survival also requires co-operation from the rich industrial nations.

The second route to development is through *industrialization*. The collapse of world trade in the 1930s encouraged *import substitution* through domestic production, often behind tariff or quota barriers. This may be a dangerous route because it entails specialization in activities in which the economy begins with a comparative disadvantage. It is thus potentially wasteful in resource terms, and there may be a limited chance of competing internationally. The hope is that import substitution will turn out to be but a preliminary phase which enables the acquisition of technical skills and experience which in the long run will lead to *export-led growth*.

Some LDCs have carved a niche for themselves in the export of manufactures, in particular a group including Brazil, Mexico, Hong Kong, South Korea, and Singapore, sometimes known as the *newly indus-*

trializing countries (NICs). However, it seems that success brings its own problems, in that such exports threaten the viability of labour-intensive manufacturing in the industrial countries. As noted in Chapter 32, this has led to a recent move back towards protectionism. The LDCs would naturally like to outlaw this and if possible have positive discrimination in their favour, but the prospects for this are not encouraging.

If LDCs cannot afford investment (or even survival) from domestic funds, the third alternative route to economic development is by *borrowing*. LDCs have traditionally been borrowers in world markets, but in recent years they have complained that the terms on which they have been allowed to borrow have been too tough. The OPEC oil shock initiated a wave of new borrowing by those LDCs without their own oil reserves, and debt accumulated rapidly. Oil-producing LDCs like Mexico were hard-hit by the decline in real oil prices in the mid-1980s.

The possibility that some LDCs might default on the repayment of debt pushed interest rates up higher. This was aggravated by the world recession and the adoption of restrictive monetary policies in the industrial nations. For many LDCs the ratio of debt to GNP rose rapidly, as did the ratio of debt to exports, which may be a better indicator of the severity of a country's debt position. The *international debt crisis* was born. Default was avoided in a number of cases by *debt rescheduling*, either by the granting of new loans or by the extension of repayment periods. The LDCs are naturally loath to adopt traditional IMF remedies for current account deficits that involve deflationary policies, as living standards are already so low, and they would prefer to receive more subsidized credit.

The final issue to consider is that of *aid*. For a single nation, it is reasonably clear that the responsibility for internal redistribution of income lies with the government. At the world level, the responsibility is less clearly defined. Yet the LDCs' interpretation of history suggests that their current plight partly reflects past exploitation by the now-rich nations, so they are entitled to assistance. Some critics of aid point to the corruption which prevents 100 per cent of aid from reaching its intended destination, but this argument cannot be sustained. Aid through freer migration does not appear politically viable in the current economic environment. What appears to be required is increased aid to enable the LDCs to invest in their future and to acquire the human skills and physical capital that is needed for them to become truly part of the world economy. This may need to be accompanied by a greater willingness in the rest of the world to allow freer trade with the LDCs, which will benefit *both* North and South in the long run.

IMPORTANT CONCEPTS AND TECHNICAL TERMS

Match each lettered concept with the appropriate numbered phrase:

(a) Import substitution
(b) Less developed countries
(c) Primary commodities
(d) Buffer stock
(e) New protectionism
(f) Export-led growth
(g) Price volatility
(h) Newly industrialized countries
(i) Export concentration
(j) Aid
(k) Industrialization
(l) Debt rescheduling
(m) New International Economic Order
(n) International debt crisis

1 An organization aiming to stabilize a commodity market, buying when the price is low and selling when the price is high.

2 Agricultural commodities, minerals, and fuels: goods that may be inputs into a production process but are not outputs from such a process.

3 International co-operation to reduce the widening gap between the developed and the developing countries—called for in a resolution passed by the General Assembly of the United Nations in 1974.

4 Recent attempts by some industrial countries to protect domestic industries from competition from LDCs.

5 Assistance from the rich North to the poor South in the form of subsidized loans, gifts of food, or machinery or technical help, and the free provision of expert advisers.

6 A situation in which LDCs have difficulty in meeting their debt repayments and interest payments, such that interest rates rise, aggravating the situation still further.

7 A phenomenon in which some LDCs depend upon a narrow range of products for export.

8 Production and income growth through exports rather than the displacement of imports.

9 A group of countries that have successfully developed local industries and are growing rapidly and exporting manufactures.

10 The low-income nations of the world, ranging from the very poor, such as China and India, to the nearly rich, such as Brazil and Mexico.

11 A policy of replacing imports by domestic production under the protection of high tariffs or import quotas.

12 A situation in which prices are subject to extreme movements from year to year.

13 A process involving the expansion of industries that produce manufactures.

14 A procedure whereby countries with difficulties in meeting their debts are either lent new money to meet existing loans or allowed to pay back the original loan over a longer time scale than originally negotiated.

EXERCISES

1 Table 35.1 lists some data relating to various welfare measures for eight countries throughout the world. (They will be identified in the 'Answers' section.) The list of countries includes low-income, lower middle-income, upper middle-income, and industrial market economies. Try to associate each country with the appropriate income category. Which of the countries would you classify as LDCs.

TABLE 35.1 Welfare indicators

Country	Average annual per cent growth rate of population 1980–87	Per cent of GDP from agriculture 1987	Life expectancy at birth (male) 1987	Infant mortality rate (aged under 1) per 1000 live births 1987	Population per nursing person 1984	Number enrolled in secondary school as percentage of the age group 1986
A	2.0	16	63	39	710	29
B	1.4	13	67	32	980	74
C	2.7	57	52	128	4680	25
D	1.0	2	72	10	70	100
E	2.5	24	62	45	2740	68
F	0.7	11	68	25	260	82
G	2.8	59	47	112	3040	4
H	0.1	2	72	9	120	85

Source: World Bank, *World Development Report*, 1989.
(In some cases, data may relate to different years.)

2 Demand for a primary product is stable, but the supply is subject to large fluctuations from year to year. The producers of the product decide to operate a buffer stock to stabilize revenue. Table 35.2 shows how demand varies with price.

TABLE 35.2 Demand for a primary product

Price per unit ($)	Quantity demanded (thousand units)
100	300
90	325
80	350
70	375
60	400
50	425
40	450
30	475
20	500

Suppose the buffer stock is operated in such a way that price is stabilized at $70 per unit.

(*a*) In the first year of the buffer stock, supply turns out to be 450 (thousand) units. What would the equilibrium price have been without the buffer stock? How must the buffer stock act to stabilize price at $70?

(*b*) Supply is 350 in the second year. Identify what equilibrium price would have been, the quantity bought or sold by the buffer stock, and the cumulative quantity of the commodity held by the buffer stock.

(*c*) In the following five years, supply turns out successively to be 375, 425, 400, 325, and 475. Trace the cumulative quantity held by the buffer stock.

(*d*) What price would on average have kept the buffer stock stable?

3 Consider the market for a primary commodity in which supply is stable, but the position of the demand schedule varies with the business cycle experienced by the industrial nations. The position is illustrated in Figure 35.1.

SS represents the supply curve. When the industrial nations are in the trough of the cycle, demand is at DD_1; at the peak, demand for the commodity is DD_2.

(*a*) Identify equilibrium price and *revenue* at the trough of the cycle.

(*b*) Identify equilibrium price and revenue at the peak of the cycle.

Suppose now that a buffer stock is established with the aim of stabilizing price at *OB*.

(*c*) Identify quantity supplied and total revenue if demand were such as to make *OB* the equilibrium price.

(*d*) Describe the actions of the buffer stock and revenue accruing to producers in the trough of the cycle.

(*e*) Describe the actions of the buffer stock and

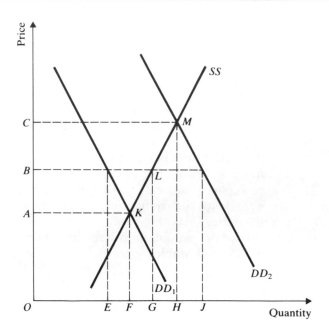

FIGURE 35.1 Commodity price stabilization

revenue accruing to producers in the peak of the cycle.

4 Consider two economies, representative of low-income and high-income nations. In the period 1965–85, the low-income country experiences a faster annual growth rate of 2.9 per cent per annum compared with 1.6 per cent per annum for the higher-income economy. Suppose the low-income country begins with GNP per capita of $380, compared with $8460 for the high-income economy. Calculate the absolute difference between GNP per capita in the two countries, and investigate whether the differential widens or narrows over a five-year period given the above growth rates.

5 Table 35.3 presents data on growth rates and the share of manufactures in exports for a selection of countries.

TABLE 35.3 Industry, growth, and trade

Country	Annual real GDP growth 1965–85 (%)	Share of manufactures in exports 1960 (%)	1985 (%)
A	4.3	3	41
B	0.2	0	1
C	2.9	0	27
D	7.6	26	60
E	1.4	29	37
F	6.1	80	92
G	−0.7	5	12
H	6.6	14	91
I	−0.2	4	7

Source: World Bank, *World Development Report*, 1984 and 1987

Identify the newly industrialized countries.

6 Which of the following would be regarded as typical features of the LDCs?
  (a) Low productivity in agriculture.
  (b) High dependence on primary commodities.
  (c) Meagre provision of infrastructure.
  (d) Low population growth.
  (e) Low propensity to import.
  (f) Rapidly expanding labour force.

7 This exercise explores issues of static and dynamic comparative advantage in the context of LDCs.
  (a) Many LDCs have a relative scarcity of physical and human capital, as compared with natural resources or unskilled labour. Where is their comparative advantage likely to rest?
  (b) Does the historical pattern of primary product prices have implications for the product specialization suggested by your answer to (a)?
  (c) Might an import substitution policy serve to alter a country's comparative advantage? What are the disadvantages of this approach?
  (d) Discuss whether export promotion is likely to be a superior strategy.

8 The transfer of aid between countries involves both (rich) donors and (poor) recipients. In this exercise, we explore some of the motivations on each side. If you find the questions to be obscure, please tackle them in conjunction with the commentary provided.
  (a) It might be argued that donors provide aid for humanitarian motives. Does your experience of the governments of industrial nations suggest this to be a sufficient explanation for aid flows?
  (b) What political motivations might donors have for granting aid?
  (c) Many aid transactions involve the movement of commodities between countries, either directly or as an indirect result of aid. How might donor countries advance their own economic self-interest through the granting of aid?
  (d) From the recipients' perspective, why might there be political reasons for accepting aid?
  (e) The economic motivation for accepting aid seems obvious ... but might there be disadvantages for an independent country?
  (f) Why should free trade be superior to aid for encouraging development?

9 Consider Table 35.4 and then relate the figures to the statements that follow.

TABLE 35.4 Debt indicators for developing countries, 1980–83

Indicators	1980	1981	1982	1983
Ratio of debt to GNP	19.2	21.9	24.9	26.7
Ratio of debt to exports	76.1	90.8	108.7	121.4
Debt service ratio[a]	13.6	16.6	19.9	20.7
Ratio of interest service to GNP	1.5	1.9	2.2	2.2
Total debt outstanding and disbursed (billions of dollars)	424.8	482.6	538.0	595.8
Official	157.5	172.3	190.9	208.5
Private	267.3	310.3	347.1	387.3

Note: Calculations are based on a sample of 90 developing countries.
[a] Ratio of interest payments plus amortization to exports.
Source: World Bank, *World Development Report*, 1984

Which of the following statements are supported by the figures in Table 35.4?
(a) The size of debt relative to GNP was increasing steadily during the period.
(b) An increasing share of exports was being taken up by the servicing of existing debt.
(c) Borrowing from commercial banks and other private sources grew in importance relative to borrowing from official sources.
(d) During the period, the amount of debt grew such that, even if an entire year's exports were devoted to paying off the debt, it would not suffice.

TRUE/FALSE

1 _____ In 1987, there were 2.5 billion people in low-income countries with an average income for the year of about £180 per person.
2 _____ A major problem of the LDCs is the lack of both physical and financial capital.
3 _____ The tribal customs prevalent in some LDCs inhibit the development of enterprise and initiative.
4 _____ The law of comparative advantage proves that the best route to prosperity is for the LDCs to export primary commodities to the rest of the world.
5 _____ The reduction of price volatility by the use of a buffer stock is most necessary and most successful when demand and supply are relatively elastic.
6 _____ Import substitution is doomed to failure because it involves the concentration of resources into industries in which an economy has a comparative disadvantage.
7 _____ On average, the NICs grew twice as rapidly as the rich industrialized nations during the 1970s.
8 _____ Debt rescheduling has avoided default by a number of LDCs on external loan repayments; such defaults would have had major repercussions on financial institutions in the leading countries.
9 _____ The quickest way to equalize world income distribution would probably be to permit free migration between countries.
10 _____ More aid is what is needed to solve the problems of the LDCs.

QUESTIONS FOR THOUGHT

1 Is it feasible for LDCs to achieve economic development without external assistance?
The increasing indebtedness of many LDCs raises the possibility that some may be forced to default. Discuss the implications of such an outcome.
2 What do you consider to be the main consequences for an economy of a sustained deterioration in its terms of trade?
(Oxford and Cambridge Schools Examination Board GCE A level Economics Paper 2, June 1989)
3 Imagine that you are asked to make an assessment of the economic performance of a number of countries. Explain why such a task would be an exercise in normative economics.
(University of London GCE Economics Special Paper, June 1988)

ANSWERS AND COMMENTS FOR CHAPTER 35

Please note Where questions are reproduced from GCE examinations, the examination boards bear no responsibility for the answers provided in this volume, which are the sole responsibility of the authors.

Important Concepts and Technical Terms

1	*d*	5	*j*	9	*h*	13	*k*
2	*c*	6	*n*	10	*b*	14	*l*
3	*m*	7	*i*	11	*a*		
4	*e*	8	*f*	12	*g*		

Exercises

1 **TABLE A35.1** GNP per capita, various countries

Country	GNP per capita (US$ 1987)
Low-income countries	
C Nepal	160
G Burundi	250
Lower middle-income countries	
E Philippines	590
A Thailand	850
Upper middle-income countries	
B Argentina	2 390
F Yugoslavia	2 480
Industrial market countries	
H United Kingdom	10 420
D United States	18 530

Normally, we would include as LDCs all low-income and middle-income countries. Hopefully, this exercise will have illustrated the wide range of conditions represented under this definition. It is easy to lose sight of this when we treat them together.

2 (a) Equilibrium price would have been $40 per unit and the buffer stock must buy up 75 (thousand) units to maintain price at $70.

(b) Equilibrium price would have been $80 per unit. The buffer stock sells 25 (thousand) units to maintain price. The buffer stock now holds 50 (thousand) units.

(c) The net additions to the buffer stock in the five years are 0, +50, +25, −50, +100. Cumulative quantities held: 50, 100, 125, 75, 175. The total cost of operating the buffer stock over the seven years amounts to 175 000 × 70 = $12.25 million—plus the costs of warehousing and storage.

(d) Average supply over the period was 400 (thousand) units per annum; a price of $60 per unit would have kept the stock stable. If the buffer stock continues to maintain the price at too high a level, stocks must build up in the long run, tying up precious resources.

3 (a) With demand DD_1, equilibrium price is OA, revenue is the area $OAKF$.

(b) With DD_2, equilibrium price is OC, revenue is $OCMH$.

(c) Quantity OG, revenue $OBLG$.

(d) Buffer stock buys EG, revenue $OBLG$.

(e) Buffer stock sells GJ, revenue $OBLG$.

4 **TABLE A35.2** Relative growth in low- and high-income countries

Period	GNP per capita		Absolute difference in GNP per capita
	Low-income country	High-income country	
Initial	380.0	8460.0	8080.0
1	391.0	8595.4	8204.3
2	402.4	8732.9	8330.5
3	414.0	8872.6	8458.6
4	426.0	9014.6	8588.5
5	438.4	9158.8	8720.4

The absolute difference between the two countries continues to widen, even though the low-income country is growing at a higher annual percentage rate.

5 The NICs included in the list are:
A Brazil
D Singapore
F Hong Kong
H Republic of Korea
On the basis of these figures, country C (Sri Lanka) also seems to be following this path. The other countries are Ethiopia (B), Uruguay (E), Jamaica (G), and Chile (I).

6 (a), (b), (c) and (f).

7 (a) Clearly, comparative advantage will *not* lie with hi-tech manufacturing industries. More sensible would seem to be labour-intensive activities, in particular primary production—either agriculture or mineral extraction.

(b) A problem with specializing in primary production is that there has been an historical tendency for the terms of trade to move against primary products, and for prices of such commodities to be highly volatile, as a result of fluctuations in either supply or demand.

(c) The 'infant industry' argument in favour of imposing tariffs has always been a tempting one: an LDC might hope that by imposing a tariff it would be possible to nurture new industries which would eventually be able to compete in world markets, after an initial period in which the country would save on imports. However, the problem has always been that the industry becomes over-protected, and never grows up. Import substitution tends to engender an inward-looking attitude on the part of domestic producers.

(d) Export promotion forces an outward-looking attitude on domestic producers. It has proved very successful for the NICs, but there is some doubt about whether the same route could be followed by *all* LDCs, especially given the increasingly protectionist attitude adopted by the industrial countries since the recession of the early 1980s.

8 (a) It might be nice to imagine that donors act purely out of humanitarian motives, but realistically this seems unlikely. By the late 1980s, only five countries in OECD (Norway, The Netherlands,

Denmark, Sweden, and France) had reached the UN target for aid as a percentage of GNP, agreed back in the 1970s. Countries like the UK and the United States were giving a much smaller proportion in 1988 than in 1965. It seems more likely that donors are partly if not mainly motivated by self-interest of one sort or another.

(b) Many political motivations exist: donors may wish to preserve the ideology in which they believe, or to strengthen their own position in a region of the world. The changes in the geographical pattern of US aid flows in the postwar period are revealing.

(c) Much of aid is 'tied' aid. For instance, bilateral aid between countries may be based on an agreement that the recipient will purchase goods from the donor in the future, sometimes at prices above the competitive world prices for similar goods. Indeed, there is evidence that some countries regard aid as being part of trade policy.

(d) Political stability is important for development—and even more important for the government in power! There have been times when aid has been used to bolster the position of the government in power. At times this has involved the use of aid for 'prestige' projects, which may improve the image of recipient or donor but do little to promote development.

(e) The economic reasons for acceptance of aid by a poor country hardly need stating, but one potential problem is that the recipient country may find itself in a position of dependency. For instance, it might be that aid lowers the domestic incentives for saving, or even production, such that the LDC cannot break out of its reliance on other countries.

(f) It has often been argued that allowing LDCs to trade on fair terms with the rest of the world would have more beneficial effects than the simple granting of aid. This may be seen in particular in terms of the incentives for the LDC economy.

9 All of them. Item (c) is worth special mention: the increasing importance of bank loans relative to official aid is a significant feature of the international debt crisis. A more detailed account of the crisis may be found in an article by George McKenzie and Steve Thomas in the *Economic Review*, March 1984.

True/False

1 True: see Section 35–1 of the main text.
2 True: see Section 35–2 of the main text.
3 Sometimes true: it takes time to develop work practices and the acceptance of factory working.
4 False: there are many problems with a heavy reliance on primary products (see Section 35–3 of the main text).
5 False: if demand and supply are relatively elastic, then price movements will tend to be small, even in the face of large demand or supply shocks. Draw a diagram to check it out.
6 False: this is too static a picture, which presumes that the pattern of comparative advantage cannot be changed over time (see Section 35–4 of the main text).
7 True.
8 True: see Section 35–5 of the main text.
9 True: see Section 35–6 of the main text. Although true, however, it is also extremely unlikely.
10 True and false: more aid is necessary but not sufficient. Freer trade is also important.

Questions for Thought

1 From the discussion of this chapter, it seems unlikely that LDCs can develop without the help (or at least the co-operation) of the rich countries. More difficult is the question of the form in which that help should come—aid, direct investment by multinationals, or freer trade? The focus of the second part of the question is on the consequences of default on international debt, which is often discussed mainly in terms of the effect on the international financial system.
2 See Section 35–3 in the main text for discussion of some of the issues.
3 The distinction between normative and positive economics was made in the first chapter of the book, and it seems appropriate that we should return to it right at the end. In assessing the economic performance of different economies, and in particular in looking at the problems of LDCs, it is very easy to become emotional, and to allow value judgements to cloud our view of the economic issues. Being aware of this may serve to minimize its effect.